GORBACHEV'S NEW THINKING AND THIRD WORLD CONFLICTS

To the Victims of Regional Conflicts.

GORBACHEV'S NEW THINKING AND THIRD WORLD CONFLICTS

Edited by
Jiri Valenta and Frank Cibulka

Transaction Publishers
New Brunswick (U.S.A.) and London (U.K.)

Copyright © 1990 by Transaction Publishers,
New Brunswick, New Jersey 08903

All rights reserved under International and Pan-American Copyright Conventions. No part of this book may be reproduced or transmitted in any form or by any means, electronic or mechanical, including photocopy, recording, or any information storage and retrieval system, without prior permission in writing from the publisher. All inquiries should be addressed to Transaction Publishers, Rutgers—The State University, New Brunswick, New Jersey 08903.

Library of Congress Catalog Number: 89-33635
ISBN: 0-88738-212-6
Printed in the United States of America

Library of Congress Cataloging-in-Publication Data
Gorbachev's new thinking and Third World Conflicts /
edited by Jiri Valenta and Frank Cibulka.
    p. cm.
  ISBN 0-88738-212-6
  1. Developing countries—Foreign relations—Soviet Union.
2. Soviet Union—Foreign relations—Developing countries.   3. Soviet Union—Foreign relations—1985-   4. Gorbachev, Mikhail Sergeevich, 1931-   .   5. Perestroika. I. Valenta, Jiri. II. Cibulka, Frank.
D888.S65G67   1989   89-33635
327.470172′4—dc20   CIP

Contents

A Note from the Senior Editor: East-South Relations	vii
Acknowledgments	ix
Introduction *Jiri Valenta and Frank Cibulka*	xi

Part One Gorbachev's "New Thinking " and Third World Regional Conflicts Conceptualized

1. Gorbachev's "New Political Thinking" and Foreign Policy   3
   Vernon Aspaturian
2. Gorbachev's "New Thinking" on Regional Conflicts:
   A Theoretical Analysis   45
   Bhabani Sen Gupta
3. Gorbachev's Policies toward the Third World: An Overview   65
   William E. Griffith
4. From Lenin to Marx in Soviet Third World Policy   77
   Jerry F. Hough

Part Two Moscow's Junior Allies and Regional Conflicts

5. U.S.S.R.-Vietnam Alliance and Regional Conflicts   91
   Douglas Pike
6. U.S.S.R.-Cuba Alliance and Regional Conflicts: Trust but Verify 103
   Howard J. Wiarda

Part Three Regional Focus: The Conflict in South Asia

7. Moscow and the Regional Conflicts: Afghanistan   125
   Ali T. Sheikh
8. Gorbachev's "New Thinking" on Regional Conflicts in
   Light of the Soviets' Afghan Experience   143
   Sabahuddin Kushkaki

Part Four Regional Focus: The Conflict in Africa

9. Africa after Gorbachev's Rise to Power: Angola and Ethiopia 159
   Colin Legum
10. The U.S.S.R. and Conflict in Southern Africa:
    Angola and Namibia   171
    H. de V. du Toit

Part Five Regional Focus: The Conflict in Southeast Asia
11. U.S.S.R., Vietnam, and the Conflict in Kampuchea 195
    Khien Theeravit
12. Gorbachev's "New Thinking" and the Philippines:
    Making of a New Regional Conflict? 213
    Frank Cibulka

Part Six Regional Focus: The Conflict in Central America
13. The "New Thinking" and Central America 237
    Alvaro Taboada

**Part Seven Superpowers and Regional Conflicts: American
            Policies and Future Options**
14. The Rise and Fall of the Reagan Doctrine 265
    Charles William Maynes
15. Soviet "New Thinking" and U.S. Foreign Policy 277
    W. Bruce Weinrod

Part Eight Overview and Evaluation
16. Moscow's "New Thinking" and Third World Regional Conflicts:
    Some Conclusions 291
    Jiri Valenta

Appendix A, Geneva Accords on Afghanistan 321
Appendix B, Agreements for Peace in Southwestern Africa 335
Biographical Sketches of the Editors and Contributors 343
Index 347

Note From the Senior Editor: East-South Relations

This volume is the first in a series that will focus on East/South relations. The most neglected, yet possibly most crucial issues in the study of the Soviet Union and other communist countries derive from their policies vis-à-vis countries of the developing world, that is, issues evolving on an East/South axis. In the last forty years, numerous studies have assessed the strategic, political, and economic components of East/West relations and the contrasts and similarities between East and West, capitalism and socialism. And in the last few decades, numerous scholars have addressed all aspects of relations between the United States and its Caribbean and South American neighbors, as well as other North/South issues.

The field of East/South relations, meanwhile, remains relatively underdeveloped. Recently, several excellent book-length studies on the origins and development of Soviet theory regarding Third World radical regimes have been published. Most other East/South issues, however, are yet rarely assessed in a systematic fashion: the impact of the "new thinking" on the behavior of the Soviet Union and that of its junior allies in the regional conflicts in Angola, Ethiopia, Nicaragua, Cambodia, and Afghanistan; the role of local forces (the revolutionary regimes and their oppositions) in these conflicts and in their resolutions; the potential for the development of new conflicts; and the intensification of Soviet and other communist countries' political and economic relations with such influential regional powers as Brazil, Argentina, Mexico, Indonesia, and Nigeria. These issues need to be addressed, as do their implications for Western policymakers.

In their present new era of cooperation, the U.S.S.R. and the United States are working to resolve the regional conflicts in and around Afghanistan, Nicaragua, Angola, and Cambodia. It will take years to find lasting, peaceful resolutions, however, for the solutions must involve not only the U.S.S.R. but also Cuba, which was shaken by an unprecedented leadership crisis in July 1989, and Vietnam, as well as various other revolutionary regimes and the forces resisting them; and any resulting agreements will require complex measures for verification that will be difficult to agree upon and difficult to enforce. As this volume demonstrates, the final word on Afghanistan has not been said, the agreed upon withdrawal of Cuban and Vietnamese forces from

Angola and Cambodia will take at least a few years, and the civil wars in those countries and in Nicaragua remain unresolved.

Meanwhile, other conflicts having varying East/South and North/South dimensions either have not been seriously tackled or may yet emerge in such countries as Ethiopia, Syria and Lebanon, El Salvador, Guatemala, Colombia, and the Philippines. In spite of the current Soviet emphasis on peaceful solutions to these types of conflicts, the "new political thinking" from which this stems remains a selective phenomenon, making it unlikely that Moscow, much less Havana and Hanoi, will uniformly cut its military ties to revolutionary allies worldwide. Some of these conflicts, furthermore, may be affected, as yet unpredictably, by new upheavals such as the turmoil in China in May and June 1989. As conflicts having East/South dimensions continue into the next decade, it makes good sense to explore their possible solutions through systematic analysis in both comparative and single-country studies.

While Mikhail Gorbachev has apparently resolved to devote a great deal of effort in the first half of the 1990s to finding diplomatic solutions to certain regional conflicts (as indicated, for example, by the time frame of the existing agreements on Afghanistan and Angola), he has also publicly supported the need for an "intensification of the East/South line," especially the development of closer Soviet and East European relations with key Third World regional powers (Brazil, Argentina, Mexico, Nigeria, Indonesia), modelled on existing Soviet relations with India. Next to the resolution of regional conflicts, the most important subfield of Soviet-Third World relations, and the main manifestation of the East/South line, appears to be in the cultivation of "the regional influentials," to use Samuel Huntington's expression, and the economically important Asian "tigers" (South Korea, Singapore, and perhaps Taiwan). It is logical that this emphasis will prevail in the first half of the 1990s, and perhaps even more so in the second half, if the "new thinking" survives and prospers in the volatile political environment of the U.S.S.R.

Acknowledgments

I would like to recognize a number of colleagues, scholars, policymakers, and institutions who have contributed to or helped ready this volume for publication. Above all, my thanks go to my coeditor Dr. Frank Cibulka of the National University of Singapore, and to my Staff Associate and absolute right hand, Ana Miyares of the Institute for Soviet and East European Studies of the Graduate School of International Studies (ISEES/GSIS). I am also grateful to Mr. M. Rajaratnam, Director of the Information and Resource Center in Singapore, who co-organized the conference that preceded this volume. During the conference, which was held in Singapore August 4-7, 1988, the staff of Mr. Rajaratnam, led by Joyce Tan, ably assisted Ms. Miyares, John D. Breidenstine (ISEES/GSIS fellow), and my research assistants, Charles Safdie and Arthur Arnau. Those who wrote chapters for the book join me in thanking Virginia Valenta for her careful editing. Dr. Herbert Bernstein, Gregg Rickman (ISEES/GSIS fellow), and my research assistant Thelvius Winieckie proofed the volume and contributed many useful comments.

I am grateful to several institutions and their officials for their sponsorship and support of this project; above all, to the United States Institute of Peace and its President, Samuel W. Lewis, and Director of Research and Studies, Dr. Kenneth Jensen; the Institute of Asian Studies of Chulalongkorn University and its Director, Professor Khien Theeravit; the United States Information Agency and its senior officials, Philip W. Arnold, Chief of Policy Staff, Dr. Robert Smith, Director, and Russel Bikoff, Program Officer, both of the Private Sector Program; the Heritage Foundation and Ed Feulner, President; and the Graduate School of International Studies of the University of Miami and GSIS Dean, Ambassador Ambler H. Moss, Jr. I also acknowledge the Social Science Research Council and the Earhart Foundation for their support of the research of two participants in this project, Ambassador Alvaro Taboada and Ali Sheikh, senior fellows and Ph.D. candidates at ISEES/GSIS. This volume is a tribute to the handsome support that allowed us to bring together outstanding scholars from four continents.

Most of those who contributed chapters to this volume are distinguished scholars needing no introduction. All were fortunate to benefit from the criticism and commentary of the following prominent analysts, a number of them former or current representatives of their governments: Professor Chan

Heng Chee, Director, The Institute of Policy Studies, and now Singapore's ambassador to the United Nations; Ambassador B. A. Clark, U.N. Regional Representative, Office of the Commissioner of Namibia, and a former Nigerian ambassador to the United Nations; Ambassador Chawat Arthayukti, Director-General, ASEAN Department at the Ministry of Foreign Affairs, Thailand; Professor Tommy Koh, Ambassador of Singapore to the United States; Ambassador Riaz Piracha, Chairman of the Board of Governors of the Institute of Strategic Studies, Islamabad, Pakistan; Ambassador Jose S. Sorzano, a former U.S. Deputy Permanent Representative to the United Nations and Special Assistant to the President for National Security Affairs; Professor Lau Teik Soon, head of the Department of Political Science, the National University of Singapore, and a member of Parliament; and Professor Surin Pitsuwan, a member of the Parliament of Thailand. Other distinguished contributors to the project were Mr. Xu Kui, Director of the Institute of Soviet and East European Studies, Beijing, China; Air Commodore Jasjit Singh, Director of the Institute of Defense Studies and Analysis, New Delhi, India; Professor Likhit Dhiravegin, Vice Rector, Thammasart University, Bangkok, Thailand; Dr. Hamzah Bin Ahmad, Senior Fellow, Institute of Strategic and International Studies, Kuala Lumpur, Malaysia; Dr. Bilveer Singh of the National University of Singapore (who also helped review the papers in this volume); Ms. Sohair Gabr, Deputy Director of Foreign Affairs for *Akhbar El Yom*, Cairo, Egypt; Mr. Thai Quang Trung, Research Director at the Information and Resource Center, Singapore; Professor Ton That Thien, the University of Quebec à Trois Rivères, Canada; Mr. Pierre du Toit Botha, Fellow, the African Institute of South Africa, Pretoria; and Dr. Rodolfo Cerdas-Cruz, Research Fellow, Political and Administrative Center for Investigation and Training (CIAPA), San Jose, Costa Rica, and Social Science Research Council Fellow.

Although we did not succeed in involving a senior Soviet analyst in this project, as we were able to do in the subsequent ISEES project on the U.S.S.R. in Angola (December 1988, Miami), we were nonetheless fortunate in that the TASS correspondent in Singapore, Mr. Vladimir Kovalenko, could participate in the initial international meeting. In the spirit of *glasnost*, may he communicate all our findings to Mikhail Gorbachev and the Soviet Politburo, with the wish of all the participants who worked to make the project a success that this volume and those to follow will serve the interests of peace in the developing world and greater understanding among all nations East and West, North and South, East and South.

Introduction

Jiri Valenta and Frank Cibulka

The second half of the 1980s has proven to be an era of dynamic change in international affairs, primarily as a result of Mikhail Gorbachev's succession to the Kremlin leadership in March 1985. Grobachev's twin reform program of domestic restructuring (*perestroika*) and "new political thinking" (*novoe politicheskoe myshlenie*) in foreign affairs, along with the associated openness (*glasnost*) evolved in response to socioeconomic stagnation (*zastoi*) on the domestic front and the prohibitive costs of the expansion of Soviet power abroad. Will the reforms allow for the transformation of the Soviet Leninist system into one that is more decent and efficient? They are already helping to revolutionize Soviet domestic politics and relations between the great powers, but the long-term results are unclear. It remains to be seen whether the reforms will condition another round of détente between the United States and the Soviet Union, this time more solidly based and presumably more enduring, or simply enable Moscow to enjoy a respite, much needed to consolidate gains on the fringes of its empire, so as to subsequently and more effectively continue the previous expansion.

In their application, the principles of the "new thinking" have affected almost every area of Soviet foreign policy, most notably superpower relations as manifested in the arms reduction process, and Soviet involvement in Third World regional conflicts, in which Moscow has taken upon itself the role of mediator/peacemaker. In 1988-1989, the changing Soviet attitudes found concrete form in the Geneva Accords (March 1988) and the stipulated Soviet military withdrawal from Afghanistan; in the accords on Angola and Namibia (December 1988), providing for the withdrawal of Cuban and South African forces from those nations; and in modest progress toward the resolution of the regional conflict in and around Cambodia.

The "new thinking" and its manifestation in the changing Soviet policy toward Third World regional conflicts, involving the Soviet Union either directly or through junior allies and proxies, was the focus of this project. The three primary objectives were: 1) to examine the changes in the Soviet foreign policy philosophy, the "new thinking," especially as manifested in Soviet policy toward the Third World; 2) to assess the sincerity of Gorbachev's leadership by looking for the signs of "new Soviet actions" toward the Third World, especially the Soviet role in seeking solutions to regional conflicts; and 3) to generate viable policy options for U.S. and other Western policymakers facing the military and diplomatic challenges presented by Moscow, its allies, and its proxies in the familiar as well as potentially new trouble spots in the Third World.

As could be expected, the project had some great strengths, but also a few problems. The timing was superb in that we began it as peace, or at least some dramatic initiatives in the direction of peace, seemed to be breaking out all over the Third World. The participants had to deal with the fresh impact of the Geneva Accords on Afghanistan, the news of the JIM-I meeting convening in late July in Jakarta, Indonesia, to discuss the Cambodian conflict, a United Nations-mediated cease-fire in the Iran-Iraq war, and a truce on Angola negotiated under U.S. auspices and in consultation with the U.S.S.R. While such military disengagements by outside powers and cease-fires do not of themselves resolve regional conflicts or guarantee lasting peace, they are significant events, especially after long years of conflict devoid of hope or progress, and their analysis seriously challenged the conference participants. Adding to the scenario was the closing in Moscow of the stormy 19th All-Union Conference of the CPSU in June/July 1988. The conference had just charted new directions for the domestic reforms and the conduct of international relations in the Soviet Union. The participants were thus forced into the difficult task of analyzing and trying to interpret the highly fluid conflict resolution process still occurring as they discussed and debated their points. The risk that this volume might produce scholarly material that would almost immediately become outdated was remedied by the updating carried out by the participants during the revision of their papers.

The major strength of the project and the volume rests with the fact that it represents, with its Singapore venue and the multinational character of its sponsors and participants, a truly international effort. The chapters in this volume were written by distinguished people of diverse backgrounds— leading scholars, policymakers, military men, and journalists, proceeding from four continents. Eight of the sixteen chapters were written by experienced Soviet experts from countries involved in the regional conflicts under discussion. Thus, the volume does not present a U.S. or U.S.-based view of the Soviet role in Third World regional conflicts, but rather a diverse set of international perceptions.

The volume has been divided into eight sections, each focusing on a different aspect of the topic. Their aggregate offers a strong mix of conceptual analyses of Soviet ideology and foreign policy and of analytical case studies of the relevant regional conflicts.

Part I contains a theoretical analysis of the "new thinking" in Soviet foreign policy and of its domestic contexts, as well as a conceptualization and an overview of the Soviet involvement in the Third World regional conflicts. Part II concentrates on the often neglected role of Moscow's junior allies— Vietnam and Cuba—as key actors in several regional conflicts: Vietnam in Cambodia and Laos and Cuba in Angola, Ethiopia and Nicaragua. Part III analyzes the Soviet occupation of Afghanistan and focuses on the current Soviet disengagement from a direct military role in the conflict. Part IV examines the civil war in Angola as well as in Ethiopia and the Cuban involvement within the context of the security and political situation in southern Africa, along with the current effort to reach a negotiated settlement in the region. This is followed in Part V by an analysis of the existing as well as potential future regional conflicts in Southeast Asia, namely in Cambodia and the Philippines. Part VI provides an analysis of the conflict in Nicaragua in the context of the U.S. and Soviet/Cuban rivalry in Central America. Part VII analyzes American approaches and policy options to the regional conflicts involving rivalry with the Soviet Union. Part VIII is a concluding chapter based primarily on original research material, but also presents a synthesis of various points of view presented at the conference.

In Chapter 1, Vernon V. Aspaturian, a distinguished American Sovietologist at Pennsylvania State University, provides what is likely to become a classical analysis of the Soviet "new thinking" in foreign policy and of the ideological context of the current Soviet attitudes toward the regional conflicts in the Third World. After assessing the foreign and military policy achievements of the Brezhnev era as "impressive in the short run but questionably durable or sustainable," Aspaturian examines the relationship between the requirements of the Soviet domestic reform and the rethinking of Soviet foreign policy. His analysis of the "new thinking" is cast in the discussion of the changing role of Soviet ideology and the changing Soviet image of the world. Aspaturian documents Gorbachev's perceptions of the failure of past Soviet policy in the Third World as well as his desire to establish more beneficial economic relations with key Third World countries.

While elucidating another overlooked key point, which is that President Ronald Reagan imposed the concept of regional conflicts on the Soviets and forced them to include it in the superpower negotiating agenda, Aspaturian notes the continuing ambiguity in the Soviet position on the "wars of national liberation," indicating that the deideologization of the Soviet foreign policy remains incomplete. Aspaturian identifies the main regional conflicts as perceived by Moscow and observes that they serve as an impediment to the improvement of Soviet relations with Western Europe and the United States. Furthermore, they continue to drain Soviet resources and aggravate Soviet relations with the Third World. The Soviet perspective on the regional conflicts suggests that they can be categorized according to a number of criteria: the nature and degree of external participation, defense and ideological saliency, risk and level of confrontation, and the leverage and strength of local regimes or movements. The mix of the above criteria determines the Soviet interests and sense of urgency for the resolution of a given conflict. Aspaturian asserts that, while Gorbachev and his advisors expressed their commitment to Soviet-American cooperation in resolving regional conflicts, this must be done with minimal damage to the interests, prestige and credibility of the Soviet Union as a global power. While allowing that the current reform movement might be just another episode in the cycle of alternative periods of expansion and consolidation/retrenchment in Soviet foreign policy, Aspaturian expresses confidence that the Soviet Union will, during the coming decade, be preoccupied with internal development and renovation, while seeking to develop into a multidimensional global power.

Noted Indian Soviet specialist Bhabani Sen Gupta offers in Chapter 2 an analysis of Moscow's "new thinking" and resulting policies toward Third World regional conflicts as viewed from nonaligned India. Gupta notes that Gorbachev's "new thinking," in a departure from the détente of the Brezhnev period, recognizes a linkage between peaceful coexistence at the central level (with the West) and in the peripheries (with the Third World), implying a Soviet commitment not to violently or radically alter the balance of power in Third World regions. In contrast to Aspaturian, Gupta concludes that the gains for the so-called Reagan Doctrine "have not been altogether positive" and the price for the United States "has been considerable." Gupta sees the "new thinking" as gaining ground primarily because it has been backed by concrete policies and has generated positive responses from other nations. He suggests that the successful solution of the regional conflicts will necessitate adopting a set of measures "from above" to be carried out by the superpowers, as well as a set of measures to be taken "from below" by the local actors. Gupta argues that in order to fully succeed, the "new thinking" will demand a cooperative response from the United States, China, and other major powers. While it has "created a positive impression upon the global mind," more concrete results will be needed in order for Moscow to win international trust and confidence.

William E. Griffith, a distinguished Soviet specialist at the Massachusetts Institute of Technology in Cambridge, provides a general overview of the Soviet foreign policy changes and of Moscow's updated position toward various regional conflicts in Chapter 3. Griffith stresses the importance of the development of the modernizing Russian intelligentsia and the personal background and qualities of Gorbachev as key factors behind his modernizing effort. He feels that Gorbachev, like other reformers before him, most likely will neither fully succeed nor fail in his policies. Griffith differs from Gupta

Introduction xv

in taking a more skeptical view of the depth and sincerity of the "new thinking." He believes that while the Soviet Union must currently, due to its relative weakness, pass through a period of retreat in foreign policy, if the regime succeeds in the country's renovation this period will have constituted only a pause until a further expansion of Soviet power takes place. In assessing the regional conflicts issue, Griffith sees the Soviet Union as adopting a selective approach to different regions based on a more realistic cost-benefit analysis of the situation. Soviet flexibility in Afghanistan, Cambodia, and Angola, where strong military and diplomatic factors dictate Soviet compromise and disengagement, contrasts with the Soviet attitude toward the Nicaraguan and Ethiopian conflicts, in which, as of early 1989, no compelling reasons for a significant change in policy exist. Griffith does not see an overall Soviet withdrawal from the Third World as imminent, citing the penetration of Soviet diplomatic and economic influence into such new areas as the Middle East and the Gulf region. He warns that an inward turn of American foreign policy would encourage more adventurous Soviet behavior in the Third World.

In Chapter 4, the provocative argument of Jerry F. Hough, a leading American expert on Soviet affairs from Duke University and the Brookings Institution, is that Mikhail Gorbachev and his associates in the Kremlin are repudiating Lenin's ideas and returning to Marx in their reform of domestic economic policy, while concurrently rejecting Lenin's view on Third World development in the belief that Karl Marx's analysis was closer to the truth. The realization that Marx correctly indicated that in the Third World, as in the more advanced Europe, growth would take place only if capitalism followed feudalism in a classical dialectic pattern, led the Soviet regime to revise its views on its participation in the world economy. Gorbachev came to realize that it would be defeatist to continue to support radical movements or regimes in Third World countries with pre-industrial economies, while ignoring the more economically developed and key capitalist-oriented countries—to use Samuel Huntington's term, "regional influentials"—such as Brazil, Egypt, and Indonesia. Hough argues that the Soviet Union is not retreating from the Third World, but rather moving away from the use of military instruments of policy and concentrating on economic ties with the Third World countries. Hough expresses his belief that, as Gorbachev leads the Soviet Union out of the isolation imposed on it by Brezhnev's errors, it is not retreating but will ultimately come to present an economic challenge to the West.

In Chapter 5, Douglas Pike—a distinguished expert on Vietnamese affairs at the University of California at Berkeley—explores the nature of the Vietnamese-Soviet relationship in the aftermath of the Vietnam War and examines its impact on the future of the Cambodian conflict. Pike conceptualizes the Hanoi-Moscow alliance as bound together by "extraordinarily close military, economic, diplomatic, and psychological ties," built up as a product of Soviet opportunism and of Vietnamese dependency. Contending that the Soviet influence over Hanoi never reached the stage of control, Pike argues that Moscow would thus not be able to impose a Cambodian settlement on the Vietnamese. While the Vietnamese version of *perestroika* does not extend into the realm of Vietnamese foreign policy, there is, according to Pike, no serious division between Hanoi and Moscow over the issue of the Cambodian conflict. While Hanoi's interest in Cambodia is that of elemental security, Moscow is torn between the impulse to serve as a peacemaker in the region and its unwillingness to become deeply involved in the conflict. The U.S.S.R. is obliged only to support a settlement that will take Vietnam's strategic interests into consideration. Pike regards the Cambodian conflict as a surrogate struggle between Vietnam and China, while considering the country's political anarchy and the specter of the return of the Khmer Rouge as far more serious problems than achieving the withdrawal of the Vietnamese troops. The movement toward Sino-Soviet rapprochement could be a contribution to the peace process, yet Pike perceives a need for a new political configuration in Phnom Penh that would incorporate all contending Khmer factions and be acceptable to outside powers, above all Vietnam and China.

In Chapter 6, Howard Wiarda, a leading Latin American specialist at the American Enterprise Institute and at the University of Massachusetts at Amherst, utilizes his analysis of Cuba's role as a Soviet junior ally to express his skepticism of Gorbachev's "new thinking." The Soviet Union can at one level champion a new détente while at another level, by backing Cuba, support the violent policies of Latin American revolutionary groups. Wiarda argues that Moscow is advancing its foreign policy goals through Cuba without "itself confronting the United States in areas that are particularly sensitive or in which the United States enjoys a local preponderance of power." Wiarda observes that, unlike Vietnam and in spite of severe internal problems and weaknesses, Cuba has repudiated both *glasnost* and *perestroika* and appears unwilling to reduce its international role. This is allegedly in part due to Fidel Castro's personal megalomania, as well as because Cuba continues to profit financially from its surrogate military role.

Wiarda considers arguments both for and against the expectation of the scaling back of the Soviet involvement in the Third World, challenging the view that the Soviets have only incurred grief and few benefits from their Third World adventurism during the past decade. He gives serious attention to the view that Moscow will seek to maintain its strategic and political gains in Cuba and Nicaragua and perhaps even attempt to advance their cause into new areas of Central America in general and El Salvador in particular. Wiarda predicts that, in spite of the considerable rhetorical change in the Soviet foreign policy, the actual policy alteration will be modest, with at best a slow and reluctant withdrawal from the strategic gains of the Brezhnev period. Relationships with junior allies such as Cuba may be subject to renegotiation, but this may not result in diminished Soviet/Cuban foreign policy ambitions, particularly in Central America. Wiarda cautions us to avoid ethnocentrism and wishful thinking in interpreting the limited evidence related to Moscow's "new thinking."

Part III contains two rather disparate chapters illuminating the Soviet involvement in Afghanistan and the process aimed at settling the conflict. In Chapter 7, Ali T. Sheikh of the Institute for Soviet and East European Studies of GSIS at the University of Miami, and the Strategic Institute of Islamabad, Pakistan, traces the Soviet willingness to aid in the resolution of Third World regional conflicts in general, and the Soviet decision to withdraw military forces from Afghanistan in particular, to Moscow's application of the principles of the "new thinking." He traces the improvement in Soviet-Pakistani relations after 1985 and the origins of the United Nations-sponsored negotiations in 1987 to the sharpening of the conflict following the introduction of Stinger missiles by the mujahideen forces. Sheikh discusses the friction between Moscow and Kabul over the issue of the Afghan version of the concept of "national reconciliation," which involves broadening the social base of the revolutionary regime while retaining a hostile, anti-imperialist posture toward the West, and has been considered incompatible with the principles of the "new thinking." He predicts the Geneva Accords by themselves will not bring an end to the fighting and most likely will result in the defeat of the communist regime and the continuation of the war in the form of fratricidal conflict among the mujahideen factions. While Sheikh gives his qualified support to the Soviet claim that the Geneva Accords could be used as a model for a negotiated resolution of other regional conflicts, he also warns that the Soviet military withdrawal from Afghanistan does not mean that Moscow has abandoned its traditional security concerns and the right to invoke them unilaterally.

Sabahuddin Kushkaki, former Minister of the Afghanistan pre-coup 1973 government and now Director of the Cultural Center of the Afghan Resistance in Islamabad, Pakistan, presents in Chapter 8 a rather different analysis of the situation in Afghanistan and of the changes in Soviet foreign policy than does his colleague from Pakistan. He labels Gorbachev's "new thinking" as "yet another version of Soviet opportunism" and views the reasons for Moscow's military withdrawal from the country as motivated solely by the success of the Afghan resistance in stalemating the war and by the sustained international pressure and sanctions imposed upon the Kremlin. In contrast to Sheikh, Kushkaki criticizes the Geneva Accords on the grounds that they failed to recognize the status of the Afghan resistance, did not involve the two parties directly engaged in the conflict—the Soviet Union and the Afghan mujahideen—

and failed to stop outside interference in the internal affairs of Afghanistan. Thus he does not consider the accords as having any relevance for other regional conflicts. He regards the "Geneva gimmick" as simply a face-saving device for pulling out Soviet troops while failing to address the inherent problems of Afghanistan. Kushkaki seems optimistic about the prospects for the seven-party alliance of the mujahideen to form a unity government, but he also discusses a more pessimistic scenario in the case of their failure to achieve unity, such as total political anarchy and absence of government, or a future partition of Afghanistan into spheres under the influence of respective neighboring countries. Kushkaki admits, despite his belief that the "new thinking" is just another version of Soviet opportunism, that the post-war regime will have to maintain a reasonable working relationship with the Soviet Union and must in no way be a security threat to the Kremlin.

In Chapter 9, Colin Legum, perhaps the most respected analyst of Soviet-African relations in the world today, examines the evolution of Soviet policy toward Africa. His central argument reveals that Mikhail Gorbachev instituted two distinctly different approaches to the conflict situations in southern Africa and in the Horn of Africa. Current Kremlin policies reflect two significant alterations toward southern Africa: its cooperative support for the American initiatives to secure a withdrawal of foreign troops from Angola and to arrange for Namibian independence through the implementation of the United Nations Security Council Resolution 435, and its endorsement of preference for a negotiated political settlement in South Africa over an intensified armed revolutionary struggle against apartheid. Its cooperation in the Angolan settlement is ascribed by Legum to the poor military position of its Angolan client and its Cuban ally there, as well as to the lack of strong Soviet strategic and economic interests in the area. In contrast, the Soviet Union under Gorbachev showed less willingness to force the Mengistu regime in Ethiopia into a negotiated settlement with its internal adversaries prior to early 1989. This was presumably due to the favorable military position of the Mengistu forces and a strong Soviet strategic interest in the country. After a series of military defeats of the Ethiopian regime in late 1988 through early 1989, Gorbachev reportedly urged upon the Mengistu regime the need for a political settlement with separatist movements. Moscow, however, continued its heavy flow of aid into Ethiopia, showing unwillingness to endanger its naval access to the strategic Red Sea ports.

General H. de V. du Toit, a prominent professor of national security affairs at the RAND Afrikaans University in Johannesburg, South Africa, and a former senior military official of the South African government, ascribes in Chapter 10, the current Soviet reform program to the need to transform the U.S.S.R. into a multifaceted superpower through the upgrading of the political, economic, and scientific-technical component of the national security of the Soviet state. Du Toit, whose chapter revolves around the impact of the "new thinking" upon the Soviet/Cuban activity in Angola and Namibia, acknowledges a genuine revision of the Soviet foreign policy ideology, citing the current Soviet use of the concept of "national reconciliation" to remove internal causes of regional conflicts as indicating a convenient way of relaxing the Soviet Union's ideological obligations in the Third World. Du Toit explains the Kremlin's flexibility in Angola as an outcome of escalating war costs due to the American application in southern Africa of the Reagan Doctrine, which dictated American support for the UNITA forces. In Professor du Toit's view, the Reagan Doctrine had a substantial impact on the Soviet attitude toward the regional conflict in southern Africa. He stresses the crucial need for the continuation of the Reagan Doctrine policies in southern Africa and elsewhere in the Third World as a means of regulating and moderating the behavior of the Soviet Union and its proxies. He calls for the continuity and coherence of the U.S. foreign policy in the form of "moral realpolitik" as well as "new thinking" on the part of the South African government.

In Chapter 11, Khien Theeravit, a leading Indochina expert at Chulalongkorn University in Bangkok and a former member of the Thai National Assembly, examines the role of the Soviet Union in the origins and perpetuation of the Cambodian conflict and assesses Moscow's contribution toward the search for a political solution of the problem. While noting, as Douglas Pike does earlier, that the U.S.S.R. is culturally alien in Southeast Asia and that Soviet interests in the region are not considered vital, Khien acknowledges the impressive Soviet expansion of influence into Indochina since 1975. Khien holds that Moscow's support for Vietnam enabled the latter to invade Cambodia and to sustain its occupation of the country. While the Gorbachev leadership appears eager to find a political settlement in Cambodia and urged Hanoi to attend the Jakarta Informal Meeting, JIM-I, in July 1988, and JIM-II in February 1989, Hanoi has remained cool and inflexible toward the diplomatic process. Khien argues that the Soviet Union is eager to improve its relationship with the ASEAN countries according to the principles of the "new thinking," but not at the cost of sacrificing its interest and present high level of influence in Indochina. That is why, according to Khien, in spite of its diplomatic maneuvering, the Soviet contribution to the resolution of the conflict remains limited. The Soviet position favors a settlement based on a process of national reconciliation and unification of all patriotic forces, while suggesting that an improvement in Sino-Vietnamese relations will be instrumental toward that goal. While Khien recognizes the unwillingness of the Soviet leadership to put excessive pressure on Hanoi for fear of being expelled from the naval facilities in Vietnam, he suggests that they can exert milder pressure by diverting aid from destructive purposes to constructive ones: from war support to aiding economic construction.

xx   Gorbachev's New Thinking and Third World Conflicts

In Chapter 12, Frank Cibulka from the National University of Singapore surveys Soviet-Philippine relations in their diplomatic and economic dimensions and analyzes their impact on the course of the National People's Army (NPA) communist insurgency in the Philippines. Cibulka interprets the current Soviet desire to harness the tide of Philippine nationalism with its growing anti-bases and anti-American sentiments and to secure an expulsion of the American military presence from the country after 1991. He dismisses allegations of Soviet support for the NPA insurgency on the grounds that Moscow would be unwilling to jeopardize the strategic and economic benefits associated with cordial relations with the Aquino administration. Cibulka warns, however, that an American military withdrawal from the Philippines and a subsequent neutralization of the country could tilt the balance of power in the Asia-Pacific region in favor of the Soviet Union. He also speculates that the resulting inevitable cutoff of American military aid would probably lead to an escalation in the civil war and the NPA's attainment of military parity with the governmental forces. Under such conditions there would arise the potential for an eventual Soviet and/or Vietnamese involvement in the conflict, as happened in Cambodia in the late 1970s. This could have serious repercussions for the superpowers' relations.

In Chapter 13, the sole chapter in Part VI, a former Sandinista ambassador to Ecuador and now a senior fellow at the Institute for Soviet and East European Studies, Alvaro Taboada, focuses upon the Soviet Union's relationship with Nicaragua's Sandinista regime and assesses the impact of the "new thinking" on the Nicaraguan revolution and its external behavior. Taboada demonstrates that the Sandinistas provided the Soviet Union with unexpected political opportunities and strategic gains in the Central American region. He conceptualizes the stages in the Soviet-Sandinista relationship and observes that, after a period of full support for the country's revolutionary-political vanguard, Moscow has, since 1985, attempted to influence Sandinista foreign policy in the direction of greater flexibility, while backing the further consolidation of the Leninist power structure internally. Taboada analyzes the scope of the diplomatic, military, and economic cooperation between the U.S.S.R. and Nicaragua, observing that it has resulted in the construction of the largest army in Central American history and provided potential strategic/political advantages for the U.S.S.R. in the region, for example in Panama. These opportunities will be increasing with the decline of the inter-American system. While the regional conflict in Central America remains unsolved, Taboada believes that its most likely outcome is that Nicaragua will become the predominant power in Central America.

Part VII contains two chapters and two dramatically different points of view about the American perceptions of, and their role in, the resolution of the Third World regional conflicts in which the U.S.S.R. is involved. In Chapter

14, the editor of the influential American journal *Foreign Policy* and a former Assistant Secretary of State, William Maynes, takes a critical look at the institutionalization of the Reagan Doctrine as the keystone of American Third World policy in the 1980s. Maynes asserts that the Reagan administration, motivated both by reasons of ideology and national interests, resolved to assist anticommunist forces in the Third World who were attempting to overthrow entrenched Leninist regimes. The Reagan Doctrine eliminated the principal weakness of Dulles's rollback doctrine of the 1950s because, by seeking to counter the Soviet empire only at its periphery (in the Third World), it avoided creating an even larger threat to the U.S. security—that of a nuclear confrontation with the U.S.S.R. Echoing a criticism raised in an earlier chapter by Bhabani Sen Gupta, Maynes critically assesses the impact of the Reagan Doctrine. He concludes that the application of the doctrine has driven American foreign policy in undesirable directions, committing U.S. resources to the aid of non-democratic forces while barring the encouragement of moderation and prospects for accommodation in the case of radical regimes that might be ready for reform and deideologization. In Maynes' view, the Third World, due to its progressive loss of military and economic value for the two superpowers, will in the future become less important as a focus of the U.S.-Soviet competition. But he remains concerned about the possibility that the current, second round of détente could still be undermined by a new Third World crisis, this suggesting that the superpowers might negotiate a joint policy of non-intervention. A key area of agreement would be the Middle East due to its high strategic value and perceived function as a barometer of the superpower intentions.

W. Bruce Weinrod, Director of Foreign Policy and Defense Studies at The Heritage Foundation, analyzes the implications of Gorbachev's "new thinking" for foreign policy. In contrast to the optimism of some contributors, Weinrod points out the superficial, unclear, and unfinished character of the Soviet reform movement, warning that its policies might still be reversed by its opponents or produce unintended consequences in the form of mass unrest or outbursts of nationalism. While acknowledging positive Soviet moves in regard to some Third World regional conflicts, Weinrod, echoing earlier views of Wiarda and Kushkaki, cautions that the Soviet Union has neither repudiated its duty to protect Leninist gains abroad, nor renounced its right to provide, directly or through its Leninist proxies, support for radical Third World insurgencies. Weinrod points out that Moscow has in the past utilized a two-track position by which it maintained normal relations with a given government while simultaneously undermining it through the provision of covert support for radical forces in that country. He also notes that the Soviet reform campaign might simply constitute a temporary pause or *peredyshka* in Soviet efforts to expand the sphere of communist domination. He suggests that the United States and its allies should respond to Gorbachev's "new thinking" with a sophisticated multidimensional and multilevel approach, including: the encouragement of the reforms leading to the pluralization of Soviet society; restraints on the transfer of military technologies to the Soviet bloc and on subsidized economic assistance; continued support for anti-Soviet insurgencies against radical Third World regimes; and open interaction with, and encouragement of, democratic forces in authoritarian regimes of both left and right.

In the concluding Chapter, Jiri Valenta, Director of the Institute for Soviet and East European Studies at the Graduate School of International Studies, University of Miami, and the principal organizer of this project, gathers and evaluates the findings of the conference and synthesizes them into a critical analysis of the Soviet "new thinking" and its impact on the Third World regional conflicts. Drawing on his own research and writing on the regional conflicts as well as on the collective wisdom of the conference, Valenta produces in his essay a balanced statement on the subject. After assessing the concepts of *perestroika*, *glasnost*, and "new thinking" and their influence on Soviet policymaking, Valenta addresses the role of Soviet junior partners Cuba and Vietnam in various regional conflicts, assessing their respective attitudes toward external military disengagement and the ultimate political resolutions of the conflicts involving their military forces. He emphasizes the Cuban and Vietnamese roles as "twin pillars of the Soviet-led interventionism on behalf of Leninist-oriented forces in the Third World" during the previous decade and points out the limits of current Soviet influence with these "voluntary allies" in the light of their distaste for Moscow's "new thinking" and under the conditions of the developing "transnational dialogue" within the Soviet alliance system.

In his discussion of the Afghan conflict, Valenta asserts that "among the regional conflicts involving the Soviet Union, the Afghan conflict is the only one in which the Soviets have taken practical, unilateral steps toward a resolution." Valenta proposes that the real test of the "new thinking" and of Gorbachev's sincerity will be whether Moscow will truly tolerate the establishment of a nonaligned government in Kabul. But he highlights the flawed nature of the Geneva Accords caused by the exclusion of the main party to the conflict, the mujahideen resistance, and suggests, though they were a catalyst for the negotiation of other regional conflicts, they may yet in fact become a model for how not to negotiate them.

After evaluating the Soviet role in the resolution of other Third World conflicts — Angola, Cambodia, and Nicaragua — Valenta turns to the discussion of policy implications for the United States. Cautioning that the changes in the U.S.S.R. are so far "neither structural nor irreversible," Valenta's argument suggests that while welcoming *perestroika*, the United

States should not subsidize it through premature granting of economic benefits to Moscow. Valenta holds that more evidence is needed before it can be concluded that "traditional Soviet imperialism is no longer a threat to the Western and truly nonaligned nations," and suggests that Western policymakers need to meet Soviet foreign policy initiatives with their own brand of innovative thinking. American foreign policy must serve above all the national interests, which dictate discouraging the creation of new pro-Soviet Leninist regimes in the Third World, while encouraging "a gradual mellowing of those already in existence." U.S. efforts to resolve Third World conflicts should include cooperation with the Soviet Union in the peace process, and ought to be based on the search for national reconciliation and power sharing among local adversaries. Such strategy would reflect the need for a reciprocal and balance-of-power oriented approach. In Valenta's words, "The U.S. relationship with Moscow is destined to be competitive for a long while," and in the long run should be based on the Churchillian notion that a strong Western alliance "must conciliate, not confront, the U.S.S.R."

Part One

Gorbachev's "New Thinking" and Third World Regional Conflicts Conceptualized

1

Gorbachev's "New Political Thinking" and Foreign Policy

Vernon V. Aspaturian

Introduction: Coping With the Brezhnev Legacy

Perestroika, the principal buzzword of the Gorbachev era, is conceived as a process cutting across all aspects of Soviet life, including ideology and foreign policy. Although Mikhail Gorbachev has meticulously avoided using the term "restructuring" in reference to ideology since this could open him up to charges of "revisionism," he has called for the application of *perestroika* in Soviet foreign policy.

> At present, a restructuring of the work of the Ministry of Foreign Affairs is underway and a reorganization of the structure of its central apparatus and foreign institutions is being carried out. This leadership is being renewed. This line must be pursued consistently, increasing the efficiency of the activity of the diplomatic service and *striving* to have it correspond fully to the vigorous international activity of the CPSU and the Soviet State.[1]

Gorbachev, however, has introduced another term, "new political thinking," which is nothing less than the application of *perestroika* to ideology. The specific application of *perestroika* to Soviet foreign policy involves the following components: (1) Recasting the ideological parameters of Soviet foreign policy and reconceptualizing perceptions of the international system, national security, defense, military doctrine, and strategy, in accordance with the "new foreign policy philosophy," essentially a subset of the "new political thinking." (2) Redirecting Soviet foreign policy goals and reordering Soviet foreign policy priorities. (3) Reorganizing the foreign policy decision-making system, involving personnel, institutions, and processes. Only the first and second components of *perestroika* in Soviet foreign policy will be treated in this analysis.

The death of Leonid Brezhnev in November 1982 after eighteen years in office, ended one of the longest periods of leadership and political stability in

4 Gorbachev's New Thinking and Third World Conflicts

the history of the Soviet Union, and marked the end of one era and the prelude to a new, potentially long period of leadership under Mikhail S. Gorbachev, who became Brezhnev's definitive successor in March 1985 after a brief two-and-a-half year interregnum of leadership uncertainty under Andropov and Chernenko. It was clear that the new Soviet leadership under Gorbachev was entering a period of uncertainty, with a legacy of both stagnation and instability that Gorbachev is determined to arrest and reverse.

There is no doubt that Brezhnev's death marked the end of a definite era in the evolution of the Soviet state and its role and status in the international system. The Brezhnev legacy is a mixture of achievements and failures in both domestic and foreign policy, with the failures accumulating toward the end of the Brezhnev incumbency. Brezhnev's death marked the beginning of a new era in the sense that the unfinished goals, frustrations, and serious unresolved chronic problems of that era were left to his successors, who in turn were confronted by a new American president determined to reverse the course of Soviet-American relations and to blunt the growth and expansion of Soviet power and influence.

Brezhnev's achievements, particularly in foreign and military policy, were impressive and extensive in the short run, but were questionably durable or sustainable. Soviet foreign policy is shaped by many variables, but among the most important and difficult to calculate is the Soviet perception of risks, opportunities, and costs in pursuing objectives, whatever they might be at any given time. When risk and cost perceptions are low and opportunity perceptions are high, Soviet Leaders are inclined to pursue their foreign policy goals more vigorously and exploit opportunities with greater alacrity, even at the expense of resolving serious domestic problems. When risk and cost perceptions are high, they are likely to behave more cautiously and prudently, consolidating and retrenching rather than expanding their power, and to concentrate on the solution of pressing internal problems rather than risk confrontation abroad.

During the decade of the seventies, as a result of the Vietnam debacle, Watergate, and general U.S. disillusionment and demoralization, the Brezhnev leadership perceived the risks and costs of acting more vigorously in foreign policy to be low. The United States appeared to enter a period of self-paralysis and incapacity to behave assertively in foreign policy, and this was viewed by many Soviet leaders as the beginning of a long period of irreversible decline for the United States. With this perception, Brezhnev decided to mortgage the immediate Soviet domestic future by investing in expanding Soviet power abroad.

It was during this period that Brezhnev's achievements manifested themselves as the Soviet Union (1) achieved status and recognition as a global power, with global interests and presence; (2) achieved and gained recognition as the political and military equal of the United States; (3) established an extended empire of dependent and client states beyond the Soviet periphery in South and Southeast Asia, the Middle East, Africa, and the Caribbean; and (4) shifted the overall world or strategic balance of power or "correlation of forces" to immense Soviet advantage.

These accomplishments were not achieved without a serious price, for which Brezhnev, posthumously, and the Soviet future will pay very dearly. Soviet successes in foreign policy generated an inevitable serious counterresponse from the United States and its allies, which in turn undercut and threatened to nullify many of Brezhnev's successes. The most serious and crippling price that the Soviet Union has paid for its immense military growth and globalist ambitions was the disorientation, dislocation, and deformation of the Soviet economy, which entered into a period of stagnation and decline, threatening to leave the Soviet Union and its East European client states far behind the United States, Western Europe, and Japan as they moved at an accelerated pace into the new era of high technology, and even threatened to undercut Soviet military prowess in the process.

The stagnation of the Soviet economy has had manifold domestic reverberations. The standard of living grew at an ominously slow pace, as both workers and managers accustomed themselves to low productivity and efficiency, and as a series of shortfalls in agricultural production created serious food problems for the country. The size of the non-Russian nationalities, particularly the Moslem groups of Central Asia, has grown at a rapid pace while the Russian and Slavic population neared zero-population growth. Such asymmetrical demographic growth threatened not only the integrity of the labor force, but the Soviet military as well. As the ethnic balance tilted in favor of the non-Slavic population, furthermore, the demand and competition for relatively diminished scarce resources and wealth among the various nationalities and republics has become sharper and more aggravated. Similar problems were generated in the Soviet Bloc as a whole, as the Stalinist socioeconomic model exhausted its potential for further constructive development. These accumulated domestic problems, of course, seriously compromised the capacity of the Soviet Union to advance its globalist ambitions abroad, which became painfully evident as the decade of the eighties unfolded.

The Brezhnev legacy, precisely because it was a mixture of grand achievements in military and foreign policy and dismal failures in domestic policies, thus became ambiguous and ambivalent in its implications for the future. Brezhnev's successors were confronted with cruel alternatives: to continue the course of enhancing military power and imperial ambitions at the expense of

6   Gorbachev's New Thinking and Third World Conflicts

further neglect and damage to the Soviet economy, or to shift priorities and effort to the resolution of serious domestic problems at the risk of suffering in the global competition with the United States abroad.

With the advent of the Reagan administration and its more assertive, even belligerent rhetoric and promise of corresponding behavior, Moscow was compelled to enter into a new phase in its competition with the United States. Squeezed between the war in Afghanistan and the political turmoil in Poland, burdened with insistent and expensive demands by its Third World clients for greater military and economic assistance as they descended into social and economic chaos, and faced with increasing guerrilla opposition supported by the United States, successive Soviet leaders were loathe to risk confrontation with the Reagan administration and engage it in a new and higher level of arms competition in the age of high technology. Thus Moscow gradually entered into a defensive and retrenchist mode as the new Reagan administration signalled that the years of low-risk, easy pickings for Moscow were over and as the U.S. pressure on Cuba and Nicaragua increased. The Soviet client regime in Grenada was forcibly overthrown, military assistance to the Afghan guerrillas and others was escalated, and intermediate-range nuclear missiles were deployed in Western Europe to counter the Soviet deployment of SS-20s. American reassertiveness, together with the prolonged leadership uncertainty and the serious domestic problems, all congealed to compel a fundamental reexamination of the Soviet agenda and its priorities in foreign and domestic policy.

Gorbachev clearly recognized that the intersection of the Soviet Union's accumulated domestic problems and the advent of a more assertive American counterresponse would lead to a catastrophic confrontation if Moscow pursued its expansionist policies. This was boldly conceptualized by Gorbachev at the 19th Communist Party conference, held in June-July, 1988.

> But, while concentrating enormous funds and attention on the military aspect of countering imperialism . . . we allowed ourselves to be drawn into an arms race, which could not but affect the country's socioeconomic developments and its international standing. . . . To put it more bluntly, without overturning the logic of this course, we could actually have found ourselves on the brink of a military confrontation. Hence, what was needed was not just a refinement of foreign policy, but its determined reshaping. This called for new political thinking.[2]

Gorbachev's rhetoric clearly reflects his sense of urgency, as both he and his supporters have emphasized that his reform program is the "last chance" the Soviet Union has to recover from its economic stagnation and torpor, which threaten to undermine not only its military prowess but its cherished role and status in the international system as one of the two global powers. This part of the Brezhnev legacy Gorbachev wished passionately to preserve, and to do this requires the repudiation of the remaining part of that legacy and the virtual inversion of Soviet priorities. How to downgrade the priority of the Soviet overseas empire acquired under Brezhnev, while simultaneously preserving the credibility of Soviet global power, emerges as one of the most vexing conundrums of the Gorbachev regime.

Restructuring Soviet Ideology

Soviet ideology over the years has increasingly become less a guide to Soviet policy than a legitimization of Soviet behavior. Since the Soviet Union is an ideologically inspired state, ideology continues to retain its importance as a source of explanation and justification of Soviet behavior. Hence, Gorbachev must still pay lip service to ideology and formulate his own program within it, otherwise he may undermine his own legitimacy.

Soviet Ideology and Foreign Policy

The exact relationship between Soviet ideology and foreign policy has been subject to great controversy, ranging from the view that it is substantially irrelevant to the conviction that foreign policy is rigidly dictated by ideology. The precise role that ideology plays in Soviet foreign policy is subject to periodic and episodic controversy, in reference to Soviet foreign policy. The most recent domestic manifestation of this periodic controversy over the relationship between Soviet foreign policy and Soviet ideology, in its broadest dimensions, was Egor Ligachev's challenge to the publicly stated positions of Gorbachev, Aleksandr Iakovlev, and Eduard Shevardnadze that Soviet foreign policy should no longer be subordinated to ideology, that the class struggle was no longer the nexus of Soviet analytical perceptions of the international scene, and that class interests would have to be subordinated to the interests of nations and mankind.[3] This had been forcefully articulated at the 19th Party Conference by Gorbachev himself:

> As we analyzed the contemporary world, we realized more clearly that international relations, without losing their class character are increasingly coming to be precisely relations between nations. We noted the enhanced role in world affairs of peoples, nations, and emerging new national entities. And this implies that there is no ignoring the diversity of interests in international affairs. . . . From the standpoint of our day—with its mounting nuclear menace, heightening of other global problems, and progressive internationalization of all the processes in a world becoming, despite all its contradictions, even more integral and interdependent—we have sought a deeper understanding of the interrelationship between working class interests and those of humanity as a whole. . . . This led to the conclusion that common human values have a priority in our age, this being the core of the new political thinking. The new political thinking has enabled us to appreciate more fully how vitally important to international relations are the moral values that have over the centuries been evolved by nations, and generalized and spelled out by humanity's great minds.[4]

8   Gorbachev's New Thinking and Third World Conflicts

Recognizing that the subordination of Soviet foreign policy to Soviet ideology, which dictated the highest priority to the class struggle in international relations, generated international conflict and tensions among states and nations, Gorbachev conceded that "stereotypes" of this character "supplied arguments to those who indulged in misrepresenting our real intentions."[5]

Every Soviet leader from Lenin to Gorbachev has made major emendations in Soviet ideology in terms of its relevance for foreign policy. Since Soviet ideology is not a unidimensional or monofunctional entity, various dimensions of Soviet ideology have been restructured periodically, to use Gorbachev's favorite term, at different times and in differing degrees. The function of Soviet ideology in setting and defining ultimate, often transcendental goals, is the best and most widely known of these functions, but sometimes thought to be its only function. Actually, Soviet ideology performs five additional distinct, interrelated, but separable, functions in Soviet behavior as follows:

1. As a system of knowledge, and as an analytical prism, it reflects an image of the existing social order and the distinctive analytical instruments (dialectical laws, and categories such as "class struggle," "historical stages," and so on) for its diagnosis and prognosis.
2. As an action strategy with which to accelerate the transformation of the existing social order into the communist millennium.
3. As a system of communication, unifying and coordinating the activities of its adherents.
4. As a system of higher rationalization to justify, obscure, or conceal the chasms that may develop between theory and practice.
5. As a symbol of continuity and legitimacy.

During the decade of the seventies, as Soviet military capabilities developed and the United States reduced its international commitments in the wake of Vietnam, appearing immobilized by the variegated traumas of the Vietnam defeat and the Watergate scandal which resulted in a series of fractured presidencies, Soviet ideological goals appeared to reassert themselves with greater force in Soviet foreign policy behavior. The resurgence of ideological imperatives was accompanied by the increasing prominence of Brezhnev in his capacity as Secretary General of the Party in Soviet foreign policy and foreign affairs.

As the Soviet Union expanded its global activities and reached into the remote regions of Asia, Africa, and Latin America to lend military support and assistance to friendly revolutionary movements and regimes, ideology was increasingly invoked to legitimize its behavior. The apparent reideologization of Soviet foreign policy found explicit expression in the Brezhnev

Constitution of 1977. An entirely new and juridically unprecedented Chapter on Foreign Policy, Article 28, in effect converted ideological commitments into state obligations by defining the goals of Soviet foreign policy as follows:

> The foreign policy of the U.S.S.R. is aimed at ensuring international conditions favorable for building communism in the U.S.S.R., safeguarding the state interests of the Soviet Union, consolidating the positions of world socialism, supporting the struggle of peoples for national liberation and social progress, preventing wars of aggression, achieving universal and complete disarmament, and consistently implementing the principle of peaceful coexistence of states with different social systems.[6]

It would be reasonable to assume that the seven distinct goals of Soviet foreign policy as enumerated above are listed in order of priority and precedence, in which case, "consolidating the positions of world socialism" (3) and "supporting the struggle . . . for national liberation" (4) have a conspicuously higher priority than either arms control and disarmament (6) or "peaceful coexistence of states with different social systems" (7), which is relegated to last. Gorbachev seeks, no less than to reorder the priority of these foreign policy goals:

> A key factor in the new thinking is the concept of freedom of choice. . . . In this situation the imposition of a social system, way of life, or policies from outside by any means, let alone military, are dangerous trappings of the past period. . . . The axis of international affairs is shifting away from confrontation towards cooperation, mutual understanding, and negotiations.[7]

And as evidence of his sincerity, Gorbachev specifically linked the INF treaty, manifesting the general improvement of Soviet-American relations, to the withdrawal of Soviet troops from Afghanistan as recognition that the improvement of Soviet-American relations and the negotiation of arms control treaties have taken higher priority in his calculations than "supporting the struggle for . . . national liberation."

It is noteworthy, however, that whereas the resolutions of the 19th Party Conference endorsed the lessening of international tensions, continued arms control negotiations, and the withdrawal of Soviet troops from Afghanistan, the closest they came to endorsing Gorbachev's view that foreign policy should be deideologized was the statement that "Perestroika requires a foreign policy adequately reflecting its humanistic essence, opening up for Soviet society broad opportunities for mutually beneficial cooperation, and diverse democratic ties with the rest of the world."[8] Nothing was said about the reconceptualization of "peaceful coexistence," the subordination of class struggle to international cooperation and the subordination of class interests to the interests of mankind. This suggests that Gorbachev's "new political thinking," in all of its manifestations, was not adopted at the 19th Party Conference as a formal Party decision, and thus accounts for Ligachev's public disputation of these issues with Gorbachev, Iakovlev, and Shevardnadze. Apparently Egor Ligachev and those who agreed with him would accept the "new political thinking" in the form of changing strategy and tactics in the pursuit of Soviet foreign policy goals, in conformity with the Leninist axiom that in foreign policy, Moscow should employ a feasible strategy in pursuit of fixed principles. Gorbachev, however, as will be elaborated below, was offering the "new political thinking" as going beyond strategy to the emendation of basic ideological principles.

The sweeping ideological tone of the foreign policy section of the 1977 Constitution is in stark contrast to the 1936 Constitution, which it superceded, in which neither a special section on foreign policy nor any extravagant statements on the aims of Soviet foreign policy was included. The 1977 Constitution, however, does seem to echo the tone of the 1924 Constitution, whose preamble was blatantly revolutionary and ideological. It began with the grandiose description of a world . . . divided into two camps . . . the camp of capitalism: national hate and inequality, colonial slavery and chauvinism, national oppression and massacres, brutalities and imperialist wars . . . [and] the camp of socialism: reciprocal confidence and peace, national liberty and equality, the peaceful coexistence and fraternal collaboration of peoples. Its final words were that

> the Union of the Soviet Socialist Republics . . . will serve as a bulwark against world capitalism and mark a new decisive step toward the union of the workers of all countries in one World Socialist Soviet Republic.[9]

Whereas the words of the 1924 Constitution reflected revolutionary bravado, ideological candor, and diplomatic naiveté, the passages of the 1977 Constitution reflected the new power and self-confidence of Brezhnev's Russia. The absence of ideological verbiage on foreign policy in the 1936 Constitution mirrored Moscow's weakness and prudence at a time of great international danger (Nazi Germany and militarist Japan), when it was still developing capabilities. Its search for allies could be seriously compromised if strident ideological and revolutionary, anti-capitalist rhetoric were included in its newly instituted constitution.

The Brezhnev constitution's chapter on foreign policy thus reflected the goals and ambitions of an ideological global power, sufficiently confident and self-assured to pronounce its ideological goals in foreign policy more openly and militantly, rather than leaving them only to Party pronouncements. Earlier, ideological goals in foreign policy were clearly separated from official state policy because their inclusion aroused strong counterreactions and responses from the outside world and could endanger the security and survival of the Soviet state. The advent of the Reagan administration in 1981, with its own ideological bent in foreign policy, would seem to reconfirm that, whenever Moscow is perceived as pursuing ideological goals in foreign policy, a strong counter-ideological response is stimulated in other countries, and state relations become entangled in ideological conflict, rendering the diplomatic settlement of outstanding issues much more difficult.

Although the growth of Soviet military capabilities would seem to make the achievement of ideological goals more realistic, the qualitative changes in military technology (nuclear weapons) render the employment of military power to achieve ideological goals more risky and even suicidal. The Soviet leaders attempted to solve this paradox by seeking a détente relationship with the United States that would neutralize or nullify nuclear weapons through deterrence, while at the same time freeing the Soviet Union to use its growing non-nuclear capabilities to achieve its foreign policy goals and purposes, a détente formula that the United States ultimately rejected.

During the Brezhnev era, the Soviet Union pursued a variation of the original Leninist-Stalinist dual-track strategy, based upon a division of labor and distribution of responsibility between the Party and the State. Foreign policy activity was divided into two spheres or realms, the sphere of interstate relations and the sphere of international class relations. In the first sphere, the Soviet state interacted with other states more or less within the parameters of traditional diplomacy, power politics, and international law. The Ministry of Foreign Affairs (formerly the Narkomindel) was the principal executing arm of state-to-state relations, and the operating tactical (later strategic) formula was that of "peaceful coexistence" between states with differing social systems. In effect, the first sphere reflected *interstate* compatibility, conflict, consensus, and cooperation, whereas the second sphere reflected inevitable *intersystem* conflict with ultimate apocalyptic consequences.

The second sphere was the domain of the Party, operating through the Comintern and foreign communist parties, as well as assorted movements, fronts, "transmission belts," and other "nonstate" activities. In this sphere the international class struggle was prosecuted. Thereby, the Party sought to undermine, subvert, or overthrow the capitalist system in the same states with whom the Soviet Union was conducting "normal" state relations. In the second sphere, the operating formula was not "peaceful coexistence" but "proletarian internationalism," the operating formula, which is translated to mean the subordination of state and national loyalty to proletarian class loyalty. Relative emphasis on one sphere or another in the conduct of Soviet foreign policy varied with circumstances, risks, and opportunities, as Moscow carefully modulated and orchestrated the two arms of its foreign policy operations.

This two-track or two-sphere approach was institutionalized in the Brezhnev constitution and was considered sacrosanct until the advent of Gorbachev's "new political thinking." Judging from Ligachev's statements, the former second secretary still subscribed to this approach, whereas Gorbachev's "new political thinking" would appear to renounce it as no longer appropriate or applicable.

The specific Brezhnev application of the two-sphere approach was based upon a recognition that pursuing the "class struggle" in Europe was risky and dangerous, whereas the newly emancipated Third World afforded ample opportunity for extending Soviet influence, power, and ideology. Thus, instead of an abstract vision of two spheres, Brezhnev conceived of two ideogeographically compartmentalized spheres. The first sphere, relations with the West, would be based upon détente as the contemporary expression of "peaceful coexistence." Moscow would seek to lessen international tensions through arms control arrangements and other inducements, appear to support the *political status quo*, postpone indefinitely any idea of altering the ideological or system *status quo*, and conduct normal relations as if the West and the socialist world existed together in separate vacuums. The SALT agreements and related arms control arrangements, the treaties with Germany, and the Helsinki Accords were the principal manifestations of Soviet foreign policy in this sphere.

Since Brezhnev assumed the conduct of Soviet foreign policy as General Secretary of the Party, the distinction between Party and state activities in international relations became increasingly blurred until their boundaries actually ceased to exist. The SALT I agreement and the Helsinki Accords, as well as other international documents, were signed by Brezhnev solely in his capacity as General Secretary of the Party, an unprecedented procedure in the history of diplomacy. Thus, unlike earlier versions of the two spheres or tracks—one Party and one State, each operating in two separate spheres, one ideological and nonstate and the other nonideological and non-Party—under Brezhnev the Soviet state pretended to pursue nonideological goals in one sphere, while openly pursuing ideological goals in the other. To be sure, the Foreign Ministry was the main operational arm of the first sphere, and the International Department of the Central Committee, the operational arm of the second, but the state was openly involved in both.

Meanwhile, in the second sphere, the Third World, neither détente, nor "peaceful coexistence," nor political or ideological *status quos* were applicable, and the Soviet Union reserved the right to pursue its policies as a state in accordance with a different set of principles and formulas: "proletarian internationalism," support for wars and movements of "national liberation," "internationalist duties," "fraternal assistance," encouraging the creation of Leninist "socialist oriented" regimes, and directly supplying political, economic, ideological, and military assistance. The culmination of this policy was the Soviet invasion of Afghanistan, where the overt subordination of Soviet foreign policy to ideology and the priority of class interests were more clearly pronounced than on any other occasion:

> The experience of the revolutionary liberation struggle of the peoples shows that at critical moments solidarity with a victorious revolution calls not only for moral support, but also for material assistance, including, under definite circumstances, military assistance. . . . Today, when there exists a system of socialist states, it would be simply ridiculous to question the right to such assistance. . . . To refuse to use the possibilities at the disposal of the socialist countries would signify virtually evading performance of the internationalist duty and returning the world to the times when imperialism could throttle at will any revolutionary movement. In the given instance, not to come to Afghanistan's aid would signify leaving the Afghan revolution and people prey to class enemies, to imperialism and feudal reaction.[10]

The United States rejected this dualistic notion of two spheres and put forth the theory of "linkage." That meant that détente was universal, and not Euro-centric, and any attempt on the part of the Soviet Union to pursue a dual-track policy of détente in Europe and expansion in the Third World would be resisted. Moscow, firm in its conviction that the United States was unable or unwilling to enforce a universal détente, acted as if Soviet behavior in the Third World would not impact adversely on its relations with the United States and the West generally.

With the appearance of an assertive American administration, however, which injected a strong dose of ideology into U.S. foreign policy, the new Soviet leader, Gorbachev, was impelled to call for a moratorium in the ideological conflict and for "removing the ideological edge from interstate relations."[11] Since Brezhnev, in the new Soviet Constitution of 1977, formally and constitutionally invested the Soviet state with ideological commitments in the prosecution of its foreign policy, it may yet be difficult for the Soviet Union to credibly maintain that it has shed its ideological edge in interstate behavior. For example, the Soviet military presence in Afghanistan was described as the fulfillment of the Soviet Union's "internationalist duty," which is essentially a self-declared and self-assumed ideological obligation. The Soviet decision to withdraw its troops from Afghanistan is an important indication that Gorbachev is serious about removing the "ideological edge" from Soviet state behavior abroad. Ultimately, Gorbachev will probably also reexamine and recast the constitutional provisions pertaining to foreign and defense policy as well, in order to bring them into conformity with his new "foreign policy philosophy."

The Changing Soviet Image of the World

Under Gorbachev, Soviet ideology in general, but in terms of its application to foreign policy in particular, is in the middle of a major restructuring process, in which all of its functional dimensions are subject to radical review and change, perhaps more far-reaching than in previous periods. It should be emphasized, however, that the process is only in its beginning and discussion state; what the ultimate consequences will be both in terms of restructuring and its relevance for foreign policy at this point remain unknown. As Gorbachev himself noted at the 19th Party Conference, "the 'new political thinking' is not a final and consummate doctrine" but subject to further refinement.[12] The removal of Ligachev from foreign policy and ideological responsibilities, and the retirement of both the late Andrei Gromyko and Anatolii Dobrynin (personal symbols of the old foreign policy, which has come under increasingly open and persistent criticism), soon after Ligachev's attempt to reaffirm the centrality of class conflict and class interests in foreign policy in his Gorky speech, strongly suggest that Gorbachev is well on the road to making his vision of international relations, that of the Soviet Party and state. Furthermore, by replacing Gromyko as the ceremonial and *de jure* head of state, Gorbachev improved his ability to transform the Soviet presidency into a new, stronger executive with defined constitutional powers over foreign policy and defense. Clearly, Gorbachev seeks to disestablish the two-spheres approach to Soviet foreign policy, an approach that is characterized as contributing to a generation of international tensions, the deterioration of Soviet-American relations, and the negative image of Soviet international behavior in general. This is now openly conceded in the Soviet media in which the following unusually candid critique of past Soviet behavior by a Soviet historian is not at all atypical:

> Could such a severe exacerbation of tension in Soviet-Western relations in the late seventies and early eighties have been avoided? Unquestionably so. It is our conviction that the crisis was caused chiefly by the miscalculations and incompetent approach of the Brezhnev leadership toward the resolution of foreign policy tasks. Though we were politically, militarily (via weapons, supplies, and advisers), and diplomatically involved in regional conflicts, we disregarded their influence on the relaxation of tension between the U.S.S.R. and the West and on their entire system of relationships.[13]

"The new political thinking" and the "new foreign policy philosophy," as the subcomponents relating to foreign policy are dubbed, for the first time promise a radical reexamination and overhaul of the analytical and epistemological dimension of Soviet ideology and for that reason can be viewed as its restructuring. Previously, the goal-orienting and action strategy components of Soviet foreign policy have been the most conspicuously tampered with, whereas the epistemological-analytical dimension has suffered relatively little change. Both Stalin and Khrushchev made substantial and critical emendations with respect to the "inevitability of war" analytical thesis and the nature of the ideological polarization and confrontation between socialism and capitalism, but their principal innovations were in the realm of strategy and approach, rather than epistemology and cognitive analysis.

The Soviet ideological prism has traditionally projected an image of a world gripped by incessant class conflict and convulsive change, in which institutions, socioeconomic structures, loyalties, and philosophies arise and decay in accordance with the pulsating rhythm of a dialectic that implacably propels it on a predetermined arc to a preordained future—world communism. This image, although amended at its margins from time to time, has been accepted as the real world by Soviet leaders. Their foreign policy has rested upon the conviction that Marxism-Leninism is a scientific system that has uncovered and revealed the fundamental and implacable laws of social evolution, and hence, afforded its adherents the unique advantage of prediction and partial control of events.

The New Political Thinking and Gorbachev's Image of the World

The "new political thinking" introduces a substantially revised image of the outside world from that of the Stalinist era and the residual Stalinism of the Brezhnev period. It builds on and extrapolates on the image that emerged during the Khrushchev period but was brushed aside by Brezhnev. This new image of the world can be found in its various stages of evolution in Gorbachev's speeches and statements, and in the speeches of his advisers and supporters, especially people like Secretariat and Politburo member Aleksandr Iakovlev, Evgenii Primakov, Alexsandr Bovin, Feodor Burlatskii, and others. Its most straightforward and clearest exposition is to be found in Gorbachev's book, *Perestroika*, especially in the chapter entitled, "How We See the World of Today."[14] This chapter summarizes in simple, clear language the basic outlines of Gorbachev's image of the world, but since the book is designed primarily for external audiences, many of the harsher edges of Soviet ideology have been burnished away, and the result is essentially a propagandistic variant of the Gorbachev vision. Particularly missing are the harsh and bitter comments about capitalism, the United States, and the West in general, which are still to be found in his speeches and reports delivered at home. He emphasizes the "positive," avoids the negative, and focuses on areas of common concern. Many of the ideas in the "new political thinking" may be new to Soviet ears and eyes, but not to Westerners, since in many respects they simply represent ideas, concepts, and themes developed in the West, coopted by Gorbachev and his supporters and given a Soviet twist. Ideas such as interdependence, mutual security, concern for ecology, environmental problems, depletion of natural resources, the unity of mankind, irrationality of nuclear war, etc., have long achieved platitudinal status in the West and are new only to the Soviet political agenda.

It should be emphasized that the summary of the "new political thinking" outlined here is still tentative, exploratory, and not definitive, since it is still in the process of evolution and definition. Furthermore, the rhetoric of the "new political thinking" has been notably absent from the speeches and statements of Egor Ligachev, Viktor Chebrikov, and other high Soviet leaders (who have paid for their criticism or lack of enthusiasm with retirement or demotion), with the conspicuous exception of Shevardnadze and Iakovlev, who appear to be the principal architects of the "new thinking." Thus these views may still not represent a consensus of the Soviet leadership, and are in fact resisted, opposed, or simply fail to be accepted by elements in the Soviet leadership and bureaucracies. Ligachev, Chebrikov, Vladimir Shcherbitskii, and Vitalii Vorotnikov, all full members of the Politburo, are opposed to many aspects of Gorbachev's "new political thinking," whereas other important members of the Politburo, like Lev Zaikov and Nikolai Ryzhkov, are essentially noncommittal. On the other hand, as the Yeltsin affair demonstrated, many aspects of the "new political thinking" in the writings of Gorbachev's supporters go beyond what Gorbachev himself may ultimately accept, when and if he does definitively consolidate his power and lay down his imprint.

Only residual elements of the old two-camp image of the world can be found in the Gorbachev outlook, just barely enough to retain a semblance of continuity in the Soviet perspective. Gorbachev still subscribes to the notion of two radically divergent dominant ideologies and social systems that seek to extend their reach into the developing Third World, which subscribes to neither but is ambivalently and episodically pulled in one direction or another. What is extraordinarily new in the Gorbachev view, for a Soviet position, is the idea that the world constitutes a material and civilizational unity, integrity, and interdependence, in spite of its contradictory, diverse, and tension-laden character, whose survival has a higher priority than the expansion of *either* of the two ideologies or social systems:

> The time is ripe for abandoning views on foreign policy which are influenced by an imperial viewpoint. Neither the Soviet Union nor the United States is able to force its will on others. It is possible to suppress, compel, bribe, break, or blast, but only for a certain period. From the point of view of long-term, big-time politics, no one will be able to subordinate others. . . . The fundamental principle of the new political outlook is very simple: Nuclear war cannot be a means of achieving political, economic, ideological, or any other goals. . . . Nuclear war is senseless; it is irrational. There would be neither winners nor losers in a global nuclear conflict: World civilization would inevitably perish.[15]

Aside from implicitly acknowledging an "imperial viewpoint" to past Soviet behavior, the revolutionary character of Gorbachev's views, from the standpoint of a Soviet leader, is that it explicitly repudiates the conviction that the worldwide victory of socialism is inevitable under any and all conditions. It thus implicitly subverts the scientific credentials of Leninism, which were hitherto based on the inescapable inevitability of the demise of capitalism and the universal triumph of socialism. The real possibility of nuclear war in the new formulation renders universal socialism only a highly likely possibility, but not a certainty. To emphasize this point, Gorbachev explicitly disavows General Karl von Clausewitz's famous dictum as being obsolete and invalid under modern conditions wherein resorting to even nonnuclear war could have catastrophic results.[16]

Noting that "no one can close down the world of capitalism . . . or the world of developed socialism," Gorbachev asserts that "the new political outlook calls for the recognition of one more simple axiom: security is indivisible."

> Universal security in our time rests upon the recognition of the rights of every nation to choose its own path of social development. . . . A nation may choose either capitalism or socialism. This is its sovereign right. Nations cannot and should not pattern their life either after the United States or the Soviet Union. Hence, political positions should be devoid of ideological intolerance.[17]

Since the "new political thinking" explicitly contradicts some fundamental and seminal elements of Marxist-Leninist cognitive and epistemological principles, Gorbachev must reconcile his new views with traditional Marxist-Leninist notions concerning dialectics, the class struggle, and class analysis in general. Otherwise he can be charged with the abandonment and even repudiation of Marxism-Leninism, charges that are now increasingly reflected in the Soviet press and implicit in Ligachev's attack. Gorbachev goes beyond simply stating that ideological conflict should not be reflected at the interstate level, a standard strategy often invoked by his predecessors, and demands that foreign policies should no longer be shaped by ideological differences, the specific point on which Ligachev's criticism was focused:

> Ideological differences should not be transferred to the sphere of interstate relations, nor should foreign policy be subordinate to them, for ideologies may be poles apart, whereas the interest of survival and prevention of war stand universal and supreme.[18]

If this view prevails, it will represent a monumental step in the repudiation of Marxism-Leninism itself, for it is an explicit admission that, first, ideological differences are a source of international tension and conflict, second, that they pose a barrier to the solution of world problems, and third, that survival and prevention of war take priority over the promotion of ideological positions.

Apparently Gorbachev is cognizant of the fact that his views are remarkably non-Marxist in nature, since they invoke supraclass concepts, based upon the premise that interests exist that rise above classes and are beyond the reach of the class struggle. Recognizing that he may be charged with the resurrection of bourgeois concepts like "eternal truths" and "universal interests," Gorbachev implicitly admits to intellectual improvisation and the restructuring of Lenin's ideas:

> A new way of thinking is not an improvisation, nor a mental exercise. . . . We draw inspiration from Lenin. Turning to him, and 'reading' his works each time in a new way . . . to see the most intricate dialectics of world processes. . . . More than once he spoke about the priority of interests common to all humanity over class interests. . . . It is they that are feeding our philosophy of international relations, and the new way of thinking. One may argue that philosophers and theologists throughout history have dealt with the ideas of 'eternal' human values. True, this is so, but then these were 'scholastic speculations' doomed to be a utopian dream. In the 1980s . . . mankind should acknowledge the vital necessity of human values and their priority.[19]

Where does this leave the "class struggle," the elemental foundation and nexus of Soviet cognitive analysis? Gorbachev came close to repudiating the class struggle, although he concedes its past validity as well as its current partial and residual validity, but clearly he recognizes that reliance on the concept of the "class struggle" as the basis of political analysis is not only a barrier to peace, but may in fact promote war and destruction:

> Since time immemorial, class interests were the cornerstone of both foreign and domestic policies. . . . Marxists . . . are convinced that in the final analysis the policy of any state or alliance of states is determined by the interests of prevailing sociopolitical forces. Acute clashes of these interests in the international arena have led to armed conflicts and wars throughout history. . . . Today, this tradition is leading directly into the nuclear abyss. . . . The backbone of the new way of thinking is the recognition of the priority of human values, or to be more precise, of humankind's survival.[20]

Then, in a remarkable series of statements, Gorbachev in his book all but concedes that dogmatic and rigid adherence to ideological orthodoxy by Soviet leaders in the past had inadvertently promoted tension and courted disaster:

> It may seem strange to some people that communists should place such strong emphasis on human interests and values. Indeed, a class-motivated approach to all phenomena of social life is the ABC's of Marxism. . . . Humanitarian notions were viewed as a function and the end result of the struggle of the working class—the last class which, ridding itself, rids the entire society of class antagonisms. But, now with the emergence of weapons of mass, that is, universal destruction, there appeared an objective limit for class confrontation in the international arena: the threat of universal destruction. For the first time ever there emerged a real, not speculative and remote, common human interest—to save humanity from disaster.[21]

The new realities compelled a revision of the Party program in a number of important particulars, which again recognized the past Soviet contribution to the generation of international tension and conflict. At the 27th Party Congress he writes, "We deemed it no longer possible to retain in it the definition of peaceful coexistence of states with different social systems as a 'specific form of class struggle'."[22] Thus, the concept of "peaceful coexistence," invented by Stalin as a "tactic" in relations with the capitalist world and converted by Khrushchev into a long-term "strategy" for dealing with the external world, was now to be transformed into a "principle" governing relations with the external world, i.e., it becomes a concept defining a *condition* rather than a process, another idea that was anathema to Ligachev.

Furthermore, according to Gorbachev, the old Leninist ideas concerning war and revolution, particularly the idea of war as the midwife of revolution, has become not only obsolete, but dangerous and must be repudiated:

> We have taken a new look at the interdependence of war and revolution. In the past, war often served to detonate revolution. . . . The First World War provoked . . . the October Revolution in our country. The Second World War evoked . . . revolutions in Eastern Europe and Asia, as well as a powerful anti-colonial revolution. All this served to re-enforce the Marxist-Leninist logic that imperialism inevitably generates major armed confrontations, while the latter naturally creates a 'critical mass' of social discontent and a revolutionary situation in a number of countries. Hence, a forecast which was long adhered to in our country: A Third World War, if unleashed by imperialism, would lead to new social upheavals which would finish off the capitalist system for good, and this would spell global peace. But when the conditions radically changed so that the only result of nuclear war could be universal destruction, we drew a conclusion about the disappearance of the cause-and-effect relationship between war and revolution.[23]

In order to underline the profundity of the Soviet change of view on the nature of the genesis, nature, and likelihood of war and revolution, and its ominous implications, Gorbachev writes:

> At the 27th CPSU Party Congress we clearly 'divorced' the revolution and war themes, excluding from the new edition of the Party Program the following two phrases: 'Should the imperialist aggressors nevertheless venture to start a new world war, the peoples will no longer tolerate a system which drags them into devastating wars. They will sweep imperialism away and bury it.' This provision, admitting in theory the possibility of a new world war, was removed as not corresponding to the realities of the nuclear era.[24]

In other words, the earlier assurances and certitudes, that even in the event of a nuclear war the world would suffer immensely but capitalism would perish while socialism would nevertheless survive, have been repudiated. Now there is not a shred of optimism left about the inevitability of the victory of socialism as long as nuclear war is possible. Gorbachev, after his recital of the new image of the world projected by the "new political thinking," asks himself the logical and rhetorical question, which not only the outside world, but his own colleagues in the communist world must be contemplating:

> Does this imply that we have given up the class analysis of the causes of the nuclear threat and of other global problems?[25]

"No," he answered. Class analysis as a basis for understanding the behavior of the capitalist world is still valid, but as a basis for concluding that nuclear war must be the inevitable result, it is not. The differences and incompatibilities between socialism and capitalism remain, but they need not eventuate in war:

> Economic, political, and ideological competition between capitalist and socialist countries is inevitable. However, it can be and must be kept within the framework of a peaceful competition which necessarily envisages cooperation. It is up to history to judge the merits of each particular system. It will sort out everything. Let every nation decide which system and which ideology is better. Let this be decided by peaceful competition, let each system prove its ability to meet man's needs and interests. The states and peoples of the Earth are very different, and it is actually good that they are so. This is an incentive for competition. This understanding, of a dialectical unity of opposites, fits into the concept of peaceful coexistence.[26]

After acknowledging that past Soviet positions on ideology were substantially contributory to the genesis and sustenance of international tensions because of their emphasis on the inevitability of war, Gorbachev asks the world to ignore and forget past Soviet statements, mentioning in particular Khrushchev's infamous boast that "we will bury you," which he called "probably the most hackneyed statement by a Soviet leader in the West."[27] This statement, he said, was not to be taken literally, then asserting disingeniously or in ignorance that it was simply a vulgarization of an old debate style during the twenties and thirties between farm experts about "who will bury whom." Gorbachev ignored the fact that this question was originally posed by Lenin as the question of questions with respect to the inevitable conflict between capitalism and socialism. "People in the West," writes Gorbachev, "must stop exploiting those few words by one who is no longer among the living, and must not present them as our position." Even less convincing is Gorbachev's assertion that neither Marx nor Lenin, nor any of the other Soviet leaders ever had intentions of "imposing communism throughout the world" or "plans for subduing the whole of Europe." Any attempt to assert the contrary, he writes, "are the fruit of crude falsification or at best ignorance."[28] Nevertheless, precisely these views are even now appearing in the Soviet press, particularly in connection with the condemnation of Stalinist policies.[29]

It is noteworthy that Gorbachev, in calling for the disavowal of ideology as a guide to the foreign policy of states, fails to mention the Soviet Constitution in this connection. As shown elsewhere, the 1977 Constitution, unlike the 1936 Constitution it replaced, includes an entire chapter on foreign policy in which ideological goals are enumerated, such as "ensuring international conditions favorable for the building of communism in the U.S.S.R. . . . consolidating the positions of world socialism, and supporting the struggle of people for national liberation and social progress." These goals have rationalized and justified the self-imposed ideological obligations of "fraternal assistance" to communist countries in the form of Soviet military invasions and "internationalist duty" to Third World countries, both used to explain the Soviet military presence in Afghanistan. The removal of passages from the Party program may eventually be accompanied by the removal of corresponding phrases from the Soviet Constitution, and then one can place more complete confidence in Gorbachev's disavowal of "subordinating foreign policy to ideology."

Gorbachev's revision of the Soviet image of the world is profound and far-reaching, but whether it becomes the definitive basis for Soviet foreign policy depends upon its acceptance by the total Soviet leadership or Gorbachev's undisputed consolidation of political power. One new perception that is bound to become controversial is the reconceptualization of modern capitalism that seems to be emerging.

The continuing vitality of capitalism in the United States, Western Europe, and Japan has been one of the great disillusionments and unpleasant surprises for the Soviet leadership. Gorbachev, in his assessments, seems to feel almost betrayed by Leninist historicism, which misled Soviet leaders into believing that both the United States and capitalism were on their last legs.

Far from being exhausted and decrepit, capitalism has exhibited extraordinary inventiveness, creativity, and productivity, in contrast to the "epoch of decline and decay" under Brezhnev. It is as if Marxism-Leninism yielded upside-down predictions in that, instead of socialism being the "cutting edge" of science and technology, it is capitalism, and instead of capitalism being in decay, it is socialism. History has seemingly played a cruel joke on the Soviet Union, as Gorbachev betrayed signs of historicist pessimism in his report to the 27th Congress, where he noted that "capitalism regarded the birth of socialism as an 'error' of history which must be 'rectified'."[30]

Gorbachev's closest academic and journalistic foreign policy advisers are even more graphic in exhibiting their profound psychological disillusionment and sense of historical betrayal, when they concede that the Soviet model of socialism stagnated, and was failing:

> Imperialist ideologues are rushing to interpret what is happening as a historic

defeat for socialism. Under the form of socialism that took shape . . . socialism's principal economic task—overtaking capitalism in labor productivity and per-capita output—was not solved. We had not created a society that in every respect was capable of serving as an example, as a model for imitation, and as a stimulus in the struggle for the socialist transformation of the world. . . . Apathy and social passivity grew . . . the management system . . . had completely exhausted its capabilities. Retaining it was causing economic stagnation, bringing our society to the brink of a crisis, and weakening the Soviet Union's prestige and influence in the international arena.[31]

Consequently, socialism lost its appeal to the developed world, and instead was being adopted by unstable Third World countries, as capitalism in contrast demonstrated remarkable strength in its competition with socialism:

At the same time, we must admit that capitalism's ability to adapt to the new historical environment has exceeded our expectations. The prospect of socialist transformations in developed capitalist countries has been put off to the indefinite future. In a number of countries that are socialist in orientation, the situation remains unstable and fraught with the possibility of backsliding; communist parties in the capitalist countries and the Third World, with few exceptions, have not been able . . . to gain the support of the majority of the working class and the working people.[32]

Soviet observers are still unable to render capitalism its due, attributing all of the rapid scientific and technological developments in the capitalist world not to capitalism itself, but to abstract historical evolution and other arcane processes. Capitalism is described as "taking advantage" of the scientific-technological revolution, instead of being correctly recognized as a tribute to, and product of, the creativity and inventiveness of capitalism as a system. Soviet writers still cannot bring themselves around to the reality that it was indeed capitalism that created the intellectual atmosphere and material conditions that gave rise to the scientific-technological revolution. Hence history and abstract social processes, not capitalism, are assigned the credit for the new scientific age of high technology, since socialism could not credibly receive the credit. Yet, one can read between the lines of current Soviet analyses that many Soviet writers are embittered by this outcome, whereby capitalism and not socialism is the cutting edge of scientific-technological progress, since it appears to historically validate capitalism and invalidate socialism at worst, or invalidate the entire Marxist-Leninist conception of historicism at best. Restructuring is designed to reverse the situation, but since old mental habits die hard, Soviet observers still think in apocalyptic terms, making references to socialism's "last chance" to renovate itself within the context of a life and death struggle with capitalism:

We must . . . clearly understand that if restructuring is not successful or is substantially limited, constrained, or again reduced to palliatives and half-measures, if the socialist countries do not rise to a new level, if capitalism, not socialism, manages to ride the new wave of scientific and technical revolution, then the worldwide balance of power could change in favor of capitalism.[33]

Gorbachev's "new political thinking" goes a long way in the tortuous process of restructuring the foundations of Soviet legitimacy, shifting it away from success in transforming the external world to success in developing Soviet society. Cheap gains in the Third World proved to be an expensive and inadequate surrogate for an exhausted and impoverished universal ideology, and a less evanescent basis for legitimacy has emerged, a legitimacy founded upon effective performance (*perestroika*) and acceptability (*glasnost-democratization*), rather than upon abstract propositions. The "new political thinking" also goes a long way in repudiating the notion that the legitimacy of the Soviet system can only be validated by the demise of capitalism, a proposition that appears not only increasingly unattainable but also one that Gorbachev recognizes can only promise to generate further international tension and conflict between the Soviet Union and the Western world. The "new political thinking" thus takes a big step in the direction of replacing the sequential concept of coexistence with a parallel concept, dissipating the Soviet conviction that only the destruction of capitalism can retroactively validate the Bolshevik Revolution and legitimize the Soviet system.

Restructuring Soviet Foreign Policy

The deideologization of Soviet foreign policy, the subordination of the international class struggle to "peaceful coexistence" and the "interests of mankind," signal the renunciation of code words for Soviet expansion, ideological militancy, and support of Third World regimes and movements in accordance with ideological criteria. For the Third World in particular it means that the Soviet Union will no longer employ ideology as the principal measuring stick for defining friends and enemies. Indeed, according to Shevardnadze, the "new political thinking" even dispenses with the concept of international "enemies."

> The "image of the enemy" in all its dimensions impedes the restructuring of international relations on the principles of morality and civilization. Having set out to lessen confrontation, we say to capitalist countries: "Let us be honest opponents but not enemies. If you are ready to settle our disputes peacefully, we can even be partners."[34]

According to Shevardnadze future Soviet foreign policy, including that in the Third World, will be shaped by "national interests" rather than ideological interests, and even traditional cost/accounting criteria may be employed to establish foreign policy priorities. Thus, the Soviet Foreign Minister, in his June 1987 address to Foreign Ministry officials, stated:

> The most important thing is that the country should not incur additional expenditures in connection with . . . its lawful foreign political interests. . . . We must enhance the profitability of our foreign policy and achieve a situation in which our mutual relations with other states burden our economy to the least possible extent.[35]

Not only did Shevardnadze again refer to the "economic profitability of foreign policy" in an even more important address to the Soviet foreign policy establishment a year later, but he emphatically reaffirmed the subordination of the international class struggle to peaceful coexistence, gave higher priority to "national interests" over "class interests," and confirmed the priority of domestic interests over foreign policy interests in Gorbachev's outlook:

> The principles of the new political thinking . . . most clearly evidences the direct dependence of a state's foreign policy on its domestic affairs. And here rising before us is that mighty range of vitally important categories brought together by the concept of "national interests." . . . National interests are a very mobile category, dynamic and constantly changing. . . . In the light of this concept, the philosophy of peaceful coexistence, as a universal principle of international relations, takes on a different content. . . . Quite validly, we refuse to see it in a specific form of class struggle. Coexistence . . . cannot be identified with the class struggle. . . . It is difficult to reconcile the equating of international relations to a class struggle with a recognition of the real possibility and inevitability of peaceful coexistence, as a higher universal principle, and mutually advantageous cooperation between states with different sociopolitical systems. . . . In order to correctly assess and ensure our national interests, it is essential to recognize the trends and understand the direction in the common movement of mankind.[36]

Gorbachev's "new political thinking" thus completely restructures the traditional relationship among development, coexistence, and expansion in Soviet calculations. It transforms what was a conceptually symbiotic relationship between coexistence and expansion into an antinomial confrontation, and relinks coexistence in a new symbiosis with internal developments. Instead of a world characterized by social systems in mortal combat, Gorbachev's "new political thinking" shifts to a more traditional image of a diverse world of nations with interests in both conflict and harmony, and thus capable of resolution.

> Our interests consist in the strengthening in every way our unique socialist individuality and essence. . . . If mankind is able to survive presently only under conditions of peaceful coexistence . . . then does not the conclusion arise that the conflict of the two systems can no longer be viewed as the leading trend in the modern world?[37]

Thus coexistence is no longer defined in the context of *peredyshka*, or "breathing space," i.e. as a staging pause preparatory for the next round of expansion, but as a necessary prerequisite and continuing foundation for *perestroika*, i.e. domestic development. But there has been another symbiosis between *development* and *expansion* that has been a hallmark of Soviet behavior. Conceptualized by Stalin in the mid-twenties, this symbiosis was designed to reconcile his program of "socialism in one country" with the Soviet commitment to support and spread world revolution. In the Stalinist conception, coexistence, development, and expansion were inseparably linked in such a way that a tactical pragmatism was married to fixed principles: Coexistence was a prerequisite for development, which in turn was a prerequisite for supporting revolution abroad.

During the Khrushchev decade, the Stalinist formula was altered to give a much higher and more immediate priority to internal development, called "building communism;" coexistence was stretched out from a tactic to a strategy; and spreading revolution was indefinitely postponed, although not abandoned. During the Brezhnev era, internal development received a lower priority, "building communism" was postponed to an indefinite future and replaced with "developed socialism," and expansion in the Third World received highest priority. Coexistence was redefined as a new form of the "class struggle" under the rubric of "détente" with the West. The Brezhnev formula thus abandoned the priority of internal development, ruptured the sequential relationship between coexistence and expansion, and substituted a strategy of simultaneous coexistence with the West (détente) and support for revolution in the Third World (expansion).

As the Soviet Union approaches the year 2000, the definitive contours of the Soviet state in foreign policy appear to be taking shape. A terminal multinational state, dominated by Great Russians and controlling its immediate periphery with strong residual messianic, if no longer precisely universalist, revolutionary reflexes, functioning as a global power, with global interests and ambitions—these are the contours of the future Soviet state. Given the nature of its multinational composition, with nearly a score of historic nationalities denied independent statehood to satisfy historic Russian security requirements and communist ideological imperatives, given its domination over more than a half-dozen adjacent communist states whose internal and external sovereignty is severely infringed upon, and given the appearance of nearly a score of client states called "socialist-oriented regimes" scattered across the Third World, the Soviet Union still has all of the earmarks of an imperial system, and will be burdened with both its benefits and disadvantages.

The Soviet overseas empire is a direct result of its growing military power during the past decades as the Soviet Union finally achieved equality with the United States in one important dimension—the military. Hence, global expansion rather than internal development assumed highest priority in Soviet calculations because of its asymmetrical capabilities. Military power gives the Soviet Union its role, status, and credentials as a global power in the international community, but also enhances the role of the military in the Soviet political process. It is this combination of a Soviet state with powerful military and military-industrial production capabilities, together with a deficient civilian economy, which posed both a danger and a challenge to the new generation of Soviet leaders and the outside world alike. Would the new Soviet leaders, armed with sufficient nuclear capability to destroy the globe unilaterally, continue to compete in the areas where they are most competitive and successful and seek to extend their global empire and influence, or would they consolidate their gains, retrench abroad, and devote greater attention and effort to remedying the deficiencies of their economy, raising the Soviet standard of living, and solving the difficult and harsh social and demographic problems that have been accumulating and now confront them?

The first several years of the Gorbachev regime suggest very strongly that the new leadership has opted for the second alternative, to consolidate and retrench abroad and to reform and upgrade at home. Gorbachev's agenda, for the most part, is still a "wish list," which arouses considerable resistance from entrenched power centers in the Soviet system and may ultimately prove to be too ambitious and utopian. When one analyzes Gorbachev's agenda, first and foremost of his objectives is to retain and consolidate power. The second item on his agenda is to implement his ambitious program designed to reform, renovate, and revitalize not only the Soviet economic system, but Soviet society as a whole. The first and second items on the agenda are, to some degree, inherently contradictory. Since his restructuring program still encounters strong resistance from entrenched bureaucracies, which constitute a potential source of political leverage for possible contenders in the leadership, in order to retain and consolidate power Gorbachev may have to compromise and modify his program. How much of his program may survive is still in question, even as he succeeds in retaining power.

The third and final item on Gorbachev's agenda is foreign policy, and here, the restructuring of Soviet-American relations assumes highest priority. The achievement of the first two items on his agenda requires the existence of a stable and predictable international environment, which would ensure the absence of confrontation, surprise, and diversion of effort and resources, particularly in dealing with issues that involve the United States. The Soviet Union will enter a prolonged period of vulnerability as it dismantles and restructures, and Gorbachev wants to minimize the possibility of the United States taking advantage of periods of vulnerability. Hence amicable relations with the United States are an indispensable prerequisite for the success of his domestic agenda.

It is at once evident that Soviet policy in the Third World has failed to measure up not only against the new criteria of "economic profitability," but has damaged the Soviet Union's international image, tarnished the *credenza* of socialism, and seriously impeded the improvement of relations with both China and the United States. Concern for the international image and prestige of the Soviet Union has assumed a conspicuous place in the attention of Soviet statesmen and scholars. Shevardnadze, in his address of July 1988, devoted considerable attention to the importance the Gorbachev leadership attaches to the image and international prestige of the Soviet Union. The image of the state, he said, defines "a nation's reputation as an important element in foreign policy and as a component of state interests and national security." Furthermore, he said:

> The image of a state, or how it is perceived by the rest of the world, develops directly and primarily from the general trend of its policy, from values and ideals that the nation defends and carries out, and from the degree to which these values and ideals conform with dominant, common human ideals and standards with its own conduct. . . . Comrades, we must not pretend that the standards and ideas of the proper or of what is termed civilized conduct in the world community do not concern us. If you wish to be accepted in it, these must be observed.[38]

The new foreign policy outlook of the Soviet Union thus requires not only a reconceptualization of its basic strategy and purposes, but a more accurate and reliable empirical picture of actual events in the world and, in particular, events in the Third World. Recent graphic evaluations of Soviet reportage on Africa and the Third World provide just a hint that the Soviet leadership's current assessment of the romanticized, often false, image of the Third World is giving way to a realization that intractable Third World problems will not yield to simplistic Leninist "solutions":

> Restructuring has made journalists who write on international topics take a sober look at the fruits of their labor. Living among myths that were created over the years led to a shortage not only of ideas but even of terms capable of reflecting rapid changes in the life of society. The journalist's basic law — reportorial honesty and devotion to principle, plus truthfulness of information — was broken. . . . Breaking down false stereotypes and banishing myths is more difficult in international journalism than in domestic reporting. The impossibility of speaking out on a whole series of highly important problems, and often a reluctance to do so, is holding back the establishment of openness. . . . It's no secret that, in conditions of openness, the reading public is losing interest in some publications specializing in international topics. . . . The main thing in these publications is not the truthful coverage of events but an interpretation of them that corresponds to the departmental line of the day. . . . All this gave rise to a kind of vicious circle: Combed-over and slicked-down information formed a distorted image of another country in the public consciousness, which in turn

created a completely real danger that inaccurate or erroneous decisions would be chosen at the state level. . . . Some stereotypes have proved so tenacious that they are not yielding even to restructuring.[39]

Thus not only did false reporting mislead decisionmakers into developing ineffective policies, but the prestige and image of the Soviet Union was being severely damaged because of the way unsavory clients or potential client regimes were being falsely portrayed. Apparently, only the Soviet leaders were unaware of the widely-known outrageous behavior of these regimes:

It is sad to read for 20 years running about one and the same country that it "has achieved definite successes on the path to the construction of a new society," when several coups have occurred there during those years, the economy is in a state of collapse, the population's standard of living has fallen, and prospects for the future are so gloomy that no one is venturing to suggest any prescriptions for the future. . . . The political struggle has brought to the top not just genuine national leaders. Among those who have wound up at the helm, there have been quite a few fortuitous individuals, venal politicians and unscrupulous demagogues. Some real maniacal murderers have come to power, people who have plunged their peoples into a never-ending nightmare of repression, killing and ruin. But there was a taboo against criticizing them. I remember how we called the Ugandan dictator Idi Amin and his clique "patriotically minded military men." . . . The Amins and the Bokassas often do irreparable damage to their peoples, and through their actions they exacerbate the international situation and discredit not only the national-liberation movement but also the ideas of socialism.[40]

Disillusionment and disappointment with the failure of events to coincide with roseate Soviet prognostications, based upon falsified information, has impelled Gorbachev to reassess the costs and benefits of Soviet policy in the Third World. Therefore, it should not be surprising to witness the Soviet Union not only arresting its expansion into the Third World and becoming further ensnared in its problems, but also engaging in selective and graduated retrenchment, in accordance with the new criteria of "profitability" in foreign policy.

These changes in Soviet foreign policy directions and priorities require not only empirical justification but elaborate and credible philosophical rationalization as well, which the "new foreign policy philosophy" is designed to serve.

Reconceptualizing Soviet Interests in the Third World: From "Wars of National Liberation" to Regional Conflicts

The concept of "regional conflicts" was initially ideologically anathema to Soviet thinking and was rejected as simply an imperialist code word that lumped together "wars of national and social liberation" and "just wars" with "imperialist wars" and "unjust wars" into a single ideologically neutral category. In the past, similar concepts like "local wars," "guerrilla wars," "low-intensity conflicts" and "counterinsurgency" wars were similarly rejected by the Soviet side. All of these Western concepts were viewed as attempts to morally equate Soviet support for movements and regimes of national liberation with U.S. support for reactionary regimes and counterrevolutionary movements. One of President Reagan's minor diplomatic accomplishments was to impose the concept of "regional conflicts" upon the Soviet Union, which Soviet writers grudgingly but indirectly acknowledge, and to force it upon the negotiating agenda together with arms control. As Evgenii Primakov, one of Gorbachev's prominent foreign policy advisers, put it, "On the eve of the Geneva Summit in November 1985 . . . U.S. spokesmen and President Reagan himself insisted upon a peculiar hierarchy: first a settlement of regional conflicts, observance of human rights, and confidence-building measures, and only then arms reduction."[41]

Although this was not the preferred Soviet ordering of the agenda, or even the preferred Soviet menu, the Soviet side accepted the menu and did not insist upon a different set of priorities, but above all it recognized that "new attitudes about the nature of regional conflicts and new approaches to their settlement have naturally become an integral part of the foreign policy strategy being elaborated in the Soviet Union." Conceding that "Soviet foreign practice has never paid so much attention to these matters as in recent years," Primakov agreed that "one should not try to give priority to arms reduction," and "that steps to stabilize international relations should be taken simultaneously along every line without any 'linkage' between the first step to the solution of one problem and the settlement of another problem, however important."[42]

Primakov, however, recognizes clearly the difficult problem of reconciling Soviet acceptance of the concept of "regional conflicts" with its previous thinking about "wars of national liberation" and "just wars," a matter which not only agitated those who considered the new formulations as abandonment of Soviet ideological commitments, but also those who think the deideologization of Soviet foreign policy remains incomplete.

> In dealing with these matters, however, one cannot avoid a vital question: If thermonuclear war threatens the existence of all human civilization, while a number of regional conflicts tend to go beyond the original framework, how should one regard the problems of armed struggle for independence or just and unjust wars? In the final count, it is a matter of whether the Soviet Union's new foreign policy philosophy can provide answers to real-life situations connected with the world's objective sociopolitical development, which is not only evolutionary but also revolutionary. Naturally, the Soviet Union's new foreign policy philosophy cannot leave out such a fundamental question as the development of the world revolutionary process in its diverse manifestations.[43]

Needless to say, Primakov fails to square this circle, and, to mix metaphors, offers an invalid syllogism as a solution. *First*, he notes, "the dynamics of regional conflicts could lead to an all-destructive global thermonuclear holocaust;" *second*, he states, "we start from the assumption . . . that war and the use of force in general should be ruled out from interstate relations, in contrast to the formula of von Clausewitz;" and therefore, third:

> None of this implies nonrecognition of the possibilities of national and social liberation forces for making use of every means at their disposal to ensure their legitimate rights. But if the use of such means is not to come into contradiction with new thinking dictated by the realities of the thermonuclear age, even more precise definitions should be given to export of revolution and export of counterrevolution.[44]

Attributing the idea of "exporting revolution" to Trotsky, but indirectly conceding that it was practiced in past Soviet foreign policy and still has it adherents, Primakov explicitly states that it is incompatible with the "new political thinking." He then attempts to draw a distinction between the "export of revolution" and support for a revolution that is the product of internal forces:

> At the same time, the denial of external assistance in creating a revolutionary situation has nothing in common with a refusal to assist revolutionary forces which rely on objective conditions in their struggle to end the national and social oppression of their peoples.[45]

Since the "new political thinking" is admittedly still in its unfinished evolutionary, improvisional, even provisional phase, its reconciliation with "old" Soviet thinking remains incomplete and not entirely satisfactory. Old foreign policy strategies and formulas are being renounced before new replacements have been completely worked out. Inconsistencies between elements of the "new political thinking" and the traditional goals and missions of Soviet foreign policy are being dismissed as simply inconsistencies between the "new thinking" and the "old strategies" rather than between the "new thinking" and the fundamental tenets of Leninism. The recognition that thermonuclear war would be universally catastrophic and must be avoided, plus the realization that regional conflicts could escalate into global conflict and therefore must be resolved, creates a serious ideological crisis for the Soviet Union since these realities conflict not only with strategies, but also with fundamental Leninist propositions concerning the unavoidability of class struggles, the inevitability of the demise of capitalism, and the certain worldwide triumph of socialism and communism. War and violence were considered to be inevitable by-products and vehicles of these processes, but with the abjuration of force, how can these processes unfold and how can the Soviet Union fulfill its historic ideological missions? Primakov addresses this matter as follows:

> How, under present conditions does the Soviet Union perform its *class mission*? Mostly (and the extreme importance of this does not require additional explanations) by ruling out war from the life of modern society. If mankind were drawn into an all-embracing thermonuclear catastrophe, none of the national or social liberation movements would have any value. At the same time, the Soviet Union's class duty is fully realized in that, while it has assumed a special responsibility for the future of universal peace . . . it has in no way given up its sympathies or its actual support for the forces of progress and construction. It has been and remains a firm opponent of any attempts to export counterrevolution to countries where progressive forces have come to power.[46]

Foreign Minister Shevardnadze has summarized matters by noting that "we, while maintaining support for the ideas of the national liberation movement, are not exporting revolution."[47] All this, however, leaves unanswered the question of how the Soviet Union will fulfill its now attenuated ideological mission of successfully deterring or countering the "export of counterrevolution," a matter not of little concern to Soviet clients in the Third World. Furthermore, what becomes of the moral distinction between "just" and "unjust" wars if both are equally capable of escalating into thermonuclear war? This, too, Primakov attempts to explicate, but does so unsatisfactorily by downplaying its significance and attributing this concern to "foreign leftists," a category that populates all of the "liberation" regimes and movements in the Third World:

> A question frequently asked, especially by foreign leftists, is whether the former division of wars into just and unjust ones is to be maintained, and if so, what are their criteria. The attitude to this problem is evidently largely connected with the fact that the Soviet Union and other socialist countries have placed all their stakes on a defensive military doctrine, a defensive military strategy, and a corresponding model for the structure of the armed forces. Non-offensive defense thus becomes the only recognized just mode of using force in interstate relations. Under these conditions, defensive wars are apparently the only ones that can be qualified as just wars between states.[48]

This explanation legitimizes the resort to self-defense on the part of "liberationist" regimes, but still leaves unanswered how a successful deterrence or rebuffing of the "export of counterrevolution" can be executed. Since a unilateral intervention on the part of one global power is insufficient to result in nuclear war, what is to prevent the U.S. from intervention and the export of counterrevolution if it is convinced that the Soviet Union will not respond for fear of confrontation and escalation to a global conflict?

If one takes Primakov's words literally, he is suggesting a tradeoff between Soviet nonexport of revolution in return for an American agreement not to export counterrevolution against incumbent regimes. This may serve to preserve existing Leninist regimes, but at the expense of not supporting "movements of national liberation" seeking power. Apparently, the fate of the latter will somehow be left to the prudence and "sense of responsibility" of external forces, who will equally and simultaneously perceive that any attempt at unilateral intervention will provoke counterintervention, and hence they will exercise self-restraint.

Apparently, those struggling against national oppression and imperialism will have to rely primarily on the prudence and "sense of responsibility" of the United States to refrain from "exporting counterrevolution."

> At the same time, the peoples have a right to struggle in defense of their national independence. The actual choice of the form of such a struggle is not limited, for no one can impose definite behavior patterns on the peoples, but a sense of responsibility here is enhanced both on the part of the forces fighting for national liberation and on the part of any other states to somehow be involved in a particular conflict. That is what should make it impossible to overstep the line that separates a just struggle for the peoples' rights from a situation fraught with disaster for the whole of mankind.[49]

Is it any wonder that words like these impelled Ligachev to retort:

> We proceed from the class character of international relations. Any other presentation of the problems sows confusion among Soviet people and among our friends abroad.[50]

Primakov's words, which are echoes of Gorbachev's ideas, and which have been again reaffirmed in important speeches by Gorbachev, Iakovlev, and Shevardnadze, as well as by various journalists and academics, appear to be preliminary rationalizations for a substantial restructuring of Soviet policy in the Third World. This requires, first of all, the resolution of regional conflicts, because in the words of Primakov, "the so-called Third World is now the most dangerous zone of conflict."[51] To be sure, Primakov's prescriptions call for elaborate "rules of conduct" to govern the behavior of the great powers with respect to regional conflict situations, and resemble more a Soviet "wish list" than realistic analysis.[52] At the same time they reenforce the impression that the Soviet Union is serious about seeking a resolution of all outstanding regional conflicts that interfere with other domestic and foreign policy goals much higher on Gorbachev's agenda than preserving the configuration of the Soviet presence in the Third World. Ever since the Soviet Union accepted the idea of "regional conflicts," the "new political thinking" has virtually co-opted the concept, which has become a routine fixture in the Soviet diplomatic lexicon and appears to have displaced earlier Soviet ideological formulations and definitions of what are now subsumed under this rubric.

The Soviet acceptance of the concept of "regional conflicts" can only mean that the concept of "national liberation" will have diminished significance as an analytical tool. Soviet disillusionment with developments in the Third World is clearly evident in the reduced attention given to "national liberation" movements, and the very concept itself may now be in jeopardy, since it appears to have been overtaken by events and developments. The concept of "national liberation," like many other Soviet concepts, is being redefined as increasingly obsolete and no longer a fruitful basis for Soviet analysis or behavior. Instead, as speeches and statements by Gorbachev and Shevardnadze and analyses by prominent academic advisers like Primakov indicate, more traditional concepts such as "national interests" and "defense," defined within a nonoffensive context, are assuming a greater conceptual and analytical role in the Soviet thinking about foreign policy. In his speech of November 2, 1987, Gorbachev for example used a more elastic concept of "national liberation" to include "liberation" through the economic development of some Third World countries into "great powers" economically and politically, thus suggesting a new line of approach to these countries.[53] Countries that would fall into this category included South Korea, Brazil, Nigeria, and Mexico. Furthermore, he noted that states and nations were emerging in the Third World that were "national states in the genuine sense," i.e., no longer dependencies of larger European powers, and he further observed that Third World nations acting in concert within various international and regional organizations were no longer as helpless and vulnerable as before. In Gorbachev's view, "national liberation" thus is no longer the main avenue for Third World countries, and the Soviet Union is apparently ready to redefine its relations with the Third World accordingly.

To some degree, Gorbachev's rethinking not only presages a restructuring of Soviet relations with Third World countries and a reexamination of the Soviet constellation of interests involved in "regional conflicts," but it also suggests a recognition that Soviet Third World policy has been more of a financial and economic drain upon Soviet resources than a source of replenishment. By treating some Third World countries as viable economic entities and genuine "nation-states" not requiring the trauma of "national liberation" and the imposition of "progressive forces," the Soviet Union is more likely to attract diplomatic support for its policies and, more importantly, establish more fruitful and beneficial economic relations. Soviet foreign trade and foreign economic relations are a disaster area, and one of the glaring deficiencies of Soviet foreign policy in the Third World has been its inability to craft a policy that could tap the rich and diverse resources of the Third World on behalf of the Soviet economy. By remaining dogmatically attached to the concept of "national liberation" and its various permutations, and by preoccupying itself with the ever-changing nature and chain of stages towards socialism—national democracy, vanguard parties, socialist-orientation, etc.— Moscow blinded itself to real developments in the Third World that not only crippled Third World countries that were ensnared, but contributed to the crippling and deformation of the Soviet economy as well. Invalid and analytically impotent concepts resulted in faulty and counterproductive policies and behavior.

Effectively junking the concept of "national liberation," which was the principal Soviet ideological code word for "regional conflict," dictated a reexamination of these conflicts and led directly to the Soviet acceptance and recognition of a concept of "regional conflict" that could become a common basis for negotiation. Regional conflicts are no longer viewed through a rigid moral prism in which the protagonists are defined in terms of "progressive" and "reactionary" forces, but are viewed increasingly in terms of conflicting interests, both of domestic players and external actors, that are susceptible to negotiation and settlement.

Afghanistan emerges as the quintessential illustration of how faulty analysis deformed Soviet foreign policy. The invasion of, and Soviet conduct in, Afghanistan has come under considerable criticism, and one prominent high-ranking Soviet military official who served in Afghanistan went so far as to even deny the revolutionary credentials of the Afghan regime, terming the so-called revolution a "military coup" devoid of any authentic revolutionary credentials.[54] He was quickly repudiated by the Soviet Foreign Ministry as expressing his personal opinion, but it is at once evident that this opinion, or some variation of it, continues to circulate in and around the Soviet leadership.[55]

The Soviet decision to withdraw from Afghanistan and Gorbachev's public suggestion that an Afghanistan settlement based upon "national reconciliation" be used as a model for settling other regional conflicts reflects these fundamental reexaminations of Soviet thought and behavior with respect to the Third World.[56] One need not accept Gorbachev's invitation to employ Moscow's vision of an Afghan settlement as a prototype or model for settling other regional conflicts—since they are not all made up of the same ingredients—in order to recognize that Soviet statements about Afghanistan are reflective of thinking about wider and more aggregated problems. (See Appendix A, "Geneva Accords on Afghanistan.")

The Soviet decision to withdraw from Afghanistan after considerable economic investment in effort, resources, and blood, brings to the fore the question of the intensity of Soviet commitment to its clients in the Third World. Since Afghanistan, for a variety of reasons, is the most proximate and important socialist-oriented country in terms of Soviet interests, what does this imply for continuing Soviet support to other client states? One cannot jump to the conclusion that since the Soviet Union is willing to withdraw from Afghanistan, its commitments elsewhere are totally unreliable, although marginal clients may have a good deal to worry about. The viability and strength of a particular movement or regime will be an important factor in measuring Soviet commitments, but they will also be calculated against other considerations. Generally speaking, the weaker and more vulnerable a regime or movement within its own domestic sociopolitical context, the more likely that Soviet support will be withdrawn. In the case of Afghanistan, even in the face of a number of factors that impinge on Soviet interests—geostrategic importance, territorial adjacency, defense considerations, nationality factors—the Soviet decision to withdraw was influenced overwhelmingly by the patent nonviability of the various Leninist regimes installed, and the relative strength of the domestic opposition forces. Where the local client regime is relatively well entrenched, as in Angola, or where the domestic opposition is weak or ineffective, as in Nicaragua, Soviet calculations may be different, irrespective of the presence of other factors.

Resolving Regional Conflicts: Prospects and Problems

High on Gorbachev's agenda of Soviet policy in the Third World is a resolution of regional conflicts, because their continued existence adversely affects so many other more important items on his priority list. An inventory of regional conflicts in which the Soviet Union is involved or has a strong interest includes the following, in descending order of importance for Soviet interests:

1. The Afghanistan conflict.
2. The Iran-Iraq conflict.
3. The Arab-Israeli conflict.
4. The Ethiopian conflict.
5. The Indochina conflict.
6. The southern Africa conflict.
7. The Nicaraguan conflict.
8. The El Salvador conflict.

These conflicts, above all, constitute an obstacle to the improvement of relations with the United States, or at least impose a limit upon the degree of Soviet-American cooperation. To a lesser extent they serve as an impediment to broadening the improvement of cooperation with Western Europe, Japan, and China. Second, they constitute a drain upon Soviet resources and contribute to the distortion of Soviet economic, domestic, and military priorities, to say nothing of mounting Soviet military casualties. Third, they have aggravated Soviet relations with the Third World and in particular have aroused anxiety among other states that border the regional conflict areas.

Although one can approach the Soviet involvement in regional conflicts on a case-by-case basis, and in each individual instance analyze it in isolation, the Soviet approach to regional conflicts is holistic in character, and the analysis of individual regional conflicts derives greater explanatory potency if it is placed in the total context of regional conflicts as a worldwide phenomenon. Certainly the Soviet literature reflects this, as Soviet writers speak of all regional conflicts as requiring resolution, while recognizing their individual differences. From the Soviet perspective, regional conflicts can be categorized in accordance with a number of criteria, which unevenly characterize individual cases. These criteria are as follows:

1. External participation.
2. Nature and degree of external participation.
3. Defense saliency.
4. Ideological saliency.
5. Risk and level of confrontation.
6. Leverage and strength of local regime or movement.

It is the number and mix of these criteria in individual cases that determine the urgency of the Soviet commitment to establish parameters and conditions for a successful resolution. Given that, the Soviet literature repeatedly emphasizes that the sense of urgency is largely shaped by the degree and nature of Soviet-American involvement. Hence, from the Soviet perspective, the resolution of the Afghan conflict has had the highest level of urgency for Moscow, and resolution of the Nicaraguan conflict has had the highest level of urgency for the United States.

The Soviet military presence in Afghanistan in particular has complicated Soviet policy in the Moslem and Arab world, particularly with respect to the more moderate regimes in the area. Finally, as Soviet writers increasingly note, the Soviet Union is the only global power involved in direct military activity in a regional conflict, and this has served to diminish the prestige and image of the Soviet Union in the international community.[57]

Furthermore, Soviet encouragement and involvement in regional conflicts are quintessential illustrations of the subordination of foreign policy to ideology that Gorbachev wishes to eliminate. Even in the case of Afghanistan, Soviet writers now concede that the impetus for the Soviet invasion was overwhelmingly ideological in character and that Soviet defense and security interests are not currently at stake.[58] Increasingly, the Soviet invasion of Afghanistan is called a "mistake" and a search for appropriate scapegoats is actively in progress.[59] Aside from the grim prospect of generating internal political conflict over the decision to intervene in Afghanistan, the intervention has served to aggravate and inflame nationality tensions, as many non-Russian nationalities express resentment about the loss of their sons in a war that can only reflect Russian imperial ambitions. As one bereaved Lithuanian mother put it, "Why is Lithuania at war with Afghanistan? We have no quarrel with Afghanistan." Particularly among Soviet Moslems and the central Asian nationalities, both resentment at the intervention and aroused Moslem consciousness can be attributed to the war in that country. These are all important factors influencing a settlement in that country.

In both the Nicaraguan and Afghan instances the defense and security interests of one of the global powers are involved, but in both cases the problem is compounded by the interests of other external participants (Cuba in the case of Nicaragua and China in the case of Afghanistan) and the divergent fate of the Soviet and American clients involved, particularly the incumbent regimes. Neither client regime betrays any evidence that it is willing to commit suicide in order to serve the interests of Moscow. This is complicated by the asymmetrical nature of the forces seeking to overthrow the incumbent regimes and the corresponding determination and level of American support. Here a further asymmetry is involved. The regional conflict that impinges most directly upon Soviet interests is Afghanistan, and its incumbent regime has only low-to-medium prospects for survival in the absence of Soviet support, whereas in Nicaragua the Contras have very low prospects for unseating the Sandinista regime.

Although both sides would emphatically deny it, the stage is set for an eventual outcome of the two conflicts that will result in the replacement of the Najibullah regime in Afghanistan with a regime made up of a mix of resistance elements, and the withdrawal of the Contras and the survival of the Sandinista regime in Nicaragua. This will come about not through deliberate and calculated negotiations, but from the near simultaneous withdrawal of outside support to the various local parties involved. The Soviet Union has already withdrawn all of its forces from Afghanistan as of February 15, 1989. Whereas the Soviet client regime there is unlikely to survive a withdrawal of Soviet forces, all effective external assistance to the Contras has ceased, and they have not demonstrated a capacity for mobilizing the necessary local forces to overthrow the incumbent regime on their own. Since Soviet security is not involved in Nicaragua and U.S. security is not involved in Afghanistan, neither side has an intensity of interest sufficient to risk confrontation by the continued support of its respective client. In both instances the final resolution of the two conflicts will depend upon a tacit Soviet-American agreement, whereby the United States will not militarily support what will be an anticommunist regime in Kabul, and the Soviet Union will stop further military assistance to the Sandinistas. Both the United States and the U.S.S.R. are secure enough to tolerate ideologically hostile regimes on or near their borders if the military presence of the other global power is not involved. The Soviet Union will, of course, seek a settlement that will allow it to maintain a modicum of influence in any future Kabul regime, based largely on a complex of domestic considerations, but its decision to withdraw, in any event appears irrevocable.

Moving to the other end of the spectrum, the regional conflict that shows few signs of resolution is the Ethiopian conflict. Here, only the Soviet Union and its client states are involved and the degree and future character of their involvement are shaped entirely by their own calculation of interests, free from external pressures. The risk of confrontation with the United States is virtually nonexistent and does not figure in as a factor; neither are the defense interests of the Soviet Union or Cuba involved. The Soviet/Cuban involvement is determined almost exclusively by global/ideological considerations. What is likely to affect the course of events in this area is the increasing Soviet sense of embarrassment in being associated with such an unsavory regime as the Mengistu government, whose character, as portrayed in the Soviet press, almost matches that of Idi Amin and Bokassa in venality, brutality, and irrationality. Furthermore, neither the Cubans nor the Soviet Union feel entirely comfortable supporting a regime that is not only oppressing its own population, but is in conflict with an Eritrean movement for independence that meets all of the standards for the kind of liberation movement that both Moscow and Havana could support. What is most likely in Ethiopia is increased Soviet pressure upon Mengistu to reform or face efforts to replace him with another leader. But in this instance, Soviet leverage may not be sufficient to prevail against both Mengistu and Cuba, who may have different reasons for resisting Soviet pressure. The other possibility, although somewhat remote, is for the Soviet Union to unilaterally withdraw its support, but this is likely only if the damage to Soviet prestige, image, and sensibilities is sufficient to outweigh the essentially diminishing interest of the Gorbachev administration in maintaining its presence in East Africa.

The situation in Angola and southern Africa, generally, is somewhat more complicated because more players are involved: the U.S.S.R., the United States, Cuba, and South Africa. Furthermore, the situation is complicated because of the Namibia factor and, to a lesser extent, the problems affecting Mozambique. As the most powerful local player in the conflict, South Africa has vital interests that are separate and distinct from those of the United States, and it is fully capable of preventing any resolution of the conflict it finds unacceptable. The external pressure on South Africa is limited while South Africa's capacity for mischief is unlimited. This is a given that all of the actors must take into account. Without the cooperation of South Africa, no resolution is likely.

The Soviet involvement is devoid of a defense or security interest and is predominantly ideological and global in character, but to a lesser degree economic interests are involved since Angola was a source of hard currency that was paid in return for Soviet support. Here again, the intensity of the Soviet commitment is waning, but its involvement is more costly and risky than in Ethiopia. The Cuban factor, however, is not an insignificant one, and it appears that Cuban ideological commitment to the Angolan regime now surpasses that of the Soviet. The threatened, continued, and possibly escalated support to the forces of Jonas Savimbi could further complicate relations with the United States. The chief barriers to an implementation of the December 22, 1988 Accords, which involve the withdrawal of Cuban troops and the independence of Namibia, are neither the United States nor the U.S.S.R., but Cuba, the MPLA regime, and South Africa. Even here, the June 1989 agreement between the MPLA and Savimbi, providing for a coalition government of national reconciliation, suggests that a general resolution of the conflicts in southern Africa could be imminent.

Cambodia represents another difficult regional conflict, not so much because of U.S. involvement and the risk of confrontation, which is very low, but because the conflicting interests of Vietnam and China are involved. A further complicating factor is the disproportionate strength of the Pol Pot Khmer Rouge forces in the ranks of the opposition to the Vietnamese-backed regime, and this raises a question as to what a new regime would look like. The withdrawal of Vietnamese troops from Cambodia and the withdrawal of Soviet troops from Afghanistan constitute two of the three preconditions for Chinese agreement to discuss the improvement of relations with Moscow. Relatively high on Gorbachev's agenda is the normalization of relations with China, which appears to be more important than preserving Vietnam's presence in Cambodia. Already the situation has improved to the point where a meeting between the Chinese and Soviet foreign ministers took place in late 1988, and Gorbachev himself went to China in May 1989. The fact that Soviet troops left Afghanistan on the preceding February 15, created an environment in which Gorbachev and Deng Xiaoping might be able eventually to reach an agreement on a resolution to the Cambodian conflict, barring unforeseen fallout from the tumultuous events of May and June in China. If these two powers can find a common ground, Vietnam is unlikely to resist and prevail by itself. The main issue would then become the nature of the regime to replace the Vietnamese-supported government, and the degree of U.S. involvement in the settlement. The stage would appear to be set for a settlement within the wider framework of the United Nations, since not only has Gorbachev suggested a greater role for the United Nations in settling issues, but also because the legitimacy and credentials of an acceptable Cambodian government are an issue.

Both Gorbachev and his most enthusiastic supporters have called for Soviet-American cooperation in resolving regional conflicts. The prospect of greater Soviet eagerness to resolve these conflicts under the rubric of greater Soviet-

American cooperation, whether real or contrived, or in the name of improving Soviet-American relations if the former is not forthcoming, is likely to gather steam if Gorbachev survives his political conflicts at home. Under existing circumstances, from Gorbachev's perspective, the continuation of any of the conflicts enumerated can no longer serve the interests of the U.S.S.R., and the resolution of all these conflicts would appear to be in Gorbachev's interest. The fact that negotiating activities involving virtually all the regional conflicts have almost simultaneously appeared strongly suggests a deliberate and coordinated Soviet approach. The chief issue for Gorbachev is how to resolve these conflicts with minimum damage to the interest, and above all the image, prestige, and credibility of the Soviet Union as a global power.

The manner and approach of the Soviet Union in extricating itself from regional turbulences or contributing to their resolutions will vary considerably, depending on the corresponding saliency of the interests of the affected powers in the region and the impact such action will have on the global balance and distribution of power. Implicit tradeoffs between Moscow and Washington are highly likely in the resolution of regional conflicts, in conformity with the relative importance and configuration of interests of the individual conflict to the two global powers. Nevertheless, there appears to be an asymmetry in the urgency and intensity of interest in resolving regional conflicts, and this will affect not only the pace of the negotiations but their outcome as well. With respect to other regional conflicts, the United States is more deeply implicated in the Iraq-Iran conflict, but Soviet interests are potentially and relatively more important because of the region's geographical propinquity. But unfortunately neither global power has any real influence, nor can either bring pressure upon any party to the conflict at the present time. More than any other regional conflict, the Arab-Israeli confrontation is susceptible to joint Soviet-American efforts and authentic cooperative action. Moscow has given many indirect indications of wishing to normalize relations with Israel and appears to be waiting only for the appropriate occasion.

Although the United States has a compelling interest in the resolution of regional conflicts, it does not have the collateral interest of resolving conflicts in a manner that preserves or enhances the global power credentials of the Soviet Union. Under President Reagan in particular, the United States could not be characterized as an equal opportunity global power. The Soviet Union is a unidimensional global power, whereas the United States is a multidimensional global power, and Washington cannot be expected to have an interest in altering the global power asymmetry of the two countries in Moscow's favor.

Given the current trajectories of both American and Soviet foreign policy, a renewed and restructured Soviet-American détente (to use a badly abused but still appropriate concept) appears to be in the offing. This is at the top of

Gorbachev's foreign policy agenda and could allow him to trim the Soviet military budget, shift allocations and resources away from the military side of the economy to the nonmilitary sector, and reduce the swollen size of the armed forces and release perhaps a million workers to participate in the labor force. There is little doubt that as in the past, this shift in allocations will provoke controversy and perhaps even domestic turbulence in the Soviet Union.

As the Soviet Union trims its global presence, it will come to rely on other forces and institutions in the international system as instruments of its foreign policy. This serves to explain Gorbachev's sudden interest in a broader and more responsible role for the United Nations and its institutions in dealing with world problems. Soviet official spokesmen have conceded publicly that Moscow's past policies with respect to the United Nations were mistaken, and they have promised to make appropriate amends. The Soviet Union not only has paid up its past financial obligations to the United Nations but has also praised its peacekeeping missions and has agreed to allow Soviet citizens to serve as authentic international civil servants in the U.N. Secretariat and other administrative agencies. Moscow has also evinced interest in joining international financial and economic organizations, which it has spurned in the past, again largely for the same purpose. Thus, the Soviet Union appears to be inching away from unilateralism towards multilateralism in accordance with Gorbachev's reinvention of the concept "interdependence."

In foreign policy, the Soviet Union in the past has gone through alternative periods of expansion, on the one hand, and consolidation/retrenchment on the other, with corresponding intensified internal development. What is happening under Gorbachev may be just another episode in this recurring cycle, to be superceded by another change in direction after the turn of the millennium, depending upon what happens in the nineties. Risks and opportunities, self-confidence and vulnerability also run in cycles, and a period of self-perceived vulnerability and lessened opportunity is by no means necessarily permanent. Indeed, some observers of the Soviet scene interpret Gorbachev's reform program as simply a phase in which the Soviet Union plays "catch up" with the West, so that it might resume its expansionist pace with greater vigor and effectiveness in the next few decades of the coming century.

Nevertheless, during the coming decade, barring any slippage of the United States into debility and irresolution, the Soviet Union is likely to be preoccupied with internal development and renovation. We have it on no less an authority than Gorbachev himself that the chief impetus to Moscow's change of direction has been his own assessment of the Soviet Union's inability to compete successfully in the modern world and to participate fully in the ongoing scientific-technological revolution, to say nothing of being its cutting edge, as a fully-fledged, multidimensional global power.

Notes

1. *Pravda*, January 28, 1987. Report to the Central Committee Plenum of January 27, 1987, "On Restructuring and the Party's Personnel Policy."
2. *Documents and Materials of the 19th All-Union Conference of the CPSU* (Washington, DC: *Soviet Life*, 1988), p. 31. (Hereafter cited as *Documents and Materials*.)
3. Speech by Ligachev at Gorky, August 5, 1988, *Sovetskaia Rossiia*, August 6, 1988.
4. *Documents and Materials*, p. 32. *Cf.* also statements by *Shevardnadze, infra.*, pp. 32 ff.
5. Ibid.
6. *Constitution of the U.S.S.R.* (Moscow: Novosti Press, 1977), pp. 31-32.
7. *Documents and Materials*, pp. 34-35.
8. Ibid., p. 129. The resolutions adopted by the 19th Party Conference in July 1988 did not have a special section on foreign policy. The resolutions approved "the international activities of the CPSU Central Committee based on new political thinking . . . efforts to . . . achieve the settlement of regional conflicts . . . [and] the decision to withdraw troops from Afghanistan." Ibid., pp. 128-129. This was the only mention of "new political thinking" in the resolutions. The resolutions did not endorse explicitly the "new political thinking," although it endorsed specific foreign policy measures, but apparently not the new philosophy that justified them.
9. *Istoriia Sovetskoi Konstitutsii, 1917-1956* (Moscow: 1951), pp. 458-460.
10. "New World Solidarity with the Afghan Revolution," *New Times*, January 1980 (No. 3), pp. 9-10.
11. Mikhail Gorbachev, *Perestroika* (New York: Harper and Row, 1987), p. 221. (Hereafter cited as *Perestroika*.)
12. *Documents and Materials*, p. 31.
13. V. Dashichev, "The Quest for New East-West Relations," *Literaturnaia Gazeta*, May 18, 1988, p. 14. Foreign Minister Shevardnadze, in his address to the Soviet foreign policy establishment on July 25, 1988, said much the same thing, but in a more muted tone. See *Vestnik Ministerstva Inostrannykh del SSSR*, August 1988 (No. 15), pp. 27-46. A shorter version of the speech can also be found in *Pravda*, July 26, 1988.
14. *Perestroika*, pp. 135-170.
15. Ibid., p. 138.
16. Ibid., p. 141. Clausewitz's dictum has been repeatedly and emphatically renounced as no longer valid by Shevardnadze, Primakov, and others.
17. Ibid., p. 143.
18. Ibid.
19. Ibid., pp. 145-146.
20. Ibid., p. 146.
21. Ibid., pp. 146-147.
22. Ibid., p. 147.
23. Ibid., pp. 147-148.
24. Ibid., p. 148.
25. Ibid.
26. Ibid.

27. Ibid., p. 150. Hackneyed though Khrushchev's words may have been, Shevardnadze referred to them derisively in his speech of July 25, 1988. Ibid., *supra.*, Note 13.
28. *Perestroika*, p. 150.
29. *Cf.*, for example, V. Dashichev, "The Quest for New East-West Relations," *Literaturnaia Gazeta*, May 18, 1988.
30. Mikhail Gorbachev, *Towards a Better World* (New York: Richardson and Steinman, 1987), p. 92.
31. Aleksander Bovin, *Izvestiia*, January 11, 1987.
32. Ibid.
33. Ibid.
34. Shevardnadze speech of July 25, 1988, as cited in Note 13.
35. Shevardnadze speech of June 1987, as reported in *Vestnik Ministerstva Inostrannykh del SSSR*, 1987 (No. 2), p. 31.
36. Shevardnadze speech of July 25, 1988, as cited in Note 13.
37. Ibid.
38. Ibid.
39. Boris Asoian, in *Literaturnaia Gazeta*, October 7, 1987, p. 14.
40. Ibid.
41. Evgenii Primakov, "U.S.S.R. Policy on Regional Conflicts," *International Affairs* (Moscow), June 1988 (No. 6), p. 3. Interestingly enough, Gorbachev had a short section in his book *Perestroika* on "Regional Conflicts," but he offered nothing conceptually significant (see pp. 173-177). For other important articles by Primakov on the "new political thinking," *Cf.* Primakov, "A New Philosophy of Foreign Policy," *Pravda*, July 10, 1987; and "The Summit Meeting: A Look into the Past and the Future," *Pravda*, January 8, 1988.
42. Ibid., pp. 3-4.
43. Ibid., p. 4.
44. Ibid.
45. Ibid., p. 5.
46. Ibid.
47. Shevardnadze speech of July 25, 1988, as cited in Note 13, *supra.*
48. Primakov, op. cit., p. 5.
49. Ibid., p. 6.
50. Ligachev speech of August 5, 1988, *Sovetskaia Rossiia*, August 6, 1988.
51. Primakov, op. cit., p. 6.
52. Ibid., p. 7. Primakov acknowledges that whereas in the past, regional conflicts had been viewed "solely through the prism of confrontation between the U.S.-S.R.and the U.S.A. " and that "confrontation between internal forces [in local states] occurs against a background of the existence of two opposite systems," he also points out that Moscow apparently no longer views regional conflicts as exclusively the product of imperialism or colonialism, but rather they may arise as a result of complex internal and external forces, and can take place whether or not outside forces are involved, or even whether opposing systems are involved. Many regional conflicts are purely local in origin and development, but unfortunately external forces intrude. Optimistically, he writes, in some conflicts if outside forces were withdrawn, a reconciliation of internal forces could take place.
53. Gorbachev's speech on the 70th anniversary of the Russian Revolution, November 2, 1987, in *Pravda*, November 3, 1987.

54. "Afghanistan: Preliminary Results: Interview with Major General Kim Tsagolov," by A. Borovik, *Ogonek*, July 1988 (No. 30), pp. 25-27. General Tsagolov was a military adviser in Afghanistan in 1981-84 and 1987, and is currently Chairman of the Department of Marxism-Leninism at the Frunze Military Academy. Not only did General Tsagolov say: "I am convinced that a military coup took place in Afghanistan on April 27, 1978," he also added: "Yet we persuaded ourselves in the late 1970s that Afghanistan was 'confidently advancing along the path of socialism.' What kind of socialism? There wasn't the slightest hint of socialism there. We were the victims of our own illusions." Furthermore, he did not think the Najibullah regime would survive the withdrawal of Soviet troops.
55. *Krasnaia Zvezda*, August 3, 1988.
56. "Speech of M. S. Gorbachev," *Pravda*, March 17, 1988.
57. *Cf.* Aleksander Prokhanov, "A Writer's Opinion: Afghan Questions," *Literaturnaia Gazeta*, February 17, 1988.
58. Ibid.
59. *Cf.* Letter by Academician O. Bogomolov, entitled, "Who was Mistaken?" Ibid., March 16, 1988.

2

Gorbachev's "New Thinking" on Regional Conflicts: A Theoretical Analysis

Bhabani Sen Gupta

The "new thinking" about international relations inaugurated by Mikhail Gorbachev in his political report to the 27th Congress of the Communist Party of the Soviet Union (CPSU), and further developed in speeches and statements thereafter, has four principal elements. First, the world is seen as an "integrated whole" rather than a whirlpool of polarized confrontations and conflicts of classes on intermeshing national and international levels. Second, in an integral and interdependent world, contradictions cannot be resolved by armed conflicts and ideological polarization, but only through negotiation and compromise. Third, the major problems that face humankind in the final years of the 20th century and will face it through the 21st—from nuclear war to environmental degeneration—can only be resolved on the basis of bilateral and multilateral cooperation. Finally, in an integrated and interdependent world, nations must think about security differently. Each nation's security is linked to the security of its rivals and adversaries. Nations therefore must think and act in terms of equal and adequate security. An international security system based on equal and adequate security is possible only if the great powers recognize each other's and every nation's legitimate security interests, and if the focus of security gradually shifts from military overpreparedness to regional and global security cooperation, yielding to the United Nations the role of conflict control and peacemaking in conflict-laden regions.

Gorbachev's report to the CPSU 27th Congress departed in several vital aspects from the reports submitted by the late Leonid Brezhnev to the three previous party congresses. Gorbachev did speak about imperialism's traditional role in provoking conflicts and wars and mentioned the many contradictions that mark intercapitalist and interimperialist relations. However, he did not identify the central contradiction as one between capitalism-imperialism and socialism and national liberation. The central contradiction in the world of today, in Gorbachev's view, is between nuclear annihilation and the survival of human civilization: a contradiction whose resolution compels global cooperation rather than confrontation. The central contradiction is also between the limitless promise of human development and well-being on a global scale through the giant strides of science and technology, and the limitless devastation that threatens humankind, regardless of national and ideological boundaries, from the overkill power of runaway nuclear war technology, which is now about to invade outer space.

Gorbachev's "new thinking" in international affairs is the other side of his "new thinking" in opening up and restructuring the Soviet society. In both areas, the "new thinking" must go with "new action" if it is to inspire national and international credibility and influence the thinking of other nations. Thus, *glasnost* and *perestroika* have to be seen in their linkage with *novoe politicheskoe myshlenie*. Neither can work without the other. If the "new thinking" in world politics appears to have shown better results than *perestroika* during the three preparatory years of the Gorbachev era, it is because the world seems to be more responsive to Gorbachev's innovative thrusts of foreign policy than is the Soviet system to Gorbachev's determined attempts at domestic political and economic reforms. At the same time, concrete fruits of the "new thinking" in foreign policy will feed *glasnost* and *perestroika* by reducing the weight of military expenditures and paving ways of economic collaboration between the U.S.S.R. and the capitalist countries.

Several major pronouncements offered the conceptual and operational substance and framework of Gorbachev's "new thinking" on foreign policy. The first major regional extrapolation came in Vladivostok in a speech of July 1986, in which Gorbachev visualized an Asian Helsinki arrangement—a framework of nonmilitary security for countries belonging to the Asia-Pacific region or with vital interests in that region, including the U.S.S.R., the United States, Japan, China, Indonesia, and India. The Vladivostok speech was an Asia-Pacific version of the larger concept of an integral, interdependent world that must learn to resolve differences short of war, through mutual negotiation and compromise.[1] Then in September 1987, in an article printed in both *Pravda* and *Izvestiia*, Gorbachev assigned a pivotal role to the United Nations Security Council in a "comprehensive system of international security." The five permanent members of the Council—the United States, the Soviet Union, China, Britain, and France—could become "guarantors of regional security," observed Gorbachev. The Security Council and the General Assembly could use the International Court of Justice for "consultative conclusions on international disputes" with its mandatory jurisdiction recognized by all on mutually agreed upon conditions.[2] This was indeed a sharp, even startling departure from the earlier Soviet policy, which used the United Nations to advance the interests of Third World countries and isolate the United States from them. An American scholar found it astonishing that a communist state like the U.S.S.R. was offering to engage in a process "involving laws and international institutions that will restrict its freedom of action."[3] It was one of the boldest challenges of "new thinking" to the democratic powers, notably the United States.

Gorbachev's "new thinking" in foreign policy recognized a linkage between peaceful coexistence at the central level of world politics and in the peripheries.[4] This, too, was a major departure from the Brezhnev line of the 1970s, and it came as a pleasant surprise to the Americans. President Richard Nixon's Moscow summit with Brezhnev had produced a set of basic principles governing Soviet-American relations. The "basic principles" were glued together with the adhesive "linkage": the détente to be backed by mutual restraint in the Third World where neither superpower was to grab unilateral advantage at the cost of the other. Implied in this formulation was a Soviet commitment not to violently or radically alter the balance of power in vital Third World regions. This implication of the linkage theory was hardly acceptable to the Brezhnev leadership. Even if Brezhnev personally wished to follow a moderate line, the Politburo took the stand that there could be no compromise on the ideological struggle, and it saw détente as a shot in the arm of the national liberation struggles. The Soviet Union extended crucial military support to the Leninist regime in Angola. It backed Vietnamese military intervention in Kampuchea, and a year later intervened in Afghanistan with a "contingent military force" to protect a wobbling Leninist regime from the mujahideen forces armed by the United States, China, Saudi Arabia, and Egypt, along with other countries, and hosted by Pakistan. In the West, all this was seen as disturbing thrusts of an expansionist foreign policy, especially with regard to the Third World. If the accounts of Arkadii N. Shevchenko, who defected to the United States when he was assistant secretary general of the United Nations, are correct, there was an acute clash of views in the CPSU Politburo about the wording of the "basic principles," as well as of the joint communique. The ideologues headed by Mikhail Suslov finally yielded to Andrei Gromyko, who had the powerful backing of Brezhnev.[5]

Gorbachev's "new thinking" on international relations has its critics and opponents in the Politburo and the Central Committee. Egor K. Ligachev, a secretary of the CPSU Central Committee who functions like a watchdog of the Soviet Union's ideological interests in the global arena, did not hide his reservations about the bold innovative thrusts of Gorbachev's "new thinking" at the Communist Party Conference in June 1988: "Policy making is not as easy as slurping down cabbage soup," he warned. "Caution should be combined with decisiveness. As the saying goes, before going into the room, make sure you can get out again."[6]

If Gorbachev's foreign policy "new thinking" is nevertheless gaining ground, it is because, in the first place, it is backed by concrete action, and, second, it has generated positive responses from other nations, particularly the United States. The most important action flowing from the "new thinking" is the decision to withdraw Soviet troops from Afghanistan in less than a year from the conclusion of the Geneva agreement on Afghanistan in April 1988. Regardless of the battlefront situation within Afghanistan, one-half of the Soviet forces were pulled out by August 15, and the rest left by February 15, 1989. As the withdrawal began, the CPSU leadership circulated a document among Central Committee members admitting that the decision to intervene in Afghanistan with military force was a mistake and revealing that it was taken by Brezhnev without consulting all the members of the Politburo. Going a step ahead of the generally cautious tone of the party document, two noted political commentators declared bluntly that the introduction of troops into Afghanistan reflected an excessive tendency to use military force in Soviet foreign policy.[7]

The acknowledgement that the intervention in Afghanistan was a policy error was an extraordinary act on the part of a great power. The Nixon administration, which withdrew American troops from Vietnam, never acknowledged that the U.S. intervention was a policy mistake. Gorbachev apparently wanted to recover as much as he could of the ground the Soviets had lost in the Third World by the Afghan intervention. By accusing their own government of an "excessive tendency to use military force" to shore up foreign policy gains, Soviet analysts drew pointed attention to the same tendency in the United States and other countries.

Gorbachev's decision to get his troops out of Afghanistan in a short span of time, regardless of political and strategic consequences, acted as a catalyst for a sudden proliferation of peace initiatives in the Third World. In May 1988, the United States was able to initiate a series of negotiations between South Africa, Angola, and Cuba with three objectives in view: withdrawal of South African troops from Angola and Mozambique, the long-delayed independence of Namibia, and withdrawal of Cuban troops from southern Africa within an agreed time frame. Accords were reached with breathtaking speed on the first two issues, while an agreed time frame for the complete pullout of 50,000 Cuban troops proved to be difficult (see Appendix B, Agreements for Peace in Southwestern Africa). Nevertheless, South Africa withdrew its 2,000 troops from Angola before September 1; the independence of Namibia was scheduled for 1989; and Fidel Castro declared that the circumstance was emerging in which he could bring the Cubans back home from Africa. It goes without saying that Gorbachev was prodding the Cuban leader to move in that direction despite Castro's coldness to *perestroika*. He was also pressing the Leninist leaders of Angola to negotiate a political settlement on the basis of the newly minted concept of national reconciliation in Third World nations torn by civil wars.

Peace continued to break out in 1988. August brought about a truce in the eight-year-old Gulf war between Iraq and Iran, with the two superpowers working together at the U.N. Security Council in an effort to convert the truce into a peace agreement. Nudged by Moscow, Vietnam announced that it would pull out 50,000 of its troops from Kampuchea in 1988 and would complete the withdrawal by the end of September 1989. It also transferred the headquarters of the intervention army from Kampuchea to Vietnamese territory. In March, Vietnam, the Kampuchean regime, and the three factions of the resistance alliance met at a "cocktail" conference in Jakarta (JIM I) under the friendly auspices of Indonesia. Though no accord was reached on a political settlement of the Kampuchean issue, the resistance alliance offered a modified peace plan.

Then, at the end of August, the Soviet Union and China got together at the level of deputy foreign ministers in Beijing to discuss Kampuchea for the first time. The spokesman of the Chinese foreign ministry told reporters on September 1, 1988, that the talks, which lasted four days, had found some common ground. It now looked like there would be a "just and reasonable" solution to the Kampuchean issue, and China would do its "best" to resolve the remaining obstacles.[8] Xinhua news agency, in a commentary dated September 1, acknowledged that there were fears among the people that the Khmer Rouge would make a bid for power after the Vietnamese took their troops back, but that would not happen. Both sides to the conflict agreed that the Kampuchean government would be reconstructed. They differed on how this was to be done. The Vietnam-backed government invited the resistance factions to join in a government of national reconciliation, while the resistance peace plan proposed that both governments be dissolved, an interim regime set up with Sihanouk as leader, and elections held under U.N. supervision.

Gorbachev's style of "new thinking" being backed by "new action" was demonstrated also in the role the Geneva Accords gave to the United Nations to supervise the withdrawal of Soviet troops. This, too, proved a catalyst. The United Nations was given the pivotal role in ending the Gulf war. The Kampuchean peace talks converged on the peacekeeping and election-supervising role that would go to the United Nations once agreements were finally reached. The United Nations was not involved in the southern African peace negotiations. But in view of its longstanding direct involvement in the independence of Namibia, it was assumed that the world organization would play a crucial role in at least the Namibian phase of an eventual southern African peace plan. The United Nations, furthermore, was invited to mediate the war over the Western Sahara between Morocco and the Polisario-Front guerrilla movement, which has been fighting for the former Spanish colony's independence.

What triggered the peace proliferation? Why did so many regional conflicts suddenly begin to bend to negotiated settlements? In the United States, most people believed that the Reagan Doctrine had worked, that the display of American military strength eventually convinced the Soviet Union that its policy of propping up Leninist regimes in the Third World could not succeed. American observers, however, examined more deeply the causes of war and peace in the peripheries, and came to the conclusion that neither superpower could afford to spend sizeable portions of its resources to perpetuate protracted Third World conflicts. Former Defense Secretary Elliot Richardson wrote that "both the United States and the Soviet Union have encountered their own reasons for wanting a stronger framework of world order. They are finding it increasingly difficult to ignore the waste inherent in their habitual modes of politico-military competition. Nine-tenths of their military capacity, both nuclear and conventional, are dedicated to preserving stalemates that could be maintained at lower force levels at far less cost. At long last, moreover, they seem ready to face up to the fact that neither has ever gained any significant advantage at the expense of the other from increasing the intensity of a local conflict."[9]

Historian Paul Kennedy's hypothesis that the United States has vastly overstretched its resources by accepting global commitments not entirely germane to its national security is broadly recognized as a fact by the American foreign policy community. Echoing widely held views, James Chase, a senior associate of the Carnegie Foundation and coauthor of *America Invulnerable*, wrote, "By the 1980s . . . both superpowers had extended themselves far beyond the safe measure of power that Thomas Jefferson had recommended for the Republic. The United States had set up a worldwide alliance system, supervised by its world's product. Forty years later, America generates less than 20 percent of that product and has become the greatest debtor country in the world, gravely dependent on foreigners to finance its living standards."[10]

A comprehensive analysis of the causes of regional conflicts, together with a portfolio of recommendations for their control and resolution, came on May 5, 1988, from a joint team of American and Soviet specialists. Sponsored by the Washington-based Institute for Soviet-American Relations and the Moscow-based U.S.A.-Canada Institute of the Soviet Academy of Sciences, the two teams—the American side headed by Arthur Cox and the Soviet side by Georgii Arbatov—took three years to produce the study, entitled *Basic Requirements of Stable Coexistence*.[11] I was told by my contacts in the International Department of the CPSU Central Committee Secretariat during the

May 1988 Reagan-Gorbachev summit in Moscow that the joint report had figured prominently in the discussion on regional conflicts at the level of aides to the two leaders.

The report noted that, while the superpowers had carefully avoided direct collision because of their shared fear of nuclear war, "both sides have attempted to advance their political goals throughout the world through measures that have frequently involved the direct and indirect use of combat military force." The "most promising road to the desired condition of stable coexistence in U.S.-Soviet relations," the report added, "lies in progressive demilitarization of U.S.-Soviet competition" in the Third World. This judgment was based on two central "truths": The arms race is stalemated by "an inescapable mutual vulnerability to nuclear destruction," and the "deepest, most enduring cause of fear and distrust is the assumption by each side that the other harbors hostile intentions, including aggressive use of military force."[12]

The U.S.-Soviet study team made several recommendations for progressive demilitarization of the superpower competition. The superpowers should avoid the commitment of combat military force to regional conflicts. They should refrain from introducing proxies of voluntary military forces or covert military forces in regional conflicts. They should also bar the transfer of sophisticated weapons to Third World nations and use their diplomatic influence to persuade other major producers of arms to ban the transfer of such weapons. And they ought to create jointly manned intelligence centers in Moscow and Washington to provide verification of agreements that may be reached to resolve specific regional conflicts.[13]

These suggestions, to be adopted "from above" by the superpowers, had complete support of the Gorbachev regime, I was told by a central secretariat official. A senior level official, who asked not to be identified, said, "We have been discussing these principles with the Americans very seriously. Informal bilateral talks on regional conflicts are going on side by side with the formal and informal negotiations in nuclear and conventional arms control and disarmament. In our view, the two are not only equally important, but they are also interlinked. For a stable and secure international order, regional peace and stability are as important as stability in the superpower relationship."[14]

In Gorbachev's thinking on regional conflicts, certain basic principles must guide regional actors themselves if conflicts are to be resolved and peace maintained. A second high-ranking official of the foreign ministry gave me an outline of six measures that are to be taken "from below"—that is, by local actors. First, parties to a regional conflict must have the political will to resolve the conflict. If political will is lacking at the regional level, the major powers might use persuasive diplomacy to help create this basic tool. Second, the parties directly involved in a regional conflict must engage in negotiations. The mechanism of talking, of creating a dialogue, is of crucial importance because dialogues not only generate mutual understanding but also narrow differences and produce areas of agreement. Third, they must agree to give and take and to compromise. Polarization can only lead to prolongation of conflicts, especially in cases where neither side is clearly superior to the other and can make its will prevail upon its weaker opponent. Fourth, the neighboring countries must observe restraint in supplying arms to the warring parties. This, my interlocutor stressed, is of particular importance because most of the regional conflicts tend to involve neighbors of the combating nations in partisan roles, and also because neighbors can be, and are, used by the major powers as proxies through whom the course of conflict can be influenced. Fifth, the great powers must observe restraint in supplying weapons so that the local combatants are forced to make do with whatever arms they themselves produce or can procure from other external sources. This would keep the level of a regional conflict low. Finally, the regional actors should use the mechanisms of the U.N. Security Council and the International Court of Justice or the good offices of the U.N. Secretary-General to bring them together to mutually acceptable compromise settlements. If the local actors are unwilling to do this on their own, the major powers should use diplomatic pressure to influence them.

Gorbachev and his aides seem to have distilled the "from above" and "from below" principles to resolve regional conflicts from the experience with these conflicts, especially in the 1980s. In each of the four regional conflicts now giving way toward solutions—in Afghanistan, southern Africa, Kampuchea, and Central America—the superpowers, their local or nonlocal allies, and directly combating parties are involved in complex webs of cooperation along rival lines. Each conflict centers around a Third World Leninist regime, inevitably weak in its bellicose and disorderly teething period, against whom powerful thrusts of the Reagan Doctrine are openly and loudly directed. The Soviets intervened directly with military force in Afghanistan to protect a wobbling Leninist regime that found itself pitted against the vast majority of its countrymen. The Afghan resistance immediately received powerful support from Pakistan and, through Pakistan, an ally in the form of the United States. Several other countries, notably Saudi Arabia and China, were also indirectly involved in helping the Afghan mujahideen.

In southern Africa, the Leninist regime in Angola was opposed from the beginning by its ideological rival, UNITA. The regime received strong indirect military support from the U.S.S.R., and UNITA received aid from the United States, though at a lower level. The Soviets financed the operation of 45,000 Cuban troops fighting on behalf of the Leninist government, while South Africa joined the combat with its own military force on behalf of UNITA. In Kampuchea, the Vietnamese intervened to oust a Leninist regime of genocidal tendencies to plant another that would be under Hanoi's influence. China rushed to the assistance of the three-party opposition alliance, whose leading force was the Khmer Rouge of the discredited Pol Pot government. Large supplies of Chinese arms and funds were supplemented by relatively modest doses of American supplies, while neighboring Thailand offered hospitality à la Pakistan in the case of the Afghan conflict. In Nicaragua, the Reagan administration armed and provided the Contras, who also received hospitality from neighboring nations, while the regime in Managua found patrons in Cuba and the U.S.S.R.

Each of these four conflicts has run for many years, sometimes longer than a decade. In each, as noted, a Leninist regime is at the center of conflict. And each conflict has utterly devastated its country. Apart from enormous costs in terms of human lives and limbs and productive resources, the conflicts have made it impossible for the regimes to address the fundamental problems of development. Together, the conflicts have imposed an extremely heavy load of tension on the international system and on world politics. They have helped create a global climate of militarization of international relations. The United States, under the Reagan administration, undertook the biggest ever military buildup program in peacetime, while the Soviet Union had been steadily rearming since the 1970s. Enormous quantities of arms and weapons, including sophisticated weapon systems, were sold to Third World nations by the arms producers—eighty percent of the transfers by the United States and the Soviet Union alone. The Soviet economy stagnated as a result of the transfer of vast resources to military production, while the United States became the world's largest debtor nation in merely three years when its impressive record of continuous economic growth during most of the 1980s was deeply overshadowed by huge budget and trade deficits. Involvement in each of the regional conflicts, and in so many of them at the same time, strained the economic resources of both superpowers, but the U.S.S.R. more than the United States. To make matters worse, none of these conflicts clearly and unequivocally produced results desired by either superpower who, between them, have invested an enormous amount of resources to achieve their desired objectives.

The last point deserves further reflection. The peace negotiations with regard to each of the four regional conflicts have displayed two aspects. The first is the disengagement of external powers, including neighbors acting in tandem with, or on behalf of, either superpower. The second is the conclusion of the internal civil war through reconciliation and compromise between the warring parties. Progress has proved to be easier with respect to the first aspect than the second. The Geneva Accords on Afghanistan provide only for the withdrawal of Soviet troops; they also prescribe certain cooperative behavior on the part of Pakistan and the United States that has not yet been observed, as seen for instance in the continued supply of arms to the Afghan resistance in the course of the Soviet pullout (see Appendix A, "Geneva Accords on Afghanistan.") A bid by Pakistan, supported by the United States, to extend the Geneva Accords to the construction of an interim government in Kabul that would be acceptable to the four to five million Afghan refugees that have taken shelter in Pakistan and Iran fell through because it was opposed by Moscow and Kabul and was, in any case, outside the province of the U.N. mediator. As a result, even as the Soviet pullout continued, two opposing plans were at work for the future of Afghanistan: the Kabul regime pressing its policy of national reconciliation, and the mujahideen, or large factions thereof, determined to bring down the Soviet-backed Leninist government.

The southern African negotiations do not extend to the civil war in Angola, which will apparently continue without external help to either side even if accords are signed and implemented, leading to external disengagement and Namibian independence. In Kampuchea, the stumbling block is the nature and composition of the government that will prevail after the Vietnamese troops have completely withdrawn. Except in Afghanistan, Leninist rule is likely to prevail in the three other conflict-laden countries. Kampuchea, Nicaragua, and Angola are not likely to be governed by non-Leninist regimes after external disengagement. Even in Afghanistan, the collapse of the Kabul regime after the pullout of Soviet troops is not entirely assured. Regardless of who rules in Kabul, the regime will be nonaligned and will be obliged to maintain friendly relations with the U.S.S.R., with which a great deal of the Afghan economy has been integrated. In sum, therefore, gains for the Reagan Doctrine have not been altogether positive. The price has been considerable.

In Gorbachev's "new thinking" on world affairs, the vacuum created by the mutual standoff of the superpowers from Third World conflicts is to be filled by the United Nations and other regional cooperation and security organizations. The United Nations is competent only in keeping the peace and, in specific cases, in helping to negotiate conflict resolution. A U.N. peacekeeping role can also be maintained only for limited periods, although, as in Cyprus, the limit may mean many years. The task of maintaining regional peace and stability can be performed only by regional organizations. Gorbachev, in his Vladivostok speech, recognized regional organizations like ASEAN and SAARC as constructive instruments of regional peace and stability. The Soviet Union likewise has supported the Arias peace plan for Central America.

To be sure, strong local bilateral rivalries render regional peace and security cooperation most difficult to achieve. In South Asia, for instance, the rivalry and antagonism that accompany India-Pakistan relations rule out a common regional approach to the Afghan conflict. India has stated clearly that the installation of a fundamentalist Islamic regime in Kabul is not acceptable to it, and yet this seems to be the objective of Pakistan's persistent support to the seven-party mujahideen alliance operating from its own territory.

The American dilemma is that, while it may have little taste for an Islamic fundamentalist regime, it is driven to support the cause of the fundamentalist mujahideen because they alone can be expected to overthrow the Soviet-backed Leninist regime in Kabul. The dilemma is sharpened by the divisions that weaken the unity of the seven factions of the mujahideen alliance set up in Peshawar, capital of the North-West Frontier Province (NWFP) of Pakistan, commonly known as the Peshawar Seven. Three of the seven groups are identified as fundamentalists determined to install an Islamic regime in Kabul; the four others are said to be more moderate, willing to participate in a government headed by Zahir Shah, the former king of Afghanistan who lives in his old age in Rome. Another complicating factor is the existence of a larger number of rebel groups within Afghanistan, 1,200 by Soviet count, who have connections with the Peshawar Seven in terms of arms supplies, but who are believed to be stubbornly independent in their respective "liberated" fiefs. Perhaps due to American pressure, the rebels did not mount sustained military operations during the withdrawal of Soviet troops. However, they made their power strongly felt by making occasional rocket attacks on Kabul and by blowing up Afghan government ammunition depots. They also reportedly captured a couple of provincial towns not distant from the Pakistani border. The future is clouded with uncertainty, as is conceded in a brief prepared in August 1988 by the Foreign Affairs and National Defense Division of the Congressional Research Service:

> Great uncertainty surrounds the future of Afghanistan. Under one scenario, the conflict will continue indefinitely with the current government retaining control of Kabul and the north, if not elsewhere. Under another, the country will be divided as in Lebanon among various contending factions, including forces loyal to the regime and regional resistance commanders. Under a third, the collapse of the Kabul government will be followed by the organization of a consensus government based on the resistance alliance, albeit one dominated by Islamic fundamentalists. Current indications are that in southern Afghanistan the withdrawal of Soviet troops is leading to a rapid deterioration of security for the government.[15]

The future political setup in Afghanistan became more complicated and uncertain after the death of General Zia-ul Haq, president and supreme ruler of Pakistan, in a plane crash on August 17, 1988, which also took the life of the American ambassador Arnold L. Raphel, the chief military attaché to the U.S. embassy, and an unspecified number of top Pakistani generals believed to be between twelve and twenty. General Zia was deeply committed to the cause of the mujahideen, especially that of the fundamentalist groups among the Peshawar Seven, and to the Reagan Doctrine. The cause of the explosion of an American-made C-130 was not disclosed even after a month of a joint U.S.-Pakistani investigation, fanning suspicion that it might have been an act of subversion by relatively junior officers in the Pakistani Army. What Zia-ul Haq's sudden removal from the scene may mean for the future of Afghanistan and for future relations between Pakistan and the U.S.S.R. and Pakistan and India is speculated upon in another brief of the Congressional Research Service:

> At stake for the United States is the continuity of Pakistan's role as a major supporter and a channel for aid to the Afghan resistance and, in a broader sense, the continuity of Pakistan's role as a strategically located ally in the vital Persian Gulf region. Another major uncertainty is whether the passing of Zia will affect Pakistan's apparent drive to acquire a capability to deploy nuclear weapons, and whether the United States will have more or less influence over the nuclear policy of Zia's successors. The future course of Pakistan-India relations, long under strain, will have an important impact on regional security. The death of Zia may cause the Soviet Union to seek better ties with Pakistan, but the Soviets are unlikely to find sufficient opportunities to increase their influence. The Soviets may hope that Pakistan's new leadership will be less enthusiastic in supporting the Afghan resistance movement's effort to topple the pro-Soviet government in Kabul.[16]

Pakistan in the next few years will probably continue to support the mujahideen and at the same time explore the possibilities of normalizing relations with the U.S.S.R., while maintaining a strong bilateral, security-oriented relationship with the United States. The drive for normal relations with Moscow gathered strength as Sino-Soviet relations became normalized following the Gorbachev-Deng summit in May 1989. In the next few years, Pakistan, in my view, will adopt the Chinese model of foreign policy. With strong bilateral relations with the United States including a security connection that does not necessarily imply supporting American interests in the Persian Gulf and the Middle East, Pakistan will most probably seek good, neighborly relations with the U.S.S.R., taking advantage of the Soviet offer of substantial participation in its development program and, more importantly, of Soviet commitment to Pakistan's territorial integrity and independence. If Pakistan-Soviet relations are normalized, regardless of what government rules in Kabul, Afghanistan cannot but have friendly relations with the U.S.S.R.

Brewing behind the façade of the Soviet withdrawal from Afghanistan and the efforts of the Pakistan-backed mujahideen to set up an Islamic fundamentalist regime in Kabul there has been an oncoming contention between Pakistan and India for influence over Afghanistan. Traditionally, Afghanistan has always been friendly with India, while having a low-level tension with Pakistan over the issue of Pakhtoonistan, a projected independent state of the

Pushtun-speaking Pathans of NWFP and the southernmost areas of Afghanistan. As noted, India's prime minister, Rajiv Gandhi, has made it clear that the installation of a fundamentalist Islamic regime in Kabul under Pakistan's influence would not be acceptable to India. Such a regime may produce an anti-Hindu impact among the Moslems of India, the world's fourth largest Moslem population, especially in Kashmir where the Moslems are an overwhelming majority. India already accuses Pakistan of helping the irridentist Khalistani movement, which perpetrates violence and terror through segments of the Sikh population. The Sikhs live in the northwestern state of Punjab, which borders Pakistan and thus provides vital transport links to Kashmir. The installation of a Pakistan-backed Islamic regime in Kabul will certainly be seen by Indians as altering the balance of power in South Asia in Pakistan's favor. Relations between Pakistan and India would become strained still further if the diminishing supply of high-technology weapons from the United States drives the new rulers of Pakistan to cross the rubicon of nuclear weapons production. On the other hand, if the United States continues to transfer high-technology weapon systems to Pakistan even after the withdrawal of Soviet troops from Afghanistan, just to keep an imaginary lid on Pakistan's nuclear weapons program, India's fledgling good relations with America will certainly come under heavy strain.

Such indeed are the stern complexities of the regional relationships in South Asia that lend a forbidding background to the political future of Afghanistan. For India, the reinstatement of the military patron-client relationship between the United States and Pakistan, almost simultaneously with the Soviet military intervention in Afghanistan, generated the great divide between the Indian and global perceptions of the Soviet action. While the world was outraged by the Soviet invasion of a small, non-aligned, landlocked nation that was traditionally friendly towards Moscow, India saw the resurrection of the America-Pakistan military patron-client relationship—especially the assumption by Pakistan of the role of a frontline state in the containment of Soviet influence in the Third World—as an immediate threat to its security and influence in South Asia. I am not suggesting that India would have joined the international community to condemn the Soviet invasion if the United States had not rushed to offer military assistance to Pakistan and the Afghan rebels. India, however, would have been openly critical of the Soviet action, and in diplomatic exchanges would have put much stronger pressure on Moscow than it actually did to cut short its military presence in Afghanistan. With a large-scale American military aid commitment to Pakistan, the Soviet military presence in Afghanistan proved to be a positive factor for India's defense-planners, who got, on a long-term basis, the best possible military procurement deal with the Soviets, matching with Soviet hardware everything that the United

States transferred to Pakistan, and, in addition, obtaining Soviet frontier military technology through the production under license of a sophisticated weapon system in India.

In January-February 1980, Indira Gandhi sent her special envoy to Islamabad, proposing to General Zia-ul Haq that Pakistan refrain from getting high-tech arms from the United States and that Pakistan and India jointly negotiate with the Soviet Union a settlement of the Afghan crisis.[17] That offer was rejected. Eight years later, on the eve of the final round of Geneva talks for the U.N.-sponsored accord on Afghanistan, Rajiv Gandhi made a second offer to General Zia of a regional settlement of the vexing question of Afghanistan's political status after the pullout of Soviet troops. His argument was that Gorbachev's February 8th announcement that Soviet troops would leave Afghanistan in twelve months meant that the time had come for eliminating superpower involvement in that country and for taking a regional approach to the savaged nation's political future. Concretely, he suggested through the foreign secretary of the Indian external affairs ministry, that the matter of the future government of Kabul be settled in talks among Pakistan, India, the mujahideen, and the Leninist regime in Kabul.

Pakistan, however, refused to allow India to "poke its nose" in Afghan affairs at that late hour. While General Zia received the Indian foreign secretary on the eve of the Geneva round, the then prime minister of Pakistan, Mohammad Khan Junejo, pleaded illness. Public opinion in Pakistan was almost unanimous to keep India out of the Afghan settlement. The Indian prime minister then took a diplomatic step that raised many eyebrows in the world. He invited the Afghan president, Dr. Najibullah, to New Delhi for a state visit and bestowed on him a glittering, red carpet welcome. Prior to that, a trusted aide to the prime minister had made a trip to Kabul and returned with the impression that the Leninist regime might survive a civil war with the mujahideen. India's foreign minister had visited Kabul in 1987 and promised Delhi's participation in Afghanistan's postwar reconstruction. Now Mr. Gandhi sent his new foreign minister to Kabul in a further gesture of India's commitment to the Leninist regime.

India has neither the means nor the intention to influence the course of events in Afghanistan. It has, however, incurred the strong antipathy of the Peshawar Seven. An India-Pakistan contention over Afghanistan will only further strain the already mutually hostile bilateral relationship. It was probably in anticipation of this kind of development that the Soviet Union in May 1988 placed the subcontinent on the list of regional conflict issues to be discussed with the United States. The two superpowers will have to act if they are to prevent Afghanistan from becoming an issue of confrontation between two rival South Asian neighbors who fought four wars between 1948 and 1972.

Now I shall turn from Afghanistan to the broader area of regional conflicts in general. To be sure, neither the "from above" policy proposals made by the joint Soviet-American team of experts nor the "from below" propositions given to me by a Soviet foreign ministry official will not necessarily foreclose revolutionary political change in Third World countries. The right of a people to choose their own form of government and society is acknowledged both by the United States and the Soviet Union. If a Leninist-oriented revolution occurs in a particular country, it should be allowed to stand on its own feet. Gorbachev's six broad principles would, however, expect the revolutionary side to accommodate its opponents to the greatest extent possible. If the superpowers do not intervene in a revolutionary civil war, either directly with arms supplies to their respective chosen clients or through proxy powers, the outcome of the civil war will be determined locally. Regional organizations and the United Nations might intervene with a view to settling the local conflict. Its intensity will remain limited, as will its destabilizing impact on international relations.

Some analysts see in the Gorbachev approach a pragmatic retreat from the revolutionary zeal of the Brezhnev and Khrushchev period. One American analyst has noted that Gorbachev and his advisers appear to view the Third World as a "tragic arena, not a region of hope and promise."[18] Others have argued that the "cost of the empire"—computed by Americans at about $35 billion—is too heavy a burden for the Soviet Union to bear, especially because the economic gains from the Third World Leninist-oriented regimes are far from significant. Each Third World country installing a Leninist regime is an additional drain on the limited resources of the U.S.S.R. The "expansionism" of the 1970s has led to an overextension of Soviet resources, without bringing in a compensating political or strategic harvest. The "expansionism" has provoked the United States to launch a unilaterally globalist and militarist foreign policy. The American armed support to contra forces in Third World Leninist-oriented countries has kept the Soviet-backed regimes engaged in fighting prolonged, expensive, and destructive civil wars. These regimes have not been able to address themselves to their countries' political and economic development. As a result, their regional and international impact has fallen far short of expectations, while large segments of their populations are becoming alienated due to economic distress and general insecurity of life. Thus, the two Leninist-oriented regimes in southern Africa—Angola and Mozambique—together have not had much of a political impact on the rest of the continent. The application of the Reagan Doctrine has not allowed these Third World Leninist regimes to consolidate their political gains.

These considerations appear to have weighed with Gorbachev and his advisers in sculpting their new approach to regional conflicts.[19] At any rate, the "new thinking" appears to be cushioned on objective realities in the Third World. Few Third World countries are pregnant with revolutionary possibilities at the end of the 1980s. The last revolutionary wave was seen in the Portuguese colonies in Africa in the wake of the collapse of Salazar's fascist imperialism. The Nicaraguan revolution was caused by the oppressive rule of the Somoza family, who enjoyed American patronage and support. It seems to have driven a stern warning to most of the ruling elites in Latin America: They must democratize their political systems, giving the people adequate political participation in freedom and with dignity. The winds of change now blowing in the Third World are of democracy and human rights, not Leninist revolutions. The Soviets clearly do not expect any Third World country to explode in a Leninist revolution in the near future.

If these considerations alone have gone into the making of Gorbachev's "new thinking" on regional conflicts, the new policy becomes largely one of convenience; necessity is made into a virtue. In this writer's view, the roots of Gorbachev's "new thinking" go deeper than opportunism. They derive from a fundamentally new approach to world affairs and from the overriding need of modernizing the Soviet system. For *glasnost* and *perestroika* to succeed, Gorbachev needs to transfer large volumes of resources from the military to the civilian side of the Soviet economy. He has to transfer thousands of scientists and engineers from military to civilian consumer goods industries. He needs to decentralize the command politicoeconomic system and blend socialism with democracy. Furthermore, he needs to lock capitalist technology and capital into his plans for economic *perestroika*. He cannot expect to achieve these objectives unless he can substantially bring down the threshold of conflict in the world arena, and strike at the foundations of Western, especially American, anti-Sovietism.

To be sure, Gorbachev's "new thinking" on regional conflicts cannot be separated from his "new thinking" on international relations as a whole. The "stable coexistence" he is trying to build with the United States in the 1980s is fundamentally different from the détente of the 1970s. The new détente is not being built entirely from above. The Soviet Union and the United States have begun to work together at hundreds of points, covering science and technology, the environment, nuclear disarmament and conventional arms control, the youth, schools, colleges and universities, communications and the performing arts. Every bold thrust of *glasnost* is a blow to the bedrock of anti-Sovietism in the United States. American anti-Sovietism is unlikely to survive a consolidation of *glasnost* and *perestroika* in the U.S.S.R., extending its reach to human rights, a larger emigration of Jews from the U.S.S.R., and the restoration of diplomatic relations with Israel. The détente of the 1980s is being built on the ruins of the détente of the 1970s, absorbing the lessons of the past. Gorbachev will not allow the new détente to collapse in the face of an American conservative anti-Soviet backlash, as Brezhnev did in the 1970s.

In another crucial respect, the détente of the 1980s is being constructed very differently from its predecessor. The West Europeans, especially the German Federal Republic, and to a lesser extent France, are inclining towards Gorbachev's "new thinking." Regionalism is flourishing more in Europe than anywhere else. The concept of "one European homeland" is steadily winning West European support. Futhermore, Gorbachev is simultaneously building a second détente—between the Soviet Union and China. The volatile dynamics of the U.S.-U.S.S.R.-China triangle, which imparted a structural instability to the détente of the early 1970s, are conspicuously absent from the relationships of stable coexistence between the superpowers and between the Soviet Union and China that are being built in the late 1980s.

Gorbachev's "new thinking," then, is not aiming at the construction of a U.S.-Soviet "duopoly" for the world. As a realist, Gorbachev attaches extraordinary importance to competitive rather than adversarial coexistence with the United States. To the extent that the world continues to be bipolar, he will work with the United States to build a framework for a stable international order. In his schema, however, the five permanent members of the U.N. Security Council are the keepers of the peace in the peripheries of the international system. The crucial role of conflict resolution and peacekeeping is assigned the United Nations. Japan is also a coveted member of the club of peacekeepers and peacebuilders. Appropriate roles are allotted to regional cooperation organizations, which will be encouraged to take charge of regional security and peace. The assumption is that once the great powers begin to conduct themselves with a sense of responsibility for stable peace, the happy contagion will spread to the entire international community. At any rate, the deviants might be brought under control relatively easily.

To succeed, Gorbachev's "new thinking" will demand cooperative responses from the United States and China, as well as the other major powers of the world. The year 1988 witnessed a hopeful beginning. Hope, however, must be tempered with caution in the wait for further developments. Gorbachev's own *glasnost* and *perestroika* so far have not become an irreversible process of change in the U.S.S.R. Gorbachev must be able to win over the strong and stubborn resistance he has been facing from the privileged elites of the system. He has to persevere with the reforms without yielding to damaging compromise. The "new thinking" has created a positive impression on the global mind. It will require a lot of flesh and blood to make the impression lasting and to win international trust and confidence.

Notes

1. See Bhabani Sen Gupta, *The Gorbachev Factor in World Affairs* (New Delhi: B.R. Publishers, November 1989).
2. The articles appeared in *Pravda* and *Izvestiia*, September 17, 1986.
3. James Chase, "The Quest for Absolute Security from 1812 to Star Wars," *Foreign Policy*, No. 70, Spring 1988, p. 10.
4. From an exclusive interview with *The Washington Post*, May 22, 1988.
5. Arkadii N. Shevchenko, *Breaking with Moscow* (New York: Alfred K. Knopf, 1985), pp. 205-8, 211-16.
6. *The New York Times*, July 3, 1988. See also Peter Reddaway, "Resisting Gorbachev," *New York Review of Books*, August 18, 1988.
7. *The New York Times*, June 17, 1988.
8. *China Report*, September 2, 1988. Gorbachev himself confirmed the good results of the August-end meeting in his speech at Krasnoiarsk, Siberia, on September 16, 1988. See *The New York Times* of September 17, 1988, and *The Christian Science Monitor*, September 19, 1988. A Sino-Soviet summit appears to be on the active bilateral agenda.
9. Elliot Richardson, "Multilateral Cooperation: The Realistic Alternative," *Journal of the United States Institute of Peace*, April 1988. See also Stephen F. Cohen, "Centrists Lack the Guts to Respond to Gorbachev," *The New York Times*, September 19, 1988.
10. Chase, *op. cit.*, pp. 8, 9.
11. The study was released in Washington and Moscow on May 5, 1988 by the Institute for Soviet-American Relations, Washington, D.C.
12. Ibid.
13. Arthur Macy Cox, "Mr. Gorbachev's Peaceful Coexistence Ploy," *The New York Times*, August 20, 1988.
14. During the May summit I was in Moscow for an Indo-Soviet dialogue that spanned history, politics, sociology, mass media, and literature. I met with a number of government and party officials as well as academic experts.
15. Richardson P. Cronin and Francis T. Miko, *Afghanistan: Status, U.S. Role, and Implications of a Soviet Withdrawal*. Washington, D.C., Congressional Research Service, updated August 25, 1988, cyclostyled.
16. Richard P. Cronin, *Pakistan After Zia: Implications for Pakistan and U.S. Interests*, Washington, D.C., Congressional Research Service, updated August 24, 1988.
17. Bhabani Sen Gupta, *The Afghan Syndrome: How to Live with Soviet Power*. (New Delhi: Vikas Publishing House, 1982).
18. Chase, op. cit., p. 9.
19. Is the withdrawal of Soviet troops prompted by "defeat" in Afghanistan? This is the prevailing theme in the United States, Western Europe, Pakistan, and other countries. This theme should perhaps be tempered with other considerations. The Soviets could have stuck it out in Afghanistan if that were the determination of the Gorbachev leadership. The war was costly more in terms of lost opportunities and lost prestige than in terms of manpower and financial resources. The Soviets could have gone on fighting, waiting for fatigue to set in in the United States and for political change in Pakistan and increasing social tension between Pakistanis and Afghan refugees. The mujahideen did not "win" the war when Gorbachev announced the decision to withdraw.

This decision was taken in 1985, with some opposition in the CPSU Politburo and none from the military, according to my reliable Soviet sources in Moscow. It was taken because Gorbachev was convinced that without a dramatic peace move in Afghanistan, he could not break the spine of the second Cold War and make an impact on the global mind with his foreign policy new thinking. In July 1986, when he described Afghanistan as a "bleeding wound" in his Vladivostok speech, he for all practical purposes notified the world of his intention to get out, and he also offered an opaque apology for mistakes committed by his predecessors. The admission of a policy error was indeed an unprecedented move by a superpower. From 1986 onward, Soviet television started to prepare the Soviet people for a withdrawal from Afghanistan by showing actual war scenes including Soviet casualties. With the singleminded follow-up of the withdrawal decision, the acknowledgement of error, the role given to the United Nations, and simultaneous cooperation with the United States to resolve other regional conflicts, Gorbachev was able to recover a lot of the damage to Soviet prestige in the Third World that had been caused by the military intervention in Afghanistan.

3

Gorbachev's Policies toward the Third World: An Overview

William E. Griffith

Mikhail Gorbachev has introduced major, perhaps even historic changes in Soviet foreign policy with respect to the Third World. These changes have been an integral part of an overall revision of Soviet foreign policy, which in turn has been a direct result of a more general overhaul of Soviet society and domestic policy. One must therefore understand Gorbachev's broad reform agenda before comprehending the changes in Soviet Third World policy.

It is impossible to know now whether, and if so how much, Gorbachev will succeed in his endeavors. Modern Russian history has had many such reforming leaders, from Tsar Peter the Great to Yuri Andropov. None of them succeeded completely in his aims, which were above all else patriotic: to transform backward Russia into a modern, fully developed great power equal to and therefore secure vis-à-vis Russia's Western opponents.

Gorbachev has profited from two important new factors. The first has been the development of a much larger and more sophisticated modernizing Russian intelligentsia. (Between 1959 and 1979 Russians with full university degrees and with secondary education tripled in number.) This intelligentsia has sought personal as well as national security, higher income, and less interference in their personal and communal lives from nonrational, incompetent, and corrupt bureaucrats. Therefore they are one important social base for Gorbachev's reforms. His other, more important social base are those sectors of the party, governmental, administrative, and police bureaucracies that because of patriotism are determined to prevent, as Gorbachev has said, the Soviet Union from entering the twenty-first century as a second-rate power.

The second factor has been Gorbachev himself. Along with his wife Raisa, he is a member of the modernizing intelligentsia, the first university-educated

Soviet party head since Vladimir Lenin. Moreover, as the Soviet general secretary he has shown intelligence, energy, uncommon communications skills, effective use of experts, quick decisiveness in adopting and revising policies, and the ability to cleverly sidetrack his opponents.

His major changes in Soviet domestic and foreign policy, foreshadowed by but more radical than Andropov's, were the result of his diagnosis of the ills that had accumulated in the Soviet society during the stagnation of the Brezhnev years. These ills, he realized, were all the more dangerous because the West and Japan had during the same period outdistanced the Soviet Union in the revolution of high technology.

Gorbachev saw Russia's main ills as declining economic growth; growing technological backwardness; increasing social strains; nearly all-pervasive corruption; the antireformism of Soviet officials (the *nomenklatura*); the overextension and self-isolation of Soviet foreign policy; and the dangers of nuclear war and ecological catastrophe. The most important of these for Gorbachev has been the threat of growing Soviet backwardness in the revolution of high technology. Hence, his "new thinking," implemented by *perestroika* (restructuring), *glasnost* (greater [but still limited] freedom of expression), and *demokratizatsiia* (democratization [but not of the Western style]).

To begin with East-West relations: Gorbachev's *novoe myshlenie* ("new thinking") in Soviet foreign policy assumes that there can be no victory in nuclear war; that military superiority is impossible; and that Soviet foreign policy should therefore give priority to Soviet-U.S. (and Sino-Soviet) détente in order to create interdependence and mutual security, rather than, as Brezhnev did, give priority to a global struggle against "imperialism," including by indirect or (as in Afghanistan) direct military intervention. Therefore, nuclear deterrence and nuclear parity should be replaced by "nuclear sufficiency" and a defensive rather then offensive strategy. These new Soviet policies would preserve strategic stability, reduce nuclear and conventional weapons arsenals by arms control treaties, and thus lead to a nonnuclear world and the nonuse of force in international relations. Gorbachev has declared moreover that the Soviet Union should become integrated into the international economy (which would imply becoming export-competitive therein, *inter alia* as a means of stimulating domestic technological progress), and should participate much more actively in international organizations.

It follows, however, from the very patriotic nature of Gorbachev's motives, that he and his associates, while realizing that the Soviet Union must go through a period of retreat in foreign policy because it is weaker than its opponent, must also realize that this period will be, if successful, only a pause until the expansion of Soviet power can be, without major risk, resumed—it is, in sum, a policy of *reculer pour mieux sauter*.[1]

Gorbachev's new foreign policies had by early 1989 led to significantly improved Soviet relations with the West, especially in the arms control field, although they have not yet led to improved Soviet relations with Japan, and they may seriously and even disastrously destabilize Great Russian rule over subject nations within the Soviet Union and in Central and Eastern Europe.

This chapter concentrates on the content, causes, and results of the new policies in another area, which also has had major significance for East-West relations and for Soviet relations with China, Japan, and Great Russia's subject nations within the "world of real socialism": the areas of Third World regional crisis.

Gorbachev's New Third World Policies

To understand Gorbachev's changes in Soviet Third World policies, one must first understand the origins, the nature, the length, and the results of the Soviet intellectual preparation for them: the more than a decade of published reassessment of Third World developments and Soviet policy toward them in specialized Soviet journals by Soviet academic experts and high party officials. This intellectual preparatory work took place, ironically, during the 1970s and early 1980s, when Brezhnev's policies in the Third World were in most respects the opposite of those that the Soviet Third World experts were increasingly recommending.

Experts of other countries have suffered the same fate. As Lord Keynes remarked, most politicians act, usually without realizing it, under the influence of long-gone economists. Was this also not the earlier fate of many British experts about India, French experts about Indochina and Algeria, and American experts about the same Indochina? What was new about the developments in Soviet Third World policy was that Gorbachev rapidly and in many areas almost completely adopted the recommendations of the experts so soon after Brezhnev had done just the contrary of what they recommended.

In the 1970s and early 1980s the primary cause for these experts' analyses and recommendations was their increasing, and increasingly public, pessimistic diagnoses of the economic and political development failures in so much of the Third World, the inability of Marxist-Leninist ideology to account for these failures, and, in part for that reason, the failures of Soviet Third World policies. Khrushchev's optimism and radicalism about the Third World had emphasized a permanent revolutionary process against capitalism and imperialism on the one hand, and in favor of political, economic, and social independence, and therefore for alliance with the Soviet Union, on the other. Beginning in 1955, he made substantial gains in the wake of Third World states gaining independence from their European colonial rulers: Nehru's India, Sukarno's Indonesia, Nasser's Egypt, Ben Bella's Algeria, Castro's Cuba, Nkrumah's Ghana, Toure's Guinea, and Keita's Mali. But he and his successors lost their influence in Indonesia, Egypt, Guinea, Ghana, and Mali; relations with Algeria became less close, and relations with Cuba were frequently strained, especially because Castro opposed détente with the United States. In general, much of the Third World became less, not more successful in political and economic development and less attracted to the Soviet model for both.[2]

Soviet Third World experts therefore increasingly concluded during the 1970s that the Third World was not an important revolutionary force, that some Third World countries chose capitalism and others socialism, and that all should be left to choose for themselves; and that the Soviet Union should no longer give so much priority to supporting socialism, especially by military force, but rather use political and diplomatic means to help solve or at least contain them.[3]

This process of change and the changing balance among Soviet Third World experts was long and bureaucratically complex. What were the differing views, and how and why did the new, revised views gradually gain more influence? Generally, one can distinguish, as Professors Galia Golan and Jerry Hough have skillfully done,[4] between two general schools of Soviet Third World thought: the orthodox-conservative and the modern-sophisticated. The former, of which Boris Ponomarev—who until Gorbachev had him retired was the long-time head of the International Department of the Soviet Central Committee—was the most authoritative figure, favored the orthodox Leninist "class" approach: leadership by communist parties and rejection of nationalist, ethnic, or religious approaches. (This approach could be used, however, to downgrade the importance of Third World "national liberation movements," because they were either communist, but small, or non-communist in their revolutionary potential.)

The latter, more sophisticated, and usually politically more junior approach (although Karen Brutents, one of Ponomarev's deputies, often seemed to support this tendency), stressed national and ethnic considerations and the roles of the petty and national bourgeoisie and nationalist intellectuals as being at least as important as the class approach. Organizationally, this meant a united national front with a (non-communist) mass political party. These theorists did not, of course, reject Leninism and the Leninist vanguard party as the sought-after long-term goal, but they maintained that a capitalist period might well intervene and that Soviet policy should be minimalist in the Third World, that is, it should be deterrent vis-à-vis the West, offering the Soviet Union as a counter-example, but generally adopting a low military posture.

Both schools of thought rejected separatism and terrorism (at least in theory, although probably not entirely in practice). In general, the policy makers responsible for ideology tended to be conservative, the International Department was split (Vadim Zagladin being conservative, Karen Brutents and

Rostislav Ulianovskii, often modernist), and the Institute on the U.S.A and Canada and especially the Institute of Oriental Studies and the Institute of World Economic and International Relations (IMEMO) were definitely modernist.

Despite these changed analyses and resultant changes in policy recommendations by Soviet Third World experts, in the early 1970s Brezhnev acted in the opposite fashion, and in the process, it seemed then, made substantial gains in Angola, Ethiopia, Nicaragua, and Indochina. Moreover, he did not prevent, and, as he probably was aware in advance, he may have encouraged the coming to power of a communist regime in Afghanistan. Finally, the overthrow of the pro-American Shah by the late Ayatollah Khomeini in Iran, although devoid of a significant Soviet role, resulted in the collapse of American influence with what had been a major American Third World ally. Initially this appeared to be yet another (potential) gain for Moscow.

However, by late 1988, the last two developments had turned into Soviet defeats. In Iran, Khomeini crushed the local Communists and denounced the Soviet Union; and while in the latter stages of the Iran-Iraq War he cooperated in improving relations with Moscow (which were furthered by Majlis Speaker Hashemi Rafsanjani's June visit to Moscow), his Islamic fundamentalism was considered a very dangerous phenomenon, especially for Moslem Soviet Central Asia. In Afghanistan, the mujahideen rebellion, which precipitated the Soviet military intervention there in December 1979, led President Carter to drastically change American policy of détente to one of confrontation with the Soviet Union and to begin a massive American military buildup, which added to the domestic Soviet problems summarized above and turned the international "correlation of forces" against the Soviet Union and in favor of the United States.

Thus, when Gorbachev became general secretary in March 1985, the analytical and policy groundwork for his approach had been laid by Soviet Third World experts whose forecasts had become increasingly valid. By that time, it had become clear that a Soviet victory in Afghanistan was not soon, if ever, to be in the cards; and in such guerrilla wars the counter-insurgent power loses if it does not win. The guerrilla based civil wars in Cambodia and Angola had not produced victories for Vietnam and Cuba, the Soviets' allies, nor for the Soviet Union itself. The crisis in Nicaragua remained a major cause of tension in Soviet-American relations. The Israeli-Egyptian peace treaty and the U.S.-Israeli "strategic relationship" had postponed any prospect of an Arab victory over Israel. And while the Ethiopian leader Lt. Colonel Mengistu Haile Mariam had defeated Somalia, with Soviet and Cuban help, the rebellions against him in Eritrea and Tigre were continuing.

Because of its domestic economic problems and its foreign overextension and isolation, Gorbachev decided that détente with the United States and the

People's Republic of China was essential for the success of Soviet economic reforms and for overcoming the widening Soviet technological gap with the West and Japan, especially in military technology, which was so dependent on nonmilitary microelectronics and computer technology. Détente also required that Moscow move toward settlement, if only through proxies, of at least some Third World regional crises in which it was involved with Washington and Beijing, and which involvement seriously hindered the Soviet objective of détente.

Two of those who led the campaign to deescalate Soviet Third World policy were Gorbachev's advisers; others that were prominent in the previous academic revisionist proposals to change Soviet Third World policy were promoted and gained influence after Gorbachev became general secretary. Evgenii Primakov, who had been head of the Institute of Oriental Studies, where most of the proposals for revising Soviet Third World policy were framed and published in the late 1970s and early 1980s, became head of IMEMO, the most important Soviet research institute on international politics and economics. More important, at the Reykjavik summit conference he was the head of the Soviet working group on regional crisis areas. In an important *Pravda* article on the foreign policy "new thinking," Primakov wrote that one should prevent regional conflicts from leading to "horizontal expansion between the U.S.S.R. and the U.S.," i.e., that overall Soviet-American relations should be insulated from becoming worse because of these regional conflicts.[5]

Another intellectual supporter of, and adviser to, Gorbachev, the well-known journalist Aleksandr Bovin, wrote at the same time:

> It should be acknowledged that capitalism's ability to adapt to new historical situations exceeded our predictions. The prospects for socialist transformations in developed capitalist counties have been shunted into the indefinite future. The situation in a number of countries of socialist persuasion remains unstable and is susceptible to regression. And in capitalist and Third World countries, communist parties, with certain exceptions, have been unable to transform themselves into mass organizations and secure the support of the bulk of the working class and working people. There are a number of reasons for this and one of them is undoubtedly the failures, contradictions, and phenomena of crisis and stagnation in the development of the Soviet Union, other socialist countries, and world socialism as a whole. Socialism has not yet been able to achieve that force of example of which V.I. Lenin spoke.
>
> That means that all socialist countries face similar tasks—the tasks of markedly increasing the efficiency of the national economy, fully restoring the position of social democracy, and improving the quality of life by improving productive relations. These tasks are being accomplished in the Soviet Union during the course of restructuring. Other socialist countries operate on the basis of their own interests and needs. Everyone's experience is open to everyone else, but what is taken from that experience, what you "transplant" into your own soil, is everywhere decided independently.[6]

Other writers pointed out that agriculture, not heavy industry, should be given priority in the Third World. Moreover, in another indication of rising priority for realpolitik over ideology, Soviet foreign policy began to pay more attention to the capitalist Latin American and Gulf countries and less to radical Third World states.

Regional Crises

I turn now to brief analyses of the various regional crisis areas as of early 1989 and Soviet policy changes concerning them. One important general point: It seems unlikely that Gorbachev intends a general withdrawal from all these areas. There have been as yet no decisive changes in Soviet policies with respect to Ethiopia or Nicaragua. In fact, Soviet Foreign Minister Eduard Shevardnadze recently visited Latin America, in advance of a future planned visit by Gorbachev, and urged regional cooperation, likely an intended means of increasing Soviet influence there. Moscow has also been establishing diplomatic relations with as many Gulf and Middle Eastern states as possible, and is interested in gradually establishing relations with Israel.

In general, Gorbachev is trying to reinsert the Soviet Union into the Middle East, no longer concentrating only on such radical states as Syria, Libya, and South Yemen (PDRY) (although he will not abandon them), but also on the more traditionalist and conservative ones, especially Saudi Arabia and the Gulf emirates. He is particularly interested in establishing full diplomatic relations with Saudi Arabia, *inter alia*, in order to exploit Saudi resentment of American support for Israel. (The Saudis in turn would probably like Soviet help with Iran.) Primarily because of his support of détente and fear of Islamic fundamentalism, however, Gorbachev did not try to match the U.S. naval deployment in the Gulf. But he did try, unsuccessfully, to transform it into a U.N. naval deployment and he armed Iraq, which the United States tilted toward and supplied with intelligence information. Thus both superpowers, sharing a desire to thwart Khomeini's Islamic fundamentalism, contributed to Iran's exhaustion and acceptance, in 1988, of a ceasefire with Iraq. That the United States had initially sent its navy to the Gulf to prevent Kuwait from accepting a Soviet offer to protect Kuwaiti tankers against Iranian attacks demonstrated the evolution of superpower confrontation toward tacit superpower parallelism, a new Middle Eastern phenomenon that led Iran to exhaust itself before Iraq.

Another major example of Gorbachev's and the U.S.S.R.'s partially successful attempt to reinsert the Soviet Union in Middle Eastern affairs was the effort to help convene and participate as co-chairman with the United States in an international Arab-Israeli conference modelled on the abortive 1975 Geneva conference. That Washington agreed to Soviet participation was a significant result of Soviet-American détente and in theory at least a partial abandonment of Henry Kissinger's determination, and the determination of his successors, to get the Soviet Union out of the Middle East and keep it out. But the American shift was more apparent than real, being largely a response to King Hussein's insistence on and Shimon Peres' support for the project. The victory of Yitzhak Shamir in the November 1988 Israeli parliamentary elections, plus the tensions within the PLO and between the Israelis and the Palestinians over the *intifada*, made the success of such a conference and of the Arab-Israeli peace process in general even less likely, but did not exclude the possibility that such a conference might eventually be convened. And the sudden U.S. agreement of December 1988 to talk with the PLO showed that the American position was still evolving.

Following the lead of some Soviet analysts of the previous era and early part of his rule, Gorbachev has also supported less than his predecessors the nonaligned movement countries and the Group of 77, primarily, it seems, because they shifted from support of Soviet foreign policy to a neutral position between the two superpowers. Whenever they can, they now seek access to better quality Western technology, not inferior Soviet equivalents, a change that has hastened the decline of Soviet support for these countries.

The conclusion of the Soviet military withdrawal from Afghanistan in February 1989 was a result of the following: 1) the Soviet failure to achieve a military victory in the face of the historic resistance of the Afghan tribes to foreign conquest; 2) the military support given the mujahideen by the United States, the People's Republic of China, Egypt, and Saudi Arabia, and Pakistan's role in getting this support to them; separate Iranian support of the Shia (Hazari) mujahideen, and later the deliveries of American-made Stinger missiles used to shoot down Soviet attack helicopters, which had caused high mujahideen casualties; 3) the rising discontent of the Soviet population with the war; and, 4) last but not least, especially of late, the war's hindrance to Soviet-American and to Soviet-Chinese détente and its damage to Moscow in the Islamic world, particularly in the Gulf.

In early 1989, after the Soviet withdrawal, the fall of Najibullah's communist government in Kabul seemed increasingly likely, and although law and order were not likely even then to break out in that devastated country, whatever civil disturbances did continue would probably be without the Afghan or Soviet Communists' active involvement.

In two other regional crisis areas, Cambodia and Angola, guerrilla wars have long been raging, and three secondary powers, Vietnam, Cuba, and South Africa, further complicate the prospects of peace—just the contrary of Afghanistan, where Soviet opponents of varying ideologies cooperated to help the mujahideen. (Settlements might already have been reached in Cambodia and Angola if the only parties needing to agree were Moscow and Washington.) In Cambodia the incentive for the Soviet Union to urge Vietnam to withdraw early had more to do with détente with China than with the United States, and increased Soviet pressure on Vietnam for this purpose played a major role in the rapid improvement of Sino-Soviet relations, which by early 1989 had led to a Vietnamese commitment to remove its troops from Cambodia by September 1989 and, even before that, to the Sino-Soviet summit meeting between Gorbachev and Deng Xiaoping in May 1989 in Beijing. However, the Khmer Rouge and Prince Sihanouk had not come to terms, and there was rising debate in the West about whether the danger of another Khmer Rouge massacre was worse than a compromise with the pro-Vietnamese regime in Phnom Penh; the prospects for internal peace in Cambodia therefore remained clouded at best.

In Angola, the situation had also evolved by early 1989 to the point where through American mediation and directly involved external powers, the Soviet Union, Cuba, and South Africa had agreed to withdraw from their involvement in the conflict (and South Africa from Namibia as well), and the MPLA government in Luanda and Savimbi's UNITA rebels accepted these governments' mediation between them.

Fidel Castro's role in Angola deserves additional attention. He was, as in the 1970s, unenthusiastic about détente with the United States (this time springing from Gorbachev's "new thinking"), but unable to prevent it, and his economy and security were vulnerable to Soviet pressure. Even so, he not only made clear his opposition to détente but persuaded Moscow to aid him in putting more Cuban troops and better fighter planes in Angola. This resulted in the failure of South Africa and Savimbi, in mid-1988, to capture a key communications point in southern Angola, Cuito Cuanavale. White South African casualties in the attempt to take the site were large enough that Pretoria became more inclined toward peace, even if it included leaving Namibia. (Thereafter, however, Namibia would be so economically dependent on South Africa and so vulnerable, like South Africa's other black neighbors, to covert South African military pressure that with Soviet and Cuban forces gone from Angola, it would not be able to defy Pretoria.) Finally, some reports indicated that Moscow was urging caution on the African National Congress (ANC).

In Nicaragua the Soviets probably would prefer a more moderate Sandinista policy. Castro, left to his own devices, probably would not. In any case, the refusal of the U.S. Congress to continue military aid to the Contras (in part as a result of the "Iran-Contra" affair) and the worsening situation for the government in El Salvador preempted any effective American pressure on Moscow to withdraw on the grounds of furthering Soviet-U.S. détente. In early 1989, it remained to be seen whether President George Bush's administration would be able and willing to exert such pressure successfully, or if it would accept the status quo.

Despite some recent reports of Soviet discontent about developments in Ethiopia, Gorbachev has shown little indication that he will abandon Mengistu, who was ushered into power by Brezhnev and Castro during a period of American inaction following the deposition of Emperor Haile Selassie. When Siad Barre, the "Marxist-Leninist" Somali leader previously allied with Moscow, invaded the southern Ethiopian province of the Ogaden in 1978 (in partial fulfillment of the obsessive Somali territorial irredentism), the Soviets sent not only weapons but a command staff, and Castro sent troops, to push the Somalis back to their borders. However, Mengistu continued to be confronted with many ethnically-based rebellions, notably in Eritrea and Tigre, and some of them scored successes in the late 1980s. The Soviets were able to use the Ethiopian Red Sea ports of Massawa (in Eritrea) and Assab, although the main railhead, Djibouti, remained under French protection even after it became independent in 1977. The Americans, who switched from supporting Ethiopia to supporting and restraining Somalia, got the previous Soviet air and naval base at Berbera, near the entrance to the Red Sea. In June 1988, after a northern Somali rebellion of the Somali National Movement (SNM) broke out against Mogadishu and was supported by Mengistu, Siad Barre felt compelled to make peace with Mengistu, but his hope that this would stop the rebellion was short-lived, for in fact it only escalated.

Conclusion

In late 1988 there were no clear signs that an overall Soviet withdrawal from the Third World was underway. Instead, Gorbachev appeared to be applying a much more realistic cost-benefit analysis than had his predecessors, following the recommendations of the more sophisticated Soviet Third World experts. This was particularly true in Afghanistan and Cambodia where the costs of Soviet adventurism to Soviet-American and Sino-Soviet détente respectively overshadowed the uncertain prospects of victory, and in Cambodia and Angola where his less pro-détente allies, Vietnam and Cuba, were hurting, rather than helping, the Soviet détente efforts. However, in Ethiopia, South Yemen, and Nicaragua, where he has been under no effective U.S. or Chinese pressure, Gorbachev seems for the moment to be keeping his cards in the game. Moreover, the gains that he made in the Middle East—in terms of Arab support and, by 1988, even U.S. support for an international conference on the Middle East with Soviet participation, and his diplomatic initiatives toward the Gulf Cooperation Council (GCC) states, and less directly toward Israel itself—clearly showed that he was trying, with considerable success, to increase Soviet influence in this region without harming Soviet-U.S détente.

Can Gorbachev's Third World policy statements be believed, or are they, as some Western conservatives say, only disinformation? Past Western experience with frequent, yawning gaps between Soviet rhetoric and actions calls for prudence. The Soviet military forces withdrew from Afghanistan, and Gorbachev is supporting compromise settlements in Angola and Cambodia. So far he has no compelling reason to withdraw from Nicaragua and Ethiopia because of Washington's blunders and executive-legislative standoff on Nicaragua and its inaction in Ethiopia, although Castro also opposes his doing so. Nevertheless, the totality of Gorbachev's foreign policy initiatives complement his Third World policy and his domestic reforms.

Even so, we do not know how Gorbachev would react if some great new Third World opportunity beckoned. He took a moderate line in the recent Gulf crisis, and he seems to want to advance Soviet influence in Europe, the Middle East, and the Far East by political and economic, not military means. By early 1989, therefore, it did not look as if Third World crises, old or new, would be likely soon to derail détente as the Soviet invasion of Afghanistan did in 1979. But caution is called for. American policymakers might turn inward, as they did after the Vietnam debacle, thus lowering Moscow's estimate of the risk of renewed Soviet adventurism. Even so, Gorbachev can hardly expect that Soviet or even East German technology will become as attractive to Third World countries as is Western technology, and the same can be said of Soviet military technology, wherein Western advances are likely to continue to outstrip the Soviet. Therefore, like all great Soviet modernizers, from Peter the Great to Khrushchev, Gorbachev is unlikely either totally to fail or totally to succeed.

Even if mass dissidence within the Soviet Union and Eastern Europe were to force Gorbachev either to harden his policies there or cause him to be replaced, it seems likely that he or his successor would concentrate on domestic and East-West affairs rather than on the Third World, much of whose intractability, as first Washington and then Moscow have learned, is as great as, although less visibly appalling than, its tragedies.

Notes

1. The above is primarily based on Chapter 1 ("Central and Eastern Europe: The Global Context") in William E. Griffith, ed., *Central and Eastern Europe and the West* (Boulder, CO: Westview, 1989). For the role of the intelligentsia today, see Jack Snyder, "The Gorbachev Revolution: A Waning of Soviet Expansionism?,"

International Security, Vol. 12, No. 3 (Winter 1987-88), pp. 93-131, at p. 112. For Gorbachev's personal role, see Stephen M. Meyer, "The Sources and Prospects of Gorbachev's New Political Thinking on Security," *ibid.*, Vol. 13, No. 2 (Fall 1988), pp. 124-163, at p. 127.
2. Bruce Porter, *The U.S.S.R. in Third World Conflicts* (Cambridge: Cambridge University Press, 1984); Elizabeth Kridl Valkenier, *The Soviet Union and the Third World: An Economic Bind* (New York: Praeger, 1983); Mark Katz, *The Third World in Soviet Military Doctrine* (Baltimore: Johns Hopkins University Press, 1982).
3. Elizabeth Kridl Valkenier, "New Soviet Thinking About the Third World," *World Policy Journal*, Vol. 4, No. 4 (Fall 1987); Elizabeth Kridl Valkenier, "Revolutionary Change in the Third World: Recent Soviet Assessments," *World Politics*, Vol. 28, No. 3, April 1986; George W. Breslauer, "Ideology and Learning in Soviet Third World Policy," *ibid.*, Vol. 39, No. 3, April 1987; Jack Snyder, *op. cit.*; and Neil MacFarlane, "The U.S.S.R. and the Third World: Continuity and Change Under Gorbachev," *The Harriman Institute Forum*, Vol. 1, No. 3 (March 1988).
4. For analysis of expert views in the Brezhnev period, see Galia Golan, *The Soviet Union and National Liberation Movements in the Third World* (Winchester, MA: Allen & Unwin, Inc., 1988); Jerry F. Hough, *The Struggle for the Third World: Soviet Debates and American Options* (Washington, D.C.: Brookings Institute, 1986); Marie Lavigne, *Les Relations Est-Sud dans L'Economie Mondiale* (Paris: Economica, 1986).
5. *Pravda*, July 10, 1987.
6. *Izvestiia*, July 11, 1987.

4

From Lenin to Marx in Soviet Third World Policy

Jerry F. Hough

Soviet Third World policy has always been multifaceted.[1] Soviet policy towards the Third World countries on the Soviet border—Turkey, Iran, Afghanistan, India, and China—has always been different from Soviet policy towards more distant areas such as South America. In recent decades, Soviet policy toward India and Afghanistan, but also Vietnam, has belied a somewhat "quadrangular" perception of politics that is bringing in more and more China and Pakistan. And Soviet policy on the Arab-Israeli question has been treated as an intimate component of Soviet-American relations, while certain Soviet actions in Africa and Latin America have been taken with seemingly scant regard for their impact on the United States.

Similarly, Soviet client states are also very diverse in terms of what they offer or take from the Soviet Union. Some, like Angola and Libya, are quite profitable to deal with from an economic point of view, for they have hard currency with which to purchase Soviet arms; others, such as South Yemen and Ethiopia, provide useful naval bases. Some others offer little in the way of profit, and rather drain the Soviet resources. Vietnam, Kampuchea, Nicaragua, and especially Afghanistan are proof of this. But Nicaragua is important in the context of Soviet-American relations, while Vietnam and Kampuchea are important for the Soviet relationship with China; and South Yemen (particularly in its revolutionary phase), for the relationship with Saudi Arabia and the Gulf states.

The variations in policy outlook and emphasis do not mean that there has been lacking a general set of assumptions that have guided Soviet policy, only that various factors have intervened to produce many exceptions to the general policy line; but we can never understand the framework in which decisions are taken until we recognize that there has indeed been a framework and until we learn its nature.

It is peculiarly important to understand the general thrust or framework of Soviet Third World policy when we think of specific Soviet policies towards client states today. First, radical revolutions are occurring only in preindustrial states whose significance pales in comparison to countries such as Brazil, Egypt, Indonesia, and even Singapore. That the Soviet Union has come to understand this means that Soviet policy towards less important client states will become more derivative of policy towards the major Third World countries.

Second, the Soviet recognition that radical revolutions have been occurring only in poor countries has produced a major change in ideology. Basically the Soviet leaders have come to reject Lenin's view of the Third World and to believe that Marx's analysis was closer to the truth. The ideological shift has had a particularly dramatic impact, because the repudiation of Lenin has also impacted profoundly on Soviet thinking about the Soviet economic system and its relationship to the world economy.

When Lenin wrote about the non-Western world in *Imperialism: The Highest Stage of Capitalism*, he asserted that the colonial areas of the world were not developing toward capitalism on the same historical path as had the West. Instead, he saw the colonial world as exploited—as forced to provide raw materials at artificially low prices and to import manufactured goods at inflated prices rather than produce them.

Lenin's original argument focused on colonies and their presumed importance for the Western countries, but it was soon extended to Third World states that were politically independent—for example, the countries of Latin America. If economically underdeveloped countries were included in the world economy, Soviet ideology contended, they would become dependent on foreign capitalists who would invest only in raw materials industries. As commodity-producing countries, they would be little different from colonies: They would bear the brunt of the inevitable business cycles of the capitalist world, and the capitalist investors would drain away more in profits than they invested in capital. This argument was implicitly also applied to Russia, for Lenin quickly repudiated the foreign debt and nationalized foreign property, thereby effectively cutting the Soviet Union off from meaningful participation in the world market. Stalin then erected an Iron Curtain against world market forces that was more impenetrable than the Iron Curtain against Western ideas.

Within this ideological framework, the only way for a Third World country to achieve rapid growth in the manufacturing sector of the economy supposedly was to follow the Soviet model that was established after 1929: to nationalize foreign property, to industrialize on the basis of internal resources, and to institute a planning system that protected the country from the capitalist business cycle.

Soviet political analysis of the Third World followed logically from this economic analysis. Clearly nationalism was a major force in the Third World, for it had toppled colonial rule. Thus, if people came to believe that capitalist development means a deferred, dependent industrial development, the forces of nationalism would surely coalesce behind the Soviet model of socialism.

This analysis was imbedded in the Soviet definition of the national liberation revolution and the national liberation movement. The Soviet Union insisted that this revolution had two stages. The first stage involved an alliance of all classes, usually under the leadership of the bourgeoisie, to liberate the country from direct colonial rule; the second stage involved an alliance of the workers and peasants (and some nationalistic intelligentsia), to liberate the country from capitalism. Once a country became politically independent, the "national liberation movement" became a synonym for the movement toward communist revolution.

Soviet leaders varied in the policy conclusions that they drew from this analysis. Stalin believed that only the Communist Party was capable of leading the second stage of the national liberation movement, and he was inclined (except when some concrete Soviet foreign policy goal such as the Japanese threat in the 1930s was an overriding consideration) to break with noncommunist forces (the "bourgeoisie") as soon as political independence was achieved. In Stalin's view, when faced with the choice between the maintenance of capitalist property and the achievement of national independence, the bourgeoisie would quickly abandon the banner of nationalism. He expressed this point very directly in his speech to the 19th Party Congress.

Khrushchev retained Stalin's basic analysis that sound Third World economic growth under capitalism was impossible, and therefore that the Third World was inherently revolutionary. However, Khrushchev thought nationalism to be even more powerful than did Stalin. He concluded that if national goals demanded communism, then many "bourgeois" elements (especially younger army officers, students, and intellectuals) would be pushed toward communism by nationalism.

Castro's experience in Cuba came to symbolize the driving forces of history in the Third World: When Castro tried to control and regulate American-owned industry, it was said, this produced such a strong American reaction that a nationalist like Castro had either to surrender or to move progressively to the left. The left-wing military revolts in countries such as Egypt and Burma, and the radicalization of their policies in the 1960s (as well as those of Sukarno in Indonesia) were seen as confirmations of this general trend.

If historical forces were on the side of revolutionary movements in the Third World, then it was sound policy for the Soviet Union to support them. But the further implication was that the Soviet Union did not have to limit itself to supporting communist parties. There were indeed many paths to socialism, and radical army officers or nationalist civilian leaders might be able to garner more public support for socialist policies than the old-line communist parties. This kind of thinking would explain Khrushchev's provision of major economic aid to countries such as India and Egypt. When Leonid Brezhnev came to power, little had occurred to undercut the Khrushchevian optimism, although events in the Arab world—especially in Iraq and Syria—had to remind any sophisticated Soviet observer that nationalism could have other consequences than economic radicalization.

The course of Soviet foreign policy behavior in the mid-1960s could possibly have been different, however, and it is likely that we need a serious rewriting of the domestic political context of Soviet foreign policy during that period. Aleksei Kosygin and Leonid Brezhnev seem to have had different positions on economic reform, Kosygin apparently being willing to consider some private enterprise in the services, and in practice Kosygin handled relations with the capitalist world in the first years while Brezhnev concentrated on relations with communist states. Soviet moderation in the Cyprus dispute and Kosygin's subsequent role in mediating the India-Pakistan dispute in Tashkent in late 1965 and early 1966 suggested the possibility of a policy that gave low priority to revolution and radical regimes. One can conclude that, if Kosygin had really been in control, the general course of Soviet Third World policy might have been different. Such a line of analysis is, however, speculative at this stage. In any case, it is absolutely certain that Kosygin did not win, for Brezhnev's responsibilities for the communist world included Vietnam, and one of his first actions was to increase Soviet aid to North Vietnam in its effort to promote revolution in the south.

In his official ideology Brezhnev did not abandon the basic Leninist interpretation of the Third World. The national revolution, it was still contended, had a socialist stage. The explanation for this definition of the national liberation revolution remained the same: Capitalist economic development in the Third World was inevitably deformed and could not satisfy the goals of national independence.

In one respect Brezhnev made the ideology even more Leninist. There was a series of disappointments on the revolutionary front in the mid-1960s—most spectacularly in Indonesia and Ghana, but also, more subtly in Egypt, where Nasser moderated his revolutionary policy. Brezhnev's solution was to accept the Leninist organizational model as well as the Leninist interpretation of Third World economic development. Thereby he suggested that a vanguard party, composed of those dedicated to socialism, was necessary to push the national liberation movement to the left after the first stage of revolution. It was the lack of such parties, it was said, that had led countries to fall off the path to socialism. Throughout the Brezhnev period, countries that had a socialist or socialist-like revolution normally had such parties, or else created them after the revolution. Where there was resistance to create a vanguard party (as in Ethopia), the Soviet Union applied great pressure to do so.

Nevertheless, all was not well in the Brezhnev analysis of the Third World or in Brezhnev's policy towards the Third World. First, many of the most radical forces in the world tended to be "new left" in one way or another. They often were more attracted to Mao Zedong and his cultural revolution in China than to Brezhnev's bureaucratic system of rule in the Soviet Union. In countries such as Nicaragua and Iran, the Sandinistas and fedajeen, respectively, basically opposed the more cauticus Nicaraguan Communist Party and the Iranian Tudeh Party as they conducted their revolutions.

Second, the revolutionary cause in the Third World did not go well in the Brezhnev era. Egypt turned completely to the right after Nasser's death, and the Chilean revolution was brought to an abrupt end by the Pinochet coup. Most important, however, the industrializing Third World countries—those that Soviet jargon said had actually started on the capitalist path—were not becoming more revolutionary, but less so. Even the shocks produced by the oil crisis of the 1970s did not produce more radical politics. In the Brezhnev era the only countries with radical revolutions were essentially preindustrial nations that by definition were not major economic-political powers, and the number of such nations is declining sharply, except perhaps in the sub-Saharan Africa.

What was most worrying of all to the Soviet Union was that the Leninist analysis of Third World economic development, which had been the basis for the prediction of the relationship between nationalism and socialism, seemed to be contradicted by the facts. The industrializing Third World countries did not remain raw materials producers but developed manufacturing centers when they integrated themselves into the world economy. The countries that grew the fastest were those that were most integrated into the world economy, especially those in the Pacific rim area. To some extent, this growth was produced by deliberate export strategies, often of items produced on licenses from Western firms. In addition, multinational corporations began changing their character. Instead of simply importing raw materials from the Third World, they increasingly wanted to utilize cheap labor to produce manufactured goods or their components. This led to the building of manufacturing capability and the development of a more sophisticated work force and managerial capability than in the past. The countries that followed a more autarchic path did not, on the whole, enjoy the same degree of industrial growth.

Third, substantially as a result of these various developments in the Third World, the center of gravity shifted drastically in the debates among Soviet specialists on the Third World. Even in the last years of the Khrushchev period, the leadership of the Institute of Oriental Studies was extremely skeptical about the revolutionary potential of the nationalist bourgeoisie. Nodari

Simoniia, the dominant intellectual force in the institute for twenty years and a specialist on the overseas Chinese in Southeast Asia, warned from the beginning that ethnic and, to a lesser extent, class divisions within the new countries made it very unlikely that countrywide nationalism would lead to socialism. Simoniia saw communism in Southeast Asia intimately related to the conflict between the overseas Chinese and the indigenous populations.

For Simoniia and the increasing number of scholars who agreed with his analysis, Third World economic and political development was following a European line of development, or at least it was not qualitatively different in the Leninist sense of being doomed to semicolonial development. Indeed, especially after the overthrow of the Shah of Iran, Simoniia argued forcefully that former colonies in Asia often developed more successfully than noncolonies precisely because the colonial powers had destroyed the political power of the preindustrial elite.

Although Simoniia himself would not phrase it in this provocative way, he was really saying that Lenin was mistaken and that Marx was right. Marx had said that the most powerful class forces produced in early industrialization wanted capitalism, that capitalism would succeed feudalism, and that it would be economically progressive for a period of time (and a period that has already lasted for a very long time in Europe). If these "laws of history" were really decisive, then they should work in the Third World as well as in Europe, and Simoniia insisted that they would.

Faced with these various considerations, Brezhnev followed a mixed policy. As already noted, he vigorously supported North Vietnam in its war policy in South Vietnam. Yet, behind all the talk about supporting national liberation movements (including their socialist phase), Brezhnev often had a choice about the nature of the national liberation movement to support, and he did, in fact, choose not to support a number of movements.

First, of course, the word "nation" is very ambiguous in the Third World. The "nation" that is represented in the United Nations is often a rather artificial unit, and the major ethnic "nations" live in territories with quite different boundaries. Except for some relatively minor covert activity, the Soviet Union generally made no attempt to gain clients by supporting the representatives of ethnic nations that were trying to break up existing countries. It did go along with the establishment of Bangladesh out of Pakistan, but it did not support the Ibos' effort to establish an independent Biafra in Nigeria.

Second, as already indicated, the most revolutionary forces in the world tended to be sympathetic in varying degrees toward China. In addition, these forces almost always were virulently anti-American. If Brezhnev was giving his top priority either to the struggle against the United States or to the promotion of world revolution, he would have supported the most revolutionary forces, despite their attitude to China.

In fact, Brezhnev treated the conflict with China as the far higher priority than either the struggle against the United States or the promotion of revolution. He turned decisively against forces that, however anti-American and revolutionary, flirted with China. Indeed, in many of the areas where Brezhnev intervened most decisively, the competition with China was at least one of the major factors. This was obviously the case in Vietnam, while in Africa, China was a major competitor at the time that the Soviet Union became actively involved. The fear of losing Afghanistan from its long-time Soviet-Indian sphere of influence to the Pakistani-Chinese was likely the decisive consideration in the Soviet decision to intervene in Afghanistan.

If one excludes the cases in which the competition with China was a decisive factor, Brezhnev was not nearly as active in the Third World as we were inclined to think at the time. We focused on countries such as Angola, Ethiopia, and Nicaragua, without giving sufficient attention to the vastly larger number of countries in which the Soviet role was quite small or, as in the case of India, nonrevolutionary. The small radical states that became Soviet clients normally seemed tied to the Soviet Union through military aid or sales. A number of Soviet scholars publicly expressed the worry that these states were merely professing revolutionary intentions in order to milk the Soviet Union for aid.

While Brezhnev was, in practice, quite cautious in promoting revolution, except in a small number of countries willing to be clients, he never seriously modified his ideological analysis. Perhaps he never assimilated the changing situation in the world and retained the simple faiths of his youth. But if he were tempted to adopt a more sophisticated evaluation of the course of events in the Third World, a powerful domestic political consideration always restrained him.

As we think of Soviet analysis of economic development in the Third World, we should never forget—for the Soviets never forget—that the analysis also applies to the Soviet Union. If integration of the Third World into the world economy leads to deformed and dependent growth, then Soviet integration into the world economy surely is not attractive, let alone necessary. But if the Soviet model of economic autarchy—no foreign investment, no free access of foreigners to the Soviet market, no pressure on manufacturers to export, no cooperation with multinational corporations on joint production—is not effective in prompting economic growth in the Third World, then the old Soviet economic model must also be of dubious utility for the Soviet Union itself. Thus, when a leading Soviet scholar made the following statement about the Third World, it surely must have been meant to apply to the Soviet Union as well:

> A course toward a closed economy or, in other words, toward economic autarchy is, as history shows, a course without a future. It is a path leading to

a dead end. . . . The higher the level of participation in the system of the international division of labor, the higher the tempos of economic growth. Extreme protectionism, carried out over an unjustifiably long time, is fraught with negative consequences (the preservation and extension of backward, non-competitive, inefficient production with high costs of production, low productivity of labor, and low quality production).[2]

It is not certain what Leonid Brezhnev was thinking about the Third World in the last years of his life, but one thing is absolutely certain: He did not want the profound economic reform inside the Soviet Union that the just-quoted statement implied. He had no intention of making a change in ideology with respect to the Third World that would legitimize economic reform at home. Moreover, he must have known that younger generations had a sense that the late Brezhnev period was featuring stagnation—*zastoi* as it is now characterized in the Soviet Union. He must have hoped that an identification with the revolutions in Afghanistan, Angola, Ethiopia, and Nicaragua would give people at home the illusion that he was more revolutionary and dynamic than he actually was.

With the death of Leonid Brezhnev and the election of Iurii Andropov, the language of the Soviet leadership towards the Third World began to change in quiet ways that were unmistakable to an insider. However, like so much in the Andropov and the Chernenko interims, the illness of the two leaders makes it very difficult to know how great a change of policy was contemplated.

With the election of Mikhail Gorbachev, a very profound change in ideology was gradually introduced. At the Geneva Summit, for example, Gorbachev sharply criticized Ronald Reagan for thinking of the Third World in East-West terms. It was a subtle way of criticizing the old Soviet class analysis, for "socialism-versus-capitalism" in the Third World was another way of saying "East-West." Then the new party program adopted at the 27th Party Congress in 1986 sharply reduced the attention given to the national liberation movement, and it removed any suggestion that socialism was a necessary stage of the national-liberation revolution.

Time after time Gorbachev emphasized the primacy of national interest and world civilization over class in international relations. He quoted Lord Palmerston's statement that England has no eternal friends or eternal enemies, only eternal interests. When he travelled to India in late 1986, he specifically said that the model for Soviet Third World policy in the future would be the policy that had been followed toward India—that is, one based on national interest considerations. This line of analysis has continued until the present day. The theses for the June 1988 Party Conference did not even mention the words "class" or "national-liberation" in the foreign policy section, and Gorbachev himself only used the word "class" once in a speech that pointed totally in the other direction. Egor Ligachev criticized this ideological tendency, but Soviet insiders said that Ligachev was not criticizing policy, but only the tendency to talk about it publicly.

The most interesting mention of the Third World by Gorbachev came indirectly in his speech on the 70th anniversary of the Bolshevik Revolution in November 1987. In this speech the General Secretary rehabilitated Nikolai Bukharin for the first time, but he continued to denounce Leon Trotsky harshly. Interestingly, however, he criticized Trotsky specifically for policies that were supported by the contemporary conservative opposition. In foreign policy, Gorbachev defined Trotskyism as support for world revolution. Indeed, he did it twice, and defined support for world revolution as "defeatism."

"Defeatism" was a very important word, which showed that Gorbachev really had accepted a Marxist view of Third World development. If capitalism was going to follow feudalism in the Third World as well as in Europe, the capitalist period in the Third World would last for some time—certainly for the period of Gorbachev's life. If this is true, then it is indeed defeatist to support radical movements in the Third World, just as it would be defeatist to base policy toward the United States, Great Britain, and West Germany on the American, British, and German communist parties respectively. It would be defeatist in the sense of choosing a losing policy. Gorbachev was saying that Brezhnev was a loser when he concentrated on Angola, Ethiopia, Nicaragua and so forth, instead of concentrating on the important Third World countries. He was also saying that policy towards Indonesia, Mexico, Egypt, Iran, Argentina, Saudi Arabia, Kuwait, and Singapore should not be revolutionary, but should be guided by the same considerations that guide Soviet policy towards the United States, West Germany, and Great Britain.

In July 1987, Eduard Shevardnadze summarized the thrust of Soviet policy very bluntly to a group of Soviet diplomats:

> The time has come . . . to "economicize" our foreign policy, if such an expression is permissible, since, until it is linked wholly with the economy, it will be unable to help in restructuring our domestic economy and society. . . . We should become a more organic part of the world economic system, and we can and are obliged to become so if we accept and assimilate the forms extant in it.[3]

One understands the full import of this statement if one understands that Gorbachev is also repudiating Lenin and returning to Marx in his domestic economic policy. Karl Marx had talked about a world in which private forms of property were replaced by socially-owned property, in which the state withered away but in which planning was carried out, and in which national boundaries became unimportant. It was a world very much like the West of the 1980s, with big socially-owned cooperatives such as General Motors and IBM, which functioned independently of national boundaries, with governmental planning by instruments such as the Federal Reserve Board, and with a minimum of state ownership.

By contrast, the Lenin-Stalin system featured state socialism, with monopolistic ministries directing the means of production in the most detailed manner. When Lenin refused in 1922 to extend the New Economic Policy (NEP) to the foreign economic sphere by ending the repudiation of the foreign debt and the nationalization of foreign property without compensation, and when he insisted (with a bitter criticism of Bukharin) that there be a monopoly of foreign trade that was stricter than a system of high tariffs, he ensured that there would be an autarchy that meant an iron curtain against the world economy, not a disappearance of national economic boundaries.

In the Soviet Union, Marx has always been a powerful symbol of an opening to the West, partly because of what he said and partly because he was a German Jew and the largest Western influence on Russia. Gorbachev's economic reform is not a return to the NEP, but a movement towards a cooperative form of socialism that is much more similar to the contemporary West than was the Soviet system under Brezhnev. In the foreign economic sphere, it will include a vigorous policy of promoting exports, joint production, and foreign investment inside the Soviet Union. In this policy, the Third World plays a very important role both as a market and as a source of supply of components and of joint production.

Within this framework the client states play a very minor role. Nicaragua, with three million people, is insignificant in comparison with a country such as Mexico with eighty million. Even Vietnam, which does have importance because of the competition with China, does not matter as much as countries such as South Korea, Taiwan, and Singapore do, at least collectively.

So long as the Soviet Union has a limited number of small countries that it is subsidizing, especially with old military equipment, it can afford to do so. We have exaggerated the financial cost of the client states. Even a Cuba is no more expensive to the Soviet Union than an Israel or Egypt is to the United States. Especially with the United States putting great pressure on countries such as Nicaragua, the cost of continued Soviet support is less than the loss of face involved in a retreat. Afghanistan was more costly, but it has always been a special case because of the competition with China and the proximity to the Soviet border.

Except in Afghanistan, the most important consideration for the Soviet Union in its policy towards the client states will be the impact of that policy on Soviet relations with the major Third World countries in the area. In Nicaragua, the seeming efforts to ensure that Nicaragua does not spread revolution, especially to the Indians of Guatemala and Mexico, and the support of the Contadora process—which really means the replacement of the United States by Mexico as the great power in Central America—is the way to woo Mexico. In Southeast Asia, the resolution of the Kampuchean issue would be important in reducing the dependence of the ASEAN countries on the United States and would make them more willing to engage in joint production and trade with the Soviet Union.

When the West feared that it was losing the Third World in the 1970s, the leading Soviet scholars all understood that it was the Soviet Union that was losing. Now even the Soviet leadership understands that. It would be a major mistake to think that the Soviet Union is now retreating from the Third World to concentrate on economic development. Instead, the Soviet Union is trying to reverse the retreat from the Third World of the Brezhnev era and to abandon the defeatist policy of supporting radical regimes. The Soviet Union is determined to activate its policy towards the important countries like South Korea, Taiwan, Singapore, and Indonesia, but to do so within the order that the United States is seeking to maintain. As Gorbachev is struggling to break out of the isolation that Lenin led the country into, we have a very different challenge to respond to.

Notes

1. For an analysis with footnotes of the evolving Soviet discussion of the Third World, see Jerry F. Hough, *The Struggle for the Third World: Soviet Debates and American Options* (Washington, D.C.: Brookings Institution, 1986).
2. A.I. Dinkevich, *Razvivaiushchiesia strany: nakoplenie i ekonomicheskii rost* (Moscow: Nauka, 1977), pp. 8, 12.
3. *Vestnik ministerstva inostrannykh del SSSR,* No. 3 (September 10, 1987).

Part Two
Moscow's Junior Allies and Regional Conflicts

5

U.S.S.R.-Vietnam Alliance and Regional Conflicts

Douglas Pike

This essay examines the continuities and the changes in Vietnamese-Soviet relations since the advent of Mikhail Gorbachev's "new thinking" about Soviet domestic and foreign policies.[1] It is divided into three parts, following this introduction. First, to provide context, comes a brief overview of the major historical and geopolitical developments in Indochina and Southeast Asia during the past decade or so. Second, there is an examination of the singular nature of the Vietnamese-Soviet relationship and an effort to describe Moscow's policies and thinking about Vietnam and, conversely, Hanoi's policies and thinking with respect to the U.S.S.R. Third comes an examination of the two major issues confronting the Hanoi-Moscow alliance: the fluidity of the triangular association that involves China, and the war in Kampuchea.

Overview

Southeast Asia during the decade that followed the end of the Vietnam War witnessed four highly influential developments which, to provide context, must be noted at the outset. The first of these were the developments triggered by the Vietnam War's end and by the manner in which it ended—which created a new strategic condition both in the region and among the major external powers. Initially in Southeast Asia a geopolitical vacuum developed, followed by a balance of power struggle that polarized the region—the ASEAN nations at one pole facing Indochina at the other. Among the three major external powers—the United States, the U.S.S.R., and China—a new relationship developed. American military exodus from the mainland of Southeast Asia, more important in psychological than in military terms, created an irresistible attraction for the U.S.S.R., luring it into the Indochina peninsula possibly further than was in its national interest. That, in turn, alarmed the Chinese and engendered a change in U.S.-PRC relations, part of a more basic response by Beijing to attempt to create an anti-U.S.S.R. united front across Asia.

The second major post-Vietnam War development in Southeast Asia was the breakup of the Asian communist brotherhood. Although these relationships were never as close or durable as most outsiders believed at the time — particularly the one between the Khmer Rouge in Cambodia and the Vietnamese Communists — no one expected their differences to devolve into bitter internecine warfare. The rupture of the Chinese-Vietnamese alliance was a product of several factors: Hanoi's growing intimacy with the U.S.S.R.; Hanoi's intrusiveness in Kampuchea, which was, the Chinese charged, designed to form a Hanoi-run Federation of Indochina; and Hanoi's mistreatment of ethnic Chinese in Vietnam. The breakup of the Hanoi-Khmer Rouge alliance essentially was the surfacing of ancient antipathies, coupled with Pol Pot's efforts to indoctrinate the next generation of Khmer with militantly hostile attitudes toward the Vietnamese, thus "reversing history" and moving Indochina away from a "special relationship." The result was Vietnam's December 1978 invasion of Kampuchea, followed by China's February 1979 punitive strike against Vietnam, which then subsided into a cold war between the two countries. At the same time, there was a resurgence of indigenous nationalism, by the Khmer with respect to the Vietnamese and by the Vietnamese with respect to the Chinese.

The third development was the utter failure of economic development in Indochina. Flushed with victory in 1975, Hanoi's prospect was for a prosperous, successful future — possibly one that threatened Southeast Asia. But soon Vietnam was beset by economic stagnation, social malaise, administrative failure, the flight of its technological class as boat people, and for a time, a two-front war. In Kampuchea, holocaust descended first with Pol Pot, then with resistance war. These developments appeared all the more stark when set against the resilience and plain good luck of the rest of Southeast Asia. It was an ironic and in some ways inexplicable phenomenon, this double helix of fortune — upward to a vastly improved condition for the ASEAN countries, downward into despair and suffering for the people of Indochina. The two spirals appear to be continuing.

The fourth development was the general rise of regionalism as an historical force in the area and worldwide. On the one hand ASEAN, as a regional association, began to flourish and has developed steadily. On the other, the Indochina Federation concept of a regional grouping moved perceptibly closer to reality. It seems clear that regionalism is now a major universal influence.

In Southeast Asia it is the area's key indicator, to be watched and measured in any attempt to determine what the future holds.

It was against this backdrop that the U.S.S.R. in 1975 looked anew on the Southeast Asian scene, perceiving new opportunities but still facing old impediments. The region itself had long held the U.S.S.R. to be a status quo European nation. Because of this alien quality and because of local nationalism, Moscow's past efforts to control events and acquire influence in the region often had been thwarted or ruined. The central approach of the U.S.S.R. in Southeast Asia throughout the earlier years had been essentially ideological, forced on it by the Maoist challenge. The determinant of its orientation in attempting to influence regional policies and behavior was (and still is) China. Most Soviet moves have been not actions but reactions, not following a well-defined and predetermined course of action, but responding to unfolding events. The result of this reactive approach was that considerable investment yielded only modest return. There were temporary moments of success, in China and Indonesia, but in general nothing seemed to work very well for the Soviets in Asia, despite expenditures of much money and years of effort. Vietnam represents a promising exception to this historical experience, and that probably is one reason why it is so important in current Moscow thinking.

Clearly the U.S.S.R. is making a determined effort to increase its naval prowess in Asia in general and Southeast Asia in particular. This is expressed largely in comparative terms, that is, against U.S. naval strength with the demand for "balance and equity" of the two fleets. Moscow's expectation is that this approach will hold, improve its global balance of power position, and translate into increased political influence in the region.

The U.S.S.R. now has in Vietnam a set of air and naval bases that represent a degree of threat to the United States and its allies. However, the extent and nature of that threat is variously interpreted by analysts and observers. A common view in influential circles in the United States and Europe is that Soviet post-Vietnam War moves in the Pacific resulted from a natural growing concern for a region that increasingly will affect Soviet security and economic interests. Soviet actions therefore were seen as normal and essentially benign, or at least not of deliberately aggressive calculation. Standing opposed to this rather sanguine view—and the preponderant opinion in the U.S. government—is the contention that Soviet bases in Vietnam do constitute a serious strategic threat, one that is essentially psychological, with the bases chiefly useful in times short of full-scale war. Most analysts believe that Moscow's strategic planners have concluded that Soviet bases in Vietnam would be ultra-vulnerable in the event of war with the United States, and therefore do not incorporate them into U.S. war planning scenarios. Short of total war, however, the bases can have great utility, they help encircle China, and would be useful in any local war. Moreover, they intimidate Asian countries, particularly Japan, both by representing direct Soviet military involvement and by identifying Vietnam with Soviet military power and thus enhancing the threat posed by Hanoi.

Hanoi-Moscow Axis

The present Soviet-Vietnamese relationship, as it has developed in the past decade, is a complicated compound of history, economics, geopolitics, and national psychology. It is neither as close nor as durable as most observers believe. There never was—in the early years before World War II or during the Vietnam War years—much warmth or empathy between Vietnamese Communists and those in Moscow. Ho Chi Minh regarded his Moscow connections as having utility, but he treated Soviet Leninism—beyond the few valuable lessons in organizational techniques and weapons technology it could teach—as irrelevant for Indochina, and even counterproductive for his purposes. Vietnamese Communist theoreticians today still consider Moscow's doctrines of limited use in their problem solving, although they do employ them as icons for their emotive value. On the other side, Lenin never thought much at all about a relationship with Southeast Asia, including Indochina, while Stalin's continental mentality kept him from developing much interest.

When Ho Chi Minh plunged into his anticolonial struggle with the French in the Viet Minh War, he expected sturdy support from Moscow. Instead, he found Moscow willing to sacrifice what for Ho were life and death interests for some marginal Soviet advantage. This left him and other ruling figures in Hanoi (many of whom still hold power) with some bitter memories and lingering distrust. During the Vietnam War, Soviet material and psychological support made it possible for the Vietnamese Communists to fight a protracted struggle, something they could not otherwise have done. However, Soviet war policy was a mixture of pragmatic self-service and judicious commitment. Moscow was wary of entrapment, fearful of escalation, conservative in risk taking, and constantly plagued by ideological dilemmas. It is clear now that throughout the war Moscow was more uncertain about its course of action than was recognized at the time. However, it managed to fund the war for Hanoi; indeed, only with Soviet help could the war have continued, devolving into confrontation with the United States.

The relationship of Vietnam and the U.S.S.R. today binds the two together with extraordinarily close military, economic, diplomatic, and psychological ties. There is today a military alliance in all but name. Becoming a member of the Council for Mutual Economic Assistance (CMEA), Vietnam in effect joined the socialist world economic system. On the international scene, the U.S.S.R. and Cuba represent Hanoi's only truly supportive associates, a fact made doubly important by the isolation of Vietnam, surrounded by adversaries and largely friendless in the world. For these and other, cultural reasons, Vietnam has great need of a relationship that provides psychic assurance, something the U.S.S.R. presently supplies.

This association was not planned by either. In 1975 Moscow rushed somewhat incautiously into the geopolitical vacuum left by the sudden end of the Vietnam War. It saw an opportunity and moved immediately—only later addressing itself to the implications and consequences of its move. The genesis of the association on Vietnam's part was a compound of blunder and miscalculation. Hanoi's leaders at the end of the war made a series of policy decisions that proved disastrous for the country and had the net effect of throwing Vietnam into a dependency on the U.S.S.R., never intended by them and not desirable from their standpoint.

Hence, the relationship is built on, and is a product of, Soviet opportunism and Vietnamese dependency. The U.S.S.R. has pursued strategic opportunity, which probably is its sole motive, and consequently the present relationship may last only so long as perceived opportunities remain. Hanoi's dependency on Moscow is economic and military. Moscow in 1988 again supplied Vietnam with grain, because food was in short supply. Since it has no arms factories, Vietnam relies on the U.S.S.R. for all the weapons and military hardware needed in Kampuchea and to defend itself against China.

In terms of their respective cultures, Russia's meeting Vietnam is a collision of opposites. There is little trust between them, no affective bonds that can be discerned. Privately the Vietnamese hold the Soviets among them in contempt, considering them racist, insensitive to things Vietnamese, and largely incapable of appreciating the subtle characteristics of the Vietnamese mind; in other words, as barbarians. For their part, those Soviets with extended first-hand experience in Vietnam say privately the Vietnamese are utterly self-centered, endlessly demanding of material goods, and entirely unappreciative of aid provided them at considerable sacrifice by the Soviet people. Possibly the relationship carries the seeds of its own destruction, as the Chinese believe, although any marked change will not occur until the present basis of the relation—opportunism and dependency—ends.

Thus, the continuity in the existing relation is Moscow's continuing perception of opportunity and Hanoi's material needs. Changes in the relationship, to whatever extent they actually have developed, lie within the domain of the "revolution" that has been launched in the U.S.S.R. by General Secretary Mikhail Gorbachev and is echoing in Vietnam (and possibly in other Leninist systems). The phenomena currently being observed in Moscow, travelling under the terms *glasnost* (openness), *perestroika* (restructuring), and "democratization," have counterparts in Hanoi, although usage is more imprecise. The general Vietnamese concept is simply "liberalization," using the terms *coi mo*, roughly *openness* and akin to *glasnost*, and *doi moi* or *renovation*, akin to *perestroika* (the Soviet "democratization" concept is rarely encountered in Vietnamese literature). It is clear that history is pushing Vietnam in the direction of reform, and this may eventually have a significant effect on Vietnam's foreign policies. However, one of the major points that this paper makes in this respect is that the "liberalization" phenomenon in Vietnam is essentially internal, having to do with the administration of the economic sector and improvement of party cadre performance. It does not have much direct meaning for Vietnamese foreign policy, including the all important relationship with the U.S.S.R. Perhaps eventually it will have impact, but it is difficult for me to see how even the long-run external relationships, which are the domain of national security interests, can be affected extensively by what is essentially an effort to alter the internal workings of the two respective societies. It is argued by some observers that these forces will prove fundamentally inimical to socialist cohesion, the force holding the Soviet empire and this alliance together. Possibly the forces for change underway in the two respective countries, if they become extensive and permanent, will prove to have at least limited effect on the external relationship.

Hanoi leaders appear not to know quite what to make of Mikhail Gorbachev. They seem to wonder whether they have another Nikita Khrushchev on their hands—the Soviet leader who saw Vietnam as a trap and was disengaging the U.S.S.R. from its association at the time when, much to the relief of Hanoi leaders, he was ousted from power. Given a tendency toward paranoia, Hanoi leaders are not sure they can trust Gorbachev—would he sell them out in exchange for a deal with China?—and while they have no evidence indicating this, doubt remains. After all, they reason, the U.S.S.R. has never fully supported them, and usually the support that was offered was for the wrong reason, to counter Chinese influence.

Finally, in this brief history and analysis of Vietnamese-Soviet relations, there remains the need to touch on the matter of Moscow's influence in Hanoi—its nature and its extent. It is a question that has long divided Vietnam specialists, arising originally in the mid-1960s within the U.S. government, between those who advocated that the United States should pressure Moscow to use its influence on Hanoi to end the war versus those who argued that even if so moved, the U.S.S.R. did not have the power to change basic Hanoi strategy. The argument continues today between those who say Moscow could force Hanoi to settle the Kampuchea problem if it chose to do so, and those who say Moscow has no such power. My view on this is on the side of the latter.

Moscow has influence in Hanoi—there is no question of that—perhaps more influence than anyone else, which may not be saying much. Soviet advice is taken seriously by the Vietnamese, and there is a genuine desire to accommodate Moscow where possible. If the suggestion regards something Hanoi is inclined to do in any case, or is a marginal matter, the Vietnamese can be counted on to accept. If it is a matter in which the Hanoi leadership is more or less equally divided, Moscow's weighing in on one side could well tip the scales. But if it is something the Vietnamese leadership does not want to do—or feels it cannot do—no amount of pressure will change this. The more pressure that is applied, the greater will be the Vietnamese intractableness. Not even force can be counted on—witness China's decade-long effort to effect a changed Hanoi policy in Kampuchea using methods far more forceful than anything Moscow would be prepared to employ (such as invasion)—and to no avail. Whether in fact the U.S.S.R. now or in the past has actually sought to influence Hanoi on major matters is another question. The fact remains that the net effect would have been the same.

Issues

The two most important issues confronting the Hanoi-Moscow association are China and the war in Kampuchea. Not exactly an issue, but a third problem that could easily become an issue, is the failed Vietnamese economy and what to do about it.

The issue around which the entire Vietnamese-Soviet relationship revolves—and this cannot be stated too strongly—is China. There are in this triangular relationship many inherent contradictions. These stem from the basic fact that in facing China, Vietnam and the U.S.S.R. have vastly different perspectives, national interests, and foreign policies. The U.S.S.R. is large and formidable; Vietnam is small and vulnerable. The cultural gulf between the U.S.S.R. and China is stark and elemental; that between Vietnam and China, complex and symbiotic.

In the short run there may be a clear identity of Soviet-Vietnamese interest with respect to China, although it appears even now that this is being quietly questioned in some circles in Moscow. However, the two will probably continue to stand in alliance at least for the next few years. As long as China maintains its present confrontational policy—and "bleeds" Vietnam—Hanoi has little room to maneuver. In the long run for Hanoi, China is simply too large and too near to permit the luxury of permanent hostility. Neither is there reason to think that China wants or expects permanent intransigence. Eventually Vietnam and China will again opt for relations that will be at least nominally amicable. This may or may not prove to be in Moscow's interest.

The Chinese have imposed a requirement on the U.S.S.R. that three obstacles must be removed before Sino-Soviet relations can improve significantly—the Soviet occupation of Afghanistan; the presence of large numbers of Soviet troops along two stretches of the Sino-Soviet frontier; and the Vietnamese occupation of Kampuchea, which Soviet pressure could help terminate. It has never been fully established that these three are in fact true obstacles to improved relations, as opposed to being Chinese excuses for not changing the relationship. Now, even the status of the obstacles has become less clear. Soviet troops have left Afghanistan; there has been a Soviet troop reduction in the border regions (to levels that may or may not be acceptable to Beijing); and Beijing may or may not be satisfied that Moscow is doing all it can to influence Hanoi's policies in Kampuchea. The Chinese publicly say they have not yet dropped the three obstacles, certainly not the one in Kampuchea. There the matter rests at the moment—in doubt.

Kampuchea's importance to the Hanoi-Moscow relationship derives both from the fact that it directly involves Hanoi's and Moscow's respective associations with China and because Kampuchea is the eye of the storm of instability in Southeast Asia. For the time being, the efforts to end the war in Kampuchea remain largely at an impasse.

One can sense in the Soviet behavior toward the Kampuchean question the tug of diametrically opposite forces. On the one hand Moscow would dearly love to be the peacemaker—the power that finally ends the long Kampuchean nightmare. To become this, however, Moscow must be prepared to become deeply involved—to wade far into the Indochina morass that has trapped so many before it. Hence the opposite pull, the caution not to get involved, certainly not become trapped by Kampuchea. This dichotomy is strongly suggested in Mikhail Gorbachev's famous speech in Vladivostok in July 1986. It stands out as a futuristic statement in which the Soviet leader addresses all issues, answers all questions, and offers a grand political vision for the entire sweep of the Pacific Basin—yet carefully circumnavigates the substance of the Kampuchea question, confining himself to minimalist comment that it is an internal Khmer matter. Clearly, Gorbachev can recognize a mine field when he sees one.

Hanoi's interest in Kampuchea is, of course, transcendental and far exceeding the interests of all other outside powers. It is the stark and elemental concern of Vietnamese national security. The strategic assessment by Hanoi's generals holds that Vietnam's geography dooms it to being extraordinarily vulnerable to threat on its flank—it has a thousand-mile coast line and is only ninety miles wide at the waist—and hence it is mandatory that there never come into power in Phnom Penh (or Vientiane for that matter) a government hostile to Vietnam. This is a firm conviction, and the Hanoi leadership is prepared to pay any price to see that this does not happen, which means any settlement in Kampuchea short of Vietnamese defeat in total war must accommodate their view. The U.S.S.R. probably shares this strategic assessment. In any case it is obliged to support it, else risk rupture of relations with Vietnam.

The central problem facing Kampuchea, and the world that seeks to help it and its people, is the fact of anarchy. The problem is not the withdrawal of Vietnamese forces, nor the security of interests of the Socialist Republic of Vietnam, although both are real factors and must be addressed. It is not Moscow's pressure on Hanoi, although clearly there is a good deal of "new thinking" in Moscow with respect to a Kampuchea settlement to build on. It is not China's cooperation, or lack of it, in the peace process. Rather it is *anarchy*, in the ordinary dictionary usage, that is, the *absence of government*. There simply is no government in Kampuchea today below the provincial level; and very little government outside of Phnom Penh except for the "military government" represented by the People's Army of Vietnam (PAVN). A governing structure must be installed that will not only prevent the return of those elements that ruled the country with Pol Pot, but will also prevent a night of long knives by their enemies seeking revenge. More important perhaps, it must be an institutional structure that will prevent governance from developing into politics with guns, into a kind of thirteenth century warlordism with a half-dozen Pol Pots, which inevitably would lead to a *de facto* partition of Kampuchea, a "balkanization" that would guarantee continued suffering by the people of Kampuchea.

Of the many ambiguous aspects of the Kampuchean scene, Vietnamese intent is not one of them. Hanoi's purposes are clear and unequivocal. It believes it can achieve victory in Kampuchea, defined as creating a ruling mechanism out of the Heng Samrin People's Republic of Kampuchea government (which individual resistance fighters are welcome to join, but not share power with); to the exclusion of all major outside influences (including China); and under conditions in which the People's Republic of Kampuchea Armed Forces will become strong enough to permit People's Army of Vietnam withdrawal. This it hopes to accomplish by 1990, although there is no great deal of assurance that it actually will be able to do so by that date.

In a broader context, the issue of war in Kampuchea appears to be something of a paradox: All participants and actors involved would like to see a settlement, but no one is willing to bring this about. A case can be made that each outside interest (that is, non-Khmer) perceives it to be in its national interest both that the war ends and that it continues. This perception applies equally to Vietnam, the U.S.S.R., China, the ASEAN states, and the United States. While the pro-peace versus pro-war balance may not be exactly equal in any one country, it is sufficiently balanced to prevent an altered policy. Logically it would have seemed that some sort of resolution would have been achieved years ago—perhaps a joint effort by all outside actors who have found it in their separate interests, for differing reasons of course, to force through a settlement. This has not happened, and the best or central reason why it has not appears to be the respective sets of offsetting national interests.

The key figure in any Kampuchean settlement scene clearly will be China.

There can be no peace without Chinese support, or at least Chinese acquiescence. Since the Chinese are masters of the art of masking true intent, we cannot be sure what the Chinese would settle for in the final resolve—whether the minimal requirement that they have presence and status in Phnom Penh, or something greater.

The Kampuchean conflict represents a surrogate struggle between Vietnam and China, a battle of wills waged by two determined combatants, experienced in the art of protracted conflict. Each means to stay the course; each means to outlast the other. Time does not appear to be a major factor for either.

Recently we have witnessed in Kampuchea something that might be called a true "peace process," although not one that holds much immediate promise. It is in the hands of the various Khmer elements rather than, as has been the case with earlier settlement ventures, in the hands of outsiders. The Khmers led by Prince Sihanouk appear to have given up on the rest of the world in efforts to end the war, and are attempting what might be called an all-Khmer approach (or perhaps a better term is a Khmer-only approach). But the forces involved—the People's Republic of Kampuchea (PRK) and the Coalition Government of Democratic Kampuchea (CGDK)—are largely surrogate—of Vietnam and China—and hence cannot actually take their fate into their own hands.

Vietnam in mid-1988 and early 1989 made a few forthcoming gestures on Kampuchea—another troop draw-down; U.N. trial balloons; and endorsement of a vague "national reconciliation" for Phnom Penh that would broaden to some degree the PRK government. Clearly what is required is a new political configuration in Phnom Penh, one that incorporates all contending Khmer factions and is acceptable to outsiders, primarily Vietnam and China.

The Kampuchean peace process in late 1988 was given some impetus by indications that Hanoi would probably adhere to its announced plan to withdraw all of its military forces from Kampuchea by sometime in 1990, but possibly by late September 1989, and by the Sino-Soviet "summit" meeting in Beijing in May 1989. These clearly were contributions to the peace process but still left many impediments.

Whether there is an acceptable settlement reached in Kampuchea or not—that is, whether the impasse continues—there will probably be little effect on Hanoi-Moscow relations. It is not an issue that divides, as far as can be determined. Rather, it appears to be regarded in both capitals as a common intractable problem that both would prefer to see resolved but also one that both can accept indefinitely. There are differences—at best nuanced differences—between the two as to what might be possible in Kampuchea. But the overriding consideration seems to be the common determination not to allow the problem to become divisive.

Final thought

Considering the unpredictability of events in Vietnamese history in this century, it would be foolish to attempt any charting of the future of Vietnamese-Soviet relations. There is, however, a clearly established fact of Vietnamese history to be noted: No nation, nor any group, has ever had an enduring, successful relationship with the Vietnamese—not the Chinese for a millennium; nor the Khmers of a once vast empire; nor the now near-extinct Cham; nor the Thais; nor the fifteenth century Burmese; nor the Montagnards of a dozen tribes; nor the French; nor the Americans. Each had moments of amicability and mutual benefit, but each also carried the seeds of its own destruction. Such is the challenge of history facing Moscow. What is past is not always prologue. Still, it is one of our best guides to the future. Therefore it would seem wisest when faced with the question of which will prevail, Moscow or history—to bet on history.

Notes

1. This paper is drawn from the author's *Vietnam and the U.S.S.R.: Anatomy of an Alliance*, Westview Press, 1987, a full-length study of the Soviet-Vietnamese relationship, which contains a bibliographic listing of about 300 entries. Since its publication in late 1987, these additional sources can be added:
Stephen M. Young, "Gorbachev's Asian Policy: Balancing the New and the Old," *Asian Survey*, March 1988.
Thai Quang Trung, "The Gorbachev Effect: A Collective but Shaky Leadership," *Vietnam Commentary*, May-June 1988.
Lewis M. Stern, "The Missing Linh: The Meaning of His Leadership," *Vietnam Commentary*, May-June 1988.
Hoang Huu Quynh, "Reformist vs. Neo-Conservative: Two Likely Premiers," *Vietnam Commentary*, May-June 1988.
Stephen Morris, "Glasnost and the Gulag: The Numbers Game," *Vietnam Commentary*, May-June 1988.
Phan Doan Nam, "Renovating Thinking about Foreign Affairs," *Tap Chi Cong San*, February, 1988.
Nayan Chanda, "A Troubled Friendship: Moscow Loses Patience," *Far Eastern Economic Review*, June 9, 1988.
"Great October Forum," *Tap Chi Cong San*, October, 1987 (JPRS-ATC 88-001). A special issue devoted to past and present Soviet-Vietnamese relations.

6

U.S.S.R.-Cuba Alliance and Regional Conflicts: Trust but Verify

Howard J. Wiarda

The world is awash with wishful thinking, wishful sociology, and wishful political analysis about the Soviet Union. President Reagan's trip to Moscow and the signing of the Intermediate Nuclear Forces (INF) agreement gave rise to an avalanche of writings arguing that the Cold War is over—even that the West has won. At another level, academic conferences and symposia are discussing the vulnerabilities of communist regimes or arguing that Marxism and Leninism no longer serve as beacons of hope in the world. Soviet agriculture and the Soviet domestic economy are in crisis, there is a sharp generational gap highlighting an already severely strained social structure, and there is a crisis of leadership and institutions, not least of all the Communist Party of the Soviet Union, which is being viewed by many as an anachronism. (Few serious persons—except perhaps in Western universities—continue to believe in the viability of Leninist ideology.) If one were to pull together the threads of these various strands, one would have to conclude that the political and social fabric of the Soviet Union is about to unravel—if not today, then certainly tomorrow.[1]

Western assessments of Soviet foreign policy—certainly at the popular level and to some extent at the official level as well—have followed a similar trajectory. Because of its current and future domestic preoccupations, the Soviet Union is thought likely to pull back from its global foreign policy role. Crisis at home and the demand of Soviet citizens for more consumer goods and greater political and societal openness, it is argued, will lead to a deemphasis on foreign adventurism in countries like Afghanistan, Grenada, Ethiopia, Vietnam, Angola, Mozambique, and Nicaragua. The Soviets cannot afford it, the argument runs, and therefore they will concentrate on priorities at home rather than on far-flung, costly, and not overly successful excursions abroad.

Therefore, we are likely to see, this line of thinking suggests, not just a new period of détente between the superpowers but a new relaxation of tensions among their bloc partners along the Iron Curtain in Central Europe as well as an end to the superpower rivalry in the Third World. As a result of the changes in the Soviet domestic situation and the West's reassessment of Soviet foreign policy possibilities, expectations about the impending end of the Cold War—the prospects of a Soviet pullback and therefore for the United States similarly to reduce its vigilance as well as its military preparedness— have reached new heights of (at least in some quarters) euphoria. The worst fears of the conservatives, that signing an arms reduction treaty with the Soviets would lead to an irresistible momentum toward a relaxation of the U.S. guard and a unilateral, possibly precipitous disarmament in the West, appear to be at least seriously contemplated, if not on the path to realization.

Some perspective is necessary. The signs of change in the Soviet Union are abundant, with internal pressures on its society, its institutions, and its official ideology. And the logic is that internal pressures will force the Soviets to reduce their international commitments, both present and future. But while the logic is clear, the facts so far do not necessarily point to a U.S. Cold War victory and a Soviet withdrawal from international commitments in the Third World and elsewhere. We should not be overly surprised if future trends do in fact point in this direction, but as yet the Soviets have shown few signs of actually reducing their aspirations to global power status or of pulling back from the very many strategic commitments they continue to honor. (They may soon, or over the long term, in ways that would make Paul Kennedy's recent book[2] applicable to a seemingly overextended Soviet global empire as well as the United States one.) The theory and logic for a Soviet withdrawal are persuasive, but the amount of real movement has been minuscule and even it could be reversed—e.g., by a sudden Soviet reentry into Afghanistan. The issue of Soviet and Soviet "junior partner" policy in Southeast Asia, southern Africa, and Central America remains even more ambiguous. Hence, for now a more cautionary and prudent posture is required by the United States, one that watches Soviet developments closely but does not allow U.S. preparedness to diminish, one that is hopeful but does not allow wishful thinking to get in the way of making realistic assessments based on hard evidence.

Logic of a Soviet Pullback

In recent statements, Soviet General Secretary Mikhail Gorbachev has stressed the need for "new thinking" in both domestic and international affairs. While most of the attention in this new international thinking has been focused on East-West affairs, a reassessment has also been underway in terms of Soviet relations with the Third World. Here we examine briefly six aspects of the new Soviet thinking with regard to the Third World: ideological statements, personnel changes, economic theory and practice, political/diplomatic relations, the models used to interpret the Third World, and preoccupation with the Soviet economy and domestic political situation. We then assess these changes in the light of other evidence.

At the ideological level a reexamination is underway in the Soviet Union regarding trends in Third World radicalism and the prospects for "national liberation"—a review, in short, of the principles of Soviet strategy over the last thirty years and more, and of the Brezhnev Doctrine.[3] In the newer Soviet literature, the Third World is seldom seen anymore as an important revolutionary force, nor is the developing nations' role in the decline of capitalism stressed. The emphasis on national liberation itself is seldom mentioned, and the Third World nations are no longer presumed to be following a path toward ultimate socialism. In the recent literature there is far less enthusiasm for the Third World as an area for future Soviet expansion and a rejection of close identification with radical, anti-American states. The Soviets are inclined to assist such regimes no longer out of the necessity and inevitability of global proletarian solidarity and international revolution, but "only to the extent of their ability." In these and other ways, the Soviet Union appears to be fashioning a new posture toward dealing with the Third World that would seem to justify its disengagement from these divisive areas, reducing its commitments, and reaching an accommodation with the United States. At the ideological level, first of all, the approach toward the Third World seems increasingly to be "hands off."

In terms of the personnel who deal with Soviet Third World policy and thinking, significant trends toward greater pragmatism and open-mindedness seem to be evident as well. The Soviet Union's leading think tank, the Institute of World Economy and International Relations, is under new direction, that of Evgenii Primakov, who has written that Third World countries can make progress even under capitalism and despite their connections with imperialism. The editor of the Communist Party's leading theoretical journal, *Kommunist*, is yet another advocate of change, in particular greater global interdependence. And Gorbachev's chief foreign affairs adviser, Aleksandr Iakovlev, argues that countries such as Brazil must be viewed as new regional powers in an increasingly multipolar world. There are others, for example, the editor of *Problemy Ekonomiki*, a leading theoretical journal of economics, who argues that it is not the continued exploitation of the Third World that explains capitalism's ongoing vitality but efficiency, rationality, and technological renovation.[4] These views are not exactly orthodox by traditional Soviet standards, yet they are voiced by the new men of influence in Soviet thinking, whose views will sooner or later be translated into foreign policy.

The third area of Soviet "new thinking" is in economic theory and policy.

The Soviet Union is eager for trade with the West and now accepts the reality of worldwide economic interdependence. Its older strategy of luring the developing countries away from capitalist markets has been modified in favor of a recognition of the strength of capitalist economies and the desire, through trade and technological transfers, to take advantage of them. The Soviet Union acknowledges that it cannot realistically substitute its own antiquated economic mechanisms for the trade and economic ties that link the developing nations with Western capitalist markets, nor does it wish or can it afford to do so. The Soviets want desperately to build up their own trade with the West, and in their relations with the Third World they are insisting that the benefits must be "mutual," another word for "profitable." It has become clear that the Soviet Union is not eager to take on and heavily subsidize very many more Third World "basket cases." The Soviets have already told such countries as Nicaragua that they should not expect very much in the way of economic assistance—although military assistance may be another matter.[5]

At the political and diplomatic level, the fourth aspect, the Soviets also seem to be scaling back. Rather than looking for new gains in the Third World, the Soviets are reevaluating and reassessing their priorities. After all, what have they gained from the adventurism in Afghanistan, Grenada, Angola, Ethiopia, Cuba, Nicaragua, and Vietnam? With one or two exceptions, the answer would have to be, not much. Most of these countries turn out to have been a drain on the Soviets instead of resulting in gains; they have been costly financially, in terms of antagonizing the United States, causing endless grief, embarrassment, and no end of troubles. The Soviets appear to have concluded that sub-Saharan Africa is hopeless and not worth spending very much time or resources in, and that Latin America is also difficult logistically, of very little strategic value to the Soviets, and perhaps not as potentially revolutionary as first appeared in 1959 (with Castro's revolution) and then again in 1979 (with successful revolutions in Grenada and Nicaragua and the potential for more in El Salvador and Guatemala).[6]

The changes in the models and interpretations by which the Soviets assess and interpret the Third World are especially interesting. Quite a number of Soviet scholars have abandoned the usual Leninist categories (except perhaps at the rhetorical level, or as a means of keeping their jobs) in favor of more pragmatic and open-minded approaches; a few are even questioning whether Leninist analysis has relevance for the Third World. There is a new emphasis on the role and persistence of national traditions in the developing nations, and on the distinctiveness of sociocultural conditions in different Third World areas. The path of Third World development, because of the strength of indigenous Third World traditions, is not likely to follow that of Western Europe or pass through the Leninist stages; and there is some questioning of whether the usual Marxian concern with the supposedly universal economic laws governing the unfolding of the historical dialectic is appropriate.

The new interpretations place great emphasis on the "specifics" of the developing nations, on what Marx referred to by the catch-all category of the "Asiatic mode of production"—i.e., one particular to the then Third World. At least one Soviet scholar has even proposed a separate political economy and method of interpretation for the Third World, one that acknowledges the diversity of the several developing areas. Not only is there a great deal of intellectual ferment in terms of how the Soviets interpret the developing nations, but at the pragmatic level as well, doubts are being raised about the advantages to the Soviet Union politically and diplomatically of radicalism and radical movements in the Third World.[7]

Finally, we must assess the situation in the Soviet Union itself. The Soviet economy is in deep trouble, the country is falling farther behind technologically, social and ethnic problems abound, agricultural production is lagging, and the political institutions enjoy less legitimacy than before. There is a sharp generational gap, a crisis of succession in several Eastern European countries (and maybe in the Soviet Union itself), a crisis of society, a crisis of ideology (few continue to actually believe the Leninist dogma), and a crisis in the agencies of the state, most particularly the Communist Party, whose absolute monopoly of political power is being challenged. Wherever one looks in the Soviet Union, at whatever institutions, one sees a new questioning, considerable disarray, fragmentation, growing incapacity, and perhaps even unravelling and potential "ungovernability."[8] Scholars who once wrote about the Soviet behemoth and "totalitarianism" are now undertaking research projects on the "crisis," the "collapse," and the "vulnerability" of communist regimes.[9]

The logic of these changes would seem to point toward a necessity for the Soviet Union to pull back from some of its global commitments. That has been the main thrust of recent academic writings in the West about the Soviet Union. With Soviet citizens now demanding more consumer goods and a Western lifestyle; with the Soviet economy, agriculture, and industrial plant management so badly in need of reform; with the Soviet political system undergoing new strains and pressures; and with the country, including its armed forces, becoming progressively less rather than more technologically competitive, it would seem incumbent on the Soviet Union to withdraw somewhat, to turn inward, and to concentrate on its need for domestic reform rather than new conquests abroad.

This logic is strong, compelling, and attractive, especially for those peoples and nations exhausted by forty years of the Cold War and wanting and hoping to go on to other things. Moreover, the results desired and predicted may well turn out to be the valid and correct ones. And yet, very little has happened so far. The Soviets have served notice that Nicaragua should not expect much in the way of economic aid, but there is no sign of a significant diminution in military assistance. Nor is there any indication that Soviet assistance, directly or via Cuba, to guerrilla groups in Guatemala, El Salvador, Peru, and Colombia on the Latin American continent is decreasing. The Soviets have withdrawn militarily from Afghanistan, but we do not as yet know by what means (a puppet regime, under immense Soviet pressures, a renewed or continued military presence, diplomacy) the Soviets will try to maintain their control of that country on their southern flank.

An agreement has been reached on Angola, but it has numerous loopholes, and so we will have to see how that is finally resolved. Soviet commitments to valued regional allies such as Cuba, Ethiopia, and Vietnam seem as strong as ever—even though the latter has recently begun to pull out of Cambodia. Nor is there any clear indication as yet that the Soviets will not use the present period of relaxation of East-West tensions, as they used the earlier period of détente, to give the appearance of rapprochement in some areas, meanwhile scoring impressive Cold War gains in others that were less visible or attracted less attention. These were chiefly Third World areas—Ethiopia, Central America, Peru, South Yemen, Angola, Mozambique, Afghanistan, Southeast Asia, the Middle East, the Caribbean—where significant victories could be scored without their receiving much publicity or disturbing the new East-West openings in Europe. Moreover, while there is a strong, perhaps valid logic to the pullback scenarios outlined above, there is an alternative logic (discussed in more detail below) that suggests that the Soviets may yet succeed in maintaining their vast new overseas empire, maybe even expanding it, by passing the costs off to the Warsaw Pact allies or to the West, which means chiefly the United States. Hence, while virtually all the scholarly and intellectual arguments and logic would seem to point toward a Soviet withdrawal from some areas of its overseas, principally Third World, empire, the conclusion may in fact not follow from the premises; it has not happened yet, and there is considerable reason to think that, even shouldering fewer costs the Soviets may not have to contract their international commitments very much, if at all, and could still score significant successes.

Cuba as a Soviet Proxy: The Impact of *Glasnost*

For a considerable period now Cuba has been functioning as a junior partner, a proxy, and a surrogate of the Soviet Union in Latin America and globally.[10] Cuba serves as a Soviet advance base, an "aircraft carrier," a link to local communities (usually black or mulatto/mestizo and Spanish or Portuguese-speaking), a military intelligence station, a guerrilla training base, and a "model" of socialist development. It is a wonderful arrangement for the Soviet Union which, at comparatively low cost and without getting itself directly involved, can use the Cubans to advance its own foreign policy goals. Moscow thus avoids confronting the United States directly in areas that are particularly sensitive to the United States or where the United States enjoys strategic local preponderance of power (such as Central America and the Caribbean), and it enables the Soviets to champion peace and détente at one level while at another having the Cubans do their "dirty work" for them. For the Cubans this arrangement has also been a good one, enabling them to earn oil, hard currency, and other sorely needed rewards at the material level; while also vaulting "little Cuba" to the position of a "superpower," with troops and paramilitary technical advisers operating in some twenty-five to thirty nations of the world, and a prestigious leader of the nonaligned movement.

Cuba has strongly opposed *glasnost* and *perestroika*, and has expressed its disapproval to the Soviets both publicly and privately. The reason for the Cuban opposition stems chiefly from the fact that its communist regime and institutions are far less firmly established than are those of the Soviet Union, and from fears that any kind of political opening may well undermine the island's shaky regime. Cuba is more vulnerable than is the Soviet Union and, in addition, its leadership is not willing to see its power reduced or be forced to share power with any other group or institution, and certainly not with the Cuban people. The Gorbachev reform program has not been at all well received in Cuba, and the Cubans are very reluctant to relax their system of controls—though there are already signs that the Cuban leadership will have to respond to the Gorbachev initiatives, most likely by appearing to "open" the system a bit without in any way affecting their absolute power.[11]

The Cuban regime is "vulnerable" in many of the same ways that the Soviet Union is or that other Leninist regimes are, and perhaps more so. And, as with the Soviet Union, the logic of Cuba's weaknesses may lead it to play a less aggressive role in the world and to return to a modest and self-effacing posture in accord with its small size and limited resources. But once again, logic is one thing and reality another. So far there is precious little indication that Cuba will pull back from its extended, virtually global commitments and again become just another small, ineffective Third World country. Logic would suggest that Cuba's foreign policy adventurism peaked in 1979, at the time of the successful Cuba-aided Grenadan and Nicaraguan revolutions, and has since been on the way down;[12] but there is virtually no evidence that the Cuban leadership at the highest levels accept that logic. Indeed, quite the contrary might be the case, as we shall see later in the chapter. As the Cubans might be inclined to put it (echoing both Will Rogers and numerous down-and-out sports teams), rumors of our imminent [foreign policy] demise are greatly exaggerated.

What precisely are the Cuban weaknesses and vulnerabilities? Herewith is a list based on both an extensive review of the literature as well as research work and interviews during two brief trips to Cuba in 1987 and 1988.[13] This list of Cuban debilities seems remarkably parallel to the earlier discussed Soviet vulnerabilities, although Cuba's weaknesses seem far greater than those of the Soviet Union:

Economy

The Cuban economy is widely thought of as deeply troubled, to have shown little or no growth since the 1950s, to have failed to keep pace not only with neighboring, more open-market economies but also with other socialist countries. Determined Cuban efforts to diversify the economy have not been notably successful. There is little fuel or traffic, little to buy, only limited industrialization, and no future whatsoever in sugar. The sense is growing among expert, less ideologically-committed observers that all the sacrifices of the earlier years of the revolution and still today may not pay off in future economic growth. Eventually the revolution must produce in terms of economic development, consumer goods, and a higher standard of living or the regime will be in some future trouble.

Leadership

The Cuban leadership, particularly Fidel Castro, is aging, becoming elder statesmen. That is, the leadership is listened to politely, even reverently at times, but it is not always taken seriously. There is a generational gap, and some say the leadership is not fully informed of the new realities. There are crude jokes about Castro's seeming desire to surpass former dictator Stroessner of Paraguay with the lengthiest regime in the history of the Western Hemisphere; and as a rule of thumb it seems fair to say that when a leadership is joked about in this way, it may have to start thinking about retirement or liquidating potential challenges to its rule, as Castro seems to have done in the trial of General Arnaldo Ochoa Sánchez in July 1989.

Social Programs

The revolution's early social programs (health, education, housing) were viewed as successful; but now there is evidence of considerable backward slippage. In some quarters the suspicion is growing that even the earlier successes may have been exaggerated.[14]

Elan

In many respects a good deal of the spirit seems to have gone out of the Cuban revolution. The élan is fading. Many Cubans appear to be going through the motions of waxing enthusiastic for the revolution, but genuine emotion seems to be absent. What was sensed as an intoxicating explosion and surge of liberation and optimism in the early days of the revolution is no longer there. By the same token, the liberating appeal that the revolution had for Latin America in 1959 is currently (except in some limited ideological and intellectual circles) wholly lacking.

Generational Differences

The generation of Cubans that was personally acquainted with and repelled by the preceding Batista regime is now mostly gone; for the newer generations the dark days of prior corruption and dictatorship are little more than revolutionary "myths" and slogans. A "new class" of Cuban leaders has grown up who only dimly (if at all) remember the revolution, who are bureaucrats and apparatchiks, and who know how to mouth the slogans and catch phrases but whose Leninism seems less than enthusiastic. By now a second generation is growing up, as in Eastern Europe, that will soon demand the freedoms and liberties of the West. There is a crisis of ideology and of generational change in all the communist systems.

Public Attitudes

Many observers have sensed a considerable amount of sullenness and cynicism in Cuba. People dislike but cannot change the system, so they have resigned and accommodated themselves to it. But as in Poland, there is in Cuba a bitterness and a resentment underneath; some estimates are that one-third of the population would leave if, a la Mariel, the boats were made available.

Distance

Cuba is far from Soviet shores; one senses little genuine affection for the Soviet Union on the island; and, unlike in Eastern Europe, there is no Soviet occupation army. A growing literature suggests that Cuba since the revolution has only changed one form of dependency for an even less advantageous one.[15] Not only is the physical distance great but a testing of attitudes and the isolation of the Soviets and Eastern Europeans in their compounds suggest that the psychological distance is great as well.

Pull of the United States

At the same time that the Soviet logistics and affinities are difficult and strained, the pull and attractiveness of the United States in Cuba are great.

Even now, almost thirty years after the revolution, the United States—its styles, music, dress, economic and political system, including its foreign policies—remains the chief Cuban outside preoccupation. It is doubtful that after three decades and strenuous efforts on the part of the regime, Cuba can actually escape the American orbit. The United States is Cuba's natural, necessary, almost inevitable market, and no amount of ideological and economic reorientation on the island will change that.

Depression

Cuba seems to visitors a not very happy country. There seems little spontaneity, enthusiasm, or *joie de vivre*. Its vitality seems to have been sapped. There is little money and not very much in the way of consumer goods on which to spend it. The system seems to be a burden that people bear, and no longer one to become optimistic over.

Divisiveness

There are great divisions in Cuba, between the generations, between the leadership and the medium and lower-level bureaucracies, between the leadership and its increasingly discontented population, and among all sections over the future course of the revolution. Only thinly disguised from the outside world, these divisions threaten Cuba with future fragmentation and perhaps a certain unravelling.

Isolation

Despite its recent diplomatic successes in establishing better relations with quite a number of Latin American countries, Cuba remains seriously isolated from the outside world, not just from North America but from Latin America, Western Europe, and Asia as well. The number of flights landing per week at Jose Martí International Airport, for instance, is less than one twentieth the number landing in nearby Puerto Rico. But I would argue that Cuba is not only isolated physically, but also politically from the main currents—democracy, economic reform, human rights, overall development—that are stirring her neighbors. It is very dangerous, especially for a Leninist regime, to be seen as out of step with history.

Glasnost and Perestroika

Cuba's mentor and *patrón*, the Soviet Union, seems to be going through a period of reform and self-examination. It needs, as we have seen, to restructure its economy and reform its system, and both domestic and international pressures are forcing it to provide greater freedom and human rights. Although the internal debate in Cuba as to how and whether it should follow the Soviet lead is continuing, thus far Cuba has shown few signs of opening up its system even partially as the Soviets have, and it has been quite critical of the Soviet initiatives. It is not difficult to conclude that this stance on Cuba's part will produce friction between it and its sponsor and remove Cuba even further from the main driving currents of the globe, which are toward democracy, human rights, and freedom in both the West (including the rest of Latin America) and now the East.[16] Cuba has rejected not only *glasnost* but also *perestroika*.

Nor has the Cuban government been thrilled by the implications of Gorbachev's "new thinking," as it affects Cuba's own foreign policy goals. Fidel Castro has emphasized that Cuba does not intend to copy the Soviet model in this regard. First, there have been precious few signs of a Cuban policy of *glasnost* or "openness." Unlike Eastern Europe or the Soviet Union, Cuba has allowed almost no freedom of expression, no press freedom, no public questioning of the regime or its practices, and no opening of the wellsprings of cultural or political expression. Journalists have criticized the waste or inefficiency of a few plant managers, but none of the intellectual ferment that is stirring the communist nations of Eastern Europe has yet to come to Cuba. Indeed, quite the reverse process may be happening: Cuba has achieved in recent years the dubious distinction of having more political prisoners per capita than any other nation in the world.

Second, the only *perestroika* seems to be *perestroika* in reverse. Rather than restructuring, what the Cubans have done under the policy of "rectification" is to centralize government economic control even further, take back from plant managers the small measure of autonomy they had in the past, and clamp down on the limited free market in agricultural products that had begun to emerge. "Moral incentives" as distinct from economic ones are again to be emphasized, but in the thirty years of the revolution moral incentives have yet to show that they can bring greater productivity to the flagging Cuban economy. Nor, finally, has the "new thinking" in foreign policy championed by Gorbachev and the Soviet innovators had much effect in Cuba; again, the contrary is true.

If one puts these several factors together and examines the whole rather than just the several parts separately, they add up to a somewhat impropitious prognosis for the future of the Cuban socialist regime. But since domestic situations and foreign policies are intimately related, possibly no less so in socialist regimes over the long term than in other kinds, the vulnerabilities listed above carry important implications for Cuban foreign policy as well. Since Cuban foreign policy in the future may not be dealing from a position of strength but of considerable weakness, the logic of the situation—as with the Soviet Union—would seem to require a pullback of Cuban forces and a considerable diminishment of Cuba's foreign policy of "international proletarian solidarity."

Unfortunately for this reasoning, as well as for U.S. interests, there is very little evidence that the logic of Cuba's various weaknesses and its implications for Cuba's foreign policy have been accepted by the Cuban leadership. One expects Cuba, on the basis of the domestic tensions and debilities listed here, to reduce its international role; but so far the signs of change have been few. Through 1988 Cuban troops in *increasing* numbers were still going to Angola (although the recent agreement has led to the beginning of a withdrawal process, the end result of which is still unknown); and Cuba's commitment to Nicaragua is as strong as ever. Cuba continues to assist terrorist and revolutionary movements elsewhere in Latin America; to provide arms and training to the El Salvadoran, Guatemalan, and other guerrillas; to coordinate the guerrilla struggles and forge unity among the otherwise contending leftist forces, and to serve both the Soviet Union's as well as Cuba's own foreign policy goals (not always exactly identical) in far-flung outposts in Southeast Asia, the Middle East, and Africa.

The fact is that Fidel Castro, who has always been a megalomaniac, *loves* to play a grand international role, loves to elevate his small island to a place of importance in the world (especially if his activities drive the United States to distraction), loves the elevated position he has enjoyed as head of the nonaligned movement, loves to be consulted as a senior statesman on global matters, loves to travel abroad (especially as his domestic revolution has proved so unsuccessful), and loves to move his troops and forces around as if he were a global chess player (which he has become). These factors make it extremely unlikely that Cuba's foreign policy will soon become less grandiose and adventurous—at least while Fidel Castro remains in power and maybe longer. Moreover, one can make the case for Cuba (although perhaps not for the Soviet Union) that as its domestic revolution has failed, its attraction to foreign involvements has increased—and may continue to do so. Additionally, the Cubans reap enormous profits from their military incursions abroad— from the Soviets and from the Angolans, for example—and would be loathe to give them up. Finally, as a Soviet proxy that is heavily dependent financially and in other ways on the Soviet Union, the Cubans might not be permitted by their Soviet masters to pull back from their international commitments even if the Cubans wanted to. Indeed, one could make the case that in an era when the Soviets seem likely to reduce their commitments abroad, an even larger role will henceforth be assigned to the Cubans as the Soviets' advance party, agents, and shock troops.[17]

An Alternative Logic

The logic that suggests that because of its domestic pressures and need for change, the Soviet Union will be obliged in the future to play a less adventurist and expansionist international role is persuasive but not fully compelling. So far there have been few definite signs of such pullbacks and very little evidence that the Soviets intend to relinquish their role as a global power. Much the same logic has been applied to Cuba, in suggesting that the problems of its revolution and its vulnerabilities will oblige it to play a less internationalist role in the world. But here again, the conclusions have not yet or necessarily followed from the logic of the premises—and may not in the future. One can, in fact, envision three possible logics and scenarios: where domestic considerations force *both* the Soviet Union and Cuba to pull back from their now extensive international commitments, where one does so (most likely the Soviet Union) but the other (Cuba) does not or is not permitted to, or where *neither* decides to reduce its international role although possibly taking steps to appear to be doing so.

There is, in fact, an alternative logic to the one presented in the first section of the paper. It suggests that while the Soviet Union and Cuba are facing domestic pressures, they may not at all lead to a diminishment of their international positions. Indeed, their positions could well be enhanced in this process, perhaps at the expense of U.S. foreign policy goals. Let us marshall the arguments.[18]

First, it may be argued that while the Soviet/Cuban domestic situation does not augur well at present for new offensive postures, this does not mean a Soviet/Cuban retreat. Rather, what we are likely to see is a holding action. There will be less Soviet economic and financial aid provided to troubled Third World countries but continued military and other forms of aid. Of course, the United States could raise the stakes in some of these areas of conflict (Central America, southern Africa), thus forcing the Soviets into a more precipitous withdrawal; but with the end of Contra aid and a new administration in power in January 1989, it seems exceedingly unlikely that the United States will do that. We may well see a new Yalta and a new era of détente that will lead to a status quo that the Soviets can often manage and take advantage of better than the United States. In this context, as in the 1970s, the United States may relax its preparedness while the Soviets continue to score gains.

Second, the Soviets have become quite adept at shifting the costs of maintaining their empire. So even if their domestic economy performs poorly, the empire—evil or otherwise—will survive. The costs may be shifted to their East European allies in the form of inflated oil prices or the requirement of absorbing larger quotas of the products of the Soviets' Third World allies. Or they may be shifted to the West in the form of economic aid to these Third World countries, who could be prompted by the Soviets to request it. We tend to think that when a Soviet-allied Leninist state requests our aid that we are weaning it away from the Soviet Union; but such requests are often only a ploy. We provide the aid and the Leninist state accepts, while usually remaining allied with the Soviet Union.

Third, even if some disengagement should occur, it will not necessarily be seen as a setback for the Soviet Union. The Soviets have been very careful lately to keep some distance from some of their erstwhile though often unreliable Third World allies, and to be discriminating in terms of who is welcomed into the club of fully fledged Leninist regimes. If there is a retreat somewhere, the Soviets can always say that it was not a communist regime anyhow. Hence, they can save face and avoid appearing to have repudiated the Brezhnev Doctrine.

Fourth, there are few signs presently of a crisis or imminent collapse of Leninist regimes in very many Third World countries. Communist regimes are in crisis in the Soviet Union and Eastern Europe but not, or not in the same way, in the Third World. There, Leninism is chiefly a formula for seizing and holding power; these Third World countries do not have the same crisis of legitimacy or such heightened expectations as in Eastern Europe or the Soviet Union. There are few signs that radicalism, anti-Americanism, and Leninism are declining in Latin America or very many other Third World countries, or that established Leninist regimes (in Cuba, Ethiopia, Vietnam, and elsewhere) are anywhere near collapse.

Fifth, it seems likely that the Soviet gains made in recent years in the Third World will continue as if on "automatic pilot." There will not be dramatic changes anytime soon. The Soviets are very busy with their domestic situation and with Eastern Europe at the present time; they have at this moment no coherent plan for expansion in the Third World. But that does not mean their present international system will collapse or be reversed; actually, the system can run on inertia for some time, until the Soviets have a new doctrine or are again ready to commit resources and energy. But a disintegration or a rollback of the empire seems unlikely. However, in some countries the Soviets may not be able to have it both ways. In both Afghanistan and Angola the Soviets would clearly like to maintain their presence and/or control, but the strength of the indigenous oppositions may make that impossible.

In the sixth place, a diminishment of Soviet assistance to a Third World ally should not always be interpreted as a new crack in the empire and a victory for the United States. Such moves represent shifts in focus rather than strategic retreats. For example, the Soviets may well reduce now their assistance to Nicaragua, but that may be not a product of Soviet weakness but of strategic reassessment. For the facts are that the Reagan administration has ended, the Contras have had their funding cut off, and the Nicaraguan Sandinista revolution is no longer threatened. Hence, it will no longer have such a great need for Soviet aid and equipment.

Indeed, what is very likely to happen—and is probably already happening—is that the arms and equipment shipped earlier to Sandinista Nicaragua for its fight with the Contras will now be shipped to the guerrillas in El Salvador, Guatemala, Colombia, and Peru. Moreover, the victory of the Sandinistas over the Contras and the United States and hence the opportunity for a consolidation of the Sandinista regime will give a morale boost to guerrilla groups in neighboring countries. Furthermore, it seems unlikely that the United States will anytime soon give the assistance and arms, or seriously propose intervention in Central America as the Reagan administration did. So not only will the Soviets be able to help consolidate the regimes of their allies in the Caribbean and Central America, but the prospects of still further successes look quite good from their point of view.

It should be remembered, seventh, that a proxy *cum* surrogate like Cuba actually profits from serving Soviet interests in southern Africa. Cuba is paid between $600 and $800 million per year by the Angolans for its help against Savimbi's UNITA. Furthermore, the African involvement brings considerable glory to Cuba, helps reduce Cuba's massive un- and under-employment problems, helps nurture Fidel Castro's megalomania, earns the Cubans credit with their Soviet patrons, and helps justify the Soviet subsidy to Cuba. These are not small reasons for the Cubans to continue in Angola and elsewhere, and for the Soviets to want to keep them there.

An eighth factor is that the Soviets do not always need a lot of money to do well internationally. For example, the Soviet Union has enhanced its position politically and diplomatically in South America and Panama in recent years but without significant outlays of funds. Unlike the United States, the Soviets do not seem to have to "buy" their way into good favor. Soviet foreign policy is not like the U.S.; it is not the product of the same kinds of forces or processes of decisionmaking, and we make a grave mistake if we think that it is. The Soviets can, among other things, hold their own and make foreign policy advances even without the outlay of large amounts of capital.

Ninth, one should not necessarily accept the argument that Soviet adventurism in the Third World in recent decades has brought it mostly grief and few benefits. There have been costs to the Soviets, to be sure, and several initiatives have backfired, but one needs also to keep in mind the gains: embarrassment of the United States, including in its own "back yard"; the sowing of further divisiveness and paralysis in the U.S. body politic over these murky Third World conflicts; new allies for the Soviets in far-flung areas of the globe; important military bases (Cuba, Vietnam) as well as other strategic assets; the tying up of U.S. forces in peripheral Third World areas, thus preventing their deployment in the main arenas; the wasting of U.S. financial and political resources in low-priority skirmishes; the prestige to the Soviets in becoming a truly global power; and so on. The list of accomplishments and successes is not small, and it seems unlikely that the Soviets will quickly or easily abandon them.[19]

Tenth, and in summary, the argument that because the Soviets are preoccupied domestically and have financial problems, they therefore cannot pursue a vigorous foreign policy, may not hold water. The Soviets don't have the economic and financial means but they have plenty of other assets—ideology, military aid, a formula for seizing and consolidating power, diplomacy, political machinations, fifth columns—that may serve just as well. It would be nice from their point of view if they also had the financial means but in its absence Moscow has done very well internationally by employing these other assets. We should not be too surprised if the Soviets continue to do so in the future.

Conclusion

Two alternative scenarios or interpretations about Soviet foreign policy behavior have been presented here. The first, which seems to be the dominant interpretation at present, argues that because the Soviet Union and its Cuban (and other) junior partners are going through a period of economic as well as institutional crisis, they are likely to be internally preoccupied and even shackled, and therefore incapable of launching new foreign policy initiatives in the Third World. They may have to pull back from previous commitments, and they will almost certainly be restrained from initiating any new international adventurism.

While this first interpretation has considerable logic and force of argument, it also suffers from that fact. That is, while the logic is persuasive, the realities as yet do not back up the conclusions reached. There is precious little evidence so far that the Soviets have in fact begun such a pullback or that they contemplate it (Afghanistan is an exception; we will have to wait and see regarding Angola). The second weakness of this argument is that it tends to interpret Soviet foreign policy through Western eyes. Because we would cut our commitments when faced with an economic decline (the *de rigueur* arguments of Paul Kennedy), we assume the Soviets will; but we have already seen that Soviet foreign policy is not like ours, may not follow the same logic, and is derived from different premises about the world. The third problem with this interpretation is that it seems to shade off at times into wishful thinking. We want so much for a relaxation of tensions, for the Cold War to be over, for a genuine détente, that our wishes may sometimes get in the way of hard analysis.

But the second interpretation presented here also has its problems. It may overstate the capacity of the Soviets to hang on to their far-flung empire, overstate their cleverness and ability to manage the present contradictions in their domestic and foreign policies, and underestimate the capacity of the United States or its Third World allies and their peoples to resist the blandishments of Soviet foreign policy and to continue opting for a democratic alternative to Leninism.[20] But this second interpretation does have the virtue of somewhat greater realism, for instead of any major pullback of the Soviet position (except in the two cases already mentioned), it seems more likely that the Soviets will seek, by means other than economic, to maintain their earlier gains abroad (Cuba), to consolidate what they have recently acquired (Nicaragua), and perhaps even to advance their cause in new areas (El Salvador, Guatemala). It is possible that the more reasoned exponents of the first position would not even quarrel very much with this interpretation.

If one looks for a balanced position between the other two positions, one would likely conclude that while there will be a great deal of verbal and rhetorical change in Soviet foreign policy, actual changes are likely to be more modest. The "new thinking" will lead the Soviets to rethink and reformulate their earlier policies in the Third World as well as the means used to achieve them, but they are not likely to withdraw from their earlier strategic gains except very slowly, reluctantly, and perhaps not at all. They will undoubtedly renegotiate their relations with their proxies, such as Cuba; but it is not at all certain that this will lead to diminished Soviet/Cuban foreign polic ambitions, and it could well result in *greater* Cuban machinations abroac, aided and abetted by the Soviets, whose role would now be more indirect. The distinct logics presented here, in short, may lead to alternative assessments and conclusions about the future, though not to any single or necessary outcome.

In light of the fact, therefore, that there is at this point limited hard evidence on which to reach a firm judgment, considerable degrees of ethnocentrism and wishful thinking about what can be expected of Soviet foreign policy behavior, and several interpretations that are quite a distance apart, a prudent strategy is the one set forth by President Reagan in Moscow during the 1988 signing of the INF agreement: "Trust but verify."

Notes

1. For a fuller discussion of these themes see the "Introduction" by Vladimir Tismaneanu and Howard J. Wiarda to the special issue of *World Affairs* focused on the theme of "Vulnerabilities of Communist Regimes" (Spring 1988).
2. Paul Kennedy, *The Rise and Fall of the Great Powers* (New York: Random House, 1988).
3. The analysis in this section relies heavily on the original Russian-language re-

search of Elizabeth Kridl Valkenier, "New Soviet Thinking About the Third World," *World Policy Journal*, IV (Fall, 1987), pp. 651-74.
4. Valkenier, "New Soviet Thinking;" also Jerry F. Hough, "The End of Russia's 'Khomeini' Period," *World Policy Journal*, IV (Fall, 1987), pp. 583-604.
5. Valkenier, "New Soviet Thinking;" see also her book, *The Soviet Union and the Third World: An Economic Bind* (New York: Praeger, 1983).
6. Howard J. Wiarda and Mark Falcoff, with Ernest Evans and Jiri and Virginia Valenta, *The Communist Challenge in the Caribbean and Central America* (Washington, D.C.: The American Enterprise Institute and the University Press of America, 1987).
7. The author of this chapter is particularly fascinated by this new approach in Soviet scholarship because he has often been critical, in a parallel fashion, of the prevailing U.S. orthodoxy on development and, again, like the new Soviet scholars, has championed local, often traditional, and indigenous forms of change. See his *Corporatism and National Development in Latin America* (Boulder, CO: Westview Press, 1981); and *Ethnocentrism in Foreign Policy: Can We Understand the Third World?* (Washington, D.C.: American Enterprise Institute, 1985).
8. For a general discussion of "ungovernability," first applied to the United States but now applicable to the Soviet Union, see Samuel P. Huntington, "The Democratic Distemper," in Nathan Glazer and Irving Kristol (eds.), *The American Commonwealth* (New York: Basic Books, 1976); see also Richard Rose and Guy Peters, *Can Government Go Bankrupt?* (New York: Basic Books, 1978). For Eastern Europe, see Vladimir Tismaneanu, *The Crisis of Marxist Ideology in Eastern Europe: The Poverty of Utopia* (London and New York: Routledge, 1988).
9. This is the subject of a large research project that the author is codirecting for the Foreign Policy Research Institute in Philadelphia; a preliminary statement of some of this work is set forth in the special issue of *World Affairs* cited in note number one.
10. See the essays by Juan del Aguila, Raymond Duncan, and Howard J. Wiarda in Roger Kanet and Edward Kolodziej (eds.), *The Limits of Soviet Power in the Developing World* (New York and London: MacMillan, 1988).
11. Based on interviews and fieldwork in Cuba in the summer of 1987 and spring, 1988.
12. William M. LeoGrande, "Foreign Policy: The Limits of Success," in Jorge L. Dominguez (ed.), *Cuba: Internal and International Affairs* (Beverly Hills, CA: Sage Publications, 1982), pp. 167-192.
13. The first trip was sponsored by the Ford Foundation and organized by the Latin American Studies Association; the second was funded by the Heinz Foundation through the Harvard Center for International Affairs.
14. Nick Eberstadt, "Health, Nutrition, and Literacy Under Communism," *Journal of Economic Growth*, 2 (Second Quarter, 1987), pp. 11-22.
15. Robert Packenham, "Capitalist Dependency and Socialist Dependency: The Case of Cuba." Paper presented at the Annual Meeting of the American Political Science Association, New Orleans, August 29-September 1, 1985.
16. Mikhail Gorbachev, *Perestroika: New Thinking for Our Country and the World* (New York: Harper and Row, 1987).
17. Based on interviews and field work in Cuba in 1987 and 1988.

18. The following analysis is based on interviews on a not-for-attribution basis with foreign policy analysts in the U.S. intelligence community and with academic experts on Soviet sponsorship of Third World radical movements.
19. Alvin Z. Rubinstein, "Soviet Success Story: The Third World," *Orbis*, 32 (fall 1988), pp. 551-567.
20. Howard J. Wiarda, *The Democratic Revolution in Latin America: Implications for U.S. Policy* (New York, NY: Holmes and Meier, A Twentieth Century Fund, forthcoming).

Part Three
Regional Focus: The Conflict in South Asia

7

Moscow and the Regional Conflicts: Afghanistan

Ali T. Sheikh

This chapter argues that the Soviet leader Mikhail Gorbachev's political démarche and strategic gambits in the Southwest Asian region are aimed at adjusting to changing political realities. By slowly distancing itself from the rigid ideological formulations and military posture of the Brezhnev years, Gorbachev's leadership seeks to take advantage of specific opportunities in both Pakistan and Afghanistan. Soviet policy is reflected not only in the completion of the Soviet withdrawal from Afghanistan, but also in Soviet efforts to simultaneously court the political mainstream in Pakistan. Gorbachev's diplomatic agility in the region can perhaps best be explained as the culmination of the evolving Soviet rubric *novoe politicheskoe myshlenie* ("new political thinking").

The section that follows discusses the changing Soviet foreign policy precepts with particular reference to their application to regional conflicts such as Afghanistan. A counterpart of the domestic reform program of *perestroika* and *glasnost*, the "new political thinking" is constantly unfolding in Soviet theoretical and foreign policy debates, and it is still uncertain what ideological expressions and geopolitical manifestations it will finally take. Soviet objectives in the region, however, and some of the changes under Gorbachev can be delineated, and they are outlined in this section. The second section is an analysis of the nature and scope of the present Soviet security policies toward Afghanistan. Soviet policy toward Pakistan is discussed only insofar as it helps us understand the new Soviet outlook on Afghanistan. Finally, we will briefly compare the Afghan conflict with some other regional conflicts in order to offer a comparative perspective for the resolution of regional conflicts on the one hand, and for the broader relevance of the "new political thinking" on the other.

"New Political Thinking" and Regional Conflicts

Gorbachev has frequently maintained that Soviet domestic reforms demand a change in the international situation and has outlined the kind of changes the Soviet Union would like to see. Many Soviet officials, analysts, and publicists have joined him in explaining how Soviet foreign political behavior should be subordinated to the domestic goals of *perestroika*, underlining that domestic reforms would have a positive spillover effect onto foreign policy. They have increasingly criticized the ideological rigidity that resulted in the "careless" application of ideological doctrines to foreign policy during the "stagnation years" of the Brezhnev period, as they are now officially referred to.

An increasingly large number of Soviet scholars have now engaged in lively discussions of hitherto forbidden foreign policy issues. This has gone so far that in more recent writings, many Soviet commentators have criticized the past leadership for various foreign policy decisions, including the decision to send forces into Afghanistan. There have also been semi-official yet unprecedented acknowledgements of the shortcomings of the international Leninist system and its contributions to the tensions and confrontations of the Cold War, the arms race, and conflicts in a number of regions of the developing world.

Security Issues: In the area of national security, there appears to be a dominating trend among Soviet writers to emphasize the interdependence of nations for mutual survival in the nuclear age. It is in fashion now to suggest that the level of military confrontation be reduced on the basis of the relative insecurity of nations and the doctrines of strategic parity and strategic sufficiency. The concept of peaceful coexistence also seems to have been redefined so as to describe not so much a form of class struggle as a long-lasting condition in which states with differing political and ideological systems "cohabit."[1] It is an all-embracing, comprehensive view of international security that cannot be achieved by military and technical means alone, but must also be pursued through political and diplomatic initiatives. This realization has opened the way for a new Soviet approach towards a flexible, compromising negotiating mode in tackling difficulties in the military, economic, and political spheres aimed at removing the sources of mistrust and tension. Such ideas and formulations have been in circulation in the Soviet Union since the mid-1970s, but only the Gorbachev leadership has granted them official sanction and legitimacy.

Institutional Restructuring: It was in the pursuit of new foreign policy directions that Gorbachev initiated structural reforms in the Soviet Foreign Ministry. In May 1986, in an address at the foreign policy conference in Moscow, his critical evaluation of Soviet diplomacy was followed by wide-ranging personnel and structural changes in the Ministry of Foreign Affairs. This has included the creation of a number of new departments to cover various geographical regions and political areas, including the Information Department, headed by Genadi Gerasimov, evidently aimed at creating better public diplomacy, in the spirit of *glasnost*, through daily press briefings. The changes in personnel have resulted in the replacement of about fifty Soviet ambassadors, including those in Pakistan and Afghanistan.

The sweeping changes in the Ministry of Foreign Affairs, however, do not necessarily presage the deideologization of Soviet foreign policy, but are aimed instead at practical realism, marked by flexibility and efficiency, as foreign policy decisionmaking seems to have shifted back to the Central Committee apparatus. Although the changes in the Soviet policy in Afghanistan were facilitated by the evolving "new thinking," the unfolding debate in the Soviet literature highlights that the "new thinking" and the accompanying changes in the decisionmaking, content and conduct of Soviet foreign policy were also largely shaped by the long and expensive Soviet involvement in Afghanistan.

Soviet Economic Interests: Moscow, under Gorbachev, has explicitly placed Soviet economic interests at the center of its foreign policy: "If the main thing for us, the Soviet people, is the development of the economy, social relations and democracy, this also determines our interests in the international arena and our foreign policy interests. . . . "[2] Eduard Shevardnadze's speech to foreign ministry officials in June 1987 went a step further, maintaining that: "The most important thing is that the country should not incur additional expenditures in connection with the need to maintain its defense capability and protect its lawful foreign political interests. . . . We must enhance the *profitability* of our foreign policy and achieve a situation in which our mutual relations with other states *burden our economy to the least possible extent and create a stable psychological atmosphere in which Soviet citizens can work in peace* (emphasis added)." [3] He further urged that it was necessary "to create the optimal conditions" for the economic and social development of the country and called upon the Soviet embassies abroad "to play the role of a forward patrol that follows everything new in the realm of scientific and technological progress, everything that could be of interest to the national economy."[4] In all, the Gorbachev leadership has displayed an unprecedented readiness to use foreign policy as a tool for accomplishing important domestic economic goals. This concern is given a visible expression in Moscow's recent dealings with Iran, India, and to a lesser extent, Pakistan.

Regional Conflicts: A disengagement from the regional conflicts and a willingness to enter various arms control agreements are looked to to provide the stability necessary to reallocate Soviet resources to economic reconstruction on the one hand, and to develop economic and technological cooperation with the West on the other. The recognition of the existence of an international multipolar and interdependent system is reflected in a growing tendency of dealing directly with the countries playing key roles in anticommunist insurgencies in various regions. Moscow has also simultaneously tried to woo other key regional actors, such as China and Japan in the Far East, Indonesia and Thailand in Southeast Asia, Iran and Pakistan in Southwest Asia, Egypt, Saudi Arabia, and Israel in the Middle East, and Mexico and Brazil in Latin America. In other words, the Gorbachev leadership is projecting a world view that seems to move away from the zero-sum game in favor of a broader, interrelated view of the world.

Consequently, Soviet public diplomacy and foreign policy have been rich in sweeping proposals on arms control, disarmament, and other measures for improving East-West relations. Moscow has shown a keen interest in strengthening the United Nations and in joining various international multilateral economic institutions such as the GATT, the IMF, and the World Bank. It has shown a particular receptivity to the Organization of Islamic Countries (OIC) and other regional groupings like the South Asian Association for Regional Cooperation (SAARC). From his July 1986 speech in Vladivostok to his September 1988 speech in Krasnoiarsk, Gorbachev has emphasized improving the Soviet position in Asia. In political terms, Moscow has offered nuclear weapon free zones (NWFZ) in various regions, including the Asia-Pacific region, the South Atlantic, the Korean Peninsula, Africa, the Balkans, Latin America, and Nordic Europe. Zones of peace and cooperation have been suggested for the South Atlantic, the Indian Ocean, and the Mediterranean. More profound proposals on Asia have involved addressing China's three conditions for improving Sino-Soviet relations, the elimination of superpower military bases from Vietnam and the Philippines, and better economic and political relations with the ASEAN countries and Japan. Moscow has also offered a number of world forums, one in particular on the Asia-Pacific region, and a Helsinki-type conference that would negotiate confidence building in the area.[5]

In pushing for the important domestic objectives of *perestroika* of the Soviet society, the Gorbachev leadership seems to have undertaken a far-reaching reassessment of its international position. The issues of *glasnost*, overall East-West relations, arms control, withdrawal from Afghanistan, and gradual disengagement from other regional conflicts all seem to be linked to the first priority of reforming the Soviet economy and rejuvenating the socialist system. Thus besides regional and international variables, domestic circumstances have helped to shape Moscow's decision to withdraw from Afghanistan.

"New Political Thinking" in Southwest Asia: While initially continuing the Soviet policy of involvement in Afghanistan and relations with Pakistan, Iran,

and India along the ideological and strategic lines inherited from various predecessors, Gorbachev in late 1985 nonetheless initiated an ideological and strategic reassessment of Soviet foreign and defense policy in the region. This could be detected in Gorbachev's report to the 27th CPSU Congress in February 1986, wherein there was missing any adverse reference to Pakistan, heretofore fashionable in such Party reports. That the "new thinking" on Afghanistan was underway could also be gleaned from the changed tone of Gorbachev's reference to that country as a *krovotochashchaia rana*[6] ("bleeding wound") and from the fact that Gorbachev, unlike Brezhnev, made no reference to the Afghan revolution or its leader, Babrak Karmal. Further, instead of criticizing Pakistan directly for supporting and housing the Afghan rebels, as had been the practice under Brezhnev, the Party report section immediately following the discussion of Afghanistan expressed a desire to improve relations with all neighbors. Contained herein was an expressed acknowledgement of worsened Soviet political relations and standing in the region as a result of the intervention in Afghanistan, but also the intention to rectify this situation.

In tackling the question of how to achieve this improvement, the Party report only outlined the broader contours of the emerging Soviet policy. More specific contours of the "new political thinking" in Soviet regional policy began to appear after mid-1986, as the debate in the Soviet literature took some definite shape.[7] There were also some significant political changes in the Afghan scene during this period, including Babrak Karmal's dismissal, the appointment of Najibullah as Party Secretary of the People's Democratic Party of Afghanistan (PDPA), his program of National Reconciliation, followed by the so-called unilateral ceasefire offers, approval of the new constitution, local bodies' elections, tribal and national *jirgas* (tribal assemblies), and the accompanying differences between Moscow and Kabul. Although many of these developments had little or no immediate and direct impact, their cumulative effect was to help determine the extent and scope of Gorbachev's "new thinking" on Afghanistan and Pakistan.

The New Policy Towards Southwest Asia

Relations with Pakistan under Gorbachev:

After the People's Democratic Party of Afghanistan seized power in Kabul in April 1978, Pakistani-Soviet relations moved from bad to worse. This changed, however, after Gorbachev's stern warnings to General Ziaul-Haq in a meeting at Chernenko's funeral. Afterward, the chill in Soviet-Pakistani relations began steadily to thaw, passing first through a formative base and then to the current phase of high diplomacy.

While continuing to pursue the previous ideologically rigid policy and militarily threatening posture towards the region during the first, formative phase, the new Soviet leadership also began to make conciliatory gestures and to transmit diplomatic and political signals regarding Afghanistan. By the time Gorbachev visited India in November 1986, this transitory phase had come to an end. Gorbachev even showed an unexpected willingness to sacrifice some of Moscow's goodwill towards New Delhi if that would help Moscow extricate itself from Afghanistan. Gorbachev also refused to commit Soviet uncategorical support for India in the case of any Sino-Indian or Indo-Pakistani conflict. Further, he displayed unusual restraint in not criticizing Pakistan for providing sanctuaries to the Afghan rebels. The second phase, marked by high diplomacy, brought Gorbachev's regional policy to the forefront. The result has been some qualitative changes in Pakistani-Soviet relations during this period.[8] The following major developments have gained momentum since late 1986 and 1987:

Foreign Policy: In the foreign policy domain, Moscow regarded General Zia's Afghanistan policy as totally subservient to the United States. Moscow's contempt was manifested in its refusal to discuss the Afghan crisis directly with Islamabad. Andrei Gromyko, in fact, personally rebuffed Pakistani foreign ministers on many occasions, insisting that the "problem around Afghanistan" was a matter to be directly discussed and resolved only by Pakistan and Afghanistan (and Iran). Under Gorbachev, however, Moscow began to acknowledge that Washington and Islamabad, although converging in their opposition to the Soviet military presence in Afghanistan, did nonetheless partake of different interests. Some of the issues on which Islamabad and Washington held different opinions seem to have been acknowledged, and sometimes even appreciated, by Moscow.

The Islamabad government has traditionally insisted in its public pronouncements that Pakistan was not a sanctuary for Afghan rebels. Even after having lost any plausible deniability, Islamabad also continued to maintain that it was not a conduit for military supplies to the rebels. (In fact, Islamabad has reportedly handled military assistance to the mujahideen directly and almost exclusively, while the United States, suspecting the Pakistani army of "creaming off" these military supplies, was said to have stepped in, in order to check, but not exclusively control, the "leaking pipeline.") Fearing Soviet reprisals, furthermore, Islamabad preferred to keep the Afghan conflict within the limits of Moscow's tolerance. Accordingly, Islamabad was reported to be against stepping up the Afghan insurgency with the introduction of U.S. heat-seeking, anti-aircraft Stinger missiles. Islamabad, moreover, has often been reluctant to allow Western journalists to cross over into Afghanistan openly, preferring that they travel incognito, and has also refused the open use of Pakistani territory to harbor the Soviet soldiers as prisoners of war. Unlike its predecessors, the Gorbachev leadership has displayed an understanding of such delicate and complex issues. By opening up a direct dialogue with Pakistan on the Afghan question, Moscow indirectly acknowledged the geopolitical compulsions of Islamabad's policy on Afghanistan, even to the extent that it suggested the signing of a peace agreement with Pakistan in Geneva that would not require the United States to participate as a guarantor.

Political Order: In the Pakistani domestic context, Moscow viewed Pakistan's imposition of martial law in July 1977 and its subsequent continuation with suspicion and reservation. Although in line with Pakistani popular public opinion, Moscow's disapproval of martial law rule created additional difficulties for conducting normal bilateral relations, which were heightened by the fact that Moscow viewed military rule in Pakistan as a transitory phase. The Gorbachev leadership, however, was quick to come to grips with emerging new realities, and it wasted no time in capturing the subtle and symbolic differences in posture and substance among the politicians, the foreign ministry, and General Zia. The adaptive, evolving attitude of the Soviets has reduced some friction and has further facilitated a formal, direct dialogue between Moscow and Islamabad, particularly since early 1986. In all, it seems that Moscow under Gorbachev has begun to realize that the military sector in Pakistan is a political force to be reckoned with and, despite the setback it suffered with the death of General Zia, well entrenched in the political culture of Pakistan.

Against this backdrop Moscow, in the nonofficial sphere, has of late tried to woo moderate, mainstream political forces in Pakistan. For the first time in the history of their bilateral relations, Moscow has publicly and officially received elements of the Pakistani political opposition and intellectual and religious elites. The political leaders have been of all ideological persuasions, and included the new Prime Minister Benazir Bhutto when she was still only an opposition leader. A stream of journalists have also been hosted in Moscow and/or Kabul. In the past, such practice was restricted to official delegations, underground factions of the illegal communist party, or regional leaders from the Pakistani provinces of the North West Frontier Province (NWFP) and Baluchistan.

Economic Relations: The diplomatic changes have been accompanied by a slow, yet perceptible change in Soviet economic policy. In recent years Soviet interest seems gradually to have expanded beyond traditional areas of economic cooperation and beyond conventional geographical regions to fully include the Punjab and the Sind. Ironically, a major reason is the influx of some three million refugees into the NWFP and Baluchistan, which occurred as a result of the Soviet intervention in Afghanistan. Other factors aside,

Moscow is not likely to consider it safe to send its personnel to conduct surveys and undertake feasibility studies of developmental projects in these provinces.

In pursuance of this emerging trend, Moscow has requested to open a trade center in Lahore, has offered assistance with the next five-year plan, and has recently installed nine power generating units in Multan in what the Soviet ambassador called "the first step" toward cooperation in the "upcountry."[9] Perhaps equally striking has been the reported Soviet interest in investing in some 150 private sector, joint venture projects. Aware of the new Soviet limitations in the provinces, the Soviet ambassador to Pakistan urged the members of the Executive Committee of the Lahore Chamber of Commerce and Industry to consider the "upcountry" for economic cooperation between the two countries. With unusual frankness, he even added: "We feel we have made a mistake by making Karachi the base of our trade activities."[10] This is perhaps also indicative of Soviet disenchantment with the Pushtun and Baluch nationalist leaderships, and perhaps also of Moscow's bitter experience with the Pathan and Baluchi revolutionaries and uncertainty over their future in the politics of the NWFP and Baluchistan.

Gorbachev's Policy in Afghanistan:

Since Gorbachev's accession to power, Moscow has attempted to integrate its political efforts and military strategies in Afghanistan with greater flexibility and clarity of purpose. In military terms, Gorbachev's accession to power coincided with the Reagan administration's decision to increase covert support for the Afghan guerrillas from some $200 million to about $600 million in 1987. Under congressional pressure, Stinger missiles were first supplied in substantial numbers starting in the fall of 1986. Subsequently, the conflict in Afghanistan sharply increased. The loss of Soviet aircraft and helicopter gunships was reported to have increased substantially in early 1987. With the introduction of sophisticated weapons, however, Soviet battlefield tactics and war strategies changed accordingly, and there emerged a renewed effort to mine and interdict guerrilla supply routes from Afghan sanctuaries in Pakistan. Thus, the war increasingly moved towards the Durand Line, the frontier that divides Afghanistan and Pakistan. As we shall now discuss briefly, the stepped-up military operations were coupled with political initiatives as the new Soviet leadership undertook sustained efforts to shed the burden of the Brezhnev years in its Southwest Asian policy.

Diplomatic Initiatives and Glasnost:

In 1987 Moscow and Kabul initiated concerted efforts to lobby the Third World countries to support a less critical resolution on Afghanistan in the

U.N. General Assembly. Kabul was able to restore diplomatic relations with Iraq and Cyprus and to establish new relations with Zimbabwe and Togo. In 1988, in an effort to break its diplomatic isolation, Kabul sent delegations to a number of countries, including Jordan, Iraq, Syria, and Lebanon, followed by Najibullah's visits first to Vietnam and Kampuchea, and then to India, Cuba, and the United Nations.

As already mentioned, the previous Soviet leadership had relegated the Afghan issue to the status of a bilateral problem among Iran, Pakistan, and Afghanistan, and had restricted negotiating for a political settlement to proximity talks in Geneva. The Gorbachev leadership, however, opened many new channels, including a direct political dialogue with Pakistan. After a lapse of four years, Moscow also resumed bilateral discussions on Afghanistan with the United States. Aside from direct discussions between Gorbachev and President Ronald Reagan during the summit meetings, Soviet Foreign Minister Eduard Shevardnadze and the U.S. Secretary of State George Shultz reportedly discussed Afghanistan in almost all of their twenty-seven meetings through September 1988. Gorbachev also explored the possibility of using third parties like the OIC and influential private individuals like Armand Hammer, who was reported to have shuttled at least six times between Kabul, Islamabad, Moscow, and Washington. Finally, Moscow established direct or indirect secret contacts with the local field commanders inside Afghanistan, moderate and fundamentalist mujahideen groups in Pakistan and Iran, and the former Afghan King Zahir Shah living in exile in Rome. Such efforts were coupled with a policy allowing greater *glasnost* in Afghanistan.

Since 1987, the Kabul regime has twice welcomed the U.N. Special Rapporteur Felix Ermacora in Kabul and allowed him access to the notorious Pule-Charkhi jail, in conjunction with the preparation of the annual reports on the human rights situation in Afghanistan. Furthermore, since early 1986 an increasingly large number of Pakistani and Western journalists have been encouraged to visit Afghanistan. This increased further after April 1988 to allow live reporting on the Soviet withdrawal from various cities and military bases. Moscow and Kabul have hoped to create a less hostile image by these visits, an exercise that was sometimes facilitated by the mujahideen's inaccurate use of long-range, ground-to-ground missiles that have often landed on the civilian areas of Kabul and Kandahar. Coupled with these actions is an official PDPA admission of past mistakes, present failures, and future uncertainty over its revolution, reforms, and leadership.

A similar, yet more pronounced *glasnost* on Afghanistan has become even more visible in the Soviet Union itself, and is reflected in the media coverage of the Afghan conflict both in Moscow and in the Central Asian republics. Many private associations of Afghan veterans have mushroomed, and there is a greater degree of debate and discussion in the U.S.S.R. Soviet leaders and diplomats have increasingly admitted that the decision to send forces into Afghanistan was a mistake—an admission that is reportedly circulated among Party cadres as part of the official Party record and history. Now, for the first time, the number of Soviet forces in Afghanistan, their casualties, performance, and difficulties have also been made public and are discussed with an unprecedented frankness. Many Soviet writers have accused, with increasing bluntness, the past leadership for its "wrong assessment" of the Afghan revolution and for sending in a "limited contingent." Some writers have even compared the war in Afghanistan with the war in Vietnam.

National Reconciliation: The basic principles of this ideological doctrine, which parallels the initial stage of national democratic revolutions, urge slowness and caution in reforms while suggesting a retreat to political pluralism, a mixed economy, and ideological blending with such popular beliefs as Islam, for example, in Afghanistan. Initially, the Soviet leadership encouraged a process whereby the Afghan ruling party should broaden what was then called "the social base of the revolution." In the second phase of Soviet political strategy, this process of broadening the "social base of the revolution" was given the new rubric of "national reconciliation" wherein the caution and slowness employed during the national democratic revolutionary stage were elevated from the level of tactical maneuver to strategic plan. Essentially this is a newer version of the earlier united front strategy—except for the obvious fact that the united front strategy was articulated with the communist movements in mind. The process of national reconciliation is primarily targeted at the national democratic revolutions and their ruling vanguard parties.

In many respects the process of national reconciliation can be viewed as a response to the anticommunist insurgencies in an era of "new political thinking." In Afghanistan, for example, the concept of national reconciliation has included movement toward a ceasefire and inclusion of non-PDPA members in the proposed national government. During 1986 and 1987, the Soviet commentators continuously lauded the concept of national reconciliation and its achievements in Afghanistan. From the first quarter of 1988, however, the Soviet media have periodically asserted that, since the PDPA has renounced its own revolutionary program, the justification for continued Soviet fraternal assistance has ceased to exist.[11] It is precisely this process of national reconciliation that has provided the Soviets with the ideological justification to withdraw fraternal assistance. In other words, the process of national reconciliation that initially was perceived as a ploy to perpetuate PDPA rule by generating greater legitimacy has in effect denied it the same.

Moscow-Kabul Friction: The concept of national reconciliation and the Soviet decision to withdraw troops from Afghanistan in nine months sharpened the differences between Kabul and Moscow. These differences were publicly aired on a host of theoretical and other issues. In political and military terms, the question of the Soviet withdrawal was perhaps the most contentious of all between Moscow and Kabul. Kabul was initially reported to be less than receptive, first to the idea of any particular promptness in the withdrawal and later to the bilateral assurances Moscow gave to Washington and Islamabad during the last phase of the Geneva negotiations. Kabul was also reported to have been in opposition to the principle of a front-loaded withdrawal, symmetrical suspension of supplies to the combatants, and later, the continuation of American supplies to the mujahideen. Add to this Moscow's disinterestedness in Kabul's desire to resolve the boundary issue with Pakistan before signing the Geneva Accords, or at least using it to extract concessions in Geneva; and Moscow's ambiguity on the question of continuation of Soviet fraternal assistance and advisors in Afghanistan. A fundamental clash of interests and strategies became so obvious that Moscow even threatened to withdraw its troops without a formal agreement. Gorbachev had to personally intervene to iron out such differences by calling the Afghan leader Najibullah to Tashkent for a joint statement.

An important area of Soviet/Afghan divergence has been over the handling of the process of national reconciliation. Kabul has focused on wooing foes in the resistance ranks, particularly the rank and file from the Peshawar-based mujahideen groups, and on the return of refugees. Though not publicly opposed to this track, Soviet strategists have emphasized the need to approach the military commanders inside Afghanistan. It was on this track that Kabul, revising its earlier decisions whereby the revolutionary court had sentenced in absentia several guerrilla commanders to death, entered into secret negotiations with many local field commanders.

In the second half of 1988, Moscow initiated three sets of negotiations with the Afghan resistance. The first consisted of direct and indirect contacts with the field commanders inside Afghanistan. These in some cases have resulted in local, temporary truces, providing Kabul with a breathing space, ensuring the safe withdrawal of Soviet troops, and guaranteeing a continued supply of Afghan gas to the Soviet Asian republics. Second, Moscow established direct contacts with the former Afghan King Zahir Shah and, through U.N. mediators, with other Afghan expatriates such as Abdul Samad Hamid, Abdul Satar Sirat, and Abdul Wakil. The primary purpose of this dialogue was to bring, through the United Nations, moderate and secular elements into the proposed coalition government. Finally, Moscow entered into direct negotiations with the Peshawar based seven-party alliance and the Iran-based eight-party alliance of the Shiite groups. The declared purpose of these negotiations was to bring these groups into a broad government in which the PDPA would also be a participant. According to the Soviet negotiator Yuri Vorontsov, the Soviet deputy foreign minister and ambassador to Kabul, the Soviet objective was also to bring them to one table to "find their views, their intentions."[12]

The mujahideen leadership perceived these Soviet negotiations as an attempt to create differences among various groups. Ironically, however, it has served more to unite the mujahideen than have previous efforts to do so by their major supporters and suppliers like Saudi Arabia, Pakistan, and the United States. In the January 1989 round of talks in Islamabad, before the mujahideen decided not to continue with such meetings, a representation of Iranian groups coordinated their negotiating strategies with the guerrillas in Islamabad. These were the first formal contacts between the Iranian- and Pakistani-based groups. Further, the two groups were represented in one delegation and since then, there have even been some efforts, so far unsuccessful, to combine the two alliances into one coalition government. Vorontsov himself acknowledged that his negotiations were "uniting them in a new government in Afghanistan."[13] These broadened Soviet negotiations with the mujahideen have, however, further added to the growing friction between Moscow and Kabul.

More fundamentally, the concept of national reconciliation and "new political thinking" are irreconcilable. An updated version of the united front strategies, national reconciliation primarily revolves around anti-imperialist slogans and strategies. The "new political thinking" in Soviet foreign policy, on the other hand, seeks an accommodation with the West and the United States. In line with the theoretical formulations of the "new political thinking," Moscow and Kabul have been more critical of alleged Pakistani violations of the Geneva Accords than of the United States, who after all has been the primary supplier of weapons to the mujahideen. In numerous protest notes it has so far filed with the United Nations Good Offices Mission in Afghanistan and Pakistan (UNGOMAP), Kabul has accused Pakistan of violating the Geneva Accords, often without directly criticizing the United States. This is in stark contrast to previous policy, wherein the accent of Soviet and Afghan pronouncements used to be on "international imperialism" and, wherein Pakistan, very often without mentioning it by name, is referred to as "the local reactionary." Further, in some respects, this accommodation with the United States is reminiscent of the World War II era, when Stalin's united front strategy against fascism sought an accommodation between the Communists in the colonies and their European colonial occupiers. It was perhaps against this background that Fidel Castro, publicly showing his reservations on the new Soviet policies in July 1988, claimed that he was now the only living anti-imperialist revolutionary.

Withdrawal: In April 1988, Islamabad and Kabul agreed in Geneva on a nine-month withdrawal period and on a "front-loaded" withdrawal. This implied the disengagement and withdrawal of about fifty percent of Soviet forces from Afghanistan by August 15, 1988, and the remaining by February 15, 1989 (See Appendix A, Geneva Accords on Afghanistan). The principle of a front-loaded withdrawal, however, had both political and military meanings, as a substantial number of Soviet air and ground forces were stationed in front garrisons in the south, along the Durand Line, in the west, and along Iran's border with Afghanistan. A front-loaded pullout also had geographical implications. The front-loaded withdrawal from the south of the Gardez-Kandahar axis and in the west along the Kandahar-Herat axis, completed by mid-August 1988, cleared almost all of the Iran-Afghan frontier and virtually all of the Afghan-Pakistani border.

In other words, the Soviet capability to initiate offensive military operations from inside Afghanistan was qualitatively reduced by August 1988. This was partially demonstrated in August when upon the withdrawal of Soviet forces, the city of Kunduz near the Soviet border temporarily fell to the resistance and the Soviets publicly refused to help Kabul reoccupy the city. During the entire period of the Soviet pullout, however, neither the withdrawing Soviet units were seriously threatened by the mujahideen nor, more importantly, did Moscow reintroduce essential combat units. Moscow did, however, undertake some air strikes from its bases in Central Asia.

The completion of the Soviet withdrawal left the Afghan garrisons with a considerably reduced capability to conduct large-scale operations. So far, it seems that the Afghan units have tried to maintain provincial headquarters by surrounding them with mine fields, air supplies, and reinforcements, and by offering financial inducements to the tribesmen in the neighboring areas. Their capability to maintain an air bridge with the military posts and garrisons would depend largely on the performance of the Afghan Air Force and the mujahideen's anti-aircraft capability—both factors dependent on external actors.

The Geneva Accords did not promise an end to the fratricidal war. In essence, the United States and the Soviet Union have continued, if not escalated, the supply of military equipment to the combatants. The Geneva Accords gave Soviet leader Mikhail Gorbachev a fig leaf to cover the recall of Soviet forces, but history may yet record this as the first Russian military humiliation in Asia since the Russo-Japanese War in 1905. It is, however, the first Soviet retreat from Asia since 1946, when Stalin withdrew from the Iranian provinces of Northern Kurdistan and Azerbaijan. Although both of the republics in northern Iran collapsed within six months, the withdrawal did not entail a renunciation of Soviet interests and objectives in Iran. However, the Soviet withdrawal from those areas was followed by a strengthening of the central (Shah's) authority in all of Iran, whereas the Afghan case has so far entailed a political and military vacuum that neither the PDPA nor the mujahideen groups are expected to effectively fill any time soon.

Afghanistan and the Other Regional Conflicts

Afghanistan is the only regional conflict that bears direct implications for the Soviet Union, as it is the only country where the Soviet interests can be traced back to the 1920s—or, for that matter, to the Tsarist times—and the only regional conflict in which the Soviet army was directly involved in active combat operations. Moreover, it is the only regional conflict whose zone is geographically contiguous to the U.S.S.R.; on both sides of the Amu Darya there live Tajiks, Kirghiz, and Turkmen. Finally, it is the only national democratic revolution in which the Soviets militarily intervened in its defense on the express grounds that they would not let the revolutionary process there be reversed as it was in Chile.

Such peculiarities of the Afghan case aside, the Soviet leadership has often stated that the Geneva Accords have set an example for the resolution of other regional conflicts. The same optimism has been expressed by many analysts in the West. Four major features that are unique to Afghanistan in this regard deserve mention.

First, besides the negotiations on Angola, the Geneva Accords were the only peace agreements whereby the combatants did not directly negotiate with each other. In two other regional negotiations (Nicaragua, Kampuchea) the warring parties have met face-to-face several times. Second, the Afghan Accords were negotiated and signed under the auspices of the United Nations. In no other peace negotiations was there any visible, direct role for the United Nations, except in the Iran-Iraq war, which falls into a different category of regional conflict. Third, the Geneva Accords in some respects have resulted in the de facto recognition of the PDPA government by Pakistan, as they indirectly negotiated but directly signed the accords and, in the future, would consult each other if there were any differences and difficulties in the peace process, and would set up joint commissions for the repatriation of the Afghan refugees. Fourth, the withdrawal of Soviet forces from Afghanistan was bilaterally decided by Kabul and Moscow and formally it was not part of the four instruments of settlement signed in Geneva. [Ironically, it was not even filed with the Geneva Accords the way the "U.S. Letter of Intent" on supplies to the mujahideen was filed.] In all, therefore, it is only with some qualifications that the Geneva Accords can be considered a "model" for the resolution of other regional conflicts. From the standpoint of their precise relevance, the Geneva Accords reflect a two-track policy on the part of Moscow:

The first track sought a quick Soviet disengagement and withdrawal from Afghanistan, while the second track continues to aspire to and explore the possibility of the continuation of PDPA rule. The first track seems to have greater relevance for the possible Cuban and Vietnamese force withdrawals from Angola and Kampuchea respectively, and the second track appears to offer greater relevance for the question of future survivability and consolidation efforts of the Leninist order in Nicaragua, Ethiopia, and perhaps South Yemen.

Conclusion

This chapter has analyzed Soviet efforts to extricate its forces from Afghanistan in the context of Gorbachev's domestic agenda of reform and restructuring. It is now argued in the Soviet Union that the level of world military confrontation be reduced on the basis of the relative insecurity of nations and the interdependence of survival. The underlying assumption is that the domestic goals of *perestroika* and *glasnost* would have a positive spillover effect in the domain of foreign policy, as economic interests are now increasingly placed at the center of Soviet foreign policy.

We have seen in this study that under the rubric of the "new thinking," Moscow aspires to see the formation of a national government in Kabul. Kabul, in an attempt to create a coalition government, has offered the mujahideen twenty-eight ministerial portfolios. The resistance formally refuses to be a partner to anything in which the present ruling party is a participant, be it the Geneva Accords or the suggested broad-based government envisioned by Moscow, Islamabad, or the United Nations. The mujahideen are likely to continue fighting, first to overthrow the PDPA regime in Kabul and second among themselves in a war of fratricidal revenge. Such infighting, already seen within the Peshawar-based mujahideen groups, between them and the field commanders, and among the field commanders inside Afghanistan, already seems to have increased.

Kabul has also offered the governorship to the "strongest" field commander in each of the thirty provinces. Depending on Kabul's survival, some commanders may use such offers to strengthen their positions vis-à-vis their Peshawar-based political leaders. Yet this offer may carry a great price—the price of inevitable squabbling that exhausts the guerrilla ranks before they reach the besieged city-state of Kabul. By deliberately allowing the smaller groups and some field commanders to overrun some of the military posts and bases, however, Kabul has sought to create many new "strongest" military commanders not only to negotiate peace and possibly co-opt them into the process of national reconciliation, but also to encourage the emergence of new warlords, who in turn would compete for influence and authority with the seven-party alliance in Pakistan.

Adjusting to the emerging uncertainties of Pakistani political order in post-Zia Pakistan, the Reagan administration sent a special envoy to Islamabad to help the Afghans step up their political and military campaigns to replace the PDPA regime. Yet, as Kabul is likely to be defended by two or three security rings and special forces, the real struggle for the capital is expected to be prolonged after completion of the Soviet pullout. Two factors will play a part in determining which groups become more serious contenders for power: first, the organizational ability to capitalize on military victories or compensate for setbacks in the battlefield; and second, the degree of unity within the ranks of the combatants. Neither the Kabul government nor the mujahideen have a particularly impressive record in this regard.

The survivability of the Kabul regime now depends less on how much weaponry it receives from Moscow and more on the performance of the Afghan combatants. The mujahideen's dependence upon international political and military support continues to be the single most important factor in their future ability to maintain both their operational effectiveness and their alliance of seven parties in Peshawar. The "Principles of Mutual Relations, in particular on Non-Interference and Non-Intervention," one of the bilateral agreements signed between Kabul and Islamabad in Geneva, envisaged a complete denial of Pakistani assistance to the guerrillas, including the possible use of its territory for American supplies. In line with the so-called "positive symmetry" (specified in the "U.S. Statement" filed with the Geneva Accords; see Appendix A), which ensures uninterrupted military supplies to the combatants, Moscow and Washington have continued to provide weapons to their clients in Kabul and Peshawar. Nor have the mujahideen groups shifted their functional headquarters to locations inside Afghanistan. If the mujahideen fail to establish a recognizable parallel government inside Afghanistan soon, the continued supplies to the two sides will only perpetuate the national civil war in Afghanistan. In either case, the prospects of a de facto partition or a "Lebanization" of Afghanistan may continue to haunt Moscow and Washington in coming years.

To a large degree, it was General Zia's personal influence over various mujahideen groups that preserved the unity of the seven-party alliance. It was because of pressure by Pakistan that the mujahideen groups did not seriously threaten the Soviet forces withdrawing from Afghanistan. Furthermore, it was through General Zia's personal preference that the fundamentalist groups were favored in receiving support from Saudi Arabia and the United States. Recent squabbling over the question of future government and operational strategies to launch frontal attacks in cities like Jalalabad, Kandahar, and Kabul shows that the traditionalist groups are now becoming more assertive in regard to their position against the fundamentalists. This has further increased since the general in charge of cross-border support through Pakistan's military intelligence was dismissed by Prime Minister Bhutto. If Zia's personal choice of supporting certain groups among the Afghan resistance fails, the fundamentalist groups among the resistance ranks might no longer prevail in terms of Pakistani backing and American supplies.

Soviet media coverage of Pakistan recently seems to have undergone subtle yet qualitative changes. Some Soviet media pronouncements have again become markedly critical of Islamabad's continued involvement in Afghanistan in violation of the Geneva Accords. Whether they have been aimed at inciting the Soviet audience or are reflective of a change in Moscow's policy in 1989 is too early to say. More important, Islamabad's continued support for the Afghan resistance is often portrayed as jeopardizing the process of normalization in Afghanistan as outlined in the process of national reconciliation. In other words, recent Soviet pronouncements seldom classify these violations as a threat to the Afghan revolution, to which recent media reports rarely reaffirm Moscow's commitment.

In this chapter we have seen that Kabul's program of national reconciliation has provided Moscow an ideological pretext for withdrawal. Since the PDPA has abandoned its initial revolutionary goals, Soviet commentators contend the justification for continued fraternal assistance no longer exists. Against this background, Moscow does not seem to have an ideological justification to reintroduce a "limited contingent" in Afghanistan. Moscow, however, has not abandoned its traditional security concerns and the right to invoke them.

The Soviet withdrawal from Afghanistan has left behind a regime in Kabul that insists on continuing its rule, with or without the mujahideen's participation in the proposed coalition government. We have noticed in this chapter the emergence of public friction between Kabul and Moscow. Feeling betrayed by Moscow's abandonment of its revolution and leadership, the party cadres and Kabul's middle classes are already jumping the sinking ship. In this sense, perhaps history will attribute Kabul's eventual fall, if and when it occurs, as much to the mujahideen's struggle as to the PDPA's bloody internal feuds, demoralization resulting from Moscow's ideological and political abandonment, and betrayal of a national democratic revolution in an era of "new political thinking." Thus, while the application of Gorbachev's "new thinking" to Afghanistan ended the war for Soviet soldiers through military disengagement, the new Soviet approach to foreign policy could not restore peace in a country torn apart by Moscow's past mistakes.

Notes

1. For Shevardnadze's comments on class struggle, see "XIX Vsesoiuznaia Konferentsiia KPSS: Vneshniaia politika i diplomatsiia," *Pravda*, July 26, 1988, p. 4.
2. Interview with TF-1, 30 September 1985, as cited in Roderic Lyne, "Making

Waves: Gorbachev's Public Diplomacy, 1985-1985," in Robbin F. Laird (ed.), *Soviet Foreign Policy, Proceedings of the Academy of Political Science* (Vol. 36, No. 4, 1987), pp. 235-253.
3. *Vestnik Ministerstva inostrannykh del S.S.S.R.*, No. 2, 1987, p. 31.
4. Cited by Milan Svec, "U.S.S.R. and Foreign Policy: *Perestroika* Begins at Home," *Christian Science Monitor*, January 28, 1988, p. 13.
5. *Pravda*, July 29, 1986.
6. *Pravda*, February 26, 1986, p. 8.
7. See, for example, Nikolai Kapchenko, "The CPSU Foreign Policy Strategy and Today's World," *International Affairs* (October 1987), pp. 65-75.
8. Parts of the following discussion are derived from my articles, "The New Political Thinking: Gorbachev's Policy Toward Afghanistan and Pakistan," *Asian Survey*, (Vol. XXVIII, No. 11, November 1988), pp. 1070-1087.
9. *Dawn*, Karachi, December 11, 1987, p. 10.
10. *The Muslim*, Islamabad, December 22, 1987, p. 10.
11. See, for example, Aleksander Prokhanov, "Afganskie voprosy," *Literaturnaia Gazeta*, February 17, 1988. For academician Oleg Bogomolov's reply see, "Kto zhe oshibalsia?", *ibid.*, March 16, 1988.
12. "Pullout depends on situation," *Dawn*, January 5, 1989, p. 5.
13. *Ibid.*, p. 5.

8

Gorbachev's "New Thinking" on Regional Conflicts in Light of the Soviets' Afghan Experience

Sabahuddin Kushkaki

Background

The Soviet decision to help bring into power the People's Democratic Party of Afghanistan (PDPA) in 1978, and later to intervene militarily in Afghanistan to sustain the gains made, have had adverse consequences for Soviet policies both at home and abroad. Western scholars are still debating the Soviet Union's involvement in the overthrow of President Mohammad Daoud's regime in April 1978, but knowledgeable Afghans can point to numerous indications of Soviet intent that emerged prior to that time. For example, even as far back as 1976 the two estranged wings of the PDPA were brought together under Soviet auspices. As the purpose of this paper is to assess the consequences of the U.S.S.R.'s new policies vis-à-vis Afghanistan, further details about the degree of Soviet involvement in the 1978 coup will not be offered here.[1]

Increasing Involvement

Until deciding to invade Afghanistan militarily, the Soviets kept a low profile in their involvement in Afghanistan because they did not want to show that the PDPA regimes of Noor Mohammad Taraki and Hafizullah Amin were actually directed by Moscow. However, a day-to-day survey of events before the Soviet invasion in December 1979 amply shows that the Soviets had already become deeply involved in Afghan daily internal affairs by sending thousands of military and civilian advisers to work in Afghanistan,[2] increasing assistance to the new government, becoming a defender of the Kabul communist regime in the international arena, and signing a mutual defense treaty with Afghanistan in December 1978. The Soviets opted for a direct intervention in Afghanistan when they realized that the client Kabul regime was no longer able to defend itself. Soviet opportunism was also conditioned by perceived weakness in the Western leadership and the absence of another power in the region to check Soviet moves. The Soviets were expecting international protests against the invasion, but not to the extent that they would mar the image of Moscow as a friend of the Third World or hinder its relationship with the West, which elected to impose boycotts and even suspended ratification of an arms limitation agreement.

Effects of Military Intervention

Internal

At home, Moscow has kept a very low profile in regard to the intervention in Afghanistan. However, with the passing of time it became impossible to hide the impact of this involvement on Soviet society. The Afghan war has cost the Soviet Union thousands of lives and, coupled with Moscow's involvement in other regions, has become a grave liability and a drain on the Soviet economy.

The claims that the Soviet army had entered Afghanistan to protect Soviet interests and to uphold a fraternal Leninist state at the invitation of its government were not sufficient to win national support for the intervention. One maxim of politics states that governments, no matter how dictatorial, cannot completely ignore public opinion for a long time. The Afghan case proves its veracity. The Soviets intervened in an Afghanistan with which they claimed they had had excellent relations for a quarter of a century, despite different social and political systems. This would explain the failure of the Soviet leadership to legitimize its military policy vis-à-vis Afghanistan to its own public, which failure in turn was an influential factor in the Soviet decision to finally leave the country.

From an economic point of view, the Soviet Union found the Afghan war a great burden. In the final stages of active Soviet military involvement, Moscow was spending billions of dollars annually to support the Kabul regime. This comprised a significant amount of the total funds that Moscow spent on its involvement in regional conflicts. The Soviets in turn benefitted from the Afghan economy, notably from vast natural gas resources; and in the event the country could be pacified, they could also benefit from iron ore reserves in the north, copper mines in the south, and reported uranium deposits in the west. Additionally, Afghanistan served as a training and testing ground for the Soviet military. Yet the overall returns did not justify the scale of Moscow's involvement. Furthermore, an unprecedented number of Soviet soldiers became addicted to drugs in Afghanistan, and this is said to be deleteriously affecting Soviet society. The vivid demonstration of the "invincible" Red Army's inability to defeat the resistance of a people with no or little arms has affected morale in the Soviet army and scarred the collective Soviet memory.

Regional

Afghan Resistance. Although the Afghan resistance forces have stated they will not undertake a hostile course against Moscow once they have established a government in Kabul, they do so only for the sake of their own interests, not from any sympathy toward the U.S.S.R. It is difficult to believe that Afghan sentiment towards the Soviet Union will be the same as before the war. Even then, despite a quarter century of mass Soviet military and economic assistance, Soviet-Afghan relations were not amicable. Afghanistan has traditionally been suspicious of Moscow, and despite Mohammad Daoud's decision in 1953 to accept large amounts of Soviet aid, the common Afghan still considers Russia an enemy of Islam.

Iran. Despite the fact that an estimated one million Afghans sought refuge in Iran[3] and the Afghan mujahideen were more or less allowed to move freely in and out of the country, relations between the Islamic republic and the Soviet Union grew steadily better while the Soviet aggression and atrocities were still at a full scale in Afghanistan. The Soviet Union, perhaps at its own turn, was very happy to see Iran engaged in a war against Iraq, because as a result, the Iranians considered winning that war their primary objective, and, in order to maintain open relations with the U.S.S.R., ignored what the Soviets were doing in Afghanistan.

Pakistan. Other than on Afghanistan itself the Soviet invasion of Afghanistan has had the largest and strongest impact on Pakistan. Pakistan has become a second home for more than three million Afghan refugees and a godfather to the Afghan jihad. Although a number of leftist parties have tried to force the Pakistani government to abandon its support for the Afghan resistance, and although the degree of this support has declined as time has passed, the fact remains that Pakistan has been the staunchest supporter of the cause, and the average Pakistani is very well aware of the dangers of a permanent Soviet presence in Afghanistan. In spite of the death of President Mohammad Zia ul-Haq, the Pakistani support of the Afghan cause is going to remain quite strong until a government supported by the resistance is formed in Kabul, because the Pakistanis (1) will not and cannot drive the refugees out of their territories; (2) are still aware of the inherent dangers of a Soviet client state in Afghanistan, which—once feeling itself secure—can serve as a springboard for further Soviet expansion in the region; and (3) will try to undermine the presence of a pro-Indian government on its western flank.

India. Although India failed to condemn the Soviet military intervention in Afghanistan in public, privately it has been said that the Indian government was urging Moscow to withdraw its troops. Meanwhile the failure of the Indian government to publicly condemn the invasion, its support of the Soviet puppet regime of Kabul, and its hostile vision of the resistance have created major stumbling blocks in Afghan-Indian relations.

China. The Soviet invasion of Afghanistan further deteriorated the already strained relations between Beijing and Moscow. The Chinese made the withdrawal of Soviet troops from Afghanistan one of the prerequisites for improvement in their relations with the Soviet Union. The Chinese not only vehemently opposed the invasion, but they did not refrain from rendering political and, reportedly, military support to the Afghan resistance.

Global

From a global point of view, the Soviet attempt to preserve the Leninist-oriented regime in Kabul boomeranged. The insignificant role that Afghanistan played in international affairs before the invasion and the low priority that the Western world attached to political and economic relations with Afghanistan were probably considerable influences in the U.S.S.R.'s decision to assist the PDPA's rise to power and then to intervene militarily to sustain the regime that was to safeguard Soviet interests.

Throughout the years since the Soviet Union invaded Afghanistan, Moscow has launched numerous public relations campaigns to induce the world to accept the Afghan situation as a fait accomplí. However, as a result of the continuous and valorous resistance of the Afghan people and sustained world rejection of the Soviet moves and policies, the Afghan issue continued to haunt the Soviet Union in international forums as well as in its bilateral relations with other countries. The Afghanistan issue was an obstacle in Soviet-American relations and, despite the remoteness of Afghanistan from U.S. interests, U.S. public opinion stood fast to deny Moscow the privileges it was seeking to gain and preserve in Afghanistan. Afghanistan assumed a central role in American thinking, especially when, in 1984, a group of hardliners in Congress forced the administration to escalate its military and humanitarian assistance to the Afghan freedom fighters.

Western Europe was reluctant in the beginning of the invasion to follow the American lead in penalizing the Soviet aggression. But as time passed, European policies also became great political and psychological deterrents to the Soviet policies in Afghanistan. Among the European countries, France, bolstered by its socialist parliament, was exceptionally critical of the Soviet war in Afghanistan.

However, other than voting in favor of resolutions urging a Soviet troop withdrawal from Afghanistan at various forums, the Third World countries, including a number of Moslem nations, did not actively try to induce the Soviets to reverse their policies in Afghanistan. Countries like India not only refrained from publicly condemning the invasion, but continued their bilateral relations with the Kabul puppet regime. A number of Islamic countries, such as Syria, Algeria, and Libya, either voted against resolutions condemning the Soviet invasion, abstained, or decided not to participate in the voting. The Palestine Liberation Organization opted to condone the invasion. A number of other Islamic countries, such as Kuwait, the United Arab Emirates, and Egypt (after the death of President Sadat) pursued policies of rapprochement with Moscow despite the ongoing Afghan war. At one stage, before the signing of the Geneva Accords on Afghanistan, Kabul's Foreign Minister was received in both Kuwait and Jordan. Iraq maintained normal, friendly diplomatic relations with Kabul. The Organization of Islamic Conference (OIC) in its final summit held in Kuwait in 1987 hardly mentioned the Afghanistan issue in its final communique, merely welcoming the peace and reconciliation program announced by the Kabul regime. Yet this program was condemned by the resistance—a resistance which the OIC had vowed to support. While the OIC suspended the membership of the Kabul regime, it refused to allow the Afghan mujahideen to represent Afghanistan.

The Gorbachev Approach

It appears that the Kremlin decision to pull its troops out of Afghanistan was based on four factors: (1) the continued stubborn resistance of the Afghan people; (2) human losses of at least 13,500 dead and 35,000 wounded as of the spring of 1988;* (3) economic losses; and (4) the staunch international and particularly American support for the Afghan resistance.

Under Gorbachev, the U.S.S.R. seems to attach top priority to its relations with the West, the United States in particular. Any factor that would not bring direct benefits or could be considered a liability or a hindrance to better superpower relations seems not to play a determining role in the Kremlin strategy. The U.S.S.R.'s relationships with the developing countries will be secondary in Moscow's strategy, especially to the extent that they drain Soviet resources.

The U.S.S.R. attaches importance to its relations with the West for the obvious reason of wanting to take advantage of opportunities to catch up in the economic sphere. Bringing the Soviet Union up to the economic standards and affluence of the twentieth century Western powers is of utmost importance to Gorbachev and his associates. The Soviet military intervention in Afghanistan was certainly a hindrance to the realization of Gorbachev's strat-

---

*The Soviet war dead reached 15,000 by the first day of the withdrawal, February 15, 1989.

egy because it negatively affected Moscow's relations with the rest of the world, but especially with the United States.

The Geneva Gimmick

Since the signing of the Geneva Accords on April 14, 1988, the Soviet Union has been claiming that the model used for solving the Afghan conflict could be applied in solving other regional issues as well. This analysis is spurious for the simple reason that the Geneva agreement was only a face-saving device for the U.S.S.R. to pull out its troops, as Moscow had already said it would withdraw regardless of whether there was an accord. In all other respects, the accords have either served the Soviet interests or have failed to solve the inherent problems of Afghanistan. Worked out under the auspices of an organization standing for the right of nations to freedom and self-determination, the Geneva Accords have (1) failed to recognize the Afghan resistance, which upheld these very principles; (2) failed to involve in the negotiations the two parties directly involved in the conflict—the Soviet Union and the Afghan mujahideen; and (3) failed to stop outside interference in the internal affairs of Afghanistan.

The Afghans consider the Geneva agreement, so much revered by the Soviets, as traitorous to their cause because it treats the Afghan issue as merely a bilateral problem between two countries and views the remarkable Afghan resistance as merely a refugee problem. The agreement fails to address the core of the problem, the cause of the Afghan insurgency. For this reason the Geneva agreement will fail to bring peace in Afghanistan or the subsequent return of the refugees to their homes. (See Appendix A, "Geneva Accords on Afghanistan.")

What's New in Gorbachev's Policy?

Now the question is, "What is *really* new in Gorbachev's policy toward Third World regional conflicts?" It would be naive to think that the U.S.S.R. will somehow abandon the opportunities it believes exist in various regions of the world unless it is forced to do so for reasons such as we saw in the Afghan case. The Soviets entered Afghanistan because they mistakenly believed that an opportunity existed for them that would entail only a small investment. They later left Afghanistan not because they thought the policy to enter the country was wrong, but because they were unable to quickly digest their prey due to its stubborn resistance and the sustained world reaction in its support and against the suffering of the common Afghan people.

In order to demonstrate that the so-called "new thinking" is yet another version of Soviet opportunism, one should phrase the argument this way: Had the Afghans not resisted and had the Soviets quickly achieved their objectives in the few months immediately after the invasion, would Gorbachev today be saying that the policy to invade Afghanistan "militarily" was basically wrong? This is doubtful. As a matter of fact, the Soviet military machine conducted the most devastating portions of its operations in Afghanistan from the time that Gorbachev came to power in 1985 until late 1988. Only when Moscow set economic development as a high priority was there talk about withdrawal and national reconciliation, which includes building a coalition government with the "opposition."

But for the sake of avoiding lengthy discussions of this issue, let me make a final observation: According to the "new thinking," Soviet involvement in regional issues should be justifiable from political, economic and strategic points of view. If it is determined that the liabilities are greater than the potential rewards, contemplated or actual involvement will certainly be curtailed. Otherwise Moscow will stick with the old line. Excepting when there are expenditures that will be considered a drain on the Soviet economy or mar Soviet relations with important third countries, there is no reason for Moscow to change its current position regarding regional issues. Neither is there any reason to think that, under the proclaimed "new thinking," there will be any fundamental change in traditional Soviet foreign policy objectives. The correlation of forces, as far as the Soviet Union is concerned, is such that Moscow has no incentive to give up its position as a superpower. Indeed, a whole series of hectic Soviet efforts to "catch up" economically is aimed exactly at enabling Moscow to achieve economic might and power equalling that of the United States.

Yet as a superpower, it is essential for the Soviet Union to maintain spheres of influence in many parts of the world, i.e., Cuba in the Western Hemisphere, Vietnam in Southeast Asia, Ethiopia in the Horn of Africa, Angola and Mozambique in Southwest and southeast Africa, Syria in the Middle East, South Yemen in the Gulf, India on the subcontinent, and possibly Kabul on the gateway to South Asia.

Gorbachev's Dilemma

It is naive to assume that the Soviet Union will adhere to a number of prescribed principles in assessing and implementing its foreign policy. The "peaceful coexistence" of Nikita Khrushchev after the Cuban missile crises, the policy of détente initiated by Brezhnev, and now the so-called "new thinking" have all been catch phrases for achieving the traditional Soviet objectives of survival and domination, and they lead to Soviet behavior that can only be characterized as opportunistic.

To be fair, however, the extent to which Gorbachev adheres to the principles of Leninism will ultimately determine the very nature of his reforms.

Communism by its very nature—the dictatorship of the proletariat on the one extreme; and a stateless society, a paradise on earth, on the other—is an unattainable utopia, which the Soviet Union tries to make seem attainable and meaningful by resorting to opportunism and often hypocrisy. The alternative is that communism will not remain true to itself, or that the Soviet Union will have to admit that true communism cannot be attained.

Clearly the Soviets are just making a number of adjustments in their policies. Opportunism in the communist system, so much evident in Soviet policy, both in theory and in practice since the time of Lenin, will continue to be a prime mover. It was this very policy of opportunism that tempted the Soviets to go into Afghanistan. A document circulated by the leadership of the CPSU in the summer of 1988 states that the Soviet leadership fundamentally erred in believing that a tribal, Islamic country like Afghanistan was ready to make the transition to socialism. But Taraki and then Amin (the first PDPA leaders after the 1978 coup) both said repeatedly that the Afghan experience was unique in the history of Leninism in that Afghanistan did not have to pass through its traditional stages to become a full-fledged Leninist state; and that the PDPA, by achieving full Leninist development in Afghanistan found a shorter route. This statement was obviously aimed at reconciling the "Afghan Revolution" with Leninist theory. But it is in reality another manifestation of Leninist opportunism.

Option for the Future

Afghanistan

The Afghans do not anticipate that the new Soviet diplomatic initiatives vis-à-vis Afghanistan will contribute to a resolution of the regional strife in and around their country. To think that the Geneva Accords—or, for that matter, the "new thinking"—provided a basis for attaining such a resolution is unrealistic. The Geneva agreement, in addition to failing even to recognize the existence of a just resistance to the type of aggression that is clearly prohibited under international law, also failed to address the issues that are believed to have induced Moscow to intervene militarily in Afghanistan. (See Appendix A, "Geneva Accords on Afghanistan.") It was because of the strong national resistance that threatened to topple the Leninist regime in Kabul that the Soviets sent in their troops. As long as that regime remains intact, the war will not end in Afghanistan. Not only will there be no peace in Afghanistan, but Pakistan and Iran, the two countries immediately affected by the Afghan situation, will not be able to return the Afghan refugees to their homes.

Currently, the Soviet Union sends all kinds of military and economic aid, short of soldiers, to save the Kabul regime. Whether this aid will succeed is debatable, and indeed doubtful, but it does clearly demonstrate a lack of consistency in public Soviet policy. If Moscow understands the vulnerability of its puppet regime, and it must, its continued support of the regime is contradictory to the professed desire for a peaceful, nonaligned and independent Afghanistan.

What will happen if there is no peaceful transition in Afghanistan after the Soviet withdrawal? If the Kabul government is violently overthrown, would the Afghan resistance forces be able to establish a government supported by the people? Right now, despite many differences, the resistance is represented in the seven-party alliance known as the Islamic Unity of Afghanistan Mujahideen (IUAM). They are as united in their determination to overthrow the Kabul regime as they are united in their war to drive the Soviets from Afghanistan. But if the resistance overthrows the Kabul regime, would the Afghans be able to agree on a philosophy and action of government? The IUAM is comprised of four "fundamentalist" factions and three "liberal" factions.[4] These factions worked out a charter and have appointed a president and twelve ministers for a transitional government. Originally they had said they would form a twenty-eight member government with half the members from the mujahideen, one quarter from the Afghan refugee community (exiles not working within the mujahideen organizations), and the remaining one quarter from "Moslems" inside Afghanistan. In addition to setting up a government, they have proposed the establishment of a seventy-five-member council, comprised of fifty-six elected members with the remaining twenty chosen by the leadership. Finally, they have promised the establishment of a reconstruction commission and have invited educated Afghans to apply for positions in this commission.

The idea of establishing a coalition with the PDPA cannot be considered by the IUAM. The diehard PDPAs are seen as part of the Soviet occupation forces, and resistance forces want PDPA members tried for war crimes or deported. The rejection of PDPA participation in the future government of Afghanistan is shared by the entire spectrum of relevant Afghan political figures.

The mujahideen proposal for the inclusion of Moslems living inside Afghanistan has not been officially explained, but as far as the resistance is concerned, this will be the maximum compromise it will be willing to make with forces currently active around the Kabul regime. It is safe to assume that this coalition would not include communist sympathizers, as the terms "communist" and "Moslem" are mutually exclusive, surely in Afghanistan.

But if the resistance succeeds in dismantling the Kabul regime and yet is unable to form a government supported by a wide spectrum of the people, will the war continue? If so, Afghanistan will relapse into another period of bloodshed and darkness. If the Afghans fail to form any kind of viable administration, two other scenarios are being suggested by some observers: (1) a no-government situation; and (2) a partitioned Afghanistan possibly divided between north and south; or along northern, southern, and western divides, each being under the influence of respective neighboring countries. The historical responsibility for evolving an effective and realistic administration lies squarely on the shoulders of the Afghans in the IUAM.

The Soviet Union

If the Soviets are sincere in their claim that they want an independent, nonaligned, and peaceful Afghanistan, they must cooperate in the establishment of a government based on the new realities of the Afghan scene emerging after ten long years of an ideologically-oriented resistance. Even if the Soviets support the formation of a government based on the will of the majority of the Afghan people, that government must in no way be a security threat to the Kremlin. The Afghans must maintain a reasonable working relationship with the Soviet Union because of interests stemming from the country's two major constraints—(1) being remote from the Western powers, and (2) being landlocked.

The future Soviet-Afghan relationship cannot have a sentimental base. It must be businesslike. The Soviets have to realize the consequences of their longstanding policy towards Afghanistan, which has resulted in utter devastation of the country, and try to build their ties with Afghanistan accordingly. The important factors that must be reckoned with are (1) the long Afghan memory of the atrocities committed against them in the war, and (2) the Afghan commitment to Islam. It would be folly for the U.S.S.R. to ignore the Islamic revival in Afghanistan, and it should therefore base its relationship with the new Afghan government on a new record. It should in no way support another communist movement or try to reverse the Islamic trends. Even during the era of communist rule in Afghanistan the Soviets realized this, and thus, the Kabul regime often had to address its "respect" for Islam, if only for tactical reasons.

The Afghans, too, have to realize and work with their country's constraints. Once the Afghan question is more or less settled, the country will no longer remain an area of vital interest for the Western powers. There might be a relapse to the pre-1978 status quo. Afghanistan, as a landlocked country with meager resources of its own, must always be concerned about opening and keeping access to the rest of the world. It must maintain some kind of working relationship with the U.S.S.R. in order to import essential items and, more important, have easy access through Soviet territory to the Western world.

The idea of gaining access to an easy route to the West from Afghanistan was very much in vogue in the early seventies when the Afghans solved their longstanding dispute with Iran over the Helmand River, which originates in Afghanistan and flows into Iran. The Afghans had just embarked on the construction of a transit route straight to Bandar-e-Abbas in Iran, where under a bilateral agreement, they would have acquired their own port facilities. But under present conditions, from a practical and economic point of view, the land route through the Soviet Union is the most feasible route for the Afghans. At any rate, even if only for the sake of having options, Afghanistan must have a transit route through the U.S.S.R. The kind of scenario worked out here is based on hard realities that have emerged in Afghan-Soviet relations. Among the Third World countries, Afghanistan presents a unique situation for the Soviet Union, and the Soviet Union has a unique status for Afghanistan. Yet one must be realistic and work out the kind of practical relationship that will deter a repetition of the unparalleled tragedy of the previous decade.

Pakistan

For Pakistan, the emergence of a brotherly Islamic regime on its western flank would be quite rewarding and would thus alleviate the threat from both East and West. What kind of Islamic state ought to emerge in Afghanistan should also be of great concern to Pakistan. The continuation of war and strife in Afghanistan will only harm Pakistani interests. Once establishing that no administrative institutions other than those reflecting Islamic values will be viable in Afghanistan, such an administration would find it easier to prevent a revival of the controversies and disputes that once marred Afghan-Pakistani relations.

Pakistan's relations with the Soviet Union after the establishment of a noncommunist Afghan government—in all probability an Islamic one— cannot expand dramatically because of Moscow's relationship with India, which is more important than its relationship with Pakistan. And for the Soviets, with the Afghan experience fresh in their minds, it will be impossible to subvert Pakistan into a client state despite the existence of certain Soviet client parties inside the country.

Pakistan will certainly be faced with new constraints in its relations with the West as well, once the Afghanistan issue is solved. The United States must find newer and more convincing justifications for rendering massive military assistance to Pakistan or risk damage to its relations with India. Once the Afghan problem or threat is solved, any substantive military aid to Pakistan will be interpreted by India as a threat. The anti-Pakistani Washington lobby will also make fresh attempts to weaken or even sabotage Pakistan's nuclear program. In short, even with the emergence of a friendly government in Kabul in the aftermath of the Soviet withdrawal, the international constraints for Pakistan, especially in its efforts to check Indian hegemony, will further increase.

India

India's belated attempts to influence Afghan internal politics have antagonized a wide spectrum of the Afghan people. India kept quiet about the Soviet military intervention and atrocities and supported the Kabul regime against the Afghan resistance. Now the Indians are trying to sustain the PDPA, or at least influence the establishment of a liberal government that will refrain from joining Pakistan to any extent in threatening India. In the future India may promote old Afghan-Pakistani disputes.

The Soviets will support India or at most will jointly work for the establishment of a government in Kabul that will not be considered an Islamabad-Kabul axis, i.e., an Islamic regime. Or maybe the Soviets and Indians both are contemplating a partitioned Afghanistan, with the provinces north of the Hindu Kush under their sway. Even a very weak Afghanistan with an ongoing and protracted civil war would be more preferable to them than an Afghan-Pakistani alliance.

Iran

Following the end of the eight-year-old Iran-Iraq war in 1988, it will be difficult to assess the nature of Iran's relations with the West. But regardless of the factors that might influence future Iranian policies toward the West or the communist bloc, taking into view the historical realities between Afghanistan and Iran, it is difficult to foresee a blossoming of relations between them.

In the case that the civil war continues in Afghanistan after the collapse of the Moscow client state in Kabul, the Iranians would certainly help the Shia sections who now have their headquarters in Iran, although two major groups of such Shias are now operating mainly from Pakistan, reportedly due to differences with the Iranian authorities.

China

China has welcomed the Soviet withdrawal from Afghanistan. The invasion and occupation were one of the official impediments that, according to the Chinese, barred improved Chinese relations with Moscow. If one of the motives for Moscow in calling off its military involvement in Afghanistan was to please China and normalize Sino-Soviet relations, it should be quite natural for the Kremlin to eliminate other obstacles that bar normal dealings between them.

To what extent the Chinese are going to have a say in Afghan political affairs is very difficult to assess. In the sixties, during the heyday of the

Cultural Revolution, the Chinese actively supported one of the factions of Afghan communism: "The New Democratic Party" or Shula-e-Javid. During the war, the Soviets and the Kabul authorities at one stage launched an intense campaign to eliminate the Shula-e-Javid elements from the ranks of forces that fought the Soviets. Abdul Majid Kalakani, whom the party claims was their leader after the downfall of the monarchy in Afghanistan in 1973, was executed in early 1980 after he was captured by the Kabul regime. For at least two years afterward many efforts were made to annihilate the remnants of the Shula-e-Javid within the ranks of mujahideen fighting the Kabul regime and the Soviets. Later the Communists attempted a rapprochement with these elements. The ups and downs of the relationship between the Kabul regime and the pro-Chinese Afghan Communists correlates with the type of relationship Moscow sought to maintain or develop with China.

China, before 1978 and especially during the last ten years of the Afghan monarchy, had a limited degree of economic and technical ties with Afghanistan. It will most likely try to upgrade those ties once a noncommunist government in Afghanistan is established. China's relationship with the resistance forces has been good, and the Chinese are said to have been rendering effective military aid to the mujahideen. Their political support for the Afghan cause has been valuable.

The World

It is essential for the rest of the world to try to determine the ultimate aim of the new Soviet policies. Are they really aimed at bringing about fair play or are they merely a tactical change aimed at bettering public relations to gain support for the Soviet economic upgrade? As suggested, when analyzing Gorbachev's "new thinking" in the context of regional affairs, one must first determine whether the Soviet Union is willing to abandon Leninist principles or whether this whole new experiment is a new tactic to obtain the same foreign policy goals.

Conclusion

The rest of the world should take advantage of the new thaw in Soviet policies but should proceed with caution. It may not be wise to give too much rope to an adversary. From a position of strength, the U.S.S.R. would again be able to challenge the rest of the world and resort to inciting "revolutionary movements" for the benefit of building up the communist empire. Afghan leaders have an old saying backed by experience: "Son, never trust the Russians."[5] The Afghan people are convinced there will never be a fundamental change in Soviet expansionist policies. If this were to happen, it would be a miracle of history.

Notes

1. The organized Afghan resistance refuses to treat the Afghanistan issue as a regional conflict, insisting it has international dimensions. The Soviets have termed it a "regional" issue to downplay its international significance.
2. The Soviet secret police were involved in the so-called Kabul government "attempt" to free the kidnapped American Ambassador Adolph Dubs, February 14, 1979.
3. One million Afghans were already in Iran, mainly as workers, before 1978.
4. None of them like to be labeled liberal because of the connotation the term carries in the West.
5. Afghan King Abdul Rahman's (1880-1901) advice to his son King Habibullah.

Part Four
Regional Focus: The Conflict in Africa

9

Africa After Gorbachev's Rise to Power: Angola and Ethiopia

Colin Legum

Introduction

Soviet policy under Mikhail Gorbachev shows two distinctly different approaches to the conflict situations in southern Africa and the Horn of Africa. This paper explores the possible reasons for these differences and examines the changes in priority-setting (if not necessarily in thinking) in Soviet policy in the subcontinent, particularly in South Africa itself. An attempt is made to clarify the relations between the U.S.S.R. and Cuba, and between the U.S.S.R. and its local allies. This chapter is divided into four parts: a brief background to the Soviet involvement in both the regions under survey; the U.S.S.R.'s role in the peace negotiations on Angola and Namibia; the U.S.S.R.'s policy toward South Africa; and, finally, an attempt to explain why Gorbachev appears to be following two different policies toward the conflicts in southern Africa and the Horn of Africa.

Southern African Background

Since the formation of the Comintern in the 1930s, there have been only three significant pro-Moscow communist parties in Africa: those in Egypt, Sudan and South Africa (the South African Communist Party [SACP]). Until the mid-1960s the SACP's role and influence were minuscule, though it was treated with exaggerated concern by successive governments because it was the only political party that advocated majority rule, attempted to organize black workers and peasants, and had close ties with Moscow. Its actual membership never reached more than a thousand or so. The reasons for its lack of success were that it was led mainly by whites and Indians but, especially, because it was viewed with hostility by the historic black nationalist movement, the African National Congress (ANC), which rejected its overtures to create a united front. However, in the 1940s, the ANC accepted a broad alliance of Congress movements, which included, not the SACP itself, but two of its front organizations; and in the 1950s it allowed black Communists to join the ANC as individual members, providing they declared an overriding loyalty to the cause of African nationalism. These two decisions were among the reasons cited by the black consciousness leader, Robert Mangaliso Sobukwe, for the breakaway of the Pan-African Congress (PAC) from the ANC in the late 1950s. Earlier leaders in the ANC Youth Wing—notably Nelson Mandela and Oliver Tambo, now the two leading figures in the ANC—were strongly opposed to all ties with the Communists.

Conflict between black nationalism and communism remained sharp until 1960 when the apartheid regime (elected in 1948) banned all the Congress movements, having earlier passed a law for the suppression of Communism. A new chapter opened in the mid-1960s when the ANC-in-exile embarked on an armed struggle and established its military wing, Umkhonto we Sizwe (MK—the Spear of the Nation). Shunned by all the Western powers, the MK turned for support to the communist world; which was readily forthcoming. This gave the SACP the opportunity to act as the link between the ANC and Moscow, which in turn opened the way for the SACP to get what it had for so long sought in vain to achieve: a close alliance with the black nationalist movement. The extent to which the SACP today exerts influence within the ANC is a matter of conjecture and controversy. The Pretoria regime takes the view that the ANC is now led by Communists and is "a tool of Moscow"—a view strongly denied by the ANC leadership itself. What is not open to question are the close ties that have developed between the ANC and the Soviet bloc.

Although the Soviet bloc also supports the armed struggle of the South West African People's Organization of Namibia (SWAPO), the Communists play little or no role in that movement. However, because the political and military headquarters of SWAPO are located in Angola, it has come to rely heavily on arms and military training from the Soviet, East German, and Cuban presence in that country.

The historic role of the U.S.S.R. in South Africa has been to encourage a revolutionary struggle with the ultimate aim of seeing a Leninist type government emerge in the country, which it regards as a Western bastion and an ally of NATO. Undermining Western influence and strategic links in South Africa has therefore been a strategic, if long-term, objective of Moscow.

Moscow's support for the anticolonial liberation movements in Africa created opportunities for extending Soviet influence to Angola and Mozambique after the collapse of Portuguese colonialism in 1974. (The situation in the two countries was actually different at the time of their independence, since the

Front for the Liberation of Mozambique (FRELIMO) was allied to the Chinese during the period of acute Sino-Soviet rivalry; but after independence, FRELIMO's leadership switched to the U.S.S.R. as a more credible strategic ally against South Africa. These links, however, were always fragile).

Cuban and Soviet military intervention in Angola at the time of independence was decisive in securing victory for the Movement of the People's Liberation of Angola (MPLA) against its two rivals for power, the Union for the Total Independence of Angola (UNITA), led by Dr. Jonas Savimbi, and the Front for the National Liberation of Angola (FNLA), led by Holden Roberto.

The spearhead of the military intervention was provided by the Cuban combat troops which, at various periods, numbered between 35,000 to 50,000. It is arguable whether the Cubans were proxies for Moscow or whether Fidel Castro acted as an independent Third World revolutionary leader; but even those who lean to the latter view do not dispute that the Cubans could not have maintained their military role without the support of the U.S.S.R.

While the role of the Cuban forces has been to help the Angolan army in the actual fighting, the Soviet bloc (especially the U.S.S.R. and East Germany) has provided the arms, military training and limited economic aid. Their aid was inadequate to meet Angola's needs for its recovery program after the withdrawal of the Portuguese, and the U.S.S.R. has actively encouraged the MPLA government to seek aid from, and to develop its trade with, the West.

Despite Cuban and Soviet military aid on an increasing scale, the Angolan army has been unable to crush UNITA's military challenge or to prevent the South African army from being freely deployed on Angolan territory in its fight against SWAPO and in support of UNITA.

After thirteen years, this prolonged and inconclusive military struggle had two major results: 1) it brought Angola to near economic collapse and prevented the MPLA from establishing its authority over the whole country and from pursuing its original aim of creating a Leninist state; and 2) it has weakened the MPLA's confidence in the ability of the U.S.S.R. and Cuba to serve as effective strategic allies and economic partners.

The Horn of Africa Background

Over the centuries, the Russians had always shown a strong interest in securing access to "blue sea ports" in the Red Sea and the Mediterranean. This perceived national interest acquired a much higher priority for the U.S.S.R. when, as an ascending superpower, it needed ports around the world to strengthen the sea power of its modern navy.

At the time of the overthrow of Emperor Haile Selassie in 1973, the U.S.S.R. had a military treaty with Ethiopia's unfriendly neighbor, Somalia, which gave its navy access to Indian Ocean ports at Berbera and Mogadishu. The military facilities offered by these ports were of relatively small value, especially as compared with those of Ethiopia, which, besides, is a country of considerable economic potential and carries political importance in the continent.

The refusal by the United States and other Western powers to meet the large military demands made by Ethiopia's post-imperial regime left an opening for the U.S.S.R. to form a military and political alliance with the struggling new regime in Addis Ababa; but this meant abandoning its alliance with Somalia which was in conflict with Ethiopia over border claims in the Ogaden province. It also meant ending Soviet support for the premier Eritrean Independence Movement (the EPLF), which the Soviets had clandestinely supported during the Emperor's reign.

Moscow's decision to switch allies in the Horn of Africa was a bold and risky venture, taken at a time when Ethiopia was in a state of considerable political turmoil with no predictable outcome of the power struggles raging in the country at the time, and with burgeoning civil wars over much of the old empire. Moreover, the Soviet-trained and equipped Somali army was readying itself to invade Ethiopia to "liberate" the Ogaden.

Nevertheless, once a treaty was secured with the military regime of Colonel Mengistu Haile Mariam in 1975, the U.S.S.R. mounted a major operation by sea and air to bring in massive quantities of arms, planes and tanks, while the Cubans dispatched an expeditionary force of 14,000 men to counter the Somali invasion of the Ogaden.

It seems clear that the high-risk decision to establish an alliance with Ethiopia was largely influenced by the Soviet military establishment, and particularly by the Admiral of the Soviet Navy, S. G. Gorschkov. His regular appearances in Ethiopia up to the time of his recent retirement suggest a close personal interest in the development of Soviet-Ethiopian relations. In his book, *The Politics of Sea Power*, and in his other writings and speeches, Admiral Gorschkov emphasized, *inter alia*, the strategic importance of the Red Sea and the Indian Ocean in maintaining the military-political role of the Navy in "protecting state interests." Other Soviet military and political writers described the region as "the epicenter of the national liberation movement." Ethiopia is therefore a significant block in the building of the U.S.S.R.'s geostrategic interests.

Moscow did not, however, confine its interests in Ethiopia to purely military affairs. For the first time in its dealings with African states it adopted a systematic policy of channeling the nascent revolution along communist lines by helping to create thousands of cadres, schooled in Leninism, capable of acting as a vanguard movement. It worked patiently, and with some positive results, in guiding Mengistu's military regime to establish a "people's democratic republic" that acknowledges the U.S.S.R. as "the leader of the world's progressive forces" (to quote President Mengistu).

Soviet policy in Ethiopia has also been radically different in some other respects from elsewhere in Africa. Apart from its considerable military aid, the Soviet Union has diverted relatively large amounts of economic and technical aid to Ethiopia, which stands fourth only to Cuba, Syria, and Vietnam as a recipient of Soviet largess—a strikingly different response from the commitment the U.S.S.R. was willing to make to either Angola or Mozambique. All of this says much for the special priority given to Ethiopia by Moscow.

The failure, thus far, to consolidate the communist revolution in Ethiopia is due in large measure to the resistance of the national movements, particularly in Eritrea and Tigre, which have become stronger rather than weaker over the past decade. Despite a series of major military offensives (usually planned by Warsaw Treaty Organization military officers), the Tigreans now control over eighty percent of their region, while the Eritrian People's Liberation Front (EPLF) has repeatedly inflicted severe defeats on the Ethiopian army. (In their largest major victory early in 1988, the EPLF captured four Soviet officers at the front.)

There is no sound reason for supposing that the regional conflicts inside Ethiopia can be suppressed by military force; the regions themselves have proved to be impermeable to the revolutionary ideas promoted by the Mengistu regime. The Soviet leadership has not been blind to the strength of feelings of the various regional forces fighting either for state autonomy within a federal system (as in the case of the Tigreans, Oromos, Danakils, and others); or for complete independence as in the case of the Eritreans. Moscow has continuously urged upon the Mengistu regime the need for a political settlement of these conflicts by addressing the question of nationalities. It is sensitive to the fact that the leaderships of the Eritreans and Tigreans have in the past professed themselves to be Marxist-Leninists who now denounce the Soviets as "imperialists." But the Soviet advice to Mengistu on this issue, as well as on the need to adopt more pragmatic economic and agrarian policies, has been mostly disregarded.

Despite the strong disagreements with Mengistu over Eritrea, the U.S.S.R. has nevertheless continued to give full military backing to the regime's attempts to crush by military force the EPLF and the Tigrean People's Liberation Front (TPLF) resistance. The Cubans, on the other hand, adopted a more principled stance. Having been largely responsible for defeating the Somali army in the Ogaden, Castro refused to allow his combat troops to be deployed in Eritrea against the EPLF, a movement which he, like Moscow, had supported during the Emperor's reign. There seems to be little doubt that if Havana had yielded to the repeated requests of Mengistu, the Cuban forces could have had a major impact on the fighting in Eritrea. Instead, Cuba's military forces have been drawn down to the point where the few hundred men still in the country are now engaged mainly in military training. The distinction made by Castro between his army's role in the Ogaden and his refusal to send them to Eritrea is that, in the former, the army was helping to defend Ethiopia against foreign attacks, whereas in the latter, where Castro recognized the existence of a genuine national resistance movement, the army would have been the outside aggressor.

The U.S.S.R.'s Role in the Political Negotiations over Angola and Namibia

Ever since Gorbachev announced his interest in cooperating with the United States to help in the peaceful settlement of regional conflicts, he has shown a positive attitude to the American efforts to secure the withdrawal of Cuban and South African troops from Angola and to secure Namibian independence through the implementation of the U.N. Security Council's Resolution 435 (SCR 435). The two principal issues in the conflict situation in Angola were the withdrawal of all foreign troops from the country, and the ending of the civil conflict between the MPLA and UNITA. The U.S.S.R. and the United States were in agreement that the latter issue is a domestic one that does not properly belong to the area of international mediation. On the issue of withdrawal by Cuban and South African troops, however, the two superpowers found themselves in full agreement.

Both privately and publicly, the U.S.S.R. encouraged the MPLA government to pursue the efforts made under American chairmanship to reach agreement over the parallel withdrawal of Cuban and South African troops, while willingly restricting its own role in the negotiations to that of an observer.

Castro, who has all along insisted that the continued presence of his combat troops would depend entirely on the wishes of the Angolan regime, proved himself to be a willing participant in the recent negotiating process even though it has meant sitting around the same table with the Pretoria regime under an American chairman.

Despite the initial objections to linking the issue of the withdrawal of foreign troops to that of Namibian independence, all the parties in the negotiations finally came to accept that linkage was an indispensable part of the negotiating process, although the Angolans and Cubans insisted on presenting the settlement in Namibia as part of parallel talks.

The U.S.S.R. played a constructive if not prominent part in the negotiations that led to the final agreement among Angola, Cuba, and South Africa on December 23, 1988 (see Appendix B, Agreements for Peace in Southwestern Africa). Its contribution was praised by the United States, which invited the Soviets to be present at the formal signing of the agreement ceremony in the United Nations. There is, as yet, insufficient hard evidence to determine whether the Soviets were in fact required to intervene at the more difficult stages of the negotiations by using their influence with either the Angolans or the Cubans; but what is clear is that without the supportive role of Mikhail Gorbachev in placing himself firmly behind the Americans' mediating role, agreement would have been unlikely, or perhaps even impossible to achieve.

The U.S.S.R.'s Policy toward South Africa

Even before Gorbachev's advent to power, Soviet policy toward the conflict in South Africa began to show signs of change in its emphasis on the need for a politically negotiated settlement. However, Moscow gave no public hint of this policy, which was conveyed through diplomatic channels to the African governments. This policy change did not involve any lessening of Soviet support for the ANC or for its armed struggle, nor was it accompanied by any softening of attitude over the question of comprehensive mandatory sanctions against South Africa.

The important changes made by Gorbachev are that he openly declared the Soviet preference for a negotiated settlement in South Africa as opposed to encouraging a violent challenge to the apartheid system through the ANC's armed struggle, and that he encouraged Soviet academics to air their views publicly on the issues raised by a more peaceful approach to Pretoria. This shift of policy was expressed in the private talks conducted bilaterally between Dr. Chester Crocker, the U.S. Assistant Secretary of State for Africa, and Anatolii Adamishin, a Soviet Deputy Foreign Minister. After one round of talks in London, Adamishin stated in an interview with the BBC that the U.S.S.R. wished "to avoid suffering . . . a bloody death in South Africa," and added: "We think we have common interests with America in stability in the region, and that sometimes we can take useful steps with the Americans."

Gorbachev himself spelled out the change of approach during talks he held with the Mozambican President, Eduardo Chissano, in Moscow in August 1987. "Soviet policy," Gorbachev told Chissano, was "not directed towards obtaining a unilateral advantage in Southern Africa." The future aid, he said, would concentrate more on humanitarian and economic projects rather than on the supply of weapons. The U.S.S.R., he added, did not support the argument of "the worse, the better."

The first public sign of independent thinking among Soviet academics on the South African question came in a paper read by Gleb Starushenko, a corresponding member of the Soviet Academy of Sciences, to a Soviet-African conference in Moscow in June 1986, in which he made proposals for compromises by the ANC to facilitate the chances of getting a negotiated settlement. He stressed the need to reassure white South Africans about their future by offering them guarantees to protect their group interests—a point of fundamental difference with the ANC—and by reducing the concerns of businessmen over future economic policies. An official Soviet spokesman confirmed that, while Starushenko was speaking as an independent academic, the general thrust of his paper's support for finding a negotiated settlement was in line with official policy but that he went too far in voicing the kind of compromises he thought should be offered.

A more authoritative view than Starushenko's was stated by Dr. Victor Goncharev, the Deputy Director of the Institute of African Studies of the Soviet Academy of Sciences in an interview with a Johannesburg publication, *Work in Progress*, in June 1987. He emphasized that the U.S.S.R. "should take into account the global problems and the global consequences of our behavior in every part of the world." While he insisted that the "fundamentals" of Soviet policy in southern Africa had not changed, since "it had never seen the region as an arena for superpower rivalry," but that "there may be changes and differences of approach to these problems . . . to behave more realistically, more flexibly, with every side participating in the resolution of the conflicts." More significantly, he expressed some doubts about ANC attempts to put the "socialist revolution before a national liberation struggle." While he felt that the ANC should not cease all "socialist propaganda," it should put more stress on the issues of national liberation; otherwise, they risked losing "potential allies" in South Africa. In a surprisingly frank forecast he expressed the view that it would take "black South Africans at least ten years to achieve their liberation, but that it could take from twenty-five to one-hundred years to bring about a socialist revolution."

The more flexible approach shown by Soviet official spokesmen and by academics coincided with a major policy statement of Joe Slovo, the secretary general of the SACP and a person who has always closely hewn the Moscow line. Supporting the need for a political settlement of the conflict in South Africa, he explained that the Leninists saw the struggle as passing through two phases: the first being the "national liberation struggle" which could be achieved through political negotiations; and the second being the "national democratic revolution" which could begin only after the national liberation struggled had been won.

The ANC itself has always favored the idea of a negotiated political settlement as being preferable to a continued armed struggle. Its differences with the Pretoria regime are over the prerequisites for ensuring meaningful negotiations to take place.

Although the Pretoria regime continues to see South Africa as the target for "a total onslaught" by Communists, there have been some recent signs of a ready willingness to test the sincerity of Gorbachev's *glasnost* policies.

An Assessment of Current Soviet Policies on Africa's Regional Conflicts

Gorbachev's policies reflect two substantial changes in Soviet policy toward some of the continent's regional conflicts: its keen support for the American initiative over Angola and Namibia; and its public endorsement of a preference for a negotiated political settlement in South Africa rather than for an intensified and prolonged armed struggle to smash the apartheid system through revolutionary force. However, Soviet policy shows no sign, as yet (early 1989), of being willing to support an initiative to deal with the conflicts in Ethiopia and the surrounding countries of the Horn of Africa (i.e. Somalia, Sudan, and Djibouti). When President Ronald Reagan briefly raised the possibility of talks over Ethiopia during the 1988 summit meeting in Moscow, his attempt was brushed aside by Gorbachev with an ambiguous answer that left the impression that he had either not yet addressed himself to the conflicts in and around Ethiopia, or that he was not prepared to approach the conflict in Ethiopia in the same way as Angola or Afghanistan.

The situation that faces the U.S.S.R. in Angola, as in Afghanistan, is considerably different from that in Ethiopia. In Angola and Afghanistan the U.S.S.R. found itself on the losing side or, at least, being pushed heavily to the defensive, leaving disengagement as an attractive way of getting itself out of possibly even greater difficulties. There was little more the U.S.S.R. could do, or was willing to do, to strengthen its position in Angola, where a continuation of the recent escalation in the fighting had threatened to result in major war between the Angolan army and the Cuban combat forces against the military power of the South Africans. In such an eventuality, the U.S.S.R. could have found itself in an extremely difficult position if called upon to save its allies from a probable humiliating military defeat. There were also economic considerations in continuing to defend the Soviet position in Angola. Moreover, the MPLA government had begun to be a shaky ally that was increasingly looking to the Americans as being a more likely diplomatic ally and capable of influencing the South Africans to quit Angola. The MPLA has long since given up any hope of finding economic salvation for the country's economic problems through reliance on the U.S.S.R. For Gorbachev, therefore, the prospect of disengaging from Angola had many more attractions than disadvantages.

The situation is quite different in Ethiopia where the U.S.S.R. is still on what seems to be a possible winning side, and where it has major strategic interests in securing for its navy access to two good ports on the Red Sea, Assab and Massawa, as well as useful facilities on the Dalik islands. Since it is fairly certain that the Soviet military establishment still sets a high priority on retaining Soviet military facilities in the Red Sea, and since the "new thinking" does not mean the U.S.S.R. is abandoning its aim of strengthening its position as a superpower which, *inter alia*, depends on strengthening the position of its navy by enabling it to travel across the seven seas with as much freedom as the American navy, it would require a major change of strategic thinking in the Kremlin before there can be any likely prospect of Gorbachev's policies leading to a weakening of Soviet support for Ethiopia. While Gorbachev seems willing to take on the reluctant conservative elements in the party bureaucracy to achieve his policies of *glasnost* and *perestroika*, it seems highly unlikely that, at this stage, he would take on his military establishment as well, and still hope to succeed.

However, the Mengistu regime is still a long way from consolidating itself in power. The wars in Eritrea and Tigre appear to be unwinnable, even with greater Soviet military aid. The likely prospect, therefore, is that the U.S.S.R. will continue to provide even more military aid for the regime in Addis Ababa (as, indeed, it was in late 1988 in preparation for yet another major offensive in Eritrea to reverse the Ethiopian army's continuing disastrous defeats.) From the Soviet point of view, the best hope lies in persuading the Mengistu regime to achieve a political settlement internally, and without the efforts of international mediators; whether Moscow can succeed in convincing Mengistu to find a political settlement, or whether a successor to Mengistu may be both willing to talk peace to the rebel movements and to rely on close ties with Moscow, remains moot. But so long as the Mengistu regime does not appear to be in any immediate danger, there seems little reason for supposing that the U.S.S.R. will be ready to include the Horn of Africa on the agenda for cooperation with the United States in working for the resolution of regional conflicts.

To sum up: the essential difference between the situations in Angola and Ethiopia is that, in the latter case, the U.S.S.R. has a strong strategic interest to develop its role as an ocean power and, at least for the time being, appears to have a strong and reliable ally; whereas in the case of Angola it has neither strong strategic nor economic interests and was engaged with an increasingly skeptical ally. So far as South Africa is concerned, the possibility of the U.S.S.R. expanding its influence is, at the very best, a long-term possibility depending on the eventual outcome of the "national democratic revolution," which is set to begin only after the "national liberation struggle" has been won, and the shortest route to achieving the first result (national democratic revolution) lies down the path of a negotiated settlement.

Ethiopia, therefore, remains a much stronger test than that offered by either

Angola or South Africa of the genuineness of the Soviet desire to promote the ending of all regional conflicts. However, should things begin to go seriously wrong for the Mengistu regime or a successor pro-Soviet regime, it is not altogether impossible to foresee a change of Gorbachev's policy, since even the Soviet military establishment is unlikely to attempt "an Afghanistan" in Ethiopia to prop up an unpopular regime.

It is only when either of the superpowers is in a relatively strong position and has no perceived major strategic or economic interests, that one can look forward, with any confidence, to their being willing to cooperate in the resolution of every single regional conflict in the world.

10

The U.S.S.R. and Conflict in Southern Africa: Angola and Namibia

H. De V. Du Toit

An important internal determinant of Soviet foreign policy is the belief that the U.S.S.R.'s status as a Marxist/Leninist superpower, achieved with much sacrifice and suffering, must be maintained but also expanded. As Erik Hoffmann put it, " . . . Brezhnev transformed the U.S.S.R. into a military superpower . . . Gorbachev is determined to create a multifaceted superpower."[1]

This entails the upgrading of the political, economic, and scientific-technical components of Soviet national security. If this does not happen, the U.S.S.R. will not be able to compete with the United States militarily, and even the presently undisputed military component of its superpower status will wane. Most important, in the words of Gorbachev at the 19th All Union Conference of the CPSU in June 1988, "Socialism will die unless we reform the political system."[2] That this is the *fons et origo* of Gorbachev's concepts of *perestroika, glasnost,* and *novoe myshlenie* is the premise of this chapter. In many statements and speeches Gorbachev addresses with frank and lucid directness the extent and causes of and the solutions for the stagnation that had set in in the national security components mentioned above.

To achieve *perestroika* of the domestic economy, the Gorbachev leadership has integrated the "new thinking" into Soviet foreign and internal affairs in a pragmatic and flexible manner according to intelligently rationalized priorities, using skillful publicity to create an image of the U.S.S.R. that is more acceptable nationally and internationally. In this process, ideology is deemphasized and its rhetoric renovated to fit the new situation. This is done without reneging on the substance of classical Marxist/Leninist ideology.

A few general remarks about present Soviet foreign policy are needed to set Gorbachev's Third World policies, and in particular his southwestern states of

Africa policy, in some perspective. The main goals and directions of the international policy of the CPSU are defined (i.a.) in the CPSU program approved in 1986 as,

> the provision of international conditions favorable to the perfection of socialist society in the U.S.S.R. and its advance to communism . . . firm protection of the interests of the Soviet people and resolute opposition to the aggressive policy of imperialism combined with a readiness for dialogue and constructive settlement of international problems through negotiations. . . . [Improved relations with] fraternal socialist countries . . . newly free countries . . . capitalist states . . . [and] internationalist solidarity with Communist and revolutionary-democratic parties, the international working-class movement and the national liberation struggle of the peoples.[3]

In his report to the 27th Party Congress, Gorbachev adds to this, stressing the necessity for the U.S.S.R. to extend its foreign relations: "As never before, it is now important to find ways for closer and more productive cooperation with governments, parties and mass organizations and movements . . . with all peoples, in order to build an all-embracing system of international security."[4]

To implement this, Gorbachev advocates the use of extensive bilateral and multilateral diplomacy and the United Nations being the "forum of the interests of states." He envisages thereby the creation of a more tranquil global environment, noting that, "people are tired of tension and confrontation. . . . We do not wish to handle international affairs in a manner that would heighten confrontation."[5]

A fundamental principle underlying this new political philosophy is the irrelevance of both nuclear and conventional war. Apparently defying Lenin and seventy years of entrenched Soviet political and military doctrine, but also practical common sense, Gorbachev makes one of his more dubious statements: "Clausewitz's dictum that war is the continuation of policy by different means . . . has grown hopelessly out of date. It now belongs to the libraries. . . . The only way to security is through political decisions and disarmament."[6] This fundamental innovation could then channel activities from the military-industrial complex into peaceful, civilian spheres. The Pentagon views all this with great skepticism:

> What has not changed is the reliance of the Soviet Union on military power to undergird its political policies and the continued willingness of the Soviet leadership to provide the resources necessary to sustain its military power. . . . While the Soviets have been on a steady course of expanding their military capabilities to underwrite their political ambitions, they have realized that high-technology programs underway in the West, if fielded, could widen the gap in advanced military capabilities, hamper all their recent gains, and impede plans for the future. Thus they have embarked on broad-based political, economic,

and active-measures programs to slow the West's efforts and gain time to acquire a more modern industrial base and vigorous economy, so as to be more competitive in the future. While clearly intending to change Western perceptions of the U.S.S.R., they have as yet shown no tangible evidence of changing their long-term goals.[7]

To avoid a repetition of the damage done to détente during the Brezhnev era due to insensitive Soviet perceptions of Western reactions to Soviet geopolitical activism in the Third World, the International Department and Foreign Ministry have been restructured and manned by Western pundits. This is to ensure that Third World relations and regional conflicts do not detract from the prime importance of East-West relations and an integrated rational formulation and implementation of foreign policy by the Politburo.

The "new thinking" has been propagated both in the U.S.S.R. and the rest of the world, especially in the West, by an extremely efficient and intelligent system of public relations spearheaded by Gorbachev and other experienced communicators. (As Richard Nixon put it, "He earned a Bachelor's degree in Law but he was born with a Master's degree in public relations.")[8] Disagreements about foreign policy conduct among the "masses of the West," already noted by Georgii Arbatov in 1955, are marked with a keen eye and exploited with great ability. Commenting on the successes of the "new thinking" in the international scene, Gorbachev notes that, "its regard for universal human values and emphasis on common sense and openness" are "destroying the stereotypes of anti-Sovietism and dispelling distrust of our initiatives and actions."[9] Aleksandr Iakovlev, one of the cognoscenti on North America, believes that the way to counteract the aggressive American propaganda machine is through effective, substantive Soviet peace proposals, "which constrain even the worst cold (war) warriors to reciprocate in order to save face with their own public."[10]

Soviet Policies Regarding Third World Regional Conflicts

Due to its enormous military build-up, the U.S.S.R. had in the beginning of the 1970s acquired a powerful global reach, prompting Andrei Gromyko to make a now famous statement that has yet to be disputed: "There is not a single significant question which today can be decided without or in defiance of the Soviet Union in the resolution of these issues. . . . "[11] And, as Gromyko noted in 1975, détente did not inhibit Soviet expansionism into the Third World. Quite the contrary, "The process of détente is opening up new opportunities and prospects for strengthening [Soviet] cooperation with developing countries."[12]

The U.S.S.R., therefore, in keeping with Leninist tenets prevalent at the time, sought geopolitical influence over a wide area including especially new nations. One such tenet concerned "wars of national liberation" against imperialism. Considered historically unavoidable, they are supported by the U.S.S.R. because they contribute to the gradual shift of the correlation of forces in favor of the Soviet-led camp. In the words of Brezhnev (1973), "We have always regarded and regard now, as our inviolable duty stemming from communist convictions, from our socialist morality, to render the widest possible support to the peoples fighting for the just cause of freedom. This has always been the case, this will be the case in the future as well."[13] The duty to support wars of national liberation is enshrined in the Soviet Constitution of 1977 (Article 28).

A second tenet, set out in the 1986 CPSU Program, and most important for our discussion, is the "inevitability" of the "advance of humanity towards socialism and communism" and the "irreversibility" of socialist-oriented states once established. In this context, " . . . the export of counterrevolution in any form . . . is a gross encroachment on the free expression of will by the peoples. . . . The Soviet Union is strongly opposed to attempts forcibly to check and reverse the march of history."[14]

Taking advantage of the Vietnam syndrome, a U.S. administration paralyzed by Watergate, the CIA in disarray, and liberal policies like the Clark Amendment prohibiting U.S. intervention in Angola, the U.S.S.R. could, without any risk, unexpectedly intervene with large surrogate Cuban forces in far away "imperialist spheres" such as Angola and Ethiopia, helping to defeat all parties except the proper socialist-oriented one. In Angola, this party instituted the "Peoples Republic of Angola," which, after some initial hesitation, was recognized by the Organization of African Unity (OAU) and the West, with the eminent exception of the United States. Without any form of legitimization by popular elections, the Angolan government and others like it could create "states of socialist orientation" led by "vanguard revolutionary parties of the working people."

During a triumphant African tour in 1977, Castro stated that "Africa is the weakest link in the imperialist chain today. . . . There are excellent perspectives there for going directly from tribalism to socialism."[15] This was not quite to be. In the quest for global power by extending its influence in the Third World, the U.S.S.R. suffered some severe setbacks, creating growing domestic skepticism about the future of Soviet relations with many new radical, progressive nations. These skeptics questioned the viability of Leninist doctrine in countries terming themselves Leninist, but where underdevelopment and ethnic, religious, and tribal divisions created such enormous barriers to radical progress that any further meaningful aid was not in the economic or political interest of the U.S.S.R.[16] General Secretary Iurii Andropov had elaborated on this problem already in 1983:

It is one thing to proclaim socialism as one's goal and another thing to build it. A certain level of productive forces, culture, and social consciousness is needed for that. Socialist countries express solidarity with these progressive countries, render assistance to them in the spheres of politics and culture, and promote the strengthening of their defense. We contribute, to the extent of our ability, to their economic development as well. But, on the whole, their economic development, just as the entire social progress of these countries, can be, of course, only the result of the work of their peoples and a correct policy of their leadership.[17]

The global reaction to Soviet Third World policies was also, on the whole, negative. Although many African countries could look to the U.S.S.R. as a dependable arms merchant and ally in their many rhetorical sorties against South Africa in the United Nations and other international forums, Soviet aid for crucial economic and social development was completely inadequate or lacking. The reaction to Angola and Afghanistan in the West was to move away from détente and, in the United States in particular, to continue to support the presidency of Ronald Reagan, whose administration promised to restore American strength and prestige in the world after an unhappy period of seeming effetism and incompetence. "The Reagan administration's adoption of a hard-line stance towards the Soviet Union went hand in hand with the regeneration of American power." This was particularly evident in the Third World, where it was observed that,

> the administration did not share Carter's aversion to the use of force in protection of American interests. Although the main targets—Grenada and Libya—were targets of convenience, American military actions nevertheless helped to convey the sense of resurgent power. This impression was intensified by the enunciation of the Reagan doctrine, which promised support for guerrilla movements fighting Leninist governments. Although the amounts of aid were fairly small, the administration made clear that it would not accept that Third World countries in which Leninist governments had come to power through revolutionary violence were irretrievably lost to the Western camp.[18]

The Reagan Doctrine, with its traditional policy of military containment and the ideal of stemming the tide of communism worldwide—which in Soviet jargon is labelled "globalism" or "neoglobalism"—is maligned in Soviet publications as the real cause of regional conflicts such as those occurring in Angola and Afghanistan. The eminent Soviet commentator Aleksandr Bovin defines "the strategy of neoglobalism" in its essence "as an attempt to halt and reverse social progress in as much as it is incompatible with the United States' 'vital interests,' with the preservation of the global United States' military and political presence, and with the United States' claims to world leadership. Relying on its tremendous resources and on its gigantic war machine, in other words, relying on strength, the United States is challenging world history, clearly in the hope of replaying it, replacing the onward march of history with a perpetual cycle of capitalist forms of societal life."[19]

The Reagan Doctrine, however, also dramatically changed the nature and focus of Soviet comment on regional conflict:

> Rather than emphasizing the desirability of such conflicts as a means of shifting the correlation of forces in favor of world socialism, Soviet spokesmen stress to an ever-increasing degree the necessity of finding political settlements to them. Clearly, one factor contributing to this shift was the strong American position on regional conflicts taken before and during the first Gorbachev-Reagan summit in Geneva in November of 1985. Judging by some of the comments by Georgii Arbatov, one of the most senior American specialists in the U.S.S.R., the issue of regional conflicts was one of the main issues raised. Given the White House's position on this score, one can safely infer that this meeting had finally convinced the Soviet leadership that progress in the realm of arms control, requiring at the very least a shift in public rhetoric on regional conflicts, was called for.[20]

In the proposal for an all-embracing system of international security, raised in his keynote speech to the 27th CPSU Congress in February 1986, Gorbachev singled out regional conflicts ("a just political settlement of international and regional conflicts").[21] And in an address at the Jubilee Meeting of the Central Committee in November 1987, he mentioned the need for a renewal of ideological formulae better reflecting reality, and for breaking away from the older Brezhnev's "addiction to habitual formulae and schemes which did not reflect the new realities." In the same speech, Gorbachev warned against unnecessary general pessimism about the "decline of the national liberation movement. . . . However, what is apparently happening is that one concept is being replaced by another, and the novelty of the situation is being ignored."[22]

To ensure that they could compete and negotiate with the West in the Third World from a position of strength, the Soviet leadership undertook a reappraisal of doctrine on the one hand and of diplomacy and state policy on the other, applying this to various conflicts in the Third World. This entailed renovating antiquated ideology in the first place. And, with regard to Leninist governments, it entailed cutting losses where the returns on the involvement did not make political sense, and also letting themselves be talked out of situations where they were bogged down and where face-saving demanded this manner of disengagement (e.g., Afghanistan), while on the other hand, standing firm in areas of inalienable influence (Vietnam) and making heavier commitments in areas where this would clearly be rewarding or potentially rewarding (Angola).

Whereas Brezhnev concentrated Soviet resources on Leninist-oriented states, Gorbachev, in accordance with the newly stated policies, is now leading the expansion of Soviet political, economic, and cultural ties with non-Leninist governments throughout the Third World. In this process the extensive sale of the latest Soviet weapons provides both hard currency and goodwill.[23] It would appear that by rationalizing its aims and means, the Soviets are recouping the setbacks of the pre-Gorbachev era in the Third World, and influence is again being extended, although selectively and at low risk.

Although the ideological rhetoric is clearly changing, the signals are still mixed. Evgenii Primakov, Director of the Institute of World Economics and International Relations (IMEMO), wrote in the *Pravda* editorial "New Philosophy of Foreign Policy" that,

> . . . to exclude the exporting of revolution is the imperative of the nuclear age. At the same time, the stabilization of the international situation cannot and must not be achieved by artificial maintenance of the social status quo, in other words by exporting counterrevolution. . . . The new philosophy of foreign politics takes into account the necessity to recognize the objective character of different countries' national interest. It also recognizes the need not to place these interests against one another, but by hard work to search for fields in which these interests can be squared with each other. . . . The new philosophy of foreign politics must include renunciation of the horizontal spreading of confrontation between the U.S.A. and the Soviet Union. In this context it is of particular importance to dispense with looking at regional conflicts through the prism of Soviet-American rivalry, which would hamper their settlement.[24]

Victor Afanasiev, editor-in-chief of *Pravda*—specifically singled out by delegates to the recent Communist Party congress as a member of the Brezhnev clique who should be removed—in an authoritative exposition of the "new thinking," "juxtaposes concepts such as 'interdependence,' 'mutual security,' and the 'unthinkablity of victory in nuclear war' on the one hand, with 'class enemies,' 'uncompromising ideological struggle,' and 'just-defensive and liberation-wars' on the other."[25]

More important, the Brezhnev Doctrine is still mentioned in some of Gorbachev's speeches.[26] However, in his Belgrade statement Gorbachev amended the doctrine drastically, saying that, "No one has a monopoly on truth" and that countries have "no claims to imposing their notions about social development on anyone."[27] The concept "freedom of choice" is also becoming prevalent. Vsevolod Ovchinnikov explains in *Pravda* that, "in the nuclear age . . . the concept of freedom of choice holds a key place in the new political thinking . . . has become an integral element of democratization of international relations. . . . The peoples of the newly-free states want to be masters of their destinies."[28] Another new concept, stemming from Soviet military literature, is that Third World revolutionary movements and radical regimes hold the principal responsibility for the defense of their revolutions.[29]

The "new thinking" implies that "security must not be gained at the expense of the other side's interest,"[30] and, as Gorbachev told a national television audience, that "one's own security cannot be ensured without taking into account the security of other states and peoples. There cannot be genuine security unless it is equal to all and comprehensive."[31] And even more explicitly, in *Perestroika*, " . . . we do not want to pursue goals inimical to Western interests. We know how important the Middle East, Asia, Latin America, other Third World regions and also South Africa are for the American and West European economies. . . . To cut these links is the last thing we want to do, and we have no desire to provoke ruptures in historically formed, mutual economic interests."[32]

Gorbachev's handling of the Afghanistan problem is an example of what could be expected from the implementation of the "new thinking" in regional conflicts. The invasion, an error in judgment from the Brezhnev era, resulted in 13,500 dead Soviet soldiers as of the spring of 1988, the cost of maintaining a 115,000-man army over eight years of fighting under difficult circumstances, worldwide international condemnation with lasting negative repercussions, a revolutionary government of minimal legitimacy, and a devastated country of little general benefit to the Soviet Union.

Three months after the invasion there was talk of a political settlement, but only nine years later and after a last effort of stepped up military activity did the Soviets finally implement their so-called program of national reconciliation. It has been characterized by the following elements:

- An effective system of amnesty.
- A coalition government including coopted non-Leninists.
- A semblance of derevolutionization effected by changing the name of the state from People's Republic of Afghanistan to Republic of Afghanistan, and by reinstating Islam as the state religion.
- The expansion of international relations to more countries in an effort to provide greater legitimacy to the Kabul government.
- A well-publicized partial withdrawal of Soviet troops.
- Negotiations resulting in a treaty with the United States and Pakistan.

What has been lacking are negotiations with the insurgent leaders. MacFarlane and Nel observe that:

> This combination of political, diplomatic, and military measures reveals a concerted attempt by the U.S.S.R. to regain the initiative in Afghanistan and, by extension, other similar situations. It also reveals the precise meaning of the concept of 'political settlements of regional conflicts.' In proposing such settlements, the Soviet leadership is not signalling a willingness to condone the loss of its influence and the power of regimes such as those in Afghanistan and Angola. (It is not by chance that the primary meaning of the Russian words for 'political settlement'—*politicheskoe uregelirovanie*—is political regulation).[33]

Primakov, in an article about the philosophy of national reconciliation, says:

At the early stages of the Afghan conflict inadequate attention was being paid to its international causes, to the balance of internal political forces. That distortion began to be corrected once the Afghan government took the line toward creating a coalition government that included the opposition forces. . . . The road to national reconciliation has been taken in Afghanistan, Nicaragua, and Kampuchea. It is a difficult road. Moreover, there are few, if any, historical analogies of civil war ending as a result of national reconciliation and the subsequent formation of corresponding coalition structures to run a country. That is why many politicians regard such a line less than effective or as holding no promise at all. But there are weighty arguments in favor of the line for national reconciliation as a means of neutralizing the internal causes of regional conflicts.[34]

The Cuban Factor

Before proceeding to an analysis of the Angolan situation, a few words about the Cuban factor, which really amounts to the Castro factor. Fidel Castro has been described as "a man of action endowed with impressive physical stature, courage and audacity . . . a leader with superior intelligence, singular determination, and strategic vision" with a "messianic purpose and drive" and a "penchant for risk taking."[35] And, "his foreign policy extends far beyond national survival and security. He ambitiously strives to be a world-class actor who can overcome Cuba's limitations and fulfill a great ideological and strategic mission, partly through the force of his own ideas and actions, and partly by using Soviet support. In all of this, Castro has always had tremendous confidence in his own power to assess, defy and get away with confronting the United States. . . . While megalomania may appear in his personality structure, there is a basis in reality for his conviction that he can, in fact, alter the correlation of forces and the course of history."[36] With this remarkable insight into Castro's psychology, Edward Gonzales, in 1986, was able to predict with uncanny accuracy and detail, the present Cuban military build-up and strategy in Angola.[37]

The U.S.S.R. seems to handle the vibrant and flamboyant Castro with great aplomb. While many of his initiatives are completely his own, his complete economic and indeed military dependency on the Soviet Union ensures that no Cuban action of major importance can occur without Soviet approval, coordination, and assistance. Such economic dependency was the reason a Cuban effort to be defiant in the 1960s had to be dropped. It may also have an effect on the present Soviet-Cuban debate about *perestroika*, about which Castro is not enthusiastic.

Being made a party to the present negotiations with South Africa has done much for Cuban prestige—especially being recognized as a pertinent factor by the U.S.A—and indications are that the Cubans will be quite agreeable to a total withdrawal of their troops, if as a result of the negotiations they are able to leave with the image of a mission triumphantly accomplished. Other concerned parties appear equally amenable to a Cuban withdrawal. Signals from Cuba seem to indicate that Castro's enthusiasm for a conquering military involvement in Angola is not shared by the Cuban people, who have in thirteen years of warfare suffered sizable casualties, with a substantive increase in 1987-88.

Given the nature of Castro's objectives and the unpredictability of their implementation, some African countries would likewise welcome the exit of the 50,000 Cuban soldiers in their midst. If it could survive on its own resources, the MPLA vanguard-party government would also prefer this. Often it is not consulted about Cuban military movements and strategy.

Although Castro is said to be against a Cuban *perestroika*, the alleged flexibility encountered from the Cuban delegation in the latest rounds of negotiations among Soviet, Cuban, South African, and Angolan technocrats, including the Cuban acceptance of the concept of "linkage" (i.e., the coupling of the implementation of U.N. Security Council Resolution 435 in Namibia and the total withdrawal of Cuban troops from Angola), which had been rejected for eight years, must therefore be due to Soviet pressure. How does one explain otherwise the abrupt change in policy?

Although South Africa is keen to have a political settlement and is willing to accommodate any Cuban face-saving involved, the present negotiations could be seriously jeopardized if politicians such as Fidel Castro and Jorge Risquet were to indulge in jingoistic, vainglorious, and much-publicized statements about Cuban "victories" over South African troops. For many reasons, clearly understood by its public, South Africa has played its military involvement at a very low key, internally and externally. But the spurious claims of Cuban "victories" and of South African "fear of Cuban troops" are starting to grate on the South African ear with possible internal political repercussions. South Africans have sometimes withdrawn from military positions for political reasons but never because of Cuban victories. Such victories have never occurred.

Angola/Namibia

What effect does the "new thinking" have on Soviet policy with regard to Namibia and Angola? The Namibian question as it regards the implementation of Resolution 435 is—with the assent of all the parties at present engaged in negotiations (Cuba, Angola, South Africa; under chairmanship of the United States and with the U.S.S.R. an informed observer)—completely linked to the withdrawal of Cuban soldiers from Angola. This obviates a further discussion of Namibia except to mention that the implementation of Resolution 435 could have the effect of improved relations between South Africa and a

Angola and Namibia   181

number of African states, with the latter exerting pressure on Angola for an internal policy of reconciliation. (See Appendix B for the principles that have been agreed on for the agenda of the meeting between South Africa, Cuba, Angola, and the United States in New York on July 13, 1988.)

In many areas of pre-Gorbachev Soviet expansionism in the Third World there has, in terms of the "new thinking," been rational retrenchment and a low level of risk taking. In Angola, under Gorbachev, there has in contrast been a great spiralling of increased Soviet aid.

An analysis of the "new thinking" as applied to Angola is therefore a pertinent and elucidating test of the essence of the new political philosophy. Two tenets of Leninist ideology are at issue: the irreversibility of a Leninist regime once established and the proletarian duty of the U.S.S.R. to maintain the status quo. How the concept of national reconciliation (see Primakov's remarks above) is dealt with can affect the classic Leninist formula of irreversibility.

The following exposition of 1980 clearly illustrates the Soviet doctrine underlying the decision to invade Afghanistan and to become involved in the Angolan conflict:

> What is the internationalist solidarity of revolutionaries? Does it consist only of moral and diplomatic support, of sincere wishes of success, or also of material assistance, including military help, given in definite, extraordinary circumstances, and especially in a situation of manifest massive outside interference? . . . Today when there exists a system of socialist states, it would be simply ridiculous to question the right to such assistance. . . . To refuse to use the possibilities at the disposal of the socialist countries would signify virtually evading performance of the internationalist duty and returning the world to the times imperialism could throttle at will any revolutionary movement.[38]

Before addressing the manner in which the "new thinking" may have altered this understanding, it is necessary to present a brief background to the Angolan situation: Although strongly Soviet-inclined and supported by the U.S.S.R. since 1964 in their struggle against Portuguese colonial rule in Angola, the MPLA was not originally a Leninist organization. Only gradually, through training in the U.S.S.R., were its leading members indoctrinated in Leninist ideology. Following a meeting between Che Guevara and Antonio Augustino Neto in 1966, numerous MPLA guerrillas and leadership cadres received military training in Cuba. Although the best organized of the three anticolonialist movements in Angola, the MPLA was numerically the smallest. Its support came from a very narrow ethnic base in the center of the country, from the city of Luanda, and from some of the 100,000 "assimilados" who held minor administrative posts in the Portuguese administration. Of the three "liberation movements," the MPLA, militarily speaking, posed no threat to the authorities. When I paid an extensive visit to the Angolan operational areas in 1973, almost all MPLA activities had been eradicated by the Portuguese security forces. The successful leftist MFA revolution in Portugal of April 25, 1974, however, changed the Marxist myth. The Marxist Vice-Admiral Antonio Rosa Coutinho ("the Red Admiral") was installed at the head of the Military Council in Angola in July 1974, and in January 1975 another Marxist, General Antonio De Silva Cardoso, was appointed High Commissioner.

These appointments facilitated the integration of ex-Katangese refugee auxiliaries from the Portuguese colonial army into the MPLA; the elimination, with Portuguese assistance, of elements hostile to the MPLA such as dissident Daniel Chipenda in February 1975; the arrival of massive Soviet arms assistance to the MPLA starting in October 1974; MPLA access to Portuguese arsenals; direct Portuguese military assistance in MPLA attacks against the FNLA and UNITA, especially in July, August, and September 1975; and finally, the arrival of Cuban troops in Soviet aircraft using airport facilities in the Azores.[39] In a public interview on Canadian TV in 1987, Rosa Coutinho proudly admitted his decisive role in bringing the MPLA to power.

In March 1975, 500 Cuban troops arrived. In October their number had risen to 7,000; in November, to 15,000; and in January 1976, to 37,000—on the whole a most impressive Soviet logistic achievement. Only toward the end of October 1975 did South African troops, which never exceeded 2,000, first enter Angola to assist UNITA and the FNLA. In spite of this readily available data, the leftist myth that the Cuban troops entered Angola only at the request of the MPLA and in reaction to a South African invasion was given wide credence by the Western media and academicians.

In January 1975 the treaty of Alvor was signed between the three liberation movements and Portugal. According to the treaty, Angola would become independent in November 1975, after national elections had been held. A transition government, which included ministers from all three movements and some Portuguese, was established on June 1, 1975.

As the MPLA did not stand a chance of winning an election, the customary Leninist takeover of the government had to be engineered. First, Augustino Neto explained that a compromise between the MPLA ("the popular progressive forces") and the FNLA and UNITA ("the puppets of the imperialists") was completely impossible.[40] On July 15 the FNLA was expelled from Luanda, and on August 11 the UNITA as well. Assisted by 10,000 Cuban soldiers, the MPLA defeated the FNLA in November 1975. The Cuban/MPLA forces also drove UNITA into the bush after the South Africans had withdrawn in the absence of promised political and logistic support from the United States. Bare-footed and in rags, UNITA forces did not at this stage have much of an organization, although they were supported by the vast majority of people in the southeast of the country.

The special circumstances of their involvement in the Angolan war of 1975-76 became a factor of psychological importance to the Soviets. Fully exploiting the golden opportunity provided by the Clark Amendment, the U.S.S.R. transported 12,000 Cuban troops and all the required weapons with impressive logistic expertise and speed to Angola. The war was "the first conflict in the Third World in which Soviet military intervention had a decisive influence on the outcome."[41] This feat has become a source of Soviet national pride, making disengagement from Angola very difficult.[42]

The OAU, after an initial fifty-fifty split on the civil war in Angola, finally recognized the completely unrepresentative MPLA government, as did—with inexplicable haste in February 1976—France, Great Britain, Italy, West Germany, and Portugal.

In May 1976, a wide-ranging Treaty of Friendship and Cooperation between the U.S.S.R. and the People's Republic of Angola was concluded, and in December 1977, the MPLA officially proclaimed Angola a Leninist state, and was recognized as such by the Soviet Union. The government and such parts of the country under MPLA control were totally reorganized on the Soviet model with a Central Committee and Politburo who convened a Party Conference. The ensuing economic disaster (aggravated but not caused by the civil war, although typical following such takeovers) is illustrated by a few figures: In spite of a positive trade balance of 15,000 million escudos in 1974, Angola incurred a debt to the Soviet Union of $2.6 billion, which had to be renegotiated when due, in 1983; maize production of 200,000 tons in 1973 fell to 18,000 tons in 1981 (through shortage of this and other basic foods, Angola, a rich agricultural country, formerly exporting food, became a major importer of food); exports of coffee decreased from 3.5 million bags a year in 1970 to about 400,000 bags in 1984; iron ore extraction (Cassinga) fell from 6.1 million tons in 1973 to none in 1985; 217,000 tons of cotton produced in 1976 fell to 21,500 tons in 1981. Oil production, mostly managed by foreign companies, now accounts for about 90% of Angola's exports and helps to pay for the presence of Cuban troops and Soviet arms.

Opposition to the MPLA did not disappear after November 1975. The FNLA in the north of the country in due course ceased to be a factor because of the ineffectual absentee leadership of Holden Roberto and many of its members making use of the MPLA offer of amnesty. Its place was taken by UNITA, whose guerrilla activities now cover almost the whole of Angola and which dominates (and administers) the southeastern corner of the country. Primarily based on the Ovimbundu (thirty-seven percent of the population) but with adherents all over Angola and under the leadership of one of Africa's most able statesmen, UNITA became a potent counterrevolutionary opponent of the MPLA regime because of several factors: South African assistance in the form of advisers, some logistic support, and, in the case of the massive conventional Cuban/FAPLA attacks of 1987, some direct military support; and American assistance, first as moral support from a sympathetic new administration in 1980, and, after the repeal of the Clark Amendment in 1985, limited arms deliveries including Stinger missiles. Savimbi's UNITA, however, has never been in any sense an artifact of South Africa and the Reagan administration. The United States and South Africa did not supply the continuing enthusiastic, grassroots support for Savimbi of thousands of Angolans over 30 years of privation and endurance, their patriotic fervor, the intelligent structuring of an efficient military force, the ingenuity by which this is maintained with minimal resources, the esprit de corps, or the courage and resourcefulness with which it fights an enemy having vastly superior resources.

The remarkable and increasing level of Soviet commitment to the MPLA is unprecedented in the short history of Soviet involvement in southern Africa.[43] In the military field the U.S.S.R. has supplied arms to the value of $700 million between 1974 and 1979, and $2.8 billion between 1980 and 1985. Between 1977 and 1985, some ten agreements were negotiated between Angola and the U.S.S.R., covering a wide range of economic and technical relations, including schemes in agriculture, irrigation, hydro-electricity, oil refineries, fisheries, harbors, trade, geological exploration, education, etc. Despite their magnitude, the assistance programs, however, were inadequate for the rapidly declining Angolan economy, creating an "erosion of relations" between the two countries. The U.S.S.R. therefore grudgingly assented to increased Angolan economic ties with the West but also concluded a ten-year assistance program of $2 billion to match the perceived swing to the capitalist countries.[44] Economic ties with the West have always been indispensible to Angola but have not yet had the effect of weaning the MPLA from their Leninist moorings. Roger Thurow of the *Wall Street Journal* reports about a recent interview in Luanda: "We have come up with a slogan," says Dumilde das Chagas Simoes Rangel, Angola's trade minister. "Develop the economy to fight the war, fight the war to defend the economy." Thus, if capitalism is what it takes to defend Leninism in Angola, so be it. "It is possible," says Mr. Nunes, "to construct socialism with rational economic means."[45]

The probably facetious statement of Soviet Foreign Ministry spokesman Genadii Gerasimov that the only thing Afghanistan and Angola had in common was the letter "A," is offset by a report of a statement by Gorbachev to Zambian President Kenneth Kaunda that the kind of progress in Afghanistan "can be applied in full in southern Africa as well."[46] In retrospect, large-scale Soviet and Cuban involvement in Angola since 1975 has been one of the main reasons why détente between the U.S.S.R. and the Western nations did not survive.[47] These problems called for a political solution or "political regulation," to use the Soviet terminology.

The Soviets and Cubans first attempted to achieve a pre-negotiations position of strength from which to negotiate or preferably to obviate the need for negotiations. Gorbachev's reply to the deteriorating situation in Angola in 1985 was therefore a great upward spiralling of Soviet efforts; massive assistance (arms, air defense systems, planning, and training by advisers), which for 1985 alone amounted to $1 billion; massive offensives in 1985 and 1987, launched by FAPLA forces revitalized by Soviet advisers in an attempt to obliterate the headquarters of UNITA; very substantial new economic and technical assistance; and a morale-boosting interchange of visits by many high-level dignitaries of both countries. During such a visit by Eduardo dos Santos to Moscow in 1986, Gorbachev declared, "We have the firm and mutual intention to perfect the form and methods of this cooperation. . . . We shall work together on making it closer and more effective. In a word, Soviet-Angolan relations have an excellent future."[48]

Second, the Soviet project was supplemented by the surreptitious import of 15,000 additional Cuban troops to occupy the southern part of Angola bordering Namibia. This could vouch for a more successful offensive against UNITA this year. It also makes the penetration of the Namibian border by SWAPO guerrillas again feasible. Such incursions had dwindled to minimal proportions when South African security forces could strike at SWAPO bases by cross-border attacks. Castro described this move as "needed to create proper conditions for a political solution."[49]

Third, the Cubans accepted the principle of linkage, which they had refused to consider for eight years. And fourth, Moscow was accepting and even encouraging the use of the good offices of the United States to act as chairman at the negotiations. The Soviets were keeping themselves informed without entering extantly into the picture.

Regarding national reconciliation, dos Santos has been very consistent. The MPLA is prepared to offer amnesty on MPLA terms (e.g., entailing the obligation of joining the MPLA) to all supporters of UNITA except Savimbi and his top aides. According to his Leninist statements and the structure of his government, there is no possibility in his thinking of any kind of coalition government. Only pressure from the U.S.S.R. and certain African states that strongly support national reconciliation and an end to the conflict in Angola could moderate his stance.

Savimbi, on the other hand, has, at least since 1974 (when he first expressed these views to me), in victory and in defeat been completely consistent about power-sharing. He is prepared in fact to serve under dos Santos. Although UNITA clearly has the support of at least 40 percent of the population of Angola, Savimbi feels that no single party has adequate national support to govern the country by itself. An equitable solution in Angola, could be the formation of a federation or a coalition, which, with Savimbi's consummate statecraft, might be the first coalition government in black Africa.

Although there are indications that the U.S.S.R. is perfectly aware of the real status of UNITA and the support it enjoys, there has up to early 1989 been much vituperation of Savimbi as a creature of South Africa and the United States. It is said that UNITA will stop being a factor in Angola when aid to them is discounted. The key point here is that ideologically, the views of Primakov, as quoted, pave the way for a more realistic approach. The rationale underlying the "new thinking" also gives Gorbachev the opportunity to phase out the concept of the irreversibility of socialist-oriented regimes and in its place promote the concept of national reconciliation, thereby gaining more influence in Angola and smoothing external relations with the West. To trigger this development, however, requires courage on the part of the West to exert the necessary pressure on the U.S.S.R. It more specifically requires a forceful application of the Reagan Doctrine by the United States in Africa. Finally, it will require that the Democratic party and its leaders replace their current advisers on Africa.

To keep on saddling one of the richest countries in Africa and a suffering captive population with all the onerous constraints of a Leninist government and state is a burden on its conscience that the West should no longer bear. It took the U.S.S.R. nine years of suffering serious worldwide international repercussions before agreeing to change the Leninist government in Afghanistan to the semblance, at least, of a non-Leninist government.

On the other hand, the West that waxed (and waxes) highly indignantly about minority rule in Rhodesia, Southwest Africa, and South Africa, finds nothing immoral in recognizing a non-elected, unrepresentative government installed and maintained by Cuban troops in Angola. With the West thus meekly accepting the status quo in Angola, what cogent reasons could Gorbachev provide to the Politburo for implementing any meaningful Soviet policy change in the war-torn country?

As mentioned, the obvious key to the solution of the problem seems to be a firm continuation of the Reagan Doctrine, but about this there appears to be an inexplicable difference of opinion in the United States. Commenting on money that Congress did not authorize for the U.N. peacekeeping force because some powerful legislators "opposed providing funds which might help UNITA," State Department spokesman Charles Redman said,

> As far as United States support for Savimbi . . . it just hasn't changed. . . . It is a longstanding view that lasting peace can come to Angola only in the context of genuine national reconciliation and direct dialogue between UNITA and the MPLA. We continue to support all efforts to promote such an outcome and we regard our assistance to UNITA as an important part of this effort and we have so informed Congress of that fact.[50]

Even Jerry Bender, for many years the most outspoken American critic of

Savimbi and an advocate of U.S. recognition of the MPLA, had to adjust his views in the light of MPLA failures. He now favors national reconciliation:

> The war in Angola is hopelessly stalemated; neither side can possibly defeat the other and there seems to be no prospect for a military solution. Thus it becomes increasingly clear that only a political solution can end the war. . . . Both internal and external perceptions of the competing parties have been based primarily on selective perceptions of external patrons. . . . In it the favored party is portrayed as enjoying broad ethnic and national support, while the other side is depicted as being a puppet of foreign powers. . . . The MPLA and its supporters view UNITA as a puppet or creature of South Africa and assume that it will wither away once its umbilical link to Pretoria is severed. UNITA and its supporters portray the MPLA as a Soviet or Cuban puppet that will collapse as soon as Havana's troops leave Angola. The truth is that neither would UNITA perish without South African support, nor would the MPLA be overrun were Cuban troops to be withdrawn.

A political solution and reconciliation are called for:

> The prospects of Namibian independence and reconciliation in Angola cannot be seen in Moscow as necessary, desirable outcomes. They would certainly result in a marked decline of Soviet influence in the region and may even call into question the raison d'être for anything more than a normal presence. Soviet models and recommendations in the economic and military fields in Angola have basically failed, at least in the eyes of the overwhelming majority of the Angolan people.[51]

A second, strong school of thought is of course still urging unconditional recognition of the MPLA, ignoring the existence of UNITA and the size of its support, and stopping all aid. Coauthors John Marcum, Helen Kitchen, and Michael Spicer contend, albeit circumspectively,

> The regional, political and economic advantages of a Benguella railway are of such potential significance that some observers believe that a future United States administration would be inclined to forsake its alignment with the UNITA insurgency in favor of pursuing long-term interests in favor of diplomatic, cultural and economic ties with a nominally (sic) Marxist governed Angola.[52]

Conclusion

All conditions being favorable, the U.S.S.R. will require at least another decade or two to become a multi-faceted superpower. In the meantime it can be expected that it will make use of the military option whenever power projection into the Third World is required.

If Gorbachev continues on his present path he could, in terms of Hedley Bull's definition of strategy (". . . the art and science of shaping means to achieve ends in any field of conflict") become the "complete strategist."

Gorbachev's praise of Reagan (for his ability to adapt his "views to the changing situation while remaining faithful to one's convictions") is even more applicable to himself. Incisive, dynamic, articulate, Gorbachev, as a dedicated Leninist, wants to develop his people and his country to their fullest communist potential. As a patriot, he acts and walks tall in his knowledge that he is the leader of a great power that could be even more powerful. As a practical man with much experience in management, he knows what this requires. In his keen grasp of Leninist tradition he will be flexible in shaping optimal means but unyielding in the ends he promotes. If the West can find a statesman sufficiently adept and knowledgeable to overcome the asymmetry that always seems to favor the Soviets in dialogue, Gorbachev is a partner through whom the West can develop a meaningful and balanced relationship with the Soviet Union.

In view of present world attitudes and the prestige that Soviet history engenders domestically, the U.S.S.R. is not compelled to take any steps that would diminish its influence in Angola.

Prima facie, the "new thinking" does tend to indicate changes of substance in Leninist ideology. Support for liberation movements and the concept of the irrreversibility of Leninist regimes now seem subject to a process of reconsideration. The "new thinking" questions the further use of vexacious ideological verbiage and unprofitable actions that divert attention from the set goal of optimizing Leninist potential. In contrast with the pre-Gorbachev era, which phrased the superpower contest within the context of a zero-sum game, the new political philosophy (especially "just political settlement of regional conflicts" and "national reconciliation") provides more flexibility of action and a greater choice of options should the Soviets be confronted with an intelligent American realpolitik intent on exerting the necessary coercion in Angola. This, in tandem with initiatives from other African states, could pave the way to a reversal of the monopoly of power of the MPLA government in Angola and the possibility of peace.

The relevant foreign policies adopted by the United States toward Third World countries and toward Soviet relationships with them are most important for the future of the Third World. The United States should give deep thought to the ways and means of achieving some intelligent continuity and coherence in its foreign policy. It should in this respect perhaps revert to an essential premise of its constitution, leaving executive matters such as the implementation of foreign policy in the hands of the elected executive. With the kind of expertise the Soviets are developing, the Congress's continued inefficient intrusion into the conduct of foreign affairs, which is blemished by all the pressures of internal determinants, spells disaster for the United States and for the Third World. The State Department should endeavour to steer the United

States in the direction of a moral realpolitik, to replace the traditional, unrealistic and therefore often (unintended) immoral "moralpolitik."

It is extremely important for the OAU countries to substitute well-worn rhetorical and symbolist agitations against South Africa on vaguely defined issues like apartheid for meaningful, realistic dialogue on sharply defined problems. South Africa has a keen wish to be a part of Africa in all respects and has indeed much to contribute to its welfare. Its government meanwhile appears to favor a *perestroika* of some sort for its own fatigued government structures and "new thinking" for a better coordinated foreign policy. The West, for its part, should seriously reflect upon the questionable morality of its policies and upon the damage it has been doing to the prospect for the recontruction of a flourishing Angola by not actively working towards a meaningful change of the status quo, national reconciliation, and a more representative, Leninist dispensation.

Notes

1. Erik P. Hoffman, "Soviet Policy from 1986 to 1991: Domestic and International Influences," in Laird R. (ed.), *Soviet Policy Toward the Third World*, Academy of Political Science, Vol. 36, No. 4, 1987, p. 254.
2. Quoted in *Time Magazine* of July 11, 1988, p. 8. I could not find the exact quotation in the officially edited version of Gorbachev's speech. See 19th All-Union Conference of the CPSU in *Documents and Materials, Report and Speeches* by Mikhail Gorbachev, Moscow, *Novosti Press*, 1988, in which on pp. 96 and 97 the essence of this quote is watered down.
3. Program of the CPSU approved by the 27th Congress of the CPSU on March 1, 1986, *New Times*, March 86, p. 41.
4. Political Report of the CPSU Central Committee to the 27th Congress of the Communist Party of the Soviet Union, delivered by General Secretary M. Gorbachev, in *New Times*, No. 9, March 10, 1986, p. 39.
5. Mikhail Gorbachev, *Perestroika: New Thinking for Our Country and the World* (London: Harper and Row, 1987), p. 139.
6. Ibid., p. 141.
7. *Soviet Military Power: An Assessment of the Threat, 1988*, Washington, D.C., pp. 10 and 17.
8. F. Barnes, "Can Gorbachev Last?," *Readers Digest*, July 1988, p. 148.
9. Mikhail Gorbachev, in Report to the Central Committee of the CPSU at their Jubilee Meeting to mark the 70th anniversary of the Great October Socialist Revolution, in Supplement to *Soviet Military Review*, No. 12, 1987, p. 23.
10. J. Snyder, "The Gorbachev Revolution: A Waning of Soviet Expansionism?," *International Security*, Winter 1987/88, Vol. 12, No. 3, p. 119.
11. *Pravda*, April 4, 1971, as quoted in Lange, K. "A Current Soviet View of Southern and South Africa," *Soviet Revue*, Vol. 4, No. 2, 1988, p. 14.
12. *Kommunist*, No. 14, 1975, as quoted in Lange, op. cit.

13. As quoted in MacFarlane and Nel, "The Prospects for Political Settlements of Regional Conflicts, Current Soviet Approaches," p. 13, in papers presented at Department of Foreign Affairs Symposium, February 23-24, 1988, Pretoria.
14. CPSU Program 1986, op. cit., p. 44.
15. E. Gonzalez and D. Ronfeldt, *Castro, Cuba and the World*, (Santa Monica, CA: Rand Corporation, 1986) p. 20.
16. G. Mirsky and V. Lee, in "Problems and Opinions," *Asia and Africa Today*, No 4, 1988, pp. 64 et. seq.
17. Quoted in Peter Clement, "Moscow and Southern Africa," in *Problems of Communism*, March-April 1985, p. 47.
18. Phil Williams, "Soviet-American Relations," in Laird, op. cit., pp. 63-64, and Marie Mengras, "Soviet Policy Toward the Third World," in Laird, op. cit., p. 172.
19. Quoted by Hoffman in Laird, op. cit., p. 268.
20. Mac Farlane and Nel, op. cit., p. 2.
21. Political Report of the CPSU 27th Congress, op. cit., p. 40.
22. Mikhail Gorbachev, Report to CPSU Jubilee Meeting, Nov. 1987, pp. 14 and 26.
23. Hoffman, in Laird, op. cit., p. 261.
24. Ibid., p. 270, and Lange, op. cit., p. 18.
25. Hoffman, op. cit., p. 258.
26. See his speech at the Polish Party Congress, June 1986, as quoted in D. Simes, "Soviet Foreign Policy under Gorbachev: Goals and Expectations—An American Perspective," in papers presented at the Department of Foreign Affairs Symposium, Feb. 23-24, 1988, Pretoria. ". . . to wrench a country away from the socialist community, means to encroach not only on the will of the people, but also on the entire postwar arrangement and, in the final analysis, on peace."
27. Quoted in *The Economist*, March 26, 1988.
28. *Pravda*, August 23, 1988.
29. Mac Farlane and Nel, op. cit., p. 37.
30. Ibid., p. 17.
31. Snyder, op. cit., p. 96.
32. Gorbachev, op. cit., p. 178.
33. Mac Farlane and Nel, op. cit., p. 37.
34. Primakov, E., "U.S.S.R. Policy on Regional Conflicts," *International Affairs*, No. 6, June 1988, p. 6.
35. Gonzales and Ronfeldt, op. cit., p. 51.
36. Ibid., p. 24.
37. Ibid., pp. 132-133.
38. J. Collins, "Soviet Policy toward Afghanistan," in Laird, op. cit., p. 199.
39. Branko Lazitch, Angola 1974-1988: *Un echec du communisme en Afrique*, Paris, 1988, pp. 23-24.
40. Ibid., p. 33.
41. P. R. Nel, *Angola: Soviet Commitment for a Settlement* (unpublished manuscript), p. 35.
42. Personal interview with Arkadii Shevchenko.
43. Nel, op. cit., p. 18.
44. Ibid., p. 18.
45. *The Wall Street Journal*, Sept. 21, 1988, p. 1.
46. Nel, op. cit., p. 9.
47. Ibid., p. 10.

48. Quoted in Nel, op. cit., p. 32.
49. *Pretoria News*, July 27, 1988.
50. SABC broadcast, October 25, 1988.
51. G. J. Bender, "The Eagle and the Bear in Angola," *Annals AAPSS*, 489 January 1987, pp. 123, 126, and 132.
52. J. Marcum, H. Kitchen, and M. Spicer, "The U.S. and the World," in Peter Berger and Bobby Godsell, *A Future South Africa and the World* (Cape Town: Human and Rousseau Tafelberg, 1988), p. 264.

Part Five
Regional Focus: The Conflict in Southeast Asia

11

U.S.S.R., Vietnam, and the Conflict in Kampuchea

Khien Theeravit

Some of the most important aims of the Soviet Union are to protect its global interests (ideological and political influence, security and economic well-being) and to expand the "socialist commonwealth" (*sotsialisticheskoe sodruzhestvo*). These goals are mutually supportive and are tied to the further objective of promoting the aforementioned interests in other areas both directly and through allied bloc countries. These aims have been pursued with a sense of mission and with the understanding that the main Soviet contender is, and will continue to be, the United States.

In Southeast Asia, the Russians are culturally alien and thus are seen as psychologically distant. Soviet interests in the area are basically not considered vital, but in its global competition with the United States Moscow has expanded and strengthened its existing interests by whatever means it could and wherever the opportunity arose in the area. Moscow has succeeded, to a certain extent, but mainly by military means and through surrogates.

Compared with other great powers' performances, the Soviet performance in Indochina has been most impressive. By 1975 the American-backed regimes in Vietnam, Cambodia, and Laos were eliminated, leaving Moscow and Beijing to share influence in the three states. And by the end of 1978, the Soviet Union remained the only outside dominant power in the region, exerting influence through its surrogate Vietnam. For nine years, however, Vietnam has been unable to subjugate Kampuchea. When Mikhail Gorbachev came to power in Moscow in 1985 he realized that time was not on the Soviet and Vietnamese side; Hanoi was not winning the war in Kampuchea, and neither was Moscow in Afghanistan.

Confronting this and other problems at home and abroad, the Soviet leadership has vigorously campaigned for a change in its domestic and foreign policies, referred to in its various aspects as *perestroika* (restructuring), *glasnost* (openness), and *novoe politicheskoe myshlenie* (the "new political thinking"). What are the implications and ramifications for peace and security in Kampuchea, which has been destroyed indirectly by Moscow through Hanoi? These and other relevant issues will be addressed in this chapter.

Moscow's Policy and Interests in Indochina in the Pre-Gorbachev Era

From World War II through 1985, Moscow advanced its interests in Indochina through the Vietnamese Communists. Thus, it would be misleading to treat Moscow's relations with Laos and Kampuchea separately from those with Vietnam. Referring to this period, Mr. Dieter Heinzing has rightly pointed out that, "The Soviet presence reached today is not the outcome of any systematically pursued policy of grand design. The Kremlin leaders' decision to make an active commitment was reached hesitantly and predominantly as a reaction to the actions of the French, Americans, Chinese, and—last but not least—Vietnamese."[1] Mr. Heinzing also stresses that Vietnam had become a member of COMECON and an ally of the Soviet Union. In this, Hanoi recognized the preponderant role of Moscow in Southeast Asia, officially acknowledged by Vietnamese Foreign Minister Nguyen Co Thach in 1980: "The U.S.S.R. renders Vietnam, Laos, and Cambodia all-round aid in the defense of their independence and security and is making its contribution towards consolidating peace and security in Southeast Asia."[2]

What Thach was really alluding to in 1980 was the Soviet role in satisfying Hanoi's desire to conquer Kampuchea. What resulted from the Soviet support of Hanoi was a state of war and instability, not peace and security, in Indochina. The following pages will demonstrate, in brief, what and how Moscow contributed to the existing conflict in Kampuchea prior to Gorbachev's rise to power.

Moscow's contributions to the Communist takeover of Vietnam, Laos, and Kampuchea were mainly political and military in nature. In the political area, Moscow consistently supported the communist movements in those countries by providing them with pro-communist propaganda along with negative propaganda about the opposing governments, the so-called American puppet regimes. Second, Moscow helped organize or sponsor various front-line organizations in the international arena to support the revolutionary movements. And third, in the United Nations and other international organizations, Moscow led the Soviet bloc's campaign to support the communist cause.

In the military field, first of all, Moscow generously provided the foreign Communists, directly or indirectly, with arms and ammunition. Second, Moscow trained the communist insurgents how to fight using Soviet weapons, some of which were quite advanced. And third, Moscow dispatched military advisers to assist the Indochinese Communists in the field.

Prior to 1960, when Moscow and Beijing were still working in harmony to promote communism in Southeast Asia, Moscow took responsibility primarily for promoting the political aspects of the struggle, while Beijing emphasized military means. Then the Soviet arms were channelled to Indochinese Communists through China. After the Sino-Soviet dispute became public in 1960, the Soviet arms were transferred to Indochina mainly through Hanoi, and largely by sea.

By virtue of their receiving various kinds of support from both the Soviet Union and China, and by skillfully employing military and diplomatic tactics, the Communists in Vietnam and Laos won final victories in 1975. The communist movement in Kampuchea outsmarted the allied movements in Vietnam and Laos, however, by being the first to capture political power. The Kampucheans had received no direct support from the Soviet Union, but the Vietnamese Communists infiltrated most of their armed units, and the Chinese Communists had provided them with political and armed support.

The dominant faction of Khmer Communists, led by Pol Pot, chose to align itself closely with Beijing in defiance of Moscow. The Pol Pot faction also deviated from its Laotian communist counterpart by challenging Vietnamese hegemony.

Capitalizing on the existing, traditional hatred by the Khmer people for the Vietnamese, the Pol Potists were able to mobilize Khmer nationalism to their advantage and eliminate other contenders, especially the Pro-Vietnamese faction. The purge was considered complete when Heng Samrin, the current top leader of the Phnom Penh regime, fled to Vietnam in May 1978.

The Vietnamese invasion and occupation of Kampuchea, undertaken at the end of 1978, was the result of convergent Soviet-Vietnamese ideological, political and military interests. Ideologically, Hanoi and Moscow share the similar goal of promoting the Soviet brand of communism. Politically, neither would tolerate the existence of a hostile government in Phnom Penh: It was the Pol Pot faction that prevented Hanoi from realizing its aim of creating the so-called "Indochinese Federation," which required a special relationship among all Indochinese states in the political, economic, and military fields. From Moscow's standpoint, the Pol Pot faction was responsible for breaking the official relationship between Moscow and Phnom Penh. In the military area, both Hanoi and Moscow saw China as the target and they helped one another mutually. For fear of a Chinese military intervention, Hanoi could not invade Kampuchea without Soviet support, while Moscow in 1978 wanted to outflank China by using the Vietnamese to apply pressure at China's southern border.

Recognizing their convergence of interests, Moscow guaranteed to defend Hanoi with a Treaty of Friendship and Cooperation, proclaimed on November 3, 1978. Article 6 of this treaty clearly binds the two countries in military alliance. The subsequent Vietnamese invasion and occupation of Kampuchea, which cost Vietnam dearly politically, economically, and militarily, could not have been maintained without Soviet support.

The Soviet propaganda machine gave unswerving support to Hanoi's causes and positions on all issues concerning Kampuchea. Moscow also promoted international forums that propagated Hanoi's stand. And in the United Nations and other international organizations, Moscow always worked diligently in Hanoi's interests.

Vietnam's admission to the Soviet-led CMEA (Council for Mutual Economic Assistance) in 1978 highlighted the special ties between the Soviet Union and Vietnam. As a member of the CMEA, Vietnam has received economic and technical assistance from other CMEA members. To reduce its own burden, Moscow has often volunteered to negotiate for aid with CMEA members on Vietnam's behalf. For Hanoi, receiving aid from countries other than the Soviet Union is significant for its image, but except for the Soviet Union, the CMEA members have had very little to contribute to Vietnam's ailing economy. The communist countries in Eastern Europe might have an objection to Hanoi's hegemonic scheme in Indochina, as they might have to the Soviet designs in their own region, but it is difficult to tell how much this stance might affect their cooperation with Vietnam. One thing is certain: They all know that they cannot expect benefits from Vietnam so long as Vietnamese troops are still in Kampuchea. In the CMEA spirit of cooperation, Hanoi has dispatched laborers to work in difficult assignments in other member countries, but that could be interpreted as a measure to relieve Hanoi's economic hardship; and the views of the host country on the matter have not always been positive.

Soviet military aid to Vietnam—in the form of arms, training, and military advisors—has greatly facilitated Hanoi's military venture in Kampuchea. The huge quantity of American arms left behind in 1975 by the Saigon regime and those accumulated by Hanoi as a result of decades of military build-up against the American military intervention in Indochina would have met normal requirements for Hanoi's defense for decades if an aggressive policy had not been adopted. Arms flows from Moscow to Hanoi increased after the Vietnamese invasion of Kampuchea in late 1978. Since then, Moscow has remained Hanoi's sole arms supplier. In anticipation of outside intervention, especially from China, Hanoi sent military personnel away for training in the Soviet Union and received Soviet military advisers, who concentrated on teaching and administrating advanced military technology. The Soviet military aid and its psychological impact on Hanoi's aggressive policy should not be underestimated.

The amount of Soviet economic and military assistance to Vietnam between 1965 and 1986 varies according to individual estimates. The most reliable estimate is by Vo Nhan Tri and Thai Quang Trung in the *Indochina Report*, which is given as follows:

Table 11.1
Soviet Aid to Hanoi, 1965-1986 (in millions of U.S. dollars)

Year	1965	1966	1967	1968	1969	1970	1971	1972	1973	1974	1975
Econ.Aid	85	150	200	240	250	345	315	365	470	480	520
Mil.Aid	210	360	505	290	220	170	215	450	230	460	280
Total	295	510	705	530	470	515	530	815	700	940	800
Year	1976	1977	1978	1979	1980	1981	1982	1983	1984	1985	1986
Econ.Aid	560	560	700	800	1000	1050	1175	1250	1400	1600	1800
Mil.Aid	450	630	720	1300	960	800	940	1150	1250	1360	1440
Total	1010	1190	1420	2100	1960	1850	2115	2400	2650	2960	3240

Source: Vo Nhan Tri and Thai Quang Trung, "Behind the Vladivostok Initiative: The Soviet Strategic Reach in Southeast Asia," *Indochina Report*, No. 8, October 1985, p. 14.

There were news, rumors, and speculation about friction between Moscow and Hanoi over the Soviet aid. One aspect of the friction stemmed from Moscow's frequent complaints about Hanoi's inefficiency in using the Soviet aid. Other friction derived from the fact that the Soviet aid was funnelled to Kampuchea directly instead of through Vietnamese handlers in Hanoi. Still another was the Soviet uneasiness about the aid being used to promote Vietnamese hegemony over Laos and Kampuchea, even though there was no serious conflict of Soviet and Vietnamese interests in the expansion of either's influence in those countries.

In short, for six years prior to Gorbachev's rise to power on March 11, 1985, Moscow shared common interests with Hanoi in its military intervention in Kampuchea and supported its stance on virtually all issues in the international arena.

Reversals of Soviet Policy in Kampuchea Under Gorbachev

After his appointment as general secretary of the Communist Party of the Soviet Union, Mikhail Gorbachev restructured the Soviet Foreign Ministry and took an unprecedented personal interest in the conduct of Soviet foreign affairs. He delivered a key foreign policy address at Vladivostok in July 1986, held summit meetings with Ronald Reagan in December 1987 and May-June 1988, and launched several new initiatives aimed at reducing international tensions. His peace posture has been favorably reported, and Kremlin observers have been generally impressed by his dynamic personality.

In judging a man's contributions to peace, one should not be misled by his appearance, dress, or even words, lest inadequate attention be paid to his deeds. As for Gorbachev's contributions to peace in Kampuchea, I propose to take select key issues into consideration and observe how much he has departed from his predecessors, who helped create the existing Kampuchean problem.

Gorbachev's Pragmatism. The Soviet Union under Gorbachev has deployed comparatively sophisticated tactics in pursuing its national interests. Gorbachev has recognized that using force (as in Afghanistan and Kampuchea) would not be to Moscow's long-term benefit. He has also rightly perceived that Soviet technology continues to stagnate and trail behind that of the highly industrialized West.

The changes in the Soviet Union underscore the emphasis on a "new thinking" leading to a new approach. But Gorbachev realized that the new ideas could not be implemented without removing Andrei Gromyko from his politically important Foreign Ministry post to the ceremonial post of Soviet president. Hence, one of the most obvious changes in Soviet diplomacy has been the expansion of contacts with a greater variety of countries—an omnidirect approach. The new foreign minister, Eduard Shevardnadze, has been active in promoting the "new thinking," as have Soviet diplomats all over the world, who have been instructed to present the U.S.S.R. to broader masses of the world.

In Southeast Asia, as in Afghanistan, the Gorbachev leadership might have come to the conclusion that, military might does not translate into real or lasting strength when confronted with nationalism. In Afghanistan, Moscow undertook direct military intervention and could thus reverse its action by its own effort. In Kampuchea, however, Moscow has to work through Hanoi.

In addition, the Gorbachev leadership has found it difficult to dissociate itself from the Brezhnev legacy. Thus Moscow is extremely cautious in making public any change of commitment vis-à-vis Vietnam and Kampuchea. In the Vladivostok speech, for example, Gorbachev made no specific reference to the Kampuchean issue and pre-empted any speculation that he might use his influence to soften the Vietnamese stand on Kampuchea, which could have paved the way for the Vietnamese normalization of relations with China. Instead, he stated that the issue of normalization was a matter of the sovereign governments and leaderships of Vietnam and China. The Vladivostok speech revealed Gorbachev's determination to expand the Soviet presence in the East Asian and Pacific regions.

The Gorbachev-Reagan summit meetings in December 1987 and in May-June 1988 paid no real attention to the Kampuchean problem. It was mentioned in general terms along with other regional issues in the joint communiqué, but this constituted no more than lip service to ASEAN in response to the latter's active lobbying. The superpowers set their own priorities.

Prior to the Moscow meeting of May-June 1988, when Premier Prem

Tinsulanonda of Thailand led the Thai delegation to Moscow, Soviet officials, from the working level to the top, were willing to discuss the Kampuchean problem, but all held to Hanoi's position when concrete issues were raised. Hence, the Thai-Soviet Joint Communiqué issued on May 23, 1988, was lacking in such precise terminology as "Vietnamese troop withdrawal" and "self-determination." Instead, the communiqué included such general and abstract terms as "The Kampuchean problem must be solved by political means," and the solution should "take into consideration the security interests of all concerned parties."

The only obvious change of Soviet attitude toward the Kampuchean problem has been the recognition of objective reality: The aggressor in Afghanistan, like the aggressor in Kampuchea, has been fighting a no-win war. Moscow and Hanoi no longer claim that time is on their side, or that the situation in Kampuchea is "irreversible." In the past, Soviet leaders had tried to force world public opinion to accept a *fait accompli* on the Vietnamese act in Kampuchea; Soviet Deputy Foreign Minister Mikhail Kapitsa had said in April 1986 that the situation in Kampuchea was irreversible, and Foreign Minister Eduard Shevardnadze repeated this in March 1987. This public position changed suddenly in April 1987 at the tenth round of Sino-Soviet talks on normalization of relations in Moscow where the Soviet delegation proved willing to discuss with its Chinese counterpart the Kampuchean and Afghan problems. Although no agreement was reached, many were enthusiastic because of the emergence of Moscow's new sensibility. The 12th round of Sino-Soviet talks on normalization of relations ended on June 20, 1988. Subsequently, the TASS news agency went still further by revealing that Moscow was ready to promote a peace settlement in Kampuchea.[3]

This change should be seen as an acceptance of reality, not an admission of wrongdoing, on the part of Moscow and Hanoi. The change, so far, is minimal and abstract in its implications. Because of contradictory interests in Southeast Asia, Moscow wants to improve and further its relations with China and ASEAN, but it also wants to support Vietnam and thereby keep the Soviet military presence alive in Southeast Asia. To make this abstract change effectively felt among politically naive observers, Moscow and Hanoi are trying to capitalize on Gorbachev's charming personality to also project themselves as champions of peace and advocates of a nuclear free zone.

Models for Talks. As soon as Moscow and Hanoi decided to talk with the Khmer resistance forces, the question of ground rules and models arose. This process in itself required time and effort among the concerned parties to reach an acceptable agreement. The Khmer resistance forces, China, and ASEAN have agreed that there must be negotiations between Vietnam and the resistance forces, they being the real conflicting parties, or that the negotiation process be sponsored by the United Nations, under the guidance of the U.N.-

sponsored International Conference on Kampuchea in New York in 1981. But these conditions were not acceptable to the Hanoi-Phnom Penh-Moscow axis.

The first strategy adopted by Hanoi and Moscow was to try to win over the Sihanoukist faction. This scheme required Sihanouk to return to Phnom Penh to assume an unspecified leadership post. This idea was perhaps initiated by Moscow. It was launched after PRK Foreign Minister Hun Sen's visit to Moscow in September 1983. This did not work simply because Sihanouk was not, and still is not easy to reconcile with; he did not even take the trouble to ask how much real power he would have in the proposed regime. If Sihanouk had accepted the proposal, the coalition government would have been split. However, the real problem would have remained unsolved, because the Democratic Kampuchea faction would still constitute a real challenge to the Phnom Penh regime.

The second attempt was to employ an improved version of the U.N.-sponsored "proximity talks" on Afghanistan, but the abnormality of this original model was serious (as were the negative implications of passing it on). The roots of the problem originated in Moscow, which invaded and occupied Afghanistan. As a consequence, Pakistan's territories bordering on Afghanistan became a haven for Afghan refugees and resistance fighters. Like Hanoi, however, Moscow was not willing to talk with the resistance. Instead, the foreign ministers of Pakistan and Afghanistan conducted negotiations by holding separate meetings with U.N. mediator, Mr. Diego Cordovez.[4] The "proximity talks" began in 1983, but an agreement was signed by the parties only on April 14, 1988, with the United States and the U.S.S.R. acting as guarantors. The agreement set the dates for the Soviet troop withdrawal between May 15, 1988, and February 15, 1989.

The Gorbachev leadership has hailed the Geneva Accords on Afghanistan as a great success and has tried to use the pledged Soviet troop withdrawal as campaign material for building the image of a peace-loving Soviet Union. Thus the Thai-Soviet Joint Communiqué issued in Moscow on May 23, 1988, included a sentence praising the Soviet act in Afghanistan: "They [the U.S.S.R.and Thailand] welcomed the signing of the Geneva Accords on April 14, [believing] that the Accords can be used as a model for settling the Kampuchean issue."

Earlier, the idea of "proximity talks" had attracted the attention of some of the ASEAN leaders, although they did not necessarily share a common understanding of its substance. After their annual meeting on July 8, 1985, the ASEAN foreign ministers proposed a solution to the Kampuchean conflict through "proximity talks." This was ignored by Hanoi, but even if Hanoi had been receptive to the proposal, there would still remain problems in identifying which groups and countries should be included in the talks.

In the final analysis, the "proximity talks" model has not been adopted.

The Soviet leadership has attempted to advance the idea of a Kampuchean resolution, but it has no desire to pressure Hanoi. As for ASEAN, divisions would be certain to surface under strong or sustained pressure, for its members could hardly agree among themselves as to which parties would participate in the proposed "proximity talks." Neither was Hanoi enthusiastic: It reacted by saying that the Afghan and Kampuchean cases were basically different. Both Hanoi and Phnom Penh have been trying to demonstrate to the world that they are independent from Moscow and that Soviet pressure on them will not work.

Another new initiative was put forward by the former Indonesian Foreign Minister, Dr. Mochtar Kusumaatmadja. In his quest to play a leading role in ASEAN he proposed the so-called cocktail party at a meeting with his Vietnamese counterpart, Nguyen Co Thach at Ho Chi Minh City in July 1987. The idea originally required that all the Kampuchean resistance factions meet informally to resolve their differences. This ran against the then position of Hanoi that the Khmer Rouge faction must be excluded from any negotiation. It also went against the well-known position of Thailand and Singapore that Vietnam must be brought to the negotiation table alongside its conflicting parties, the Khmer resistance forces. The Ho Chi Minh City agreement was later revised at the ASEAN foreign ministers' meeting in Bangkok. There it was decided that the Vietnamese should participate in the second stage of the proposed informal meeting, immediately after the meeting among the Khmer fighting factions.

The timing was ripe: Moscow and Hanoi had become weary of their respective wars in Afghanistan and Kampuchea. Originally, Hanoi accepted the idea of a cocktail party without its own participation as long as Khmer Rouge (K.R.) representation was also excluded. That position, however, was strongly opposed by Bangkok and Beijing. Hanoi agreed, probably with some Soviet prodding, to take part in the cocktail party immediately after the meeting of the four Khmer factions, which was scheduled to be held in Jakarta beginning on July 25, 1988. Concessions, trivial as they were, were made step by step, with Phnom Penh, Hanoi, and Moscow in close consultation. The latest concession was acceptance that the Khmer Rouge, without the "Pol Potists," could be a party to the Jakarta talks and to any future national reconciliation settlement. This meant that Khieu Samphan, currently vice president of the Coalition Government of Democratic Kampuchea (CGDK) in charge of foreign affairs, could represent the KR faction in any future negotiation.

National Reconciliation. The idea behind the cocktail party was to work out a national Kampuchean reconciliation. The essential part of this process was to get all fighting parties to talk and settle their differences, and to find ways in which to form a Kampuchean coalition government acceptable to all.

For seven years after the Vietnamese invasion of Kampuchea, the resistance forces did not want to talk with the "Vietnamese puppet regime" in Phnom Penh. Instead they demanded to talk directly with Hanoi. Similarly, Hanoi and Phnom Penh did not want to talk to any "rebel group." By 1987, moves to break this deadlock came from both sides. Moscow seemed to put pressure on the People's Republic of Kampuchea (PRK)—initially over Hanoi's head—to talk with Sihanouk, President of the CGDK. Meanwhile, the French worked hard—over the heads of Beijing and ASEAN—to convince Sihanouk to talk with the PRK. Because of the latter, and because of the urging of his compatriots and other Khmer sympathizers who wanted to see Sihanouk's faction being dissociated completely from the KR, Sihanouk agreed to talk with a Phnom Penh representative, despite his knowledge that the move was opposed by his friends and allies. He went ahead with his plan to meet Hun Sen in France twice (December 2-4, 1987 and January 20-21, 1988) and to do so, asked for a year-long leave of absence from the CGDK presidency. The Sihanouk-Hun Sen talks later proved to be a failure.

Although they did not lead to Sihanouk's direct negotiations with Hanoi, as Sihanouk had hoped, the two rounds of talks encouraged Indochinese symphathizers, as well as opportunists, to place themselves in prominant positions on the peace bandwagon. The Jakarta Informal Meeting (JIM) was part of this move.

Moscow seemed to be eager to settle, by whatever means necessary, both the Afghan and Kampuchean problems. This readiness to consider everything was apparent in Gorbachev's consultations with Nguyen Van Linh in Moscow in May 1987. In his banquet speech, Gorbachev stressed that the Kampuchean problem could be resolved only on the basis of the unification of all national patriotic forces. This indicated that he and Linh might have agreed at that point that the KR could be included in the peace settlement process.

Moscow's motive behind this move cannot be seen as separate from the Soviet overall global strategy, as mentioned earlier. Furthermore, Moscow seemed to believe that the Vietnamese troop withdrawal from Kampuchea, scheduled to be completed in 1990, was genuine, and it was concerned about the consequences of such a unilateral withdrawal. The Soviet Premier Nikolai Ryzhkov was said to have told Thailand's Premier Prem Tinsulanonda in May 1988 that all interested parties should work out measures to prevent a power vacuum after the Vietnamese troop withdrawal. It is instructive to note that Moscow had shown no such concerns over its troop withdrawal from Afghanistan.

Hanoi has been seen as less than enthusiastic about making its share of concessions. This can be interpreted in various ways. One is that Hanoi sincerely believes that the PRK forces will be strong enough to prevent a power vacuum. The other is that Hanoi had never seriously considered a genuine troop withdrawal.

The PRK had no choice but to bend with the Moscow-Hanoi wind. While it had to accept the strategy of a diplomatic offensive, it was fully aware of the weaknesses thereof, and was deeply concerned about the uncertainty of the outcome of the brewing power games. As early as June 1987, the Phnom Penh regime had devised strategies for maintaining its own interests through diplomatic struggles. It is said that Hun Sen, the PRK Prime Minister, told a gathering of nineteen Kampuchean ministers and governors in Phnom Penh on June 18, 1987, that during the period of negotiation the PRK could adopt a strategy of "talk-fight-talk": It would cooperate with the Soviet Union and the Eastern bloc countries in an attempt to normalize relations between China and Vietnam and thereby halt the Chinese international influence; it would provoke disunity among the rank and file of Pol Pot's enemies and thereby destroy the Pol Pot forces; and it would try to use Sihanouk to attack China, the United States, etc.[5]

Paris's motive is less understood. The French were believed to have successfully convinced Sihanouk to meet PRK Premier Hun Sen. They also delivered ASEAN a heavy blow by persuading Sihanouk to resign abruptly from the CGDK Presidency on July 11, 1988, two weeks before the JIM was scheduled to be held on July 25. These two acts seemed contradictory from the standpoint of Kampuchean interests. Indochina watchers asked whether the French were attempting to recover their lost influence in Indochina. Why were they working to discredit ASEAN by sabotaging the ASEAN-promoted JIM? Were they interested only in getting rid of the KR faction? And were they working in private capacity or with the backing of the French government?

In any case, the JIM took place as scheduled and Sihanouk was represented by his son. The various Khmer factions, and Vietnam, while having different motives for attending the JIM, at least stopped quibbling about the formula under which their delegations would attend.

The Vietnamese Troop Withdrawal. Moscow has also supported Hanoi's plan to withdraw the Vietnamese troops from Kampuchea. This plan seemed to undergo quantitative as well as qualitative changes. At first, no date was set for a complete withdrawal. Later, the year 1990 was clearly marked, but with some conditions attached, and finally, the year 1990 was set, without condition. In principle, this has represented a major concession on the part of the Phnom Penh-Hanoi-Moscow axis.

In practice, a monitoring system is necessary. Hanoi's announcement of a unilateral withdrawal was not guided by its own conscience but mainly by strong international pressures, especially the economic boycott. Since 1982, annual troop withdrawals were conducted with fanfare. Meanwhile, fresh troops were secretly dispatched across the Kampuchean-Vietnamese border, whenever and wherever Hanoi so wished. This was clearly confirmed by research conducted in 1985 by the Chulalongkorn University Institute of Asian Studies. It is also believed that the stage was set to cheat world public opinion. Without impartial observers to monitor foreign troop movements in Kampuchea, there is no way to confirm or deny whether troop withdrawals after 1985 were genuine or not.

On May 26, 1988, Vietnam's Deputy Foreign Minister Tran Quang announced that Vietnam would withdraw 50,000 "volunteers" from Kampuchea by the end of 1988. It was later reported that on June 30, Hanoi recalled its high command and all military advisers from Kampuchea.[6] The troops remaining in Kampuchea were said to be placed under the command of the PRK and would be entirely repatriated by 1990.

These claims were later denounced as deceptive by the DK, whose guerrilla forces have been effectively penetrating nearly all parts of Kampuchea in their struggle against the Vietnamese forces and their "puppets." A press release circulated by the DK UNESCO office in Paris on July 8, 1988, contended that between the 26th and 29th of June 1988, the Democratic Kampuchea (DK) intelligence saw seventy-eight truckloads of fresh Vietnamese troops being transported from Vietnam to Kampuchea. Details of the traffic routes were given.[7]

The DK's claim has not been confirmed by independent sources. In the past, though, its news releases have usually been trustworthy, though subject to exaggeration. If the Vietnamese troop withdrawal in this case was genuine, it would be a departure from the past. Hanoi has poor records to support its claims. It would be hard, indeed, for one to believe that the PRK forces would be in a position to command the remaining Vietnamese forces.

The Soviet Interests. Moscow has shown increasing interest in Southeast Asia. Its influence in Indochina has reached a maximum level, and that level must be maintained. Moscow has come to the conclusion that the trends stemming from the past policy did not favor Moscow's and Hanoi's interests. Thus Moscow has demonstrated its willingness to make strategic changes regarding its own actions in Afghanistan. Hanoi now is expected to adopt a similar approach in Kampuchea.

Part of Moscow's new scheme of thinking has been targeted on ASEAN. Its desire to improve relations with ASEAN is noticeable. In Moscow in May 1988, the Soviet leadership expressed a desire to the Thai delegation led by Premier Prem to become a partner in the ASEAN dialogue (as are the United States, Australia, Japan, and the European Economic Community Countries [EEC]). When Premier Prem was in Budapest, Moscow also tried to impress him by allowing him to be the first to receive the message about the Vietnamese decision to withdraw an additional 50,000 troops from Kampuchea.

Moscow is well aware that, so long as the Kampuchean problem remains unsolved, it will face difficulties in its relations with ASEAN. It would be misleading to suggest, however, that Moscow is now prepared to sacrifice its interests in Indochina in favor of ASEAN. It is not realistic to say that Moscow is more willing to balance its interests between the two sub-regions. The Gorbachev leadership may have calculated that ASEAN can effectively further or counter Moscow's interests vis-à-vis other contending powers such as the United States, China, and Japan.

Another reason for the recent change in Soviet strategy regarding Southeast Asia has to do with the waning influence of the United States. In recent years Moscow has found its own potential in gaining greater acceptance among ASEAN by exploiting negative problems created by Washington (e.g. military bases, copyright controversies, trade restrictions). The ASEAN peoples are now diversifying their interests, which were before heavily tied to the United States. Moscow under Gorbachev wants to show ASEAN that there is a better alternative, that superpowers are not always narrow-minded. These considerations could be detected in various attempts by Moscow to fish in troubled waters.

The new Soviet leadership believes in the effectiveness of peaceful means over military means in gaining further influence in Southeast Asia, at least under the present conditions. Only time will tell whether this is a tactical move or a sincere change in the Soviet outlook. Moscow's problem is that in the past it allowed its Vietnamese surrogates to terrorize Southeast Asia, and Moscow reaped more benefits from the unrest in Indochina than any other external power. Now, if Moscow is serious about peaceful coexistence with the Southeast Asian peoples, it has to prove it is so through its Vietnamese surrogates. This may be a difficult task. If Hanoi, in its own interest, is not willing to correct past wrongdoings, Moscow may have to be content with its current gains.

The Real Issues

We have witnessed the objective reality of the logic of aggression. Moscow and Hanoi's aggressive schemes in Kampuchea have been stopped on the battlefield, and a new device on the diplomatic front has been opened. The following points are good reminders to all Indochina watchers wary of being misled by various kinds of diplomatic maneuvering.

Any Soviet Contribution? If Gorbachev has a policy on the Kampuchean conflict, it is vague, and he has not yet found the means to implement it. Whatever his policy turns out to be, he does not want to do anything that could be interpreted as putting pressure on Hanoi. When General Prem visited Moscow in May 1988, he found that his Soviet counterparts were willing to discuss the Vietnamese troop withdrawal and Kampuchean self-determination, but that they insisted on excluding such terms in the Joint Communiqué to avoid embarrassing their Vietnamese ally.

Why is it that Moscow cannot be more concrete in exerting influence over Hanoi, especially in the light of its massive aid to Hanoi? The answer lies undoubtedly in calculated Soviet national interests. Moscow is aware of the bargaining power of Hanoi should Moscow fail to support its important positions. The Soviet military bases in Vietnam may be more important to Moscow than any improvement of relations with ASEAN and China.

In the final analysis, in spite of the diplomatic maneuvering, Soviet contributions to the settlement of the Kampuchean conflict remain limited. Moscow's positions on the matter can be summarized as follows: First, Moscow has been, and still wants to be, supportive of Hanoi's positions. Second, Moscow, especially under Gorbachev, has expressed its interest, and will continue to do so, to seek a settlement of the Kampuchean conflict. Third, Moscow wants to see the improvement of Sino-Vietnamese relations, thinking that this will consequently lead to a settlement of the Kampuchean problem. Finally, Moscow believes that a solution to the problem itself lies in a process of national reconciliation and unification of all patriotic forces in Kampuchea.

An Alternative. Moscow's above outlined positions have not revealed a fundamental change in Soviet foreign policy. The basic issue of the Kampuchean conflict is the international principle of self-determination. It is not clear whether the Gorbachev leadership is in favor of this recognized principle. Hanoi, in any case, has not learned how to live with it.

Moscow does not have to pressure Vietnam to the extent that such pressure will jeopardize Moscow's own interests vis-à-vis that country, but it can persuade Hanoi to abandon the present destructive course. The flow of Soviet aid can be diverted from evidently destructive purposes to constructive ones, especially economic development. There is no other better way for the Soviet Union to convince its potential friends, ASEAN and China, that Moscow is genuinely serious in working for peace. This requirement is highly justified in view of the fact that the Kampuchean problem is partly of the Soviet making. Gorbachev should undo Brezhnev's mistaken policy by detaching himself from his predecessor's practices and adopting concrete new policy initiatives.

Vietnamese Pride. The Vietnamese appreciate the massive Soviet aid, which has increased even as Moscow proceeds to normalize relations with China. However, from the Vietnamese point of view, Hanoi is not expected to be indebted to Moscow, or to owe it gratitude. The Vietnamese believe that Moscow's support serves solely to further Soviet interests. Moscow got what it wanted—military bases and the encirclement of China.

In other words, the moral incentive behind Moscow's behavior is not strong enough to convince Vietnam to share Moscow's sentiments. If Moscow shows any sign of selling out Vietnam, the latter would demonstrate its independent status by forcing the Soviets out of the military bases, which, incidentally, would be seen as an heroic act by the Vietnamese people. The Soviets seem to have tried their best to prevent that from happening.

So, the Soviet role is essentially limited. Hanoi is still in command as far as its relations with Kampuchea are concerned. It is believed that the partial Vietnamese troop withdrawal since 1982, although deceitful, was initiated by Hanoi in an attempt to end its diplomatic isolation and economic difficulties. But Hanoi's announcement on May 26, 1988, of a plan to withdraw 50,000 troops from Kampuchea by the end of 1988 was perhaps influenced by Moscow. The decision was made in Moscow during the visit of Thach and immediately after Prem's visit. The largest ever troop withdrawal, including some 300 field commanders and advisers, was carried out as early as June 1988. It remains to be seen whether this troop withdrawal is genuine or just another round of troop rotations.

There is no clear evidence to demonstrate that Hanoi has changed its illegitimate objectives in its relations with Kampuchea. But there is now clear recognition of the difficulties involved. Political isolation, economic boycotts, and a weakening economy have strongly challenged Vietnam's national survival and one of the most important causes of these troubles is the invasion and occupation of Kampuchea.

Perhaps the most disturbing fact of this conflict is the great loss of life and low morale in the war with Kampuchea. Following the Soviet example, Hanoi has now disclosed, for the first time in its nine-year war in Kampuchea, the figures of its war casualties. Lieutenant General Le Kha Phieu, Deputy Commander of the Vietnamese Forces in Kampuchea, said in Phnom Penh on June 30, 1988, that about 55,000 Vietnamese troops have been killed since 1977 and that an equal number of men have been wounded.[8]

There is a sense of urgency on the part of the Vietnamese leadership to do something to alleviate the aforementioned suffering. With or without Soviet advice (pressure or persuasion), Hanoi is seeking change. Time is not on the Vietnamese side—the advocates of the Vietnamese cause must now realize that it is difficult, psychologically, to force the Vietnamese leadership to accept that the Kampuchean situation is reversible.

All these conditions drove Hanoi to the decision to attend the so-called cocktail party in Indonesia. But Nguyen Co Thach led his delegation to the talks to reiterate his long-held position that the world community must help him to get rid of the "Pol Potists," rather than promote Kampuchean self-determination.

The Chinese Connection. General Secretary Gorbachev has made the improvement of Sino-Soviet relations a high priority. Although under his leadership the Soviet Union has improved relations with China significantly in the fields of trade and culture, major obstacles to political relations persist. Beijing has specifically named three major stumbling blocks, one of which is the

Vietnamese occupation of Kampuchea. Beijing believes that Hanoi would not have entangled itself in Kampuchea without Soviet support, and it argues that Moscow has enough influence on Hanoi to urge it to withdraw its troops from Kampuchea. Beijing has publicly announced that this obstacle is the most important of all.

The high priority that Gorbachev assigns to the improvement of Sino-Soviet relations is based on several arguments. One is rooted in a strategic view that China is too powerful for the Soviets to ignore: Its growing military strength and increasing cooperation with the United States are potentially threatening to the Soviet Union. For this and other reasons, Gorbachev has tried his best to compromise with the Chinese leadership. Inevitably, then, he has to work through Hanoi to reach his goal of normalization with China.

The Vietnamese have their own order of priorities. But in dealing with greater powers, such as China and the Soviet Union, Hanoi has had to work out tactics and strategies to retain its vital interests, reordering other subordinate priorities as the prevailing conditions allow.

Territorial integrity is a matter of vital interest to all countries. As an ally, Hanoi has no doubt expected the Soviet Union to be more supportive of the Vietnamese cause in the Sino-Vietnamese dispute over the Spratly Islands. So far, Soviet support has been confined to providing satellite and signal intelligence on Chinese ship movements. In response to the Sino-Vietnamese clash over the the Spratlys in March 1988, the Soviet daily newspaper *Pravda* expressed concern but called on both sides to refrain from the use of force. The *Far Eastern Economic Review* noted that Moscow seemed to show its even-handed policy: Moscow radio commented that "the Soviet people cherish friendly feelings for both the Vietnamese and the Chinese and want to see a quick settlement to the territorial dispute."[9]

This can hardly satisfy Hanoi. Repeated calls by Moscow for normalization of Sino-Vietnamese relations in the midst of territorial disputes can be easily interpreted by Hanoi as a form of Soviet pressure. In an effort to press Vietnam for a total troop withdrawal from Kampuchea, China has, in a sense, scored some success in putting pressure on Hanoi through Moscow.

A Question About Motives: A Change of Policy or Tactics?

Apparently, Moscow, Hanoi, and Phnom Penh have been making a concerted effort to project a positive image in championing peace and a nuclear-free zone in Southeast Asia.

Have they really changed? Have Moscow and Hanoi changed their goals—world and regional domination—in favor of *perestroika* and *glasnost*, or are they simply making tactical moves to seek gains? This is a question of motives that is difficult to answer one way or the other. Further monitoring efforts are required to match words with deeds. So far, though, the two rounds of talks between Sihanouk and Hun Sen seem to have provided the Soviet bloc with further gains. The JIM-I at the end of July 1988, as well as the JIM-II in February 1989, seem to have done the same.

It seems that there is a general consensus that Moscow and Hanoi want to cut back on foreign military ventures but are not yet willing to abandon what they have illegally gained by military means. It is too burdensome for them to continue their present strategy, so now they want the international community to take over the burden. Moscow is asking for concessions from ASEAN for a political settlement in Kampuchea, holding up the specter of the Lebanese disaster as a threat. Meanwhile Hanoi demands that the "Pol Potists" be eliminated to prevent more disasters. Other countries should be aware of the pitfalls inherent in these postures, for if they are not cautious they may end up helping the aggressors preserve unjustly gotten gains.

In his book, *Perestroika*, Gorbachev claims to be a diligent follower of Lenin and quotes Lenin's *Selected Works* extensively. Just like Lenin in the last years of his life, Gorbachev is confronted with serious internal and external problems. For his regime, this is not a good time to preach communism, but it is a time to consolidate, to infiltrate and soften the enemy, instead of attacking it. This line of argument deserves careful consideration. Genuine peacelovers should never allow Moscow and Hanoi to use their illegal gains as bargaining chips in seeking further gains.

Notes

1. Dieter Heinzing, "The Role and Interests of the U.S.S.R. in Indochina," in *Indochina and Problems of Security and Stability in Southeast Asia*, Khien Theeravit and MacAlister Brown, eds.(Bangkok: Chulalongkorn University Press, 1981, 1983), pp. 141-142.
2. Ibid., p. 137.
3. *Nation* (Afternoon Extra) (Bangkok), June 21, 1988, p. 3.
4. There was no direct negotiation, because Pakistan does not recognize the Kabul regime as a legitimate government.
5. The contents of Hun Sen's speech were allegedly leaked by a DK agent through DK authorities. Although the authenticity of the speech still needs to be verified, the writer of this paper is convinced that the substance of the speech is in line with general PRK policy currently practiced.
6. *Nation* (Bangkok), July 1, 1988, p. 1.
7. Press Release No. 041/88 (July 8, 1988) by Permanent Delegation of Democratic Kampuchea to UNESCO.
8. In Afghanistan, 13,310 Soviets were killed and 35,478 were wounded during the nine-year Soviet war. The number of Americans killed in the Vietnam War is estimated to be 58,000. See *Nation*, July 1, 1988, p. 1.
9. *Far East Economic Review*, June 9, 1988, p. 17.

12

Gorbachev's "New Thinking" and the Philippines: Making of a New Regional Conflict?

Frank Cibulka

Introduction

The second half of the 1980s has emerged as an era of significant change in the international relations arena. Its catalyst can be found in the dramatic developments currently taking place in the Soviet Union. The elevation of Mikhail Gorbachev to the Kremlin leadership in March 1985 and his subsequent launching of the twin reform campaigns of *glasnost* (openness) and *perestroika* (restructuring) were extended into the area of foreign policy through the articulation of the principles of the "new political thinking." The "new thinking" has been strongly conditioned by Gorbachev's domestic priorities and reform vision since only a calm international environment and avoidance of a further superpower arms race will allow a revitalization of the moribund Soviet economy. At the same time, the new approach to Soviet foreign policy can also be seen as an outcome of the process of critical reevaluation of the Soviet Union's role in the international arena and its more realistic adaptation to the changing world. Moscow has promoted as the principal ideological components of the "new thinking" the concepts of impermissibility of war in the nuclear era, of recognition of the existence of global problems, and of stress on the interdependence of states in the modern world, along with emphasis on new approaches to arms control and willingness to contribute to the resolution of Third World regional conflicts.[1] Without constituting a renunciation of the Soviet Union's ultimate revolutionary and ideological goals, the "new thinking" has come to be regarded by Soviet scholars as a continuation of the international class struggle in its "civilized forms."[2] What initially seemed only to constitute changes in the style of Soviet foreign policy conduct gradually metamorphosed into significant modifications in its substance. Among the new initiatives, the renewed superpower détente and the arms reduction process have been pursued vigorously through a series of summit meetings between President Ronald Reagan and General Secretary Mikhail Gorbachev, culminating in December 1987 in Washington, where the Intermediate Range Nuclear Forces (INF) Treaty was signed. The INF Treaty, for the first time in history, provided for the elimination of an entire class of nuclear weapons through the destruction of intermediate and shorter-range missiles. The continuing negotiations between the superpowers are now primarily focused in the Strategic Arms Reduction Talks (START), aimed at halving the superpower's long-range nuclear missile arsenals.

The "new thinking" also brought about revisions in Soviet Third World policy. While Moscow steadfastly retains its expensive Third World habit—the commitment to support chronically troubled Third World Leninist allies, such as Cuba and Vietnam—it appears to be less willing to pursue the more adventurist policies associated with Nikita Khrushchev and Leonid Brezhnev. The Soviet Union has not abandoned its military, material, and political support of revolutionary, socialist-oriented developing states such as Afghanistan, Nicaragua, Angola, Ethiopia, Cambodia and South Yemen, but it has become wary of accepting new Third World commitments, as can be seen from its ambivalent attitude toward Libya. The Gorbachev leadership has also indicated greater willingness to seek a negotiated solution to major regional conflicts in which it is involved directly or through a Leninist proxy. This has been demonstrated by the signing in April 1987 of the Geneva Accords on a political settlement in Afghanistan, which provided for a withdrawal of Soviet troops from that country. Furthermore, Moscow has recently expressed an interest in a negotiated resolution of the conflicts in Kampuchea and Angola, and appears to be successfully pressuring Vietnam and Cuba to work to that end.

The pragmatic basis for the Soviet approach to regional conflicts has been recently articulated by Gorbachev's adviser academician Evgenii Primakov:

> Regional conflicts which are in full blaze or which are still smoldering but could flare up at any moment cost human lives, cause immense material destruction, obstruct the progress of many countries and peoples, and destabilize international relations. Obviously, such conflicts are evidently characterized as regional in order to distinguish them from a direct global confrontation between the U.S.S.R. and the U.S.A, between the Warsaw Treaty countries and NATO. But the great powers are already involved or could eventually be involved in various regional conflicts. . . . Most important, however, is that under persisting international tension regional conflicts could upset the military-political stability in the world and pose a real threat to universal security. In light of all

"New Thinking" and the Philippines 215

that, new attitudes about the nature of regional conflicts and new approaches to their settlement have naturally become an integral part of the foreign policy strategy being elaborated in the Soviet Union since the CPSU Central Committee's Plenary Meeting in April 1985.[3]

The changes in the Soviet Third World policy must be ascribed to the high costs and unsatisfactory score sheet of the Soviet war in Afghanistan and involvement in radical African states during the 1970s and 1980s, as well as to the declining role of ideology in the formulation of Soviet foreign policy, and to the top personnel changes in the CPSU International Department. The new top personnel of the International Department have supervised a policy shift to the "right" in redirecting emphasis away from burdensome self-proclaimed Leninist regimes to geopolitically important countries with relatively well-developed capitalist economies like Mexico, Brazil, and India.[4]

While this has not entailed a rapid abandonment of existing commitments in the Third World, the Soviet Union appears to be scaling down its material support for revolutionary movements around the globe. Although the new Communist Party Program lists "international solidarity with Communist and revolutionary-democratic parties, with the international working class movement and with the national liberation struggle of the peoples throughout the world" as one of "the main goals and directions of the international policy of the CPSU,"[5] another section of the party program bluntly declares: "The CPSU has always believed and continues to believe that the 'export' of revolution, the imposition of revolution on anyone from the outside, is in principle unacceptable."[6]

Given the ambiguities of the "new thinking" in the Soviet Third World policy, one should turn toward Southeast Asia with a twin set of regional concerns. One relates to the question of the prospects for the eventual resolution of the protracted Kampuchean conflict. The second concern, which constitutes the theme of this paper, addresses the following question: Given the current military, political, and economic situation in the Philippines, what are the prospects that the protracted Communist Party of the Philippines/New People's Army (CPP/NPA) insurgency war will attract direct Soviet or proxy support, thus becoming a new regional conflict with a superpower involvement?

In the twenty years since its founding in 1968, the Communist Party of the Philippines (CPP) has evolved from a small breakaway group of young Maoist dissidents from the discredited, orthodox Moscow-oriented Partido Komunistang Pilipinas (PKP) into a powerful armed revolutionary movement posing a threat to the survival of the established Philippine political order. The new party, under the leadership of its founding chairman, Jose Maria Sison, charged the old PKP with fundamental ideological deviations and strategic errors, and adopted a Maoist strategy of waging the people's war in the countryside.[7]

Aided by its military wing, the New People's Army (NPA), and by its societal united front organization, the National Democratic Front (NDF), the communist party has progressively strengthened its power position. The CPP currently claims a membership of 30,000,[8] while its NDF mass base of support is said to number around two million. The NPA itself currently consists of 25,000 soldiers.

The last years of the Marcos dictatorship facilitated a rapid growth in the military and political strength of the CPP/NPA insurgency. The "People's Power" revolution, which in February 1986 installed Corazon Aquino as the new president of the Philippines, came after three years of political chaos and rapid socioeconomic decline in the wake of the assassination of the popular opposition leader Benigno S. Aquino, Jr. in August 1983. His widow, Corazon Aquino, assumed the presidency at a time of deep national crisis characterized by a weak economy and widespread poverty, rampant corruption and military factionalism, and invigorated communist guerrilla war.

With the increasing threat of the communist victory comes the inevitable speculation about Soviet ties with the insurgents and charges of Moscow's alleged support for their revolutionary war. Such support by the Soviet Union or Vietnam, as its regional ally, could serve to ultimately transform a civil war in the Philippines into another protracted regional conflict in Southeast Asia, with the two superpowers involved to degrees in providing direct or indirect support for the respective combatants. Such new regional conflict could seriously damage the currently improving relations between the two superpowers and could result in increased tensions and militarization of the Asia-Pacific region. The focus of this paper will rest upon the Soviet Union's relations with the Aquino administration and with the communist insurgency in the Philippines, as well as upon the prospects for an escalation of the civil war into a major regional conflict.

The Background of Soviet-Philippine Relations

Soviet Strategic Objectives in the Philippines

The Philippine archipelago is located on the rim of the South China Sea, astride the key sea lanes of communications connecting the Persian Gulf and the Indian Ocean with the waters of Northeast Asia. The Philippines host two large U.S. military facilities, the Clark Air Base and the Subic Bay Naval Base, both in northern Luzon. These facilities have, for the past forty years, supported the U.S. military operations in the Western Pacific, the South China Sea, and the Indian Ocean. They now constitute the last American military foothold in Southeast Asia. The bases play a critical role in the maintenance of U.S. forward-deployment strategy in the region, and in supporting U.S. forces assigned to protect vital interests in the Indian Ocean and the Persian Gulf.[9] The facilities at Subic Bay offer major repair and maintenance facilities for the U.S. Seventh Fleet, and hold large stockpiles of fuel, ammunition, and consumables. With the establishment of the Soviet naval and air presence in the South China Sea at Cam Ranh Bay, the importance of the Philippine bases has grown. Since the 1979 border war between the People's Republic of China and Vietnam, and following the signing of the Soviet-Vietnamese Treaty of Friendship and Cooperation in the same year, the Soviet Union has made regular use of the Vietnamese naval facilities at Cam Ranh Bay and Danang. In the years following, Cam Ranh Bay evolved into a major staging complex for the Soviet Pacific Fleet's submarines, ships, and aircraft. By 1985 it had effectively become a Soviet base with only symbolic administration by the Vietnamese. The Soviet forces there pose a direct threat to lines of communication to and from the Indian Ocean and thus, the American facilities in the Philippines play a key role in ensuring uninterrupted flow of oil and other resources to Japan and other regional actors.

Thus, accordingly, the primary Soviet policy objective in the Philippines is the removal of the American military presence and political neutralization of the country. While the prospect for ultimate Soviet access to the military facilities at Clark and Subic Bay—facilities that are far superior to the vulnerable Soviet installations at Cam Ranh Bay and Danang—may rank among the long-range goals of Soviet military planners, it is the emasculation of the American bases through the adoption by the Philippine Congress of a nonnuclear status and ultimately their removal from Philippine soil, that motivates Moscow in its policies toward Manila. Prospects for increased economic cooperation become a distant second among the Soviet priorities in the Philippines and are subordinated to strategic and military factors.

Overview of Past Soviet-Philippine Relations

The history of relations between the Soviet Union and the Republic of the Philippines during the first thirty years after the proclamation of independence in 1946 could be characterized as a period of deep-seated suspicions on the part of Manila and of relative indifference on the part of Moscow. This has resulted in the absence of formal diplomatic ties and a ban upon trade between the two countries. This situation must primarily be ascribed to the Philippine status as a former colony and loyal ally of the United States during the period of the Cold War. The strong anticommunist element in the Philippine political culture and the fears raised by the Huk rebellion during the 1940s and 1950s accounted for the openly anti-Soviet policies during the administrations of Presidents Carlos Garcia and Diosdado Macapagal. In 1957 the Philippine Congress formally embodied the country's ideological stand against communism into a law by passing Republic Act No. 1700, which outlawed the Communist Party of the Philippines (PKP).[10]

After a decade of cautious diplomatic flirtation and limited economic cooperation, formal diplomatic relations were established during President Ferdinand Marcos's official visit to Moscow in June 1976. In the coming years, relations stagnated due to geopolitical factors and realities of contentious regional alliances, constraints imposed by divergent ideologies, the Filipino political culture, as well as the steady socioeconomic decline in the Philippines under the burden of Marcos's dictatorship.

As American pressure on President Marcos increased during the final years of his rule, he attempted to play the Soviet card by professing his willingness to seek the increased friendship of Moscow. Soviet policy in the Philippines was based on strong support for Marcos, even in light of his blatant abuses of power and the rapidly growing opposition to his rule. American criticism of Marcos was portrayed in the Soviet media as an interference in Philippine domestic affairs. The object of the Soviet diplomacy was to position Moscow close enough to the Marcos regime in order to later reap benefits from the expected rift between Washington and Manila. Ultimately, this strategy backfired in an embarrassing way when, following the fraudulent reelection of Marcos to the presidency in February 1986, the newly-appointed Soviet Ambassador to Manila, Vadim I. Shabalin, became the only foreign diplomat to congratulate the President on his controversial victory, when he called upon Marcos to present his credentials in the final days of his rule. The congratulations, which were required by protocol, received maximum publicity from the government-controlled Philippine media.[11]

The Soviet Relations With the Aquino Administration

The Soviet Union rapidly launched a diplomatic offensive designed to restore Philippine goodwill toward the communist superpower. Only a few weeks after President Aquino assumed power in February 1986, the Soviet Deputy Foreign Minister, Mikhail Kapitsa, visited Manila, and the new administration reciprocated by sending Deputy Foreign Affairs Secretary, Leticia Ramos Shahani, on a mission to Moscow during the same year. Later contacts included a visit by officials of the Soviet War Veterans association and the establishment of the "twin-city" program between Moscow and Manila. The Philippine perceptions of the Soviet Union further improved after Mikhail Gorbachev's Vladivostok speech in July 1986, in which he declared that the Soviet Union was "in favor of building together, new fair relations in Asia and the Pacific," and specifically referred to the Philippines as one of the countries with which Moscow is "prepared to expand its ties."[12]

In March 1988, Soviet Deputy Foreign Minister for Asia and the South Pacific Igor Rogachev spent four days in Manila in political consultations, meeting with President Aquino and Foreign Secretary Raul Manglapus. The two countries also proceeded with the exchange of goodwill visits by congressional delegations. A high-ranking Supreme Soviet delegation visited Manila in April 1988, while a twelve-member delegation of the Philippine Congress, led by Senator Orlando Mercado, visited the Soviet Union on July 4-13, 1988.

Economic Relations Between the U.S.S.R. and the Philippines

Philippine desire for expanded trade relations ranks as the primary reason for Manila's interest in the upgrading of ties with the Soviet Union. The Philippine government and business circles are keen to gain access for the country's exportable products to the large Soviet and East European markets. The trade between the two countries opened in 1972 when the Philippines exported $1.2 million worth of goods to the U.S.S.R. In 1976, with the establishment of diplomatic relations, a formal trade agreement was signed in Moscow, providing both sides with most-favored nation treatment in the areas of customs duties, internal taxation, and the issuance of import and export licenses. After that, mutual trade grew rapidly, culminating in 1980 with the total volume of $212.8 million, divided into $189.3 million of Philippine exports and $23.5 million of imports from the U.S.S.R.[13] As the internal political and economic situation deteriorated in the Philippines, so did the volume of trade. A low point in the amount of commerce was reached in 1986, with the total volume of $31.4 million.[14] The situation improved in 1987 with the total trade volume reaching $40.4 million, consisting of $26.7 million of Philippine exports and $13.7 million of imports from the Soviet Union.[15]

With the improving state of the Philippine economy, the trade volume is likely to grow again, although serious obstacles remain. In the past, one of the irritants has been the uneven nature of the trading relationship, with the Philippines holding a favorable balance of trade until 1986, when the relationship became almost even. The Soviet side would prefer reliance on barter trade (or countertrade), but this idea has so far met with resistance from both the private sector and governmental authorities in Manila. Another Soviet suggestion was for Moscow to be paid for its goods and services in Philippine pesos deposited in a Philippine bank account, which in turn would be their source of payment for the desired Philippine products.[16]

The Philippine exports to the Soviet Union include raw materials such as nickel, copper, magnetite, sugar, coconut products, tobacco products, foodstuffs such as fruits and vegetables, shrimp, fish, beer, rum and gin, wood manufactures, garments, footwear, ceramic products, and carpeting. Philippine imports from the Soviet Union include zinc, aluminum, coal, oil, tools, machinery and equipment for forging and pressing, power generation, mining, and metallurgy.[17] The Soviet Union is also interested in purchasing fertilizers and, as Soviet oil production begins to stagnate or decline, Moscow is looking forward to buying products from the developing Philippine petroleum industry.

The Soviet side is also greatly interested in becoming involved in a number of developmental projects in the Philippines. Foremost among these ranks the proposed Soviet construction of a coal-fired power station worth $150 million in the Isabela province in northern Luzon. Soviet officials also offered to rehabilitate the idle Nonoc Nickel Refinery and to use the Batangas and Cebu shipyards for repair and servicing of Soviet commercial and fishing vessels. Moscow is also interested in a joint venture in deep sea fishing in the Philippine waters, in rehabilitating the Philippine National Railways, and in gaining landing rights for Aeroflot in Manila.[18] According to Senator Aquilino Pimentel, Jr., during the recent visit by the Philippine Congressional delegation to Moscow, the Soviet side offered to provide farm equipment for the Philippine land reform program in exchange for sugar, copra, oil, and other natural resources.[19]

The most controversial proposal from the U.S.S.R. has been an offer by a Finnish company, Fin-Stroi, made to the Filipino Contractors International Cooperation (FCIC), to utilize Filipino manpower in ten possible projects undertaken in the Soviet Union. This proposal, which would involve several thousand Filipino workers, has been received with great suspicion in the Philippines, even though it appears to have been a brainchild of the Philippine Ambassador to Moscow, Alejandro Melchor.

In spite of the unquestionable economic benefits that could be derived from Soviet economic cooperative offers, they all currently remain under consideration and the outcome of the governmental decision remains in doubt. While President Aquino's closest civilian advisers favor closer economic relations with the Soviet Union, the country's military and intelligence community allegedly remains skeptical about Soviet motives for suggested project aid and cooperation.

The "Soviet Card" and the Bases Issue

There is little doubt that Moscow's primary goal in the Philippines is to remove the American military presence and to encourage the Philippines to move into a nonaligned, neutralistic posture. Such developments would result in a severe strategic setback for the United States and allay the long-expressed Soviet fears of potential militarization of ASEAN. A prominent Soviet observer recently expressed Soviet perceptions of the American intentions in the Asia-Pacific region:

The U.S. aim is to turn the Asia-Pacific region into yet another arena for military and political confrontation with the Soviet Union and the forces of national liberation. In particular, the U.S. seeks to make Japan a key link on the anti-Soviet "eastern front," to turn its bilateral military relationship with Tokyo and Seoul into a triangle, and to stop anti-nuclear feeling spreading in the South Pacific, and to give military and political overtones to Pacific integration, drawing the Association of South-Asian Nations (ASEAN) into a closed "community."[20]

Mikhail Gorbachev himself promoted this theme during his meeting with Kim Il Sung in October 1986:

> ... in the Far East, in the Asian Pacific region ... is deployed a major American force of 360,000 men. Japan has 32 American military bases, South Korea has 40. To this must be added plans to knock together the Washington-Tokyo-Seoul bloc and attempts to draw in other states. By all indications, they aim at creating an "Eastern NATO."[21]

Moscow's concern about the American military bases in the Philippines was even reflected in General Secretary Gorbachev's Vladivostok address, when he suggested that "if the United States gave up its military presence, say in the Philippines, we would not leave this step unanswered."[22] This section of Gorbachev's speech, although rather vague, has been interpreted in the West as an offer to remove Soviet military presence from Cam Ranh Bay in Vietnam in return for the American military withdrawal from the Philippines. The Soviet leader addressed the issue in a more specific way during his Krasnoyarsk speech on September 16, 1988. In offering his seven proposals to promote all-Asian security, Gorbachev stated:

> If the United States agrees to eliminate military bases in the Philippines, the Soviet Union will be ready, on agreement with the government of the Socialist Republic of Vietnam, to give up the fleet's material and technical supply station in Cam Ranh Bay.[23]

Given the Soviet strategic interest in the region, it should come as no surprise that Moscow greatly stepped up its diplomatic offensive in the Philippines just as the U.S.-Philippine review of the Military Bases Agreement (MBA), presided over by the Foreign Secretary Raul Manglapus and the U.S. Ambassador in Manila Nicholas Platt, was about to commence on April 5, 1988. After stormy, emotional, and often acrimonious negotiations, the American and Philippine officials agreed on terms for the continued operation of the two bases in the Philippines for the next two years. The agreement signed on October 17, 1988, provided for $481 million in annual compensation for 1989 and 1990, up sharply from the current $180 million a year, but far short of Manila's demand for $1.2 billion in annual compensation.[24] The successful completion of the MBA review was necessary before initiating the difficult negotiations over the ultimate future of the bases after the expiration of the MBA in 1991.

The Soviet offer of mutual superpower withdrawal from their respective bases in the region came at the height of the review negotiations and was seen as an attempt to influence their outcome, consistent with previous Soviet behavior.

The official Soviet position is that the U.S.S.R. and the Philippines are in a stage of "laying a foundation" for their future relationship, and that the "bases issue" is a private matter between the United States and the Philippines in which the U.S.S.R. does not interfere.[25] The activities of the Soviet diplomatic staff in Manila, however, seem to contradict this claim.

On March 22, 1988, Soviet Deputy Foreign Minister for Asia and the South Pacific Igor Rogachev arrived in Manila for four days of "political consultations." Prior to Rogachev's arrival, the Soviet embassy's deputy chief of mission Minister-Counsellor Alexander Losyukov stated that while the question of the U.S. bases is "a bilateral issue" between the Philippines and the United States, it would be "quite natural" that this would crop up during discussions on regional security.[26] Rogachev declared upon his arrival in Manila that while the Soviet Union favors the removal of the U.S. bases in the country, his government would not intervene in the forthcoming base talks.[27] In welcoming him, however, Secretary Manglapus rather astonishingly declared: "You come at a time when we are discussing the U.S. bases and, in a way, your presence is useful."[28] Rogachev had also asserted that the American bases have been responsible for "stepping up tension" in Southeast Asia and that their removal would make the region more secure. He would not give a categorical reply when asked if the Soviet Union was prepared to simultaneously pull out its forces from Cam Ranh Bay in case of American military withdrawal from the Philippines, saying "it's a matter of talks between the U.S. and the U.S.S.R."[29]

Toward the end of his stay, Rogachev unveiled his boldest proposal by announcing that the Soviet Union would "consider" a request from the Philippines to help with the verification of the possible presence of nuclear arms in the American military facilities in the country. He argued that an inspection of the U.S. bases in the Philippines might be possible once an agreement between the Soviet Union and the United States for on-site inspection of the bases, including those in the Asia-Pacific countries, was concluded.[30] Rogachev's proposal constitutes a dramatic application of Moscow's policy position, which he conveyed to Secretary Manglapus during their talks. Rogachev stressed that the Soviet Union favors a "drastic reduction of the foreign military presence in the region." This would include the scaling down of naval activities in the region and limitation upon entry of nuclear-armed vessels.[31]

In the subsequent weeks, encouraged by the anti-American tone adopted by Secretary Manglapus and by the anti-bases position taken by roughly one-half of the members of the Philippine Senate, the Soviet diplomatic pronouncements grew less cautious and more direct, in effect shedding the pretense of noninterference in U.S.-Philippine relations. In late April, Soviet Ambassador Oleg Sokolov, speaking at a forum sponsored by the Philippine Columbian Association, posed a charged question:

> Do you really believe that the very concept of the (U.S.) policy to neither confirm nor deny the existence of nuclear weapons would have been invented in the first place had it not been for the presence of covering something?[32]

Moscow placed high hopes on the passage of the Senate anti-nuclear bill, which prohibits the entry into Philippine territory of nuclear-powered and nuclear-equipped vessels and planes. Should this bill be passed by the Philippine House of Representatives and signed into law by President Aquino, it would make it virtually impossible for American forces to operate in the Philippines. In the words of Senator Juan Ponce Enrile, the enactment into law of the Tanada-Pimentel bill would "emasculate" the Military Bases Agreement.[33] Soviet diplomats were therefore stung by the statement of President Aquino's Justice Secretary Sedfrey Ordonez that she has the right to disregard a constitutional ban on nuclear weapons on Philippine soil. The outspoken Soviet Minister-Counsellor, Losyukov, responded on July 21 by declaring that Soviet military strategists believe the United States stores nuclear weapons in the Philippines despite a U.S. refusal to confirm or deny their presence. "I am not assuming it," Mr. Losyukov told reporters at the Soviet Embassy's regular press conference, referring to the presence of the American nuclear weapons. "I can say that our military experts are sure of that."[34] Losyukov further claimed that there was an imbalance of military forces in Southeast Asia in favor of the United States and declared "we are viewing with grave concern the intensification of American naval activity in this area." He also insisted that the Soviet Union does not maintain nuclear weapons in Vietnam.[35]

The aggressiveness of the Soviet rhetoric was not limited to military issues. In the news conference held on May 12, 1988, Losyukov served notice that the Soviet Union will oppose the proposed U.S. $10 billion international aid plan for the Philippines if it is used to prolong the presence of American military facilities there. Losyukov agreed that the aid plan would be "a fruitful undertaking" if it helped the Philippines to attain economic recovery.

But he warned that "if such a plan is devised to promote the prolongation of the stay of the U.S. bases in the Philippines, our attitude will be negative to that."[36] Losyukov revealed that the Soviet Union did not intend to help fund the U.S.-sponsored aid plan or offer a similar program to the Philippines. Instead, he argued, the Soviet Union is interested in further developing bilateral economic relations with the Philippines.[37] The Soviet diplomat's comments provoked a negative reaction in the Philippine media and resulted in calls for Losyukov's removal on the grounds of interference in the country's internal affairs.[38]

The Soviet strategy of disrupting the U.S.-Philippine military relationship may, in part, be responsible for the keen interest on the part of Moscow for exchange of legislative delegations. The twelve-member group of Philippine Congressmen visiting the Soviet Union in July 1988 included three Senators strongly opposed to the retention of the American military presence in the Philippines—Wigberto Tanada, Aquilino Pimentel, Jr., and Teofisto Guingona. Senators Tanada and Pimentel, who authored the recently approved antinuclear Senate resolution, attended an antinuclear conference in East Berlin before proceeding to Moscow.[39] Western diplomats viewed the congressional visit as part of the Soviet strategy to undercut support for the American military bases among the political leaders in Manila, especially in the Senate, where a two-thirds majority is required for the approval of any new MBA Treaty extension after 1991.[40] According to a statement issued upon the delegation's return to Manila, the two sides agreed "to undertake concrete measures to strengthen peace and security in the Asia and Pacific region." They were said to be "in favor of reducing the military threat and strengthening universal peace and security by putting an end to the arms race, both nuclear and conventional."[41]

The Soviets are hoping for further diplomatic and political gains to result from the long-anticipated visit of President Aquino to the Soviet Union. The President has accepted in principle the invitation for a state visit, although she is not expected to travel to Moscow before early 1990.[42]

Moscow and the Communist Insurgency in the Philippines

The question of the Soviet relationship with the communist insurgency in the Philippines addresses one of the most significant and controversial aspects of Soviet Third World policy. During the past few years an inconclusive debate revolved around the issue of alleged Soviet support for the CPP/NPA. This question is of great importance since a massive infusion of Soviet weapons and financial help would have a significant impact upon the combat capability of the NPA forces and thus, ultimately, upon the outcome of the civil war in the Philippines, which in turn could be transformed into another regional conflict in the 1990s.

Soviet Ties with the PKP

The Partido Komunista ng Pilipinas (PKP) is currently a weak and shadowy wreck of the original pro-Soviet communist party organized in the Philippines in 1930 by Crisanto Evangelista. Discredited in its revolutionary role, it languishes in obscurity of its semi-legal status and occupies an ill-defined political space. Its 200 remaining members are led by the aged survivors of the old Lavaist leadership.

The Soviet Union does not attempt to deny its links with the PKP. In the eyes of the Kremlin leaders, the PKP remains a fraternal party that adopts an "internationalistic position" on relevant issues. PKP official pronouncements closely follow Soviet foreign policy issues in the Philippines. The party pledged loyalty to the Aquino administration, but remains strongly opposed to an American military and political presence in the country. The PKP has also strongly championed a favored Soviet cause in the Philippines—the bases issue. The party's general secretary, Felicisimo Macapagal, declared in a recent interview that the American Secretary of State George Shultz's statement regarding the U.S. unwillingness to pay rent for continued access to the bases proved:

> ... American arrogance and intransigence. It should be countered by all patriotic Filipinos with a renewed drive to end all manifestations of U.S. domination. The Philippines has no choice but to terminate the Military Bases Agreement by 1991 and immediately implement the nuclear weapons-free provision of the 1987 Constitution.[43]

While the Soviet ties might seem insignificant due to the PKP's weakness, they should not be completely dismissed. For example, at the University of the Philippines in Manila, where many PKP and NDF activities intertwine in shared causes such as human rights and anti-bases and anti-nuclear issues, the Soviet Union has a discreet but steady presence. The University of the Philippines served in late 1984 as a venue for the first International Conference on Peace and Security in East Asia and the Pacific. The conference was sponsored by the Soviet front organization, the World Peace Council (WPC), and its Philippine affiliate, the Philippine Peace and Solidarity Council.[44]

Soviet Ties with the CPP/NPA

The Soviet Communist Party (CPSU) officially maintains no direct links with the CPP. This situation dates back to the CPP origins, when, under the leadership of Jose Maria Sison it split away as a Maoist, Chinese-oriented faction, away from the old pro-Soviet PKP. The party's Maoist visage has not yet been officially repudiated, although the CPP has, in recent years, purposely adopted an increasingly more vague ideological posture. There are reports that the 1987 Party Conference, which allegedly elected the party's founder and chief ideologist Sison as Chairman in absentia, produced a draft constitution dropping the Maoist doctrine of "protracted people's war" and embracing a classical Leninist position.

Shortly after his arrival in Manila as the new Soviet Ambassador to the Philippines, Oleg Sokolov declared in November 1987: "The U.S.S.R. is not supplying any arms to the rebels."[45] The late Soviet President Andrei Gromyko, receiving the delegation of visiting Philippine congressmen in the Kremlin on July 4, 1988, was asked by Senator Mercado about the Soviet ties to the Philippine insurgency. He replied:

> Since Lenin's time a significant part of our foreign policy has come to be non-interference in the internal affairs of states. Non-interference, non-interference, and once more non-interference. We have always been guided by this principle and we are guided by it also currently.[46]

Significantly, this exchange was reported in the party newspaper, *Pravda*. Soviet diplomats in Manila are also fond of pointing out that the CPP has yet to shed its formal Maoist identity.

The proponents of the theory of Soviet support for the CPP/NPA argue that a shift of the international position within the CPP leadership began during the late 1970s after the arrest of the party's Maoist founder and Chairman, Sison. The assumption of the CPP leadership by Rodolfo Salas in 1977 closely followed the normalization of relations between the United States and China and the resulting alienation of the CPP from Beijing. The CPP, under the Salas leadership, allegedly commenced its international reorientation in 1979, while publicly still retaining an anti-Soviet position. In 1984, direct links were allegedly established between the CPP and the U.S.S.R. in Vietnam. Moscow then supposedly channelled aid to the CPP in the form of funds processed through the NDF offices in Western Europe. This money then reached the revolutionaries in the Philippines through a variety of religious or human rights groups and solidarity organizations. This argument was developed by the American Sovietologist, Leif Rosenberg, who was given the opportunity to interview Salas in detention after his arrest in 1986.[47] On the basis of the Rosenberg interview and a discussion between Salas and a Japanese journalist, it has been argued that the CPP negotiated with Moscow and Hanoi through mediators in the Philippines and abroad during 1984 and 1985. Both the Soviets and the Vietnamese allegedly offered the CPP arms and money, but the party claims to have rejected the offer because of unacceptable conditions attached.[48] Similar allegations were made by other captured NPA commanders. In one case, the Japanese Communist Party reportedly financed a shipment of weapons from the Soviet base at Cam Ranh Bay via Malaysia.[49]

In the early 1980s another shipment of Soviet or East European arms reached the NPA through South Yemen apparently with Libyan involvement.

A somewhat more guarded statement came from the CPP Central Committee official, Armando Liwanagn, who declared in a newspaper interview in October 1987 that due to the increased American "interference in domestic affairs," the party was forced to seek external assistance. He revealed in the *Ang Bayan* interview that his representatives had been sent abroad to establish "state-to-state relations" in Eastern Europe. He said that the party had forged links with all the communist parties in Eastern Europe except for the Soviet Union. Liwanagn explained his party's shift away from self-reliance: "The revolutionary struggle of the Filipino people has not been able to get as much international support as it should."[50]

Soviet funds were reportedly given to the CPP-controlled trade union Kilusang Mayo Uno (The May First Movement-KMU), in 1987. The sum of two to three million pesos ($100,000–$150,000) was delivered through intermediate organizations.[51] No evidence exists, however, of a large-scale transfer of Soviet funds to the CPP/NPA itself. While roughly seventy-five percent of the funds available to the party come from foreign sources, those that could be traced were found to have originated from Western Europe, Australia, New Zealand, and Japan.

There is no doubt that a massive infusion of Soviet weapons to the NPA would have a dramatic effect upon their fighting capability. Of the estimated 25,000 NPA soldiers, approximately 15,000 carry firearms, while their total lack of sophisticated antiaircraft and antitank weapons make the rebels highly vulnerable to the AFP helicopter assaults. No such massive deliveries of Soviet weapons are in evidence, and the NPA relies almost exclusively on firearms seized from the Philippine military. Weapons smuggling into the Philippines presents severe difficulty due to the insular nature of the republic, resulting in an absence of safe guerrilla transportation links to the outside world.

Reports of weapons deliveries by Soviet and Vietnamese submarines are discounted by the military intelligence as unverifiable. Similarly, reports of the presence of Soviet advisors with the NPA forces in Mindanao and in the Bicol region of southern Luzon do not appear to be credible. The westerners seen with the insurgents invariably come to be identified as West Europeans or Australians who, for ideological and solidarity reasons, spend some time with the NPA as a part of an "immersion program" of participation in revolutionary activity.

A significant amount of information emerged from the Bicol region of south Luzon, which contains one of the most extensive guerrilla fronts. During 1986, user manuals for the Soviet-made B-40 rockets were among documents captured from an NPA camp. These surface-to-air shoulder-held missiles are similar to the U.S.-supplied Stinger missiles, which so fundamentally improved the mujahideen's position during the war in Afghanistan.[52] In a related incident, in March 1988 the AFP forces operating in Albay province captured a prototype of the RPG-7 recoilless antitank gun, which can also be used against helicopters or low-flying aircraft.[53] Acquisition of either one of these weapons by the NPA would be very significant since it would enable them to effectively cripple the AFP use of helicopters in mopping up operations.

While such weapons have so far not been used by the NPA in Bicol or elsewhere in the Philippines, the presence of the user manuals and of the prototype weapon gives one the impression that the insurgents are familiarizing themselves with the weapons in preparation for their eventual delivery. One can speculate whether the Soviet Union did not make a preliminary commitment during the 1984-86 period to provide significant material support to the NPA, only to reverse or postpone such involvement due to the internal leadership and policy changes in the Soviet Union and the Philippines.

The Role of Soviet Client States

Several Soviet client states in the Third World have, with varying accuracy, been accused of playing a proxy role for Moscow in maintaining subversive ties with the Philippine communist insurgency. These are Vietnam, Cuba, North Korea, and Nicaragua. Except for Vietnam, however, the potential impact of their activities must be seen as not negligible yet peripheral to the domestic factors affecting the insurgency situation in the Philippines.

Vietnam, which has been called the "Cuba of the Orient" and whose doctrinal pronouncements have over the years hinted at wider regional ambitions outside of Indochina, would appear to be the most logical candidate for the proxy role in the Philippines. As was already indicated, Vietnam was implicated in several weapons shipments to the NPA during the early 1980s. But Vietnam's current domestic situation and external position are highly unfavorable toward sustaining an additional revolutionary commitment. Vietnam's disastrous economy and its inability to conclude the draining occupation of Kampuchea will certainly discourage it from providing large-scale support to the Philippine insurgents. During a visit to Manila by the Vietnamese Vice Minister of Foreign Affairs, Tran Quang Co, in April 1988, such allegations were vehemently denied. The Vietnamese official declared that his government is not giving aid to local communist insurgents since "all our thinking, efforts and resources are concentrated in building our country socially and economically."[54]

The documents seized in the raids on CPP safe houses in Manila in April 1988 revealed the Nicaraguan government's support for the New People's

Army. Captured letters of senior NPA members to the Sandinista leadership, dating back to 1986, indicated than an NPA official "Miguel Santiago" paid a visit to Nicaragua in order to promote further ties. In his letter, Santiago thanked the Sandinistas for introducing him to Cuban and Salvadorean "comrades" during his trip, and for the offer to train two NPA doctors in Nicaragua. He also indicated that the NPA plans to send its cadres to El Salvador to observe guerrilla operations there.[55] These disclosures resulted in an unsuccessful protest against the invitation extended to Nicaragua to participate in the June 1988 International Conference of Newly Restored Democracies in Manila.

According to Nicaraguan sources, there has also been an upsurge of Cuban activity in Manila, involving contacts with the urban NDF groups.[56] In assessing the behavior and capabilities of the three radical Soviet client states, it seems likely that at the present time, it will be Cuba and Nicaragua, rather than nearby Vietnam, that will seek closer fraternal links with the CPP/NPA and thus be in a position to serve as proxies or intermediaries between Moscow and the Philippine insurgents.

Prospects for a New Regional Conflict

Regionalization of the conflict in the Philippines would most likely result from direct Soviet or Vietnamese involvement in the country's civil war. The available evidence at this time does not indicate a large-scale transfer of Soviet funds or arms to the CPP/NPA insurgents. Neither does it point to any Soviet or Vietnamese personnel involvement in the conflict. The Soviet Union obviously monitors the fortunes of the insurgency campaign and very likely maintains discreet contacts with the revolutionaries. But the Soviet Union does not wish to endanger its improving state relations with the Republic of the Philippines and thus lose its growing influence on its political scene. The victory of the Philippine Communists remains an uncertain and ambiguous prospect for the Soviet Union. Moscow learned the hard way that newly established communist regimes do not always become Soviet allies. Moscow cannot control the direction of the Philippine revolutionary process and cannot predict the kind of ideological orientation that Jose Maria Sison would embrace in victory.

The Kremlin has other priorities—namely the removal of the American military presence from the Philippines and a neutralization of the country. Moscow is actively seeking to influence the outcome of the stormy Military Bases Review negotiations, as well as encourage the passage of the antinuclear bill through the Philippine Congress. The practical effect of the antinuclear law on the U.S. military presence in the Philippines and in Southeast Asia must seem extremely desirable for the Soviet Union. The American military withdrawal from Southeast Asia could tilt the balance of power in the Asia-Pacific region in favor of the Soviet Union. Moscow's diplomacy skillfully harnesses the tide of Filipino nationalism and anti-Americanism among Manila's democratic political elite and simultaneously cultivates extensive contacts with the Left—the PKP, the various above-the-ground NDF urban organizations, and radical student groups.

A critical point for Soviet policy will come when the issue of the American military presence in the Philippines is resolved with a degree of permanence. The future of the American bases in the Philippines after 1991 will be determined by protracted and difficult negotiations, a possible referendum and a certain struggle for ratification in the Philippine Senate, as well as by the constraints of the American budgetary process. Should the Soviet Union interfere too heavily in the negotiating process, or should it, in the near future, visibly provide significant support for the NPA insurgency, the result would almost certainly be a resolve, both in Manila and Washington, to continue their close military relationship. Until the future of the American bases is determined, Moscow will, at the most, pursue a "double track" strategy, cultivating contacts with the revolutionary groups in the Philippines and providing them with small amounts of covert aid as a symbolic gesture.

Should the lease on the U.S. bases be extended beyond 1991, Moscow would no longer be constrained diplomatically, as its worst fears would have materialized already, and might well show its frustration with the outcome by providing substantial military and financial aid to the insurgents. With the American military presence in the country, however, this would not result in a collapse of the democratic regime, but rather prolong and intensify the civil war.

The danger of a regional conflict would be greatest should the United States be forced to abandon its military facilities. Such a decision in Manila would almost certainly result in the reduction or termination of American military aid to the Philippines, thus effectively crippling the anti-insurgency campaign of the country's armed forces. An increasing weakness of the military might bring about a realization of the next stage of the insurgency, in which the NPA would attain military parity with the Philippine military. This stage, labelled "strategic stalemate," has rather optimistically been predicted by the CPP leaders for the late 1980s, but has yet to come close to completion. It would constitute a full-blown situation of civil war, with a movement away from the guerrilla strategy to a more conventional warfare between two standing armies.

At this point the Kremlin would be faced with a decision whether to proceed with massive military support for the insurgents in order to tip the military situation in their favor. Such a decision would be made on the basis of consideration of the following factors:

"New Thinking" and the Philippines   231

1. The ideological orientation of the CPP at the time and the prospects for the future relationship between the Soviet Union and the CPP/NPA following their assumption of power, especially the feasibility of future Soviet use of former American military facilities at Clark and Subic Bay.
2. The risk of provoking the return of the American military presence—that is, the likelihood of direct or indirect American intervention in the Philippines in order to save the democratic regime.
3. The prospects for a regional response, especially in terms of the potential damage to Moscow's ties with China, Japan, and the ASEAN countries.
4. The potential domestic political costs of yet another protracted and expensive Third World commitment, should the reform process still be underway in the Soviet Union.

While the above-mentioned analysis of risks, costs, and benefits would be instrumental in determining Soviet policy, the situation might present lesser risks for Moscow should the "strategic stalemate" be followed not by a military NPA struggle until victory, but rather by the use of a "united front" strategy through the formation and gradual takeover of a progressive coalition government with the democratic forces. The Soviet Union might also attempt to limit the impact of its involvement in the Philippines upon the superpower relations by encouraging Vietnam to assume a proxy role and carry out the more visible support activities for the NPA. The prospect still remains, however, that the NPA insurgency campaign in the Philippines might be transformed into a major regional conflict with possible entanglement of both superpowers.

The final issue to be addressed is the degree to which Gorbachev's policy toward the Philippines deviates from past Soviet approaches. It can, in fact, be argued that there is a great deal of continuity in Moscow's policy toward Manila. What has changed are the stakes of the game and the constraints upon the mutual relationship. The "new thinking" did not bring a dramatic change in Soviet policy because *perestroika* in Soviet-Philippine relations had already started as far back as the mid-1970s with the normalization of diplomatic ties under Marcos. Soviet policy toward the Philippines has for more than a decade been multidimensional, embracing political, military, economic, and cultural factors, while being infused with a strong dose of opportunism. During the 1970s, the warmth of mutual ties between Moscow and Manila was rather exceptional in the Southeast Asian region outside Indochina, and very much reflected the personal motivations of Ferdinand and Imelda Marcos. Today, in the spirit of new approaches springing forth from the "new thinking" and from the Vladivostok initiative, Moscow's ties with Manila are no longer exceptional in the region and resemble those with Malaysia, and to a lesser extent Indonesia and Thailand. But their significance is much greater because of the stakes raised by the gravity of the NPA communist insurrection and the nationalistic movement to expel the American bases from the country. At the same time, constraints have been lifted with the coming to power of a more neutralistic Aquino administration and with the new flexibility and openness of the Soviet polity and foreign policy. Relations between the two countries, therefore, remain on an old course, but have gained intensity and vitality, and their future contains both a promise of a more significant cooperation and a threat of an opportunistic abuse leading up to a new regional conflict.

Notes

1. See Charles Glickham, "New Directions for Soviet Foreign Policy," RFE-RL, Radio Liberty Research Bulletin, RL Supplement 2/86, September 6, 1986.
2. Viktor Yasmann, "The 'New Political Thinking' and the 'Civilized Class Struggle,'" Radio Free Europe-Radio Liberty, *Radio Liberty Research Bulletin* (Munich), No. 30 (3443), July 29, 1987, p. 5.
3. Evgenii Primakov, "U.S.S.R. Policy on Regional Conflicts," *International Affairs*, No. 6, 1988, p. 3.
4. Francis Fukuyama, "Gorbachev and the Third World," *Foreign Affairs*, Vol. 64, No. 4 (Spring 1986), p. 271.
5. *The Programme of the Communist Party of the Soviet Union. A New Edition.* (Moscow: Novosti Press Agency Publishing House, 1985), p. 85.
6. Ibid., p. 94.
7. Gareth Porter, "Philippine Communism," *Problems of Communism* (September-October 1987), p. 14.
8. Ibid., p. 22.
9. *Soviet Military Power 1988* (U.S. Department of Defense, 1985), p. 124.
10. Diosdado Macapagal, *A Stone for Edifice: Memoirs of A President* (Quezon City: Mac Publishing House, 1968), p. 1.
11. Wilfrido V. Villacorta, "Changing Philippine Perceptions of the Soviet Union," *Foreign Relations Journal*, Vol. 2, No. 1 (May 1987), p. 74.
12. *Speech by Mikhail Gorbachev in Vladivostok* (Moscow: Novosti Press Agency Publishing House, 1986), pp. 27, 29.
13. Alex Brillantes, Jr., "Perceptions of Philippine-Soviet Relations," *Foreign Relations Journal*, Vol. 1, No. 4 (December 1986), p. 136.
14. International Monetary Fund, *Directory of Statistics Yearbook*, 1988, p. 320.
15. *The Manila Times*, December 24, 1988, p. 6.
16. Confidential report to President Aquino, 1987.
17. Brillantes, op. cit., p. 137.
18. The above discussion is derived from the confidential report to President Aquino (1987). See also Armando Fernandez, "Getting the most out of the U.S.S.R. ties," *Manila Chronicle*, May 26, 1988, p. 5.
19. *Straits Times*, July 17, 1988, p. 11.
20. Evgenii Rumiantsev, *Perestroika: Asian Dimension* (India: Allied Publishers Private Limited, 1988), p. 13.
21. Quoted in P. Barakhta and Y. Zharkikh, "Asian Pacific Region and Security in Asia," *Far Eastern Affairs*, No. 4, 1987, p. 50.
22. Vladivostok speech, op. cit., p. 36.

"New Thinking" and the Philippines   233

23. Mikhail Gorbachev, *Time for Action, Time for Practical Work. Speech by the General Secretary of the CPSU Central Committee in Krasnoyarsk* (Moscow: Novosti Press Agency Publishing House, 1988), p. 26.
24. *International Herald Tribune*, October 17, 1988, p. 1.
25. Interview with high-ranking officials of the Soviet Embassy in Manila, February 28, 1988.
26. *Manila Chronicle*, March 6, 1988, p. 1.
27. *Manila Chronicle*, March 25, 1988, p. 1.
28. Ibid., p. 8.
29. *Manila Chronicle*, March 24, 1988, p. 1.
30. *Manila Chronicle*, March 26, 1988, p. 1.
31. Ibid., p. 3.
32. *Manila Chronicle*, April 28, 1988, p. 1.
33. Gaspar Balthazar, "Soviet Diplomacy and the Bases," *Manila Bulletin*, July 12, 1988, p. 16.
34. *Straits Times*, July 22, 1988, p. 10.
35. Ibid., p. 10.
36. *Manila Chronicle*, May 13, 1988, p. 1.
37. Ibid., p. 8.
38. *Manila Bulletin*, May 23, 1988, p. 1.
39. *Manila Bulletin*, July 12, 1988, p. 16.
40. *Straits Times*, July 3, 1988, p. 11.
41. *Straits Times*, July 17, 1988, p. 11.
42. *Straits Times*, July 21, 1989, p. 15.
43. *Manila Bulletin*, June 23, 1988, p. 1.
44. Leif Rosenberg, "Philippine Communism and the Soviet Union," *Survey*, Vol. 29, No. 1 (Spring 1985), p. 144.
45. *Straits Times*, November 27, 1987, p. 15.
46. *Pravda*, July 5, 1988, p. 5.
47. Leif Rosenberg, "The Soviets' Hidden Hand," *Asian Wall Street Journal*, July 1, 1987.
48. Porter, op. cit., p. 17.
49. *ASEAN Forecast*, Vol. 7, No. 8 (August 1987), p. 95.
50. *Straits Times*, October 13, 1987, p. 8.
51. Interview with a former AFP intelligence officer, Manila, October 1987.
52. Interview with a former AFP provincial commander, Manila, April 1988.
53. Interview with high-ranking AFP officers at the Regional and Provincial Command in Legaspi, Albay Province, April 1988.
54. *The Philippine Star*, April 26, 1988, p. 1.
55. *Manila Bulletin*, May 30, 1988, pp. 1, 16.
56. Interview with a former official of the National Intelligence Coordinating Agency (NICA), Manila, April 1988.

Part Six

Regional Focus: The Conflict in Central America

13

The "New Thinking" and Central America

Alvaro Taboada

This chapter will: 1) provide an overview of the diplomatic, economic, and military cooperation between the Soviet Union and Nicaragua and its projection on Central America; 2) assess the Soviet interest in consolidating the Soviet-backed Sandinista regime; and 3) evaluate the impact of the Soviet "new thinking" on Soviet-Nicaraguan relations. In regard to the third issue, attention will be devoted to ascertaining whether there is in the "new thinking" a theoretical approach different from the traditional Soviet approach to U.S.-Third World relations, and more specifically, U.S. relations with the Central American countries. In its conclusions, the chapter assesses the possible outcome of the situation created by Soviet-Sandinista political, ideological, economic, and military ties, which have introduced an East-West dimension into the complex and originally indigenous Central American crisis.

The Origins and Evolution of the Soviet-Sandinista Alliance

Springing from long-standing indigenous factors of the Central American environment and fanned by persistent inconsistencies in U.S. foreign policy, the erosion of the oldest sphere of influence in the world—American hegemony in Central America and the Caribbean—seems to be accelerating. As U.S. influence over the region declines, other actors move onto the stage. Perhaps the most important of these is the Soviet Union, which only a few years ago seemed separated from Central America by unbridgeable historical and geographical distances. Even if the Soviets in the past ordered the small communist parties of the region to follow a hard-line policy (1920-1935) or tactics of the Popular Front (1935-1945), they acknowledged that Central America and the Caribbean were too close to the United States not to be subject to its powerful influence, a fact that contributed to barring Soviet involvement in the area.

The situation changed dramatically after the Cuban Revolution and would undergo further transformation twenty years later during the 1979 Sandinista revolution. Led by the Sandinista Front (Frente Sandinista)—a revolutionary, political-military vanguard—the Nicaraguan Revolution would take a radical course. Since its beginnings, the Sandinista power structure was built around the Leninist concept of a people's revolutionary democracy, centralization, and the dominant role of the party in relation to the state and society. Sandinista strategic goals, as expressed in key documents such as the 1977 *General Political–Military Platform*, point out that the Sandinista vanguard is guided by the scientific doctrine of the proletariat.[1] The ultimate cause of the Sandinista party, their platform states, is "the same sacred cause proclaimed by Marx, Engels, Lenin, and Sandino."[2] (Ironically, Sandino himself was slandered by the Comintern in 1929 because he refused to turn his nationalist war into a chapter of the struggle for world socialism).

The National Directorate of the Sandinista Front, roughly the equivalent of the Soviet Politburo, was strengthened after 1969 and provided the nucleus of a rigidly structured party that practiced democratic centralism as well as proletarian internationalism in the struggle against capitalist imperialism.[3] The loss of legitimacy of the Somoza dictatorship in Nicaragua precipitated a national, multiclass revolt.[4] That facilitated for the then small but well organized Sandinista vanguard a chance to capture power. Victory was achieved through the skillful manipulation of the alliances and the control of the armed forces, state security, and other repressive organizations.[5] The tactics used by the Sandinistas recall some of the tactics used by the communist parties of Czechoslovakia and Hungary (1945-1948) to manipulate their democratic "allies" enroute to power.[6]

The Sandinista revolution would provide the Soviet Union with unexpected political opportunities and potentially strategic gains in the Middle American region. Despite the well-known Leninist affiliation of the Frente Sandinista since the 1960s, Soviet diplomacy was very cautious toward the Frente once it took power as part of a broad national alliance in 1979.

Many analysts would argue that the Soviet Union has perceived the Third World as a periphery from which capitalism can be undermined. Soviet incursions in the Third World began actively in the 1960s and have given the Soviets mixed results, among them the status of a global power no longer restricted to the continental Euro-Asian land mass.[7] Now political as well as military contests can be carried on through surrogates in Third World countries without risking a major war. This would not be the case if similar confrontations were to take place in a rigidly defined, nuclear overstocked Europe. Nonetheless, the Soviets have been very careful when becoming politically or economically involved in the Third World: Negative experiences such as those in Egypt and Somalia have not been overlooked.

The 1979-1980 period comprises the first phase of Soviet-Sandinista relations. During this period, the Soviets were very cautious. The Sandinistas, on their part, were able to meet the minimum standards that the Soviets required of a revolutionary group recently in power and that were necessary before the Soviets would establish party-to-party and state-to-state relations with it. The Frente Sandinista proved that it was rapidly establishing a Leninist-inspired power structure that pushed radical reforms internally and aggressively pursued proletarian internationalism and an active anti-U.S. foreign policy.

In 1980, the U.S.S.R. initiated the second phase of its approach to Nicaragua, establishing open links with the Sandinistas. In doing so Moscow had to reconsider its own views on armed vanguards such as the Sandinista Front, which, emerging from the radical New Left, had been critical of the traditional, Moscow-backed communist parties in Latin America. The Caribbean and Central America in the early 1980s seemed a promising region from the Soviet perspective. The Cuban Revolution had been successfully confronting the United States for twenty-one years; Grenada, at that time under a radically oriented regime, had formed a political wedge in the English-speaking Caribbean; Nicaragua was under the guidance of a revolutionary political-military vanguard; and Sandinista-supported guerrillas seemed headed toward victory in El Salvador.

Departing from a position that had perceived revolutionary vanguards as extremist groups, Moscow saw that the Sandinista vanguard was correct in presenting itself as an example for the people of the region who were struggling for freedom from the yoke of imperialism and its regional allies. Moscow maintained this position from approximately 1980 to 1984.

During this period of open, revolutionary enthusiasm over Central America, among other significant public gestures, the Soviets hosted Shafik Handal, Chairman of El Salvador's Communist Party, which had turned to guerrilla warfare in 1980. However, in October 1983, following the invasion of Grenada by joint U.S.-OECS forces and the downfall of the New Jewel Movement, Soviet diplomacy backed off and curbed its heated rhetoric regarding the Sandinistas and Central America, while Soviet military support to the Sandinista regime, however, increased.

Since 1985, and particularly between 1987 and 1988, the Soviet statements on Central America have emphasized a peaceful arrangement that would guarantee the Sandinistas' peaceful coexistence with other Central American countries and with the United States. In the meantime, however, the Soviet Union has continued its military and economic support of the Sandinista regime, backing its Leninist power structure.

Since Iurii Andropov's days in office, the Soviet Union has suggested a quid pro quo, Afghanistan for Nicaragua, an arrangement that would have decreased the political costs of a Soviet retreat from Afghanistan. The Soviet presence in the latter country would have been subject to consideration, while the Nicaraguan regime would have received a full set of security guarantees from the United States. For its part, Nicaragua would moderate its international behavior but would maintain its internal political structure. Whether such guarantees were finally secretly granted to the Sandinistas by the Americans in recent months is an intriguing question. Some analysts would say the Reagan administration, turned down by the U.S. Congress in its request for assistance to the Nicaraguan rebels and frustrated by the indecision of some Central American countries, may have been forced to negotiate with Nicaragua.

In this way, the United States could have obtained concrete results concerning Afghanistan, while using an apparently lost cause (Nicaragua) for leverage in other negotiations. Other analysts would argue that such an agreement was not necessary: While the Soviets were forced to start their retreat from Afghanistan in the face of multiple pressures, both political and military, they were able to contribute decisively to the Sandinista survival in Central America.

In addition to the possible Nicaraguan-Afghan linkages, a post-Brezhnev Soviet Union was interested in avoiding precarious situations that would hamper Soviet-U.S. negotiations over nuclear weapons and much needed, eventual cooperation in areas such as technology transfer. Within this general framework, Moscow seems to have suggested a more moderate foreign policy to Managua. Although their input is difficult to estimate precisely, the Soviets were influential in Managua's decisions to sign the Esquipulas Agreement (August 1987), the San Jose Agreement (January 1988), and the Sapoa Accord (April 1988), the last being between the Nicaraguan rebels and the Sandinista government. Sandinista participation in the Central American negotiations apparently took place with a considerable degree of coordination with the Soviets at the global level.

So far I have discussed three successive general approaches of Soviet policy vis-à-vis the Sandinistas from 1979 to the present. To assess properly the Soviet commitment and interests in Nicaragua, it is necessary to address some of the relevant aspects of Soviet-Nicaraguan cooperation in the political, economic, and military fields.

Contemporary Dimensions of Soviet-Nicaraguan Relations

Diplomatic Cooperation

An initial, mandatory comment on this subject concerns the traditional framework in which Soviet-Sandinista cooperation takes place vis-à-vis the different possibilities or modalities for carrying out international relations.

The old perspective of power and security interests, which takes place on an exclusively state-to-state or party-to-party basis, is foremost in Soviet-Sandinista cooperation. Different ministries and organizations are involved, such as the Soviet Ministries of Defense and Foreign Affairs and the Committee for Foreign Economic Relations. Nicaragua's cooperation with the U.S.S.R. has been carried out by the ministries of Foreign Relations, Economic Planning, and Defense. The main agency handling cooperation with the Soviet Union is the Soviet-Nicaraguan Inter-Governmental Commission on Economic, Commercial, and Technical Cooperation, which manages virtually all interchanges between the countries.

Sandinista-CPSU relations are conducted mainly through the International Department of the Central Committee of the Communist Party of the Soviet Union, and its equivalent in Nicaragua, the Directorate for International Relations (DRI) of the Sandinista Party. In effect, the most sensitive issues dealing with the Soviet Union and Cuba are handled by the DRI and not by the Ministry of Foreign Relations.

Intermediate Nicaraguan and Soviet organizations that communicate with one another are always state or party organisms, or peripheral to them. Participation of strictly civilian institutions is nonexistent in Soviet-Nicaraguan relations.

It is not only the institutional setting that determines the development of relations between the Soviet Union and Nicaragua along the narrow, traditional lines of national security and strict state-to-state cooperation. Reinforcing this situation is the underlying ideology existing within the ruling elite of both countries. We will see later that the Nicaraguan government continues perceiving the relations between the Third World and the capitalist industrial nations according to the tenets of traditional Leninist thought, even if there are some signs of reform on this particular issue on the Soviet side of the equation: The international arena is thus perceived as a setting in which conflicts are not only common occurrences, but a necessity for liberating the exploited countries from capitalist oppression. Recent developments would indicate that orthodox Soviet treatment of the Nicaraguan case is undergoing an incipient process of change whose range and depth are the subject of lively debate.

As early as January 1980, a Soviet delegation arrived in Managua to arrange the visit of a high-level Sandinista delegation to Moscow. Tomas Borge, Henry Ruiz and Humberto Ortega (Ministers of the Interior, Economic Planning and Defense, respectively) were received in Moscow by Boris Ponomarev, Ivan Arkhipov, Georgii Kornienko and others. Ortega met with Andrei Gromyko and Marshall Dimitrii Ustinov. The Sandinistas brought back to Managua the promises of party-to-party and state-to-state cooperation. Agreements on trade and economic assistance were signed as were agreements on military cooperation, since it is improbable that the Soviets would provide massive military assistance to the Sandinistas without a carefully devised arrangement. Since the visit of the first Sandinista delegation to the U.S.S.R., cooperation between Managua and Moscow has grown impressively. In the diplomatic field, the Soviet press and Soviet diplomacy have steadily backed Sandinista foreign policy in its three constant goals:

1) At the regional level, the signing of bilateral agreements with each of the Central American governments. Bilateralism would mean several gains for the Sandinistas. One is derived from the Sandinista's military superiority vis-à-vis any individual Central American country in terms of military force, but also military power, the political influence that derives from military strength.[8] Unrivaled military force has provided the Sandinistas with additional political leverage over the entire region. There are analysts who believe that the Sandinistas will probably never need to use military force to achieve their strategic objectives in the region since their military power guarantees them, among other things, an edge at the negotiation table, and also impunity while engaging in subversive activities throughout Central America.

A major regional actor and the main ideological ally and tutor of the Sandinista revolution is the militant Cuban regime. Castro-Sandinista links date back to the inception of the Frente Sandinista in 1962. Since those days, Cuba provided ideological and military training to the Sandinista guerrillas. And when they took power, Cuba sought cooperation with the new Nicaraguan government in the fields of security, armed forces, education, and health. The Sandinista regime became the only true friend of socialist Cuba in the whole hemisphere, particularly after the fall of the radical Grenadan regime in October 1983. Later, as could be expected, Cuba tried to rally Nicaragua in the opposition to *perestroika*. In late 1988 Castro met with Nicaraguan, Vietnamese, and Afghan leaders to assess the situation. The Sandinistas, however, for reasons discussed later in this chapter, do not need to oppose *perestroika* militantly in order to preserve their basic power structure. In contrast, Castro has openly questioned *perestroika* and the "new thinking," remaining faithful to proletarian internationalism both in thinking and in practice up to the present.[9] The topic of Nicaraguan-Cuban relations is extremely important for a proper understanding of the current Central American situation. To elaborate on it, however, would exceed the scope of this chapter.

2) At the level of bilateral U.S.-Sandinista relations, the pursuit of a pact that would guarantee Sandinista survival. The Sandinistas pursue a U.S. guarantee of nonintervention similar to that granted by the United States to Castro in 1962.

3) At the level of U.S.-regional relations, to press for the removal of the U.S. political influence and military presence from Central America and the Caribbean.

In all of these issues, the Soviet press and Soviet diplomacy have strongly supported Sandinista foreign policy. Not only Ortega, but the Soviet press and Soviet foreign service as well have denounced every U.S. military maneuver in the Caribbean and Central America as imperialist provocations against the Sandinistas.[10] Soviet and Sandinista condemnations of the 1986 and joint 1987 Honduran-U.S. Terencio Sierra military exercises and the Solid Shield U.S. navy exercises are among many examples of Soviet-Nicaraguan diplomatic coordination. Soviet diplomacy has lauded the Sandinista's radical rhetoric in the most diverse international forums, including the Nonaligned Movement. In turn, the Sandinistas have constantly supported Soviet foreign policy, dating back to 1979 when they kept an uneasy silence in the face of the invasion of Afghanistan. The Sandinistas—at high political cost—have also supported such activities as the Vietnamese occupation of Kampuchea; and they have consistently backed all Soviet proposals on nuclear weapons as well as Soviet denunciations of the alleged militarization of space by the machinations of the U.S. military-industrial complex.

When, because of the political events in the region, the Sandinista regime changed from a bilateral strategy to multilateral negotiations, the Soviets again backed all Sandinista diplomatic maneuvers, including the proposals within the already exhausted Contadora group and within the ailing Esquipulas process. These processes provided vital relief to the Sandinistas, while the Nicaraguan rebels became increasingly diplomatically isolated. The Sandinista regime skillfully used the Esquipulas Agreement to deliver a devastating diplomatic blow to the rebels. After taking the tactical initiative in the war in 1987, the resistance forces were cut off from all military aid and were forced to retreat. This outcome enabled the Sandinista regime to increase again its aid to the Salvadorean guerrillas in 1988, according to reports from the government of El Salvador.

In general terms, Soviet diplomacy has correctly assessed the situation in Central America, where new political opportunities and prospects for eventual strategic advances are opening without any major effort or risk on the Soviet side. While U.S. policy in Central America seems to lack a long-term strategy, and while American help to the anti-Sandinista rebels is intermittent, scarce, and unpredictable, the Soviet Union, in terms of political-military cooperation, has been a consistent and reliable friend to the Sandinista regime.

Military and Economic Cooperation

The details of the Soviet-Nicaraguan agreement on military cooperation are secret. They must surely resemble, however, a secret agreement signed by the U.S.S.R. with the Bishop Government of Grenada, as it seems that this type of accord contains some standard clauses.[11] While the full extent of Soviet-Sandinista military cooperation is not known exactly, there is considerable data on this from the Sandinistas, and also from the State Department.

The Soviet Union has supplied the Sandinistas with what most observers term, considering Nicaragua's small population and the military status of other countries in the region, an impressive arsenal. The Sandinistas have more than 120,000 infantry troops (reserves included), all equipped with Soviet-made AK-47 assault rifles. By 1984, the Soviets had already delivered over 110 T-55 tanks. Lenin Cerna, head of State Security, stated in a meeting with Sandinista diplomats in February 1981 that eventually the Sandinista army would have more armored equipment than Mexico. In 1984, the Sandinistas had five armored battalions and had also received at least 30 amphibious PT-76 light tanks, and over 250 BTR-60 and BTR-152 armored personnel carriers. By 1987, the Sandinistas had two mechanized infantry brigades, fully equipped with Soviet-made armaments.

Support equipment includes at least 3,500 IFA-50 East German military trucks. The Sandinista artillery is equally impressive by regional standards. The Sandinista air force is mainly defensive, and is equipped with some 40 MI8-HIP Soviet-made helicopters and at least twelve powerful MI-14 HINDs, among other material. The Soviet Union has also contributed to the formation of the small Sandinista navy. From 1982 to 1988, the Soviet Union delivered to the Sandinista regime the equivalent of U.S. $2.4 billion in military equipment, equalling more than 110,000 metric tons, with the flow of arms continuing uninterrupted during 1988.[12] Soviet military aid during 1988 has been estimated at $40 million per month. During the first five months of 1987 the Soviets sent 9,040 metric tons of weapons to Nicaragua. That amount declined to 5,500 metric tons during the first five months of 1988. The reported decrease in Soviet military support for the Sandinistas may be attributed to two main factors: 1) the virtual abandonment of the Nicaraguan resistance by its allies; and 2) the diplomatic leverage that the Soviets may acquire by ostensibly promoting peace while the Sandinistas consolidate their power. By diminishing military aid to the Sandinistas, the Soviets may in return ask for a U.S. guarantee not to threaten the Sandinistas' survival. The net result would be a resounding diplomatic and political victory for the Sandinistas and their allies at the very door of the United States.

Before concluding the discussion of Soviet-Sandinista military cooperation, it is necessary to note that the Sandinista regime has either built or enlarged airports with military capabilities in Managua, Montelimar, Punta Huete, La Rosita, Blue-fields, and Puerto Cabezas. All of Central America and almost all of the continental United States could potentially be reached from those airfields, if the Soviet Union were to bring in its most modern aircraft, for which these airfields are well-prepared. Also, electronic information-gathering facilities useful for the U.S.S.R. have been built in Masaya, Managua, Rio Blanco, Esteli, and San Juan del Sur on the Pacific coast of Nicaragua.

Here again one should note the political role of Sandinista military strength, which emphasizes, as John Garnett explained at a general and conceptual level, "a political relationship between potential adversaries rather than a catalogue of military capabilities."[13] The Soviet-backed Sandinista regime has exploited in a rather sophisticated way its military power without military force being used outside of Nicaragua.

Exceeding 120,000 heavily equipped men, Sandinista military power contrasts with underequipped Guatemalan, Salvadoran, and Honduran armies (43,000, 49,000 and 22,000 troops, respectively). Costa Rica, with no fighting capability, has eight thousand policemen and civil and rural guards. Old antagonisms within the area such as Honduran-Salvadoran territorial disputes have prevented effective military cooperation among the Central American countries vis-à-vis the Sandinistas and their allies in the region, such as the Salvadorean guerrillas.

It is worth mentioning that the United States has given the following military aid [in U.S. $ million] to Central American countries during the 1980-1988 period: Guatemala, 21; Honduras, 401; El Salvador, 800.1; Costa Rica, 34. Additionally, there was aid for the anti-Sandinista resistance forces: 272. The total amount of military aid to the Central American region, including the Nicaraguan resistance forces was $1.5 billion. The military aid provided by the Soviet bloc to the Sandinistas alone during the same period was the equivalent of $2.4 billion, almost 160% of the total military aid provided by the United States to the entire region!

American economic aid to Central America (1980-1988) totalled $5.33 billion, or 6.6 times the amount of military aid to the region. Soviet economic aid to the regime in Managua (1980-1988) was $2.8 billion, a proportion of almost 1:1 to the Soviet military aid to the regime.[14]

The political impact of Soviet-backed Sandinista military power on the Central America region is notorious, and it continues to grow. As early as 1985, a survey made by a Gallup International affiliate based in Costa Rica found that 92% of Costa Ricans, 88% of Hondurans, 63% of Salvadorans, and 47% of Guatemalans perceived the Sandinista regime as a military threat to Central America. The presence in Nicaragua of some 2,000 Cuban military and civilian advisers, plus the presence of unknown numbers of "internationalists" from North Korea, Vietnam, Libya, and radical organizations, have compounded the issue.

Soviet cooperation has made possible the construction of the largest army in Central American history. The impact of that army on the region could well be an important political (not simply military) factor for an eventual "Finlandization" of Central America, in the face of continuing U.S. foreign policy inconsistencies. For these reasons it seems that a U.S. strategy limited to preventing a direct Soviet military presence (be it nuclear or conventional) in Central America exhibits a very superficial understanding of the complexities, nature, and implications of that regional conflict and its global impact.

Economic cooperation with the Soviet Union involves a multiplicity of projects in the areas of agriculture, fishing, education, etc. In 1986, a study was completed for Soviet-Nicaraguan cooperation through the year 2000. From 1979 to 1986, the Soviet Union provided more than two billion U.S. dollars in economic aid to Nicaragua. During 1987, the Sandinista regime received an additional $900 million from the Soviets.

The Decline of the Inter-American System: An Opportunity for the U.S.S.R. as a New Actor in the Region

Given Soviet interests in the consolidation of the Sandinista regime, and due to power and security issues as well as internationalist solidarity and prestige, Soviet and Sandinista goals are complex ones. Both parties pursue goals that may be divided into political and military-strategic. These goals have either an actual or a potential regional impact with global implications.

Even if the actual and most visible international consequences of Soviet-Sandinista cooperation must be sought in the political domain, actual or potential military-strategic advantages are not out of sight for the Soviet Union. Geographically, the distance between Managua and Mexico City is shorter than the distance between the latter and Northern Baja California. Miami and New Orleans are closer to Managua than they are to Seattle or Portland. Between southern Nicaragua and the Panama Canal there are only 500 kilometers (312 miles).

American strategists insist on the key importance of the Caribbean Sea for the United States and for South American countries as well. Forty-five percent of U.S. imports and exports, fifty percent of U.S. crude oil imports, and sixty percent of NATO resupplies flow through the Caribbean. Cuban presence in that sea, the facilities for Soviet submarines at Cienfuegos, and the intelligence complex at Lourdes are significant gains for the Soviet Union. The above mentioned Nicaraguan airports built by the Sandinistas and port facilities on both the Pacific and the Caribbean coasts are potential military threats.

Nonetheless, the most important consequences of Soviet-Sandinista cooperation are of a political nature. The confrontation of Sandinismo with other Central American countries and with the United States has contributed to the deterioration of the already declining inter-American system. This is a political issue that involves long-range consequences. Not infrequently accused in the past of being a "ministry of colonies" under the aegis of the United States, the inter-American system is the oldest existing regional set of institutions ruled by international law. The system has its roots in the Panamerican Union (1889-1948). The present-day Organization of American States, inaugurated in 1948, regulates subjects such as the fundamental rights and duties of the states; the pacific settlement of disputes; collective security; economic norms; social norms; and norms on education, science, and culture.

Many dangerous frictions among the Latin American nations were peacefully resolved through OAS consultation meetings. Thus, notwithstanding its shortcomings, the system contributed to a generally governed behavior of the states in the region.

The Organization of American States, however, started declining, leaving behind a growing regional vacuum particularly affecting U.S. regional influence. This phenomenom would stem from a number of complex factors. The Cuban Revolution and President Kennedy's dealings with it as a consequence of the October 1962 Missile Crisis were negative events for the OAS. Social, economic, and political developments in the region after 1962 led toward an increasingly independent role of Latin American nations within the inter-American system. This positive step was not accompanied by a process of adaptation of the system to changing circumstances. A serious blow to the Inter-American Treaty for Reciprocal Assistance (TIAR), a defense treaty older than NATO or the Warsaw Pact, was delivered by the Malvinas/Falkland War in 1982. Anti-U.S. feelings grew in the region, where many argued that TIAR was not an instrument for hemispheric security, but a tool of American foreign policy.

The presence of the Sandinista regime has imposed further pressures on the regional system, worsening its semiparalysis. Even if the Leninist orientation of the Sandinistas is increasingly clearer, the response that they have stimulated in the region has been diverse.

Mexico, which has traditionally maintained an independent foreign policy, has opposed the U.S. approach to the Sandinista Revolution and has consistently backed Managua. Most South American countries have taken a similar position. Anti-Americanism has played an important role in the Mexican and South American backing of the Sandinistas. Anchored in old historical causes, economic stagnation, social inequalities, and frustration in the face of developmental differences vis-à-vis the United States, and fueled by the present weight of an enormous foreign debt, Latin American countries are distancing themselves from their powerful and rich Northern neighbor.

On the other hand, Central American governments, geographically much closer to Nicaragua and feeling the impulses of Sandinista proletarian internationalism, have tried policies more responsive—although not consistently so—to Sandinistas international behavior. Guatemala, El Salvador, Honduras, and Costa Rica formed in January 1982 the Central American Democratic Community, a move aimed at pressuring the Sandinistas. Nonetheless, poor intra-Central American coordination appeared soon. By 1984, Guatemala, under the de facto government of General Mejia Victores, proclaimed that the Sandinista revolution could coexist with democratic governments in the area. Guatemala, which did not want to sign the October 1984 Tegucigalpa Accord (a critical response to the first Contadora Act of September 1984), thus moved to a neutral position. Costa Rica also moved toward neutrality. However, the region remains full of tensions.

The perception of the role that Sandinistas and their allies should play in international relations in the region, conceived by them as a new arena of the global confrontation between socialism and capitalism, appears in countless Sandinista documents from 1979 to 1988, starting with Daniel Ortega's speech at the United Nations on September 28, 1979. This not to mention much older internal circulars and political programs of the Frente Sandinista before its coming to power in 1979.

Given the existence of different perspectives in the hemisphere on how to handle the Central American crisis, the inter-American system has not been able to cope with it. The system has been further debilitated by the emergence of ad-hoc groups that have tried to work out some type of solution for Central America. This is the underlying cause of diplomatic processes such as Contadora and Esquipulas. Regarding the former, regional leadership aspirations from Mexico and Venezuela must also be accounted for.

Where would Soviet interests and expectations fit in an apparently strictly regional scenario in whose developments Soviet influence had been marginal at best? Many observers would argue that the deterioration of the inter-American system has political as well as security implications for the hemisphere, negatively affecting the United States and thus opening new options to a competing power, the Soviet Union. While the Soviet Union would have been by itself mostly an observer of the inter-American system's erosion, the Sandinista regime has proved to be a useful junior ally through which the U.S.S.R. indirectly plays an important role in the above-mentioned process of erosion.

The Act of Contadora in all of its three successive drafts (1984, 1985, and 1986) proposed the prohibition to non-Central American states to participate in the military maneuvers in the region. The cited dispositions were aimed at weakening the scope of Articles 27 and 28 of the OAS Charter and much of the spirit of TIAR, which presupposes a certain degree of military capability and cooperation among the countries of the hemisphere. (If TIAR is by now in crisis, South American participation in a South Atlantic Treaty Organization (SATO), an important project given South Africa's uncertain future, is dead for good.)

The Sandinista regime was the staunchest supporter of the Contadora Group's proposition regarding Central America's neutralization. Soviet diplomacy in turn has enthusiastically backed the Sandinistas wherever discussion turns to the neutralization of Central America and the Caribbean. The consolidation of a junior partner of the Soviet Union and the virtual expulsion of the United States from that nation could certainly be an important victory for the U.S.S.R. in terms of global policies.

The Esquipulas Accord stated that security matters as well as those of verification, control, and arms limitation would follow Contadora's proposals, thus continuing the trend toward the neutralization of the area. Neutralization could have a positive effect on the region if there existed military balance plus the desire for political coexistence. It could be argued, on the one hand, that the latter has poor prospects in the face of the well-known Sandinista commitment to proletarian internationalism. On the other hand, Sandinista military might has thrown new military and political ingredients into the region's heated situation, a fact already addressed. That the Soviet Union has not devised every aspect of the ongoing process in Central America and the Caribbean does not mean that it has not actively participated through Cuba and Nicaragua, following an intelligent strategy that takes advantage of opportunities.

At the beginning of the 1980s the Soviet Union had not only a valuable ally in the Caribbean (Cuba), but also a new friend: the socialist-oriented regime in Grenada. The secret party-to-party agreement signed by the New Jewel Movement and the CPSU, which appears in a document captured in October 1983, includes a commitment to "regularly exchange delegations of party workers, to conduct consultations and exchanges of opinion on international matters, problems of the world revolutionary process and other matters of mutual interest."[15] The agreement also aimed toward promoting "all around development of interstate relations and ties between mass organizations of their countries." Again, Soviet relations with a Third World country were understood in a security and power context, where the actors are states and ruling parties. Obviously, Grenada's interest in the revolutionary movements was concentrated in the English speaking Caribbean.

In Central America, at the outset of the 1980s, revolutionary Nicaragua represented the first socialist-oriented country on the American mainland, opening new opportunities to the Soviet Union, some of which have been discussed. A guerrilla victory in El Salvador would have quickly tilted the Central American balance toward the Sandinistas and their allies. Cuba, Grenada, Nicaragua, and the U.S.S.R. were working together closely. Military, economic, and political agreements signed by the New Jewel Government with Nicaragua, Cuba, and the Soviet Union are clear cases of cooperation. Cuba, Nicaragua, and Grenada were actively coordinating with Leninist guerrillas like the Salvadoran FMLN and other groups in the region, as may be safely concluded from documents like the one on the secret regional caucus held in Managua in January 1983.[16] Even after the setback in Grenada and the frustration of a rapid victory by the Sandinista-supported guerrillas in El Salvador, the Soviet Union has today a much stronger influence than it ever had in the Central American-Caribbean area through the fraternal collaboration of the Nicaraguan and Cuban regimes.

A cautious but firm Soviet approach to this area, its ability to take advantage of opportunities, and the perception it has created of being a steadfast ally, are factors that open further political opportunities for the Soviet Union in a region where the United States is increasingly perceived as a retreating power.

The nature of the Soviet approach to South American giants such as Brazil and Argentina differs from the tactics used in Central America, relying in the former cases on commercial and cultural exchange and on extremely formal and well-conducted diplomatic relations. This chapter will not elaborate on issues pertaining to South America; however it should be mentioned that the Soviet perception of some of Latin America's realities is becoming more sophisticated and effective, thus helping the Soviets to carry on a successful foreign policy in that complex region of the world.

The Impact of the "New Thinking" on Soviet-Sandinista Relations and Its Consequences for Central America

Few societies in history have been as thoroughly influenced by an official ideology as the Soviet society. Ideology, understood from a Leninist perspective as the set of concepts or ideas from a given social class, has provided the Soviet leadership with a general frame of reference for long range, strategic political decisions. That Leninist ideology has deeply influenced political praxis in the Soviet Union is a proposition that may hardly be contended. Leninism has often been used by the ruling elite as authority for its own legitimization and political dominance. For these reasons, references to the scientific nature of Leninism pervade every aspect of Soviet life.

It is rather difficult to foresee longrange mutations in the substance of Soviet foreign policy if there is not a previous or at least a concomitant change in the ideology that establishes the paradigm defining the nature, content, and goals of international relations. While Soviet foreign relations have been very pragmatic (many would remember the Von Ribbentrop-Molotov Treaty as a foremost example of such pragmatism), the most important general goals of Soviet foreign policy have always been illuminated by the "dialectic conception" of history. One of the issues briefly addressed here is whether changes have already occurred in the general conceptual framework through which

Soviet policymakers perceive foreign relations, particularly those existing between industrialized capitalist nations and Third World countries (the United States, Nicaragua, and the rest of Central America in this specific case).

Soviet decisionmakers on foreign policy have perceived international relations between industrial and nonindustrial nations from a perspective derived from Leninist thought. (Lenin's *Two Tactics of German Social-Democracy in the Democratic Revolution, Marxism and Revisionism, Notes on Imperialism,* and his well-known *Imperialism, the Higher Stage of Capitalism,* constitute a body of thought that continues being a main source of theory for the CPSU and in turn, for the party-dominated Soviet state.)

According to Soviet thought following Lenin, international relations since late in the 19th century have been mainly forged by the competition between capitalist-imperialist powers. However, after the victory of the October Revolution, the international struggle has had as its fundamental expression the contest between socialism and imperialism.

Since World War I and due to the process of decolonization, imperialism took on a new form. Since then, it is based on economic dominance rather than institutional settings or military presence. Given the fact, according to traditional Soviet thought, that there is a global and inevitable antagonism between capitalism and growing socialism, helping peripheral countries in their struggle against imperialism is in the interest of both Soviet security and the Soviet historical mission. When Stalin emphasized socialism in one country, he was not fleeing from orthodox tenets but was securing the survival of the first communist nation that would eventually project power over its borders.

Leninist tenets on international relations have been followed by Soviet foreign policymakers, even if at certain moments survival or the possibility of important gains in diverse fields have made the Soviets take very pragmatic positions. At the March 12, 1985 Plenary Meeting of the Central Committee of the Communist Party held in Moscow, it was, again, reaffirmed that,

> The Soviet Union has always supported the struggle of the people for liberation from colonial oppression. Today our sympathy is with the countries of Asia, Africa and Latin America, who are following the road of consolidating their independence and social rejuvenation. For us, they are friends and partners in the struggle for a durable peace, for better and just relations between nations. As to relations with capitalist states, we will firmly follow the Leninist course of peace and peaceful coexistence. The Soviet Union will always respond to goodwill with goodwill, to trust with trust. But everyone should know that we will never relinquish the interests of our Motherland and those of our allies.

Certainly *glasnost, perestroika,* and the "new thinking" were not yet in currency at that time. Nonetheless, while questioning how new is the "new thinking," in terms of its conceptual framework for assessing relations between the capitalist nations and the Third World, as well as the Soviet role in those relations, it must be remembered that *glasnost* and *perestroika* originated only in 1985 and are primarily aimed at domestic reforms in the Soviet Union.

On the other hand, it is obvious that domestic policies have a profound influence on the foreign policy of any country. It remains an open question as to how much of an impact *glasnost* and *perestroika* will have not only on Soviet foreign policy, but also on junior allies and socialist-oriented states such as Nicaragua. In contrast to the totally state-owned Soviet economy, which *perestroika* is revising, in Nicaragua some 35 percent to 40 percent of the gross national product is still private enterprise-generated, despite the existence of a Leninist power structure. Soviet administrative changes and political opening are not likely to have a deep impact in a country like Nicaragua that still has, even if vanishing, a mixed economy. Further centralization of the Nicaraguan economy presumably will not be encouraged by the new Soviet policy, especially in the face of Nicaragua's unprecedented inflation, increasing poverty, and political oppression. (Per capita consumption by Nicaraguans has fallen to the level existing more than thirty years ago, while there are over 300,000 exiles and refugees out of a total population of 3 million.) Nonetheless, Sandinista policy is not following Soviet trends: It has accelerated the nationalization process since July 1988, while political repression has increased. Part of the Sandinista regime's behavior might be explained in the light of political competition within the Sandinista National Directorate, where it seems that hardliners have consolidated power. In addition to this, the Sandinistas are probably testing their degree of autonomy vis-à-vis the Soviet Union, as the Cubans did in the 1960s. Possibly the U.S.S.R. will not push its Third World clients and friends as strongly for openness and restructuring as it will for a more flexible foreign policy along the lines of the "new political thinking." This is probably one of the reasons why the Sandinistas remain, at least tactically, committed to regional peace plans.

Soviet specialists on Third World countries are influential in policy decision making in the Soviet Union. Their perspective in international relations, as it appears in the literature from 1986 to this day, remains predominantly faithful to orthodoxy. Even the partially Leninist-based theory of *dependencia*, to which Latin American writers have made key contributions, is perceived by Soviet political scientists such as Vladimir Davidov as deviating from the scientific truth of Leninism.[17] Latin American *"dependentistas"* such as Theotonio dos Santos, Ruy Mauro Marini, and others have been criticized by Soviet Latin Americanists on such grounds as the arbitrary creation of a "dependent mode of production."

The classification by Victor Volskii of Latin American countries and their relations in the international arena answers traditional Soviet patterns of thought.[18] Latin American countries are simply subjected to capitalist imperialism even though some of them (Brazil and Mexico) might compete with capitalist nations in mercantile and industrial ventures. Anatolii Glinkin perceives Latin America's main role in international relations as a struggle against imperialism, rather than emphasizing intraregional cooperation or the evolution of U.S.-Latin American links.[19] For Vladimir Gavrilov, underdevelopment and repression in Central America derive simply from U.S.-imposed socioeconomic models. War in Central America is U.S.-created and the U.S. contribution to Central American peace plans has been to boycott the plans. On the other hand, Ilia Bulichov would portray the Frente Sandinista of Nicaragua as an organization that perceives Sandinismo as a revolutionary science applied to concrete reality but which still tries to unite its fundamental principles with the general laws of the world-liberating revolutionary movements. Soviet Latin Americanists such as Marina Chumakova, Tatiana Gonchareva, and others sustain similarly traditional views.

While Soviet specialists thus continue perceiving the aforementioned international relations within an orthodox Leninist conceptual framework and from a power and security perspective, Soviet press and Soviet diplomacy have followed in the specific case of Nicaragua and Central America a behavior consistent with their traditional perceptions. This assertion is supported by the actual Soviet backing of the Sandinista regime at the diplomatic, economic, and military level as mentioned in this chapter. It is very significant that Gorbachev did not promise to reduce or cut military aid to Nicaragua, unless the United States did the same with other Central American countries. If successful, this strategy would eventually completely erode U.S. influence in the region, where asymmetrical American, Sandinista, and Soviet interests tend to be equated by the Soviets and Sandinistas, who have developed firm foreign policies and effective cooperation.

Another very important case that underlines Soviet conduct in a global context is the Soviet approach to Panama. While the United States has not found a way to deal effectively with the Noriega regime, the Soviet Union at the very moment of the "new thinking's" blossoming is offering Panama economic assistance and possibly even security advice through Cuba, reasserting the idea that the "new thinking" does not exclude long-term goals and competition with capitalism in Third World areas. The "new thinking" aims to improve Soviet relations with the United States. This approach could mean technological and financial cooperation between the Soviet Union and its most advanced rival.

Another Soviet goal is easing the pressure on the Soviet military budget, given the increasing technological and economic gap that exists between a stagnant Soviet Union and its prosperous capitalist opponent. The "new thinking," however, does not preclude American-Soviet rivalry. On the other hand, there are hints from the Soviets that they would like to limit their commitment to the moribund Nicaraguan economy. This attitude also has political implications. Pavel Bogomolov, *Pravda* correspondent in Central America, made subtle criticism of Sandinista radicalism.[20] More direct were his views on Soviet/Sandinista economic cooperation: "As regards cooperation with socialist countries, whether bilateral or multilateral . . . I think it should have quantitative limits for each particular period and encourage a search for internal economic reserves by the Nicaraguans themselves rather than feeding them artificially for years."[21] Limited resources and the need to cope with priorities place objective constraints on Soviet foreign policy, a reality that, although very marginally, has started to influence Soviet-Sandinista relations. Therefore this chapter does not pretend to deny the possibility of strategic changes in Soviet foreign policy, thought, and practice in the future vis-à-vis the Third World. Soviet retreat from Afghanistan, Cuban-South African-Angolan agreements on Namibia and on the Cuban withdrawal from Angola, and Vietnamese potential compromise on Kampuchea are realities that point toward change.

The effects of the treaty on Angola and Namibia as well as the effects of the Cuban withdrawal, doubtlessly influenced by the Soviets, are still unclear. Many complex factors are involved: indigenous African organizations, both radical and democratic; the role to be played by an independent Namibia, which most probably will fall under the domination of Leninist-oriented SWAPO; the relocation of Cuban troops, and the role to be played by U.S.-supported UNITA, which is now being abandoned regardless of its political and military effectiveness. Finally, it is difficult to forecast how all these developments would affect strategically located and mineral-endowed South Africa, a country in the throes of dramatic change.

The relocation of Cuban troops also poses a serious question. Cuba's faltering economy and declining social system can ill afford to absorb at once over 50,000 veterans who would possibly ask privileges from their government. On top of that, the Cuban regime would lose substantial revenues (some analysts estimate them to be around $700 million) from Angola as payment for Cuban military services.

The possibility of sending a part of those troops to Nicaragua cannot be entirely ruled out. Such action could, however, worsen the already volatile political climate of Central America.

The Soviet Union will possibly act flexibly and energetically in most regional conflicts, keeping its influence in those areas that are politically or strategically important, even in the face of a growing new détente. Soviet foreign policy changes will become irreversible, and not only in long-range strategic maneuvering, when the conceptual framework of a highly ideological power machinery has shifted to a new paradigm regarding the nature, functions, goals, and outcomes of international relations. In such a change in international relations, the depth and stability of today's incipient *glasnost* and *perestroika* will certainly have a powerful impact.[22]

Many Soviet specialists point to the fact that explicit rejection of the fundamental tenets of Leninism would be unnecessary and politically suicidal for the reformist Gorbachev regime. These observations cannot be taken lightly. Additionally, the acknowledgement by the Soviets that the threat of nuclear weapons is more pressing than the class struggle, and their admission that capitalism's historical vitality is stronger than previously thought, have introduced new elements in the Soviet strategic perception. However, it may be argued from a strictly Leninist perception that the nuclear threat is of a historically mechanical nature, and that such a threat may be dealt with through diplomacy and accommodation, while the fire of class struggle (having a dialectic nature) continues burning and undermining the rival's periphery and entrails. Soviet "new thinking" must go further to forge an irreversible path towards cooperation. New domestic developments in the U.S.S.R., such as the demotion of Egor Ligachev and the removal of other important members of the old guard leadership, point to the depth of the political and administrative renovation in this country. However, turning to foreign relations, the "new thinking" has not yet produced any substantial change in the particular case of Nicaragua and Central America. Possibly the Soviets will continue pressing in the region with cautious energy, safeguarding their influence over the Sandinistas as a political asset in the strategic neighborhood of the United States. The different treatment given by the Soviets to cases such as Nicaragua and Afghanistan shows the flexibility of the "new thinking" in practice.

Conclusion

Although the Soviet Union's presence in the Central American area is new, it is a growing reality. Soviet influence has been gained through a concatenation of factors: internal conditions of Central America and the Caribbean, inconsistent U.S. foreign policies, and steadfast Soviet behavior that has taken advantage of ongoing regional political processes. The Soviet Union's close cooperation with its junior allies—Cuba in the Caribbean and Nicaragua in Central America—is a key factor in providing leverage to Soviet policies in a region that is peripheral to the Soviets but strategically important to the United States. The extent of Soviet-Nicaraguan cooperation in the diplomatic, economic, and military arenas is indicative of a long-term commitment by both parties, whose relations developed, up to this day, in three general stages: 1) close observation of the Sandinistas by the Soviets (1979); 2) full support for their revolutionary, political-military vanguard (1980-1984); and 3) Soviet influence over Sandinista foreign policy in the direction of greater flexibility, while backing their domestic consolidation as a Leninist power structure (1985 to the present). Nonetheless, there are indications that the Soviets will avoid any economic overcommitment to the Sandinista regime, possibly having in mind their Cuban experience. An assessment of the new political developments in the Soviet Union regarding their influence over Soviet-Nicaraguan relations and their impact in Central America would take into consideration that restructuring and openness are strategies primarily aimed at Soviet domestic realities, although they are also influencing Soviet foreign policy. On the other hand, the "new thinking," which is essentially aimed at international relations, is primarily concerned with U.S.-Soviet relations. While the "new thinking" has had some important manifestations in Soviet-Third World relations (Afghanistan, and to a lesser degree, Kampuchea and Angola are good examples), the Third World, even with the "new thinking," remains an area where both superpowers continue competing and even confronting one another through surrogates, as is presently occurring in Central America. Cooperation does not exclude competition in international relations. Nonetheless, the internationally overcommitted and overextended Soviet Union is expected to act more carefully in the Third World, where it will assess more realistically its priorities. Soviet foreign policy is thus significantly departing from Brezhnev's rhetoric and policies. Economic considerations will weigh more heavily on Soviet international behavior.

Despite what has been said, the Soviet conceptual framework regarding international relations continues to be an orthodox Leninist paradigm according to which exploitation of the Third World nations by imperialist capitalism and the struggle of the former for its liberation are important aspects of the international arena in which the rivalry between socialism and imperialism is a basic although now moderated feature. Given that perspective, international relations in the long run respond to power and security interests. This assertion must be qualified, taking into consideration that Soviet foreign policy seems to become less ideologically and more pragmatically oriented under Gorbachev. Nonetheless, "scientific ideology" still provides a general framework for Soviet leaders, and no noticeable change has occurred in Leninist epistemology. No fundamental changes have yet occurred in the Central American conflict, the Sandinista policies, or the Soviet behavior toward the region. Nonetheless, there are some trends that must be taken into account for a fair assessment of the situation.

First is the already mentioned fact of a Soviet-stated willingness to reduce arms deliveries to Nicaragua. Two of the motivations for this new attitude were also discussed above (decreasing military capabilities of the resistance forces and the possibility to enhance Soviet and Sandinista diplomatic flexibility). Soviet Ambassador to Managua Valerii Nikolaienko, following this line of thought, reiterated in February 1989 that the Soviet Union is ready for a more detailed assessment of the level of military supplies to Nicaragua because "this regional problem has to be solved not militarily but through negotiations."[23]

Additionally, and given the economic difficulties that the Soviet Union itself is experiencing, Soviet aid to Nicaragua is very likely to be reduced. It is of common interest, both for the Sandinistas and Soviets, to show moderation in the region. This will facilitate obtaining financial help for the Sandinistas in Western Europe, Latin America, and the United States, thus relieving the Soviets (at least partially) from the economic burden that is the inept and corrupt Sandinista administration.

Second is the important apparent political opening offered by the Sandinistas in February 1989. It is important to note that by offering some concessions to the opposition, the Sandinistas are moving along the lines of political reforms (even if these are peripheral and tactical), thus following a more harmonious relationship with Moscow than Cuba, where Fidel Castro (the Sandinista's closest ally) has flatly rejected "new thinking" and *perestroika*.

Notwithstanding what has been explained, the outcome of the regional conflict in Central America remains uncertain. One extreme scenario would be the overthrow of the Sandinista regime by a combination of domestic decomposition and external pressures. Any Soviet reaction to the overthrow of the Sandinistas would have little chance to go beyond rhetoric, given the geographical location of Nicaragua. This scenario may have been practically ruled out after the U.S. Congress voted one more time for the abandonment of the Nicaraguan insurgents in early 1988. The rebel forces, which had won the tactical initiative in the war during 1987, are now ill-armed, ill-fed, and in the process of disintegration.

A second scenario is that the Frente Sandinista remains in power and evolves toward less repressive structures domestically and a less militant posture internationally. The well-known trend toward increased repression during 1988 leaves little room for hope at the domestic level, while growing Sandinista aid to the Salvadoran guerrillas (as denounced by Salvadoran authorities) leads one to think that the Sandinistas are not abandoning proletarian internationalism.

On the other hand, Nicaragua's ruinous economy has continued to decline at an alarming pace: During 1988 inflation reached between 20,000 and 27,000 percent. Exports were less than $200 million. By contrast, in 1979, the year of widespread civil war, when Somoza was overthrown, Nicaragua was still able to export approximately $700 million.

Massive cuts in the bureaucracy and even in the military during February 1989 have increased the unpopularity of Sandinismo. These factors might produce powerful social and political pressures against the Sandinistas. For these reasons, the Sandinistas are searching again for tactical alliances domestically, while maneuvering at the regional level, delaying the democratic settlement prescribed by the Esquipulas agreement. Nonetheless, no Leninist regime has ever fallen due strictly to economic factors, regardless of the level of deterioration of the standard of living of its people. Had the military resistance continued its pressure against the Sandinistas, it would have placed on the Soviets an increasing economic cost, especially in terms of Soviet military hardware supplied to the Sandinista regime. The economic, political, and military pressures would have led to a profound transformation of the Sandinista regime or to its overthrow in the long run. Cutting funds to the resistance was an important step permitting the consolidation of the Sandinista regime. The Sandinistas' remaining in power seems to be the most likely possibility, despite popular disenchantment and the increased flow of emigrants from all sectors of the Nicaraguan society. Power consolidation will give to the Sandinistas a predominant influence in Central America. This development is already eroding U.S. credibility and influence in the area. Recently, a close ally of the United States, Honduran President José Azcona Hoyo, stated that Honduras may set aside the wishes of the United States to negotiate a settlement in Central America. That attitude is symptomatic of the perceptions of many Central Americans regarding U.S. foreign policy in the region.

An important development took place in San Salvador, El Salvador during the meeting of the five Central American presidents on February 13-14, 1989. The San Salvador agreement called for the relocation within Nicaragua, or in third countries, of approximately 10,000 Nicaraguan resistance fighters. Many of them are in Honduran camps waiting for renewed military aid (which probably will never come) to the struggle against the Sandinistas. In exchange for the destruction of the military opposition, the Sandinista Directorate, speaking through Daniel Ortega, agreed to call for presidential elections in February 1990. The disbandment of the resistance forces would take place within ninety days of the agreement. To ensure that no military activities will take place along the Nicaraguan-Honduran and Nicaraguan-Costa Rican borders, a special commission from strictly neutral countries (Germany, Spain, and Canada) would be appointed by the United Nations. The Sandinistas would permit freedom of speech, would permit (this time seriously, they argue) a free press, and would call for international observers to watch the elections. Certainly, observing the events during the election day is a most incomplete procedure to assess the fairness of a process that requires long preparations, including voter registration and electoral identification cards, free access to the press from all parties involved, and other important conditions.

Among the many weaknesses of the San Salvador agreement is the total silence regarding the nature and control of the Sandinista armed forces and security, which are party institutions, and not really national organizations. Observers argue that, even excluding the many previous instances in which the Sandinistas have not fulfilled basic political agreements regarding the democratization of Nicaragua, the fact remains that as long as the military and security forces continue being party instruments, political power will stay in Sandinista hands, regardless of electoral processes. The opposition may participate in the administrative area, in state posts, but not in the real power structure and substantive policymaking.

The uncertainty of the results of the anti-Sandinista struggle, the erosion of U.S. support, the problems that would arise from the indefinite presence of large numbers of anti-Sandinista guerrillas in Honduran territory, the hope that the permanent presence of a radical regime will ensure a continued flow of U.S. aid to countries such as Costa Rica, the resistance leadership's political limitations, and the short-term easy road to accommodation are some of the factors that may help to explain the most relevant aspects of the San Salvador agreement. This happened when the perspectives of a politico-military victory over the Sandinistas had become more uncertain to the eyes of a vast proportion of Nicaraguans. It is also important to note that while guerrilla activities increase in El Salvador and Honduras to include the recent assassination of retired General Gustavo Alvarez, the Salvadoran civil war was not treated as extensively as the Nicaraguan case during the Central American presidential meeting. Some observers argue that the Central American presidents are weary of the protracted struggle involving their countries.

The Nicaraguan resistance received the news from San Salvador with a heterogeneous response. Some refuted the agreement. Others welcomed it as a victory derived from the military pressures that the resistance was able to exert in the past. A fact that cannot be dismissed is that, given the disastrous state of the Nicaraguan economy, the Sandinista government will open business opportunities for the private sector, and probably will also leave many important state posts (without effective power) for the opposition in the near future. Even if these steps are tactical and insincere, they represent a tempting opportunity that will be explored by many anti-Sandinistas, some of them stage-hungry politicians. The Sandinistas have shown considerable political flexibility in the face of the circumstances, making peripheral concessions seemingly spectacular, but actually very limited as to ensure their permanence in power, a fact that will have a profound impact on the whole region. Be it coincidental or not, Sandinista flexibility in El Salvador kept pace with the new flexibility shown by the Soviets in other areas.

In regard to the Soviets, it may be argued that the Soviet Union will most likely continue evaluating each regional conflict in accordance with its own national interests, carefully assessing the costs against the political and strategic advantages that may be obtained in each particular case. The Soviet leadership, even in their "new thinking," can ignore neither the costs and risks, nor the opportunities that lie ahead in Central America.

Notes

1. *Plataforma General Político-Militar Del Frente Sandinista De Liberación Nacional (FSLN) Para El Triunfo De La Revolución Popular Sandinista.* (General Political-Military Platform of the FSLN for the Triumph of the Popular Sandinista Revolution). National Directorate of the FSLN, "Somewhere in Nicaragua," May 4, 1977. This key document was first published in English as Appendix A in Jiri Valenta and Esperanza Duran, eds., *Conflict in Nicaragua: A Multidimensional Perspective* (Boston: Allen & Unwin, 1987), pp. 301-302.
2. Op. cit., p. 302.
3. The historic program of the FSLN (1969). National Directorate of the FSLN. See Valenta and Duran, eds., *Conflict in Nicaragua* (Internal Circular), National Directorate of the FSLN. April 1978, pp. 6-23.
4. On the subject of the breadth of the democratic alliance against Somocismo, among many analyses by Sandinistas, Julio Lopez, Orlando Nuñez et. al. *La Caida Del Somocismo y La Lucha Sandinista en Nicaragua* (The Downfall of Somocismo and the Sandinista Struggle in Nicaragua), (San Jose, Costa Rica: Educa, 1979), pp. 302-319.
5. I have analyzed this issue in my chapter, "Aspects of the Evolution of Law in Sandinista Nicaragua." Valenta and Duran, eds., *Conflict in Nicaragua*, pp. 67-88.
6. For an analysis of the different roads to power used by Leninist organizations, see Thomas T. Hammond, ed., *The Anatomy of Communist Takeovers* (New Haven: Yale University Press, 1975), pp. 1-45.
7. See Jerry F. Hough, *The Struggle for the Third World: Soviet Debates and American Options* (Washington D.C.: The Brookings Institution, 1985), pp. 226-257.
8. John Garnett, "The Role of Military Power," in Michael Smith, Richard Little, and Michael Shackleton, eds., *Perspectives on World Politics* (London: The Open University Press, 1981), pp. 63-75.
9. On March 4, 1988, the Communist Party of Cuba held a conference with the participation of representatives from the Communist Parties of Bulgaria, Hungary, Vietnam, East Germany, Korea, Mongolia, Poland, Romania, the U.S.S.R., and Czechoslovakia. The declaration pleased and rewarded the Cuban insistence on reaffirming the unshakable solidarity with the struggles for national liberation. See *Pravda*, No. 65 (25417), Moscow, March 5, 1988, p. 4. Castro's behavior as well as his abundant rhetoric continues unabated to the present day.
10. The *Foreign Broadcast Information Service FBIS-Soviet Union* provides abundant information from July 1979 to this day on the mutual diplomatic support by the Soviets and the Sandinistas. Particularly interesting are Radio Moscow's commentaries and the *Pravda* articles.
11. See "Secret Protocol of the Military Collaboration Between the Government of the Republic of Cuba and the People's Revolutionary Government of Grenada," undated. This is one of the thousands of documents captured in Grenada, October 1983, by U.S.A.-OECS forces. It appears in Jiri Valenta and Herbert Ellison,

eds., *Grenada and Soviet/Cuban Policy: Internal Crisis and U.S./OECS Intervention* (Boulder, Co: Westview Press, 1986), pp. 385-388.
12. Sources: U.S. State Department and Pentagon data. See Sam Dillon, "Latin America Course Changed Little in '80s," *The Miami Herald*. Monday, December 12, 1988, p. 13A.
13. Garnett, op. cit., p. 71.
14. Dillon, op. cit., p. 13A.
15. Agreement on cooperation between the New Jewel Movement and the Communist Party of the Soviet Union, July 27, 1982. Valenta and Ellison, *Grenada and Soviet-Cuban Policy*, p. 319.
16. Report on Meeting on Secret Regional Caucus of SI (Socialist International) held in Managua, January, 6-7, 1983. Op. cit., pp. 479-484.
17. Vladimir Davidov, "What is Dependencia Theory," *America Latina* (Moscow), No. 2, 1986, pp. 29-41.
18. Victor Volskii, "Latin America in the Present Day World," *America Latina* (Moscow), No. 6, 1986, pp. 4-6.
19. Anatolii Glinkin, "Latin America in 20th Century International Relations," *America Latina*, No. 6., 1986, pp. 39-46.
20. Pavel Bogomolov, "Nicaragua: A Thorny Path of the Revolution," *International Affairs*, Moscow, Jan. 1989, p. 54.
21. Ibid., p. 56
22. During 1988, Gorbachev's political power progressed toward consolidation, as most specialists in Soviet domestic politics would admit. At moments, the opposition to Gorbachev's reformism seemed to grow as many analysts inferred, for instance, from an article in the daily *Sovetskaia Rossiia*, which advocated pre-*glasnost* principles. Nonetheless, solid defense of *perestroika* appeared later in *Pravda*, April 5, 1988, p. 2. During a conference held in Miami under the auspices of the Institute for Soviet and East European Studies, Graduate School of International Studies of the University of Miami, Abel Aganbegian, a senior economic advisor to Gorbachev, explained that Gorbachev's power is firm. However, Aganbegian said concrete results from the reforms will be seen only within a few years.
23. In October 1989, the Soviets appeared committed to reducing arms deliveries to the Sandinistas—whose military warehouses are already overstocked—until the February 25, 1990 Nicaraguan elections. However, military deliveries to Nicaragua via Cuba and East Germany were said to be continuing.

Part Seven

Superpowers and Regional Conflicts: American Policies and Future Options

14

The Rise and Fall of the Reagan Doctrine

Charles William Maynes

Since the Moscow summit in May 1988 the leaderships in both Moscow and Washington seem determined to enter into what might be called Détente II. Like Détente I, which took place during the Nixon administration, the centerpiece of the relationship is likely to become the issue of arms control. But in this second effort at superpower accommodation, as in the first, the question of conflicting superpower interests in the Third World will hover over the relationship like a black cloud. Different superpower interests in or perceptions of developments in one of the Third World hot spots could derail Détente II as crises in the Middle East and southern Africa derailed Détente I. It is therefore very important to understand the current policies of the two great powers in dealing with Third World crises.

In this essay I will assess the reasons behind the development of the so-called Reagan Doctrine, which has guided U.S. policy toward the critical issues of Afghanistan, Angola, Cambodia, and Nicaragua during the Reagan administration. Then I will much more briefly assess the current Soviet approach toward Third World conflict areas. Finally, I will offer some suggestions regarding steps the two superpowers could take to manage their differences in dealing with crisis in Third World countries.

The Reagan Doctrine

In any discussion of the Reagan Doctrine, it is important to state that officially the doctrine does not exist. The terminology was invented by American journalists in order to describe what they recognized to be a policy change by the Reagan administration. It was clear that the administration was determined, as much for reasons of ideology as national interests, to assist anticommunist resistance forces in key Third World countries attempting to overthrow entrenched Leninist governments. The primary goal was to disprove the communist doctrine of historical inevitability. The Reagan administration hoped for the first time since the crushing of the Bela Kun government in Hungary in 1919 to roll back the "Red tide." American journalists began to notice this new shift in policy and gave it a name, but it is a name the U.S. government never uses.

The shift in policy represented by the so-called Reagan Doctrine centered on the issue of ideology. The Carter administration also had concluded that it was in U.S. interests to assist the Afghan resistance in its fight against the invading Soviet forces. And it provided indirect support to the Cambodian resistance struggling against the invading Vietnamese forces by refusing to recognize the new government in Phnom Penh and by providing greater assistance to Thailand, which in turn was aiding the Cambodian forces directly.

In its final days, the Carter administration also had developed increasingly hostile relations with the Sandinista government in Managua, which was then, quite openly, sending military assistance to the guerrilla forces in El Salvador. Key officials in the Carter administration in its final days debated very seriously the dispatch of American military advisers to El Salvador to assist the government in its struggle. There is little doubt that had Carter won reelection, those officials would have prevailed and a Democratic administration would have sent the advisers.

Nor did the Carter administration ever succeed in establishing normal relations with the government of Angola. It twice accused the government in Luanda and its Cuban allies of assisting invasion forces entering Zaire in the province of Shaba, and Carter three times turned down a proposal to establish formal diplomatic relations with Angola.

These similarities notwithstanding, the Carter administration's policy toward these four countries did differ from that of the Reagan administration. The Carter administration was primarily concerned with the external behavior of the countries in question. It was pursuing diplomatic objectives. Its primary goal in Afghanistan was the withdrawal of Soviet troops. Regarding Cambodia it seemed to argue that Vietnam had no right to invade regardless of the number of people Pol Pot murdered. It was willing to live with the regimes in Luanda and Managua provided certain foreign policy issues could be resolved. By contrast, the Reagan administration was as interested in the internal composition of the governments in Afghanistan, Angola, Cambodia, and Nicaragua as in the external behavior of these states. Its objectives were both ideological and diplomatic. In trying to understand why, we have to explore the principal motivations that lie behind the development of the Reagan Doctrine in the first place. There appear to be several key factors:

First, many conservatives in America, particularly those self-labelled as neoconservatives, have never really been comfortable with the postwar American doctrine of containment. They object to its passive character. After all, the goal of containment is to limit the spread of "evil," not extirpate it. For many conservatives the very existence of communism anywhere in the world poses a serious threat to American security. Why they feel this way about countries as insignificant as some small states in Africa is not always clear. It may reflect a conservative fear about the potential attraction of communist ideology, its current moribund state notwithstanding. Alternatively, the feelings conservatives harbor may betray historical fears rooted in postwar events. Thus, since 1945, even though containment has succeeded in limiting the Soviet Union to the gain of a few countries a decade, there have been gains; and given enough decades and enough countries perhaps the Soviet Union could succeed in tipping the global balance of power. Conservatives believe the United States must go on the offensive to reverse this historical trend. The Reagan Doctrine permits the United States to do this.

Second, the Reagan Doctrine meets the test of realism and prudent restraint. During the 1950s the Eisenhower administration also proclaimed its desire to pull down the Iron Curtain and roll back the communist threat to the Soviet borders and perhaps beyond. But the Hungarian uprising in 1956 proved the rollback doctrine to be totally hollow. Dulles at the time attempted to explain American failure to come to the aid of the Hungarians: "The only way we can save Hungary at this time would be through an all-out nuclear war. Does anyone in his right senses want us to start a nuclear war over Hungary? As for simply sending American divisions into Hungary, they would be wiped out by superior Soviet ground forces."[1] The Reagan Doctrine eliminates the principal weakness of the rollback doctrine—namely, the articulation of a goal that if seriously pursued simply creates an even bigger threat to American security. Under the Reagan Doctrine the United States has attempted to counter the Soviet empire only at its periphery, that is to say, only in countries that are not really vital to Soviet security interests. A U.S. success might weaken the Soviet Union but it would not threaten Soviet survival. Hence, the Soviet Union should have no or little incentive to strike back militarily with its own troops.

Third, the distinction between authoritarian and totalitarian states, which Jeane Kirkpatrick borrowed from fellow academics and made even more famous or infamous in an article in *Commentary** magazine, also played a key role in the development of the Reagan Doctrine. According to Kirkpatrick, authoritarian regimes are susceptible to reform from within, however slow it may come. Totalitarian regimes, however, remain beyond the reach of reform. Because totalitarian controls are by definition total, the future of the

---

*"Dictatorships and Double Standards," November 1979.

people under such a system is hopeless. This is why the Soviet menace is so threatening. Whatever the Soviets gain is forever lost. The "Red tide" may move slowly but it moves inexorably. In a sense, if one accepts the Kirkpatrick thesis, one believes that Lenin succeeded in developing a political system that stops history. The Bolshevik Revolution is the final revolution. Once under the communist yoke, a people can never be freed by its own efforts. Given this thesis, it becomes psychologically very important that the Soviet Union suffer a political setback somewhere. It cannot happen in Eastern Europe. An attempt there would be too dangerous and might set off World War III. So the attempt has to take place in a Third World country. Again, one arrives at the Reagan Doctrine.

Fourth, the Carter human rights policy played a role in the evolution of the Reagan Doctrine. Jimmy Carter did not begin his presidential campaign in 1976 with the intention of making human rights a major political issue. According to those who campaigned with him, he discovered the issue while on the hustings. He found that after the humiliation of Vietnam and Watergate, the American people were looking for a leader who would tell them that the basic core values of the country were good. That indeed was Jimmy Carter's message: "We can have a country as good as the American people." When Carter went on to suggest that American values could find expression not only in domestic policy but also in the country's foreign policy, the public response was strong and positive. Concern over human rights, always an important component of American foreign policy, became a leading component.

At first, the Reagan administration tried to ignore this Carter legacy. But it soon recognized that its effort was a mistake. So part of the Reagan Doctrine has been a belief or an assertion that the United States is battling for human rights and democracy in assisting the resistance forces in such countries as Afghanistan, Angola, Cambodia, and Nicaragua.

There is a final component to the Reagan Doctrine—a national desire for revenge that is bipartisan in nature. The United States suffered greatly in Vietnam—militarily, politically, and psychologically. There is among American leaders a strong desire to see the Soviet Union suffer a setback of similar magnitude—a desire that is unrelated to any geopolitical design.

Against this backdrop, what can we say about the various countries in which the Reagan Doctrine has been applied?

Afghanistan: The Reagan administration doubtless will claim the Soviet agreement to withdraw from that country as the major achievement of the Reagan Doctrine. For the third time since World War II, Soviet troops have withdrawn from a country under pressure. But in Iran and Austria the pressure was political. Here the Soviet army seems to have suffered significant casualties— at least 13,000 dead. In Afghanistan, the United States thus obtains the satisfaction of watching the other superpower humiliated by a Third World state. But in other respects the victory seems less a tribute to the Reagan Doctrine than to the norms of the United Nations Charter in their categorical prohibition on the use of force except in self defense. It was in defense of those norms that the Carter administration decided to aid the resistance. A Reagan Doctrine was not needed to justify support.

The reaction inside the United States to the news of the Afghan settlement suggests the hidden agendas of different constituencies. Those interested in a diplomatic victory applauded the agreement because it called for withdrawal of Soviet troops. Those interested in an ideological victory denounced the agreement because their real objective was the elimination of another Leninist government in the Third World.

Angola: An examination of the Reagan administration's policy toward Angola also helps to reveal the real but hidden agenda of different groups. On the basis of statements on the public record, there is very little to choose between the political objectives of the government in power in Luanda, which is supported by Cuba and the Soviet Union, and the political goals of the resistance forces of UNITA, which is supported by South Africa and the United States. In his public career, UNITA leader Jonas Savimbi has flirted with Maoism, Marxism, and black power. Indeed, at one point in the Angolan struggle, many American black power advocates favored Savimbi because, unlike his Cuban-backed opposition, he did not share power with whites and mulattos. Now Savimbi is aligned with the South African government. What emerges from the overall record is a man gifted in political maneuver. There is little doubt that he has a future in Angolan politics. He is talented, he has shown a capacity to survive, and he enjoys considerable support in certain sections of Angola. But he is far from being a principled democrat or committed market capitalist.

The government in Luanda is anxious to have relations with the United States. It works cooperatively with American businesses and has even assigned Cuban troops to guard American oil installations inside Angola. Like Mozambique, it is in need of outside assistance that only the West can offer. Consequently, it is ripe for a change in its relationship with Western countries.

Recognizing this reality, the Reagan administration's own State Department for some time resisted the logic of the Reagan Doctrine, precisely because it is a doctrine that tends to encourage its adherents to press for more consistency in policy application than a sound understanding of the national interest often allows. The logic of the Reagan Doctrine calls for the United States to support Savimbi because he is opposing a Leninist government in power. The administration reluctantly succumbed to this logic when it instituted a covert operation to assist Savimbi's UNITA forces.

Recent events might persuade some that the policy is succeeding. In late 1988, under U.S. mediation, Angolan, Cuban, and South African diplomats reached agreement on a settlement of the Angolan and Namibian problems. Cuba will withdraw its troops from Angola, and South Africa will finally permit implementation of U.N. proposals leading to an independent Namibia. The history of this region suggests, however, more caution is in order than is shown by most commentators on the recent diplomatic breakthrough. In the Carter administration South Africa also accepted the U.N. proposals for Namibia and then found a multitude of reasons not to implement them. The final withdrawal of Cuban troops from Angola may be affected by the internal strength of the regime in Luanda. Nevertheless, it is true that in late 1988 progress was made. The question is, why?

Adherents of the Reagan Doctrine claim the answer was found in the U.S. decision to aid Savimbi. That move pushed the Angolans to the bargaining table. State Department officials privately acknowledge a different explanation for success. In clashes, South Africa suffered serious reverses for the first time. White casualties were unpopular in South Africa, whose army is manned with conscripts; and increased pressure on the government to enter into talks was the result. In short, the Reagan Doctrine resulting in aid to Savimbi had, by these accounts, little to do with the diplomatic breakthrough. If anything, it may have slowed up "progress."

Cambodia: In Cambodia the Reagan administration was a last minute convert to the logic of the Reagan Doctrine. Having taken a public position in favor of assisting resistance groups trying to overthrow Leninist governments, the administration put Democratic forces in the Congress on the defensive. Attacked by the administration for not being sufficiently resolute in combatting radical forces in Central America or southern Africa, the Democrats in Congress looked around for a resistance movement they could support in addition to the Afghan freedom fighters. They settled on the Cambodian resistance movement, minus the Pol Pot forces, regrettably the heart of the resistance.

The administration initially resisted the Democratic proposal to support forces allied with the Khmer Rouge. But it ultimately retreated and the United States now provides a small amount of assistance to the anticommunist resistance forces based in Thailand trying to overthrow the government in Phnom Penh.

Recently, the Vietnamese have shown more flexibility concerning Cambodia. Vietnamese officials have announced that by 1990 they will withdraw all of their troops from that country. They have offered to withdraw sooner if a peace settlement can be arranged, but contend that in any event they will leave by 1990. The recent improvement in Sino-Soviet relations guarantees that the Vietnamese will be under increasing diplomatic pressure to put an end to their occupation of Cambodia.

These developments, however, present the West with a different dilemma. If the Vietnamese do withdraw and are unable to shore up the regime in Phnom Penh to a point where it can prevail, then the resistance will overthrow the government in Phnom Penh and the notorious Pol Pot will return to power with Western assistance, direct or indirect, since his forces are by far the strongest in the resistance. His return will set off a storm of protest among Western publics and might even justify a decision by Vietnam to send troops back into Cambodia. If the Vietnamese do succeed in helping the authorities in Phnom Penh to prevail, then the West, in its refusal to have anything to do with the government in that capital, may be losing an opportunity to negotiate better arrangements for the non-communist opposition in Cambodia while there is still time. Another possibility, in fact the most likely, is that Cambodia will descend into civil war with the current government in Cambodia able to hold on to power but unable to establish peace. In that case, the main victims will continue to be the Cambodian people.

Nicaragua: Finally, there is the case of Nicaragua. Barring some extraordinary turn of events, the Contra cause has been lost. The issue is the degree to which the Sandinista government, seeking international and regional acceptance, is still willing to offer some larger political space for a genuine opposition. The causes of the American failure are many but one appears to be key—the sharp contradiction between the public goal announced and the private goal pursued. The public goal was diplomatic. Publicly, the United States announced that its policy was designed to bring pressure on the Sandinista government to persuade it to leave its neighbors alone and to limit its ties to Cuba and the Soviet Union. The private goal, however, was political— the overthrow of the regime in Managua.

The administration could never acknowledge publicly its private agenda because the instruments at hand—namely, the Contras—were so obviously inadequate for the task. Even if one believes that they were a nuisance of sufficient force to induce the Sandinistas to open negotiations, they never had any prospect of accomplishing their main goal—a counterrevolution in Nicaragua. Implementation of the administration's private agenda would therefore have required the use of American troops. But public opinion polls repeatedly demonstrated that such a policy was extremely unpopular.

Yet it may be that the administration's public agenda can still be saved. The United States cannot extirpate revolution in Nicaragua. But it may be able to negotiate with the regime in Managua some limits on the foreign policy that the Sandinistas will pursue—the nature of their ties to the Soviet Union and their policies within the region. The Nicaraguans have repeatedly made clear that although they will not negotiate with the United States on a plan to end the revolution in Nicaragua, they are ready to negotiate with the United States on the latter's security concerns.

General Lessons

When one looks at these four cases, then, it seems fairly clear that the Reagan Doctrine has either led to failures or required the United States to take steps many of its own foreign policy specialists thought were unwise. The Soviets are leaving Afghanistan, but American support for the resistance started in the Carter administration and is defensible in terms of the United Nations Charter. The Reagan Doctrine, however, pushed U.S. policy in directions that could snatch defeat from the jaws of victory in Afghanistan. The Bush administration is concerned that a strongly anti-American, theocratic regime could take power in Kabul. But it was proponents of the Reagan Doctrine who pushed the U.S. Government to accord aid without conditions even to fanatical pro-Islamic groups. In the three other countries under discussion, the Reagan Doctrine again drove U.S. policy beyond the line between engagement and excess. Thus, without the Reagan Doctrine the United States probably would not have supported UNITA, probably would have been more willing to work with the regime in Phnom Penh, and probably would have been satisfied with a diplomatic agenda in Central America.

It is worth asking why the Doctrine forced its adherents to cross the line mentioned. In retrospect, it is clear that the Doctrine's adherents misread both the nature of communist states and the nature of the resistance in the four countries in question. It is ironic that about the time prominent Western academics developed the theory of the totalitarian state, the totalitarian age was coming to an end in much of the communist world. The Soviet Union has not been a true totalitarian state since the late 1950s. The Eastern European states began to move out of the totalitarian period about the same time. The key development occurred when governments that had been totalitarian began to develop limits on the measures they were willing to take to compel obedience. In the Soviet Union mass terror ended with the death of Stalin. The state still remained extremely oppressive. It did not hesitate to harass or imprison critics, but in general it ceased killing them. From that moment on, dissent began to grow among the courageous, and the totalitarian model began a process of terminal decline.

In Eastern Europe ordinary citizens with increasing regularity are deciding that they no longer fear their own authorities or the Soviet army. The result has been a growing pluralism throughout the European communist world. Democracy is far off and indeed it may never come. But the label "totalitarian" no longer explains adequately the East European reality.

Events have developed differently in Asia, to be sure. The communist revolutions there have been more recent and traditions of pluralism were even more rare. Nevertheless, in Asia as well one sees similar developments. There is growing pluralism in Vietnam, for example, as there was in China until June 3, 1989. Today, perhaps the only truly totalitarian states remain Albania and North Korea.

The second misjudgment concerned the character of the resistance forces. Although there were some democratic forces among the resistance groups, in none of the movements were such forces dominant. From the beginning the chance that any of the four countries would become democratic if the resistance forces won has been almost nil. If the resistance manages to take power in Afghanistan, we may see there a political authority much like that in Teheran. In Angola we have a resistance leader who in 1982 announced that there were no fundamental ideological conflicts between UNITA and the Angolan government, who in 1964 denounced those who worked with the United States as lackeys, and whose political base is primarily tribal.

In Cambodia the leading figure among the noncommunist forces is Prince Norodom Sihanouk. Should he return to power, he is likely to reestablish the same personalistic and authoritarian regime that he once gave his country. It would be, without question, an enormous improvement over the Pol Pot government and the current regime in Phnom Penh but it would not be democracy.

Finally, there is Nicaragua. Power among the Contras resides with military figures who trace their origins to the detested National Guard. It is indicative of their political attitudes that the Argentine military, more renowned for systematic torture than sound military doctrine, first came to their assistance.

This is not to say that there are no democratic elements in the Nicaraguan resistance. Figures like Arturo Cruz, Senior do represent a genuine democratic point of view. But these figures have repeatedly been pushed aside by the men with guns. If the resistance achieves a military victory, therefore, we are likely to see the kind of political order now prevailing in Guatemala, where the army retains power but presents the outside world with a formalistic facade to calm the American Congress during the aid cycle.

The Soviet Position: We have discussed the U.S. position at length. What about the position of the Soviet Union? Here there is no clear pattern. In the case of Angola and Nicaragua, the Soviet position appears not to have changed. The Soviet Union has repeatedly stated its support of a diplomatic settlement. U.S. officials credit the Soviet government with a helpful role in the negotiations regarding Angola and Namibia. At the same time the Soviet Union has not decreased its levels of aid to Angola and Nicaragua. Indeed, in the case of Angola, it appears to have increased its level of military aid to a point where the Angolans were able to bloody the nose of the South Africans. In Nicaragua, the aid continues to flow.

Regarding the crises in Afghanistan and Cambodia, the Soviet position in favor of diplomatic solutions seems even more pronounced. The Soviet Union has agreed to an accord negotiated by the United Nations leading to Soviet withdrawal from Afghanistan. And after signing that accord, Soviet officials have suggested that the arrangements in Afghanistan could serve as a model for Cambodia.

Soviet rhetoric regarding the Third World has undergone a transformation. Most American analysts of Soviet policy in the Third World concur in this judgment. Soviet policy is focusing on the large, intrinsically important countries regardless of their political orientation—countries like India, Brazil, or Indonesia. There is a recognition in the Soviet literature that these countries remain a part of the capitalist world order and are unlikely to move to the socialist world in the foreseeable future. There are fewer official expressions of a willingness to provide military assistance to Third World revolutionaries. And Soviet analysts are focusing less on such nonclass factors as regionalism or nationalism.[2]

Yet if analysts agree on the direction of current Soviet commentary about the Third World, they are divided on its significance. What will be the practical effects of the change in focus? Will Soviet policy toward the Third World reverse to former patterns sometime in the future?

There can be no definitive answer to these questions. But in concluding this chapter, I would like to suggest reasons why both superpowers are likely to accord Third World countries less attention in the future than in the past.

Militarily, Third World countries are becoming less important in terms of the superpower competition and more dangerous in terms of superpower involvement. As technology changes, both the East and the West are likely to become less interested in Third World countries as military assets. Immediately after World War II, the United States, for example, needed bases in Third World countries in order to maintain a credible nuclear threat against the Soviet Union. U.S. missiles were not transcontinental in range and U.S. aircraft based close to the Soviet Union were more likely to arrive on target than aircraft based in the United States. But as the ranges of rockets and submarines have increased, the United States has responded by closing down foreign bases from Ethiopia to Scotland.

The Soviet Union was never as dependent on foreign military bases as the United States. The difference is explained by geography. But the advances in technology also affect the Soviet Union. Moreover, to the degree that the United States is less interested in Third World states as a military asset, the Soviet Union is also likely to be less interested since these areas are no longer as much a source of military threat to the Soviet Union.

Economically as well, the Third World is becoming less vital. As plastics replace steel, as glass fiber optics substitute for copper, and as countries see knowledge as more important to development than resources, the place of the

Third World in international development begins to shift. Developed countries worry less about a secure supply of resources than about an open market. Concern about supply pushes states to try to control territory. Concern about markets pushes states to compromise in order to maintain access.

Add to this mix the possibility that the ideological struggle between the superpowers will lessen in intensity. Then it should be possible for the superpowers to take a more relaxed view about political and economic change in many Third World countries. It should be possible for them to agree that only in a few Third World countries is the international balance of power really a question. They might even agree that neither side had major security interests in certain parts of the Third World and they might then negotiate, in effect, a joint policy of non-intervention.

The trends mentioned are powerful and will grow in force over time. But whether the United States and the U.S.S.R. will be able to understand them and act on them in the near future is another question. A key to any conceptual breakthrough is likely to be the Middle East. Superpower misunderstanding and confrontation there are likely to color attitudes in both Moscow and Washington toward other parts of the developing world. Yet for a variety of reasons—not the least of which is the unwillingness of Israeli and Palestinian leaders even to talk to one another except under conditions the other side will not accept—progress is difficult. The apparent decision of Iran to seek an end to the war with Iraq might offer an opportunity for the United States and the U.S.S.R. to experiment in working together in the volatile Middle East. The Bush administration might explore with the Soviet Union whether the two sides can reach agreement on security arrangements in the Gulf that would secure Western access to oil and take into account legitimate Soviet security interests in an area so close to its borders.

These are possible directions in the approach that the superpowers might take toward Third World crises. They are directions that would serve the interests of both and would offer Third World states greater opportunity to control their own affairs and to concentrate on their real task—economic development. They are therefore directions that all of us should urge the superpowers to explore seriously and sympathetically.

Notes

1. See Jiri Valenta, "The Explosive Soviet Periphery," *Foreign Policy* 351, Summer 1983, pp. 84-100.
2. Francis Fukuyama, *Problems of Communism*, September-October 1987; and Neil MacFarlane, *The Harriman Institute Forum*, Vol. 1, No. 3, March 1988.

15

Soviet "New Thinking" and U.S. Foreign Policy

W. Bruce Weinrod

Overview

The Soviet Union under General Secretary Mikhail Gorbachev is a fascinating object of study. It is particularly so because of the stark contrast between Brezhnevian torpor and the sometimes frenetic energy unleashed recently.

But energy and motion are not necessarily synonymous with real change. In some cases, they can take the place of change. Current developments in the U.S.S.R. may result in a more positive Soviet international role, but this hope must not lead us beyond what is actually happening. Thus, it is necessary to take a close and realistic look at the U.S.S.R. under Gorbachev.

Before entering into a discussion of the specifics of Soviet foreign policy and the U.S. response, let me lay out the basic framework for my analysis:

1. The Soviet Union since 1971, owing to a combination of traditional Russian expansionism and an overlay of Leninist ideology, has posed a threat to democracy and freedom.
2. Soviet expansionism has manifested itself in many ways, but one of the most significant—particularly in recent years—has been the quest for influence in the developing world through indirect aggression. As Soviet specialist Bruce Porter has noted:

   > By advancing incrementally and by carefully choosing the places and times of its development in the Third World conflicts, the Soviet Union has substantially increased its latitude of action in the world. The cumulative effect has been an evolutionary erosion of the postwar international order, a gradual change in the nature of the game itself.[1]

3. Moscow does not necessarily directly cause the problems that lead to turmoil in the developing world; they mostly have indigenous roots. However, the Soviet Union on occasion seeks to take advantage of internal

popular dissatisfaction in developing nations resulting from domestic problems to expand its influence; Moscow has been known to provide directly, or through allies and proxies, material support for revolutionary forces that identify with Leninism. The fragility of institutions in many developing nations can make it possible for Moscow and its proxies to shift a delicate internal balance of forces by a relatively small degree of outside involvement.

4. As long as the U.S.S.R. asserts a right to provide military assistance—directly and through proxies—to assist communist revolutionaries seeking to gain or consolidate power in developing nations, the United States and its allies have the right, both under international law and as a matter of realpolitik, to respond defensively in a proportional manner.

5. There is probably a relationship between the domestic and international dimensions of Soviet policy in the sense that fundamental and long-lasting domestic changes in the direction of an open society would most likely lead to a less expansionist Soviet foreign policy.

6. A variety of factors have led to new, interesting, and potentially important developments in the U.S.S.R. These include: 1) the economic and social stagnation caused by a collectivist economy and one-party rule; 2) consistent and tough policies by the United States and its allies, which ended easy Soviet access to Western credit and technology, and which, by supporting anti-Soviet insurgencies in the Third World (a policy also followed by China), substantially increased the costs to Moscow of its overseas empire; and 3) the accession to power of a new generation of Soviet leaders who concluded that something different had to be tried to deal with the U.S.S.R.'s problems.

7. It is still a time for caution and watchful waiting with respect to Soviet policies. Domestic changes are not yet structural or irreversible, although Soviet rhetoric concerning its foreign and defense policies has changed, and there has been a shift of position in several areas—such as on-site inspection of arms control agreements, for example. But, in the past, Soviet foreign policy has gone through cycles of expansionism and pause; and while Moscow is more willing than before to talk about some contentious issues, such as regional conflicts, it has as yet done very little to actually change those policies that have contributed significantly to the commencement or continuation of these conflicts.

8. The United States and its friends must continue to be vigilant. Whatever positive developments are occurring in Kremlin policy are due at least in part to a sustained policy of active response to Soviet expansionism. The worst thing the United States could do at this point would be to remove those pressures. Such a course of action would allow the Soviets to avoid making painful and difficult choices between its overseas ambitions and domestic reform. The United States should also continue to engage the

Soviets in discussion to probe for fundamental change, and should be ready to respond positively if and when there occur genuine and long-lasting changes in Soviet international behaviour.

Determinants of Change

Let us now examine in more detail three important issues: the nature and meaning of current Soviet domestic developments; the extent and significance of changes in Soviet international behavior, particularly in the developing world; and appropriate policy responses by the United States and its allies to Soviet policies.

There are three possible basic explanations for current domestic developments in the U.S.S.R.—all of them plausible given what we now know. Possibility one: Gorbachev is a genuine reformer; he has decided in his own mind that he wants to make the Soviet Union into a modern industrial power and he realizes that to do this will require structural changes in the Soviet system. Possibility two: Gorbachev basically believes in the traditional Soviet system but also has concluded that it needs a carefully managed and controlled shake-up to invigorate it, along with a modest loosening of controls—at least temporarily—in order to provide incentives for economic development. Possibility three: Gorbachev does not have a master plan guiding his actions, but rather is pragmatically trying different approaches—some of them inconsistent with one another—hoping he will eventually press the right combination of buttons leading to economic development.

Regardless of which of the above three explanations is closest to the truth, Gorbachev's policies—whatever their intent—could unleash an internal dynamic of mass unrest and nationalism that could get out of control of the authorities and lead to unintended consequences.

It should also be noted that domestic change *per se* may not necessarily lead to less bellicose Soviet international policies. One need only recall that at the same time when Krushchev was engineering a domestic "thaw" in the late 1950s and early 1960s, he was also engaged in international saber-rattling, proclamation of Soviet support for wars of national liberation, and initiating the 1961 Berlin Crisis and the 1962 placement of Soviet missiles in Cuba.

Five other important points should be made briefly concerning Soviet domestic developments: First, the changes that have thus far occurred, while significant, are limited in key respects. They are not at this point structural, firmly entrenched, or widespread at the regional and local levels; Second, there are many forces in Soviet society either currently or potentially in opposition to fundamental change, including sectors of the KGB and the military, in addition to regional and local officials, the *nomenklatura*, and the party bureaucracy; Third, if Gorbachev's changes do not go far enough, there is a real possibility he could encounter the worst of both worlds—a Soviet society in which reactionary forces have been aroused and workers dislocated, but in which the economy is actually worse off than before because the changes made were not fundamental enough; Fourth, there have been apparent Soviet reforms and openings before—Lenin's New Economic Policy (N.E.P.) and Khrushchev's "thaw" for example—which were heralded by many in the West as the beginning of a new Soviet era. But they turned out to be merely phases of an essentially constant system; Fifth, nothing that Gorbachev has done thus far indicates he is willing to tackle the fundamental causes of Soviet problems—such as the Communist party monopoly control of the political, economic, and sociocultural realms. A free flow of people, goods, and ideas is essential to a modern society and economy but that would end Communist Party domination. Whether Gorbachev will try to move—or can succeed in moving—in this direction is an open question.

Soviet domestic developments have been analyzed in some detail for two important reasons: First, it is more likely than not that there is some connection between Soviet domestic and foreign policy; more important, a genuinely more open Soviet system would probably be less expansionist.

Second, the appearance of domestic change has led some observers to conclude that *ipso facto* this means Soviet international behavior is also changing to the extent that the United States and its allies can safely shift their policies. This would, however, be a mistake.

Soviet Policy: New Thinking versus New Behavior

Despite all of the above-mentioned constraints on fundamental Soviet change, it is still essential to examine current Soviet international policies and behavior. It is possible, though unlikely, that such behavior could change even if the Soviet domestic system remains essentially unchanged.

There has indeed been a change in Soviet rhetoric about Soviet international policies. Ideology and strident language have been downplayed. Reasonable-sounding speeches are given and policy initiatives are offered at international conferences. Soviet spokesmen seem to have had charm school lessons, and phrases such as "new thinking" and "defensive sufficiency" are presented as evidence of Soviet policy changes. In addition, some recent Communist Party personnel changes have elevated theorists identified with a shift toward working with established governments rather than radical insurgencies and factions.

There is also some evidence in Soviet academic writings—dating back to the pre-Gorbachev period and in more recent official statements—indicating a critical rethinking of Soviet overseas commitments. The State Department's Francis Fukuyama, formerly with the RAND Corporation, has identified three themes in these Soviet pronouncements: 1) The pressure of economic constraints on Soviet foreign policy and the need to focus on the Soviet Union's own development; 2) An awareness of the damaging effect of past Soviet Third World activities on U.S.-Soviet relations, and the fact that increased superpower tension (particularly since the Reagan administration took office) inhibits Moscow's ability to support progressive forces in the Third World; 3) A critique of the Leninist vanguard party approach as the best way to secure long-term Soviet influence in the Third World.

It is by no means clear that this new rhetoric signals any fundamental change in Soviet objectives in the Third World or in the tactics used to achieve them. As with Soviet domestic policy, there is more than one plausible explanation for the new Soviet rhetoric. It could, of course, indicate genuine changes in the Soviet approach to international politics. But it could also be a calculated attempt to use the language and terminology of the West to give the appearance of change without the reality.

There is, indeed, an impressive new flexibility to Soviet tactics. There has also been a willingness to shift positions on specific issues. After flatly rejecting arms control on-site inspection for decades, Moscow accepted it in the INF Treaty. The Soviets have completed a troop withdrawal from Afghanistan—although they have not necessarily abandoned the hope of Soviet domination—and have been seemingly more cooperative in encouraging regional conflict negotiations concerning Angola and Cambodia.

But even at the level of policy rhetoric, some very important things have not yet changed in Soviet foreign policy. First, there has been no repudiation of the Soviet obligation to protect the gains of "socialism." When questioned directly on this point in July 1988, while in Poland, Gorbachev eschewed the opportunity to go on record flatly rejecting Soviet military intervention to block movement away from communism, but said he would respond later in writing. Second, Soviet official spokesmen have refused, when pressed, to say that Moscow no longer believes it has the right to provide military and proxy support to pro-communist Third World insurgencies or regimes.

It should also be remembered that ideas and rhetoric are more easily manipulated in a closed society such as the U.S.S.R. than in the West. In such a society, it is possible for an outward display of rhetorical flexibility towards the West to coexist with tight controls on the actual conduct of policy by those who control the levers of power. In a closed society based on ideology, ideas are often viewed as weapons in the struggle against the designated enemy.

Soviet Policy in the Developing World

Many others in this volume present their views on actual Soviet behavior in the developing world. I will, therefore, confine myself to a few observations.

The most significant Soviet development in Third World behavior is, of course, the Soviet troop withdrawal from Afghanistan. But if the Soviet-imposed government retains control, then Moscow's most basic geopolitical objective will have been gained. Thus, it remains to be seen whether Moscow will encourage or even permit the emergence of a neutral and independent, popularly-elected government (perhaps on the Austrian State Treaty Model) or will continue to seek dominance via massive military supplies to the Kabul communist regime.

In any event, Afghanistan was a blatant case of open cross-border aggression. Soviet expansionism in the Third World has usually been carried out in a more suitable manner—through what has variously been termed "indirect," "undeclared," or "covert" aggression. Such expansionism, as practiced by Moscow, has included:

- sponsorship and support of guerrilla warfare, insurgencies and other forms of "low-intensity" conflict aimed at overthrowing governments;
- aid to terrorist groups in Western Europe, the Middle East, Latin America, and elsewhere, in the form of arms, training, and the provision of false documents and sanctuary;
- support of violent coups to install more pliable regimes; in particular, the use of "vanguard parties" modelled on Leninist precedents to establish and consolidate communist rule;
- support for acts of assassination and political intimidation against foreign leaders and high-profile defectors and dissidents.

Soviet expansionism also has involved the use of "proxy forces." While regimes such as Cuba, East Germany, Bulgaria, and Czechoslovakia, which are a part of this Soviet international "socialist division of labor," may at times be seeking to advance their interests more than Moscow's, the practical effect has been to help the Soviets extend their control of movements or regimes in the Third World.[2]

In a recent volume, nine main Soviet "instruments of influence" in seeking influence in developing nations were noted:

1. Conventional Soviet diplomatic activity, including the use of Soviet diplomatic personnel for overt and covert objectives.
2. Coordinated political action carried out by, for example, communist parties, front organizations, and covert political operations.
3. Propaganda activities employing all forms of the media; again, covert media activities are important.
4. Intelligence gathering, analysis, dissemination, and operations; counterintelligence activities including active measures designed to manipulate and deceive.
5. Provision of internal security services for local regimes, together with military and nonmilitary advisers and experts.

"New Thinking" and U.S. Foreign Policy   283

6. The transfer of arms and related supplies and maintenance capability.
7. The transfer of resources in the form of goods in kind (for example, oil), as well as cash and credit.
8. External combat forces from non-Soviet sources (such as Cuba, North Korea, Vietnam, or Libya), and, less frequently, from the Soviet Union itself.
9. Overt and covert support of terrorist groups and activities.

The analysts concluded that:

> The conduct of political-paramilitary war by the Soviet Union, acting in concert with its partners, appears to be constrained mainly by the fluctuating appearance of opportunities for these orchestrated operations. . . . It is also true that the Soviet Union does not take advantage of every opportunity that presents itself. But the Soviet government does stand committed by its very constitution to the so-called wars of national liberation, and Soviet theorists have developed a doctrine of "proletarian internationalism" to justify external intervention in support of "progressive forces" all over the world. . . . [3]

Unfortunately, there is little evidence thus far of any fundamental changes in either Soviet indirect aggression or the use of proxy forces. While it does appear that Moscow has been encouraging client states such as Vietnam and Angola to negotiate with their internal opponents, this may be with the intent to consolidate their grip on power rather than to dilute it or yield control.

Furthermore, Soviet military aid, and the involvement of Soviet bloc military forces in Nicaragua, is unchanged; and Moscow continues to pour military aid into Vietnam. As the Democratic majority on the House Armed Services Committee concluded in a September 13, 1988 report, "Soviet assistance to client states has not appreciably changed under Gorbachev and its willingness to resolve through negotiation several regional conflicts has yet to be demonstrated."

It is true that there has been no new example of Soviet indirect aggression since 1981. But this already was true before Gorbachev came to power, and thus the absence of new expansionism can plausibly be attributed as much to tough U.S. policies and the weak Soviet economy as to Gorbachev's "new thinking."

Moscow has in fact seemingly moved away from an emphasis on close ties to radical movements, "vanguard parties," and communist rhetoric on the Third World, toward a more conventional diplomacy in which it seeks normal state-to-state relations with capitalist-oriented developing nations such as Argentina and Brazil. But two important questions arise: First, is this shift permanent or merely a temporary tactical move? As Francis Fukuyama notified us, Soviet foreign policy has oscillated a number of times between periods of active expansion and periods of militant fraternal relations with communist partners and more conventional diplomacy. Based on this history, observers are entitled to skepticism and to ask whether this new Soviet approach is merely another phase rather than a genuine change.

Second, it is also by no means clear whether this Kremlin approach is an either/or proposition. Moscow has in the past utilized a two-track approach by which it maintains normal relations with a given government while simultaneously undermining it through support for radical forces in that nation. Because Moscow often utilizes proxy forces in such a situation, it becomes difficult to determine whether the Kremlin has in fact abandoned its old two-track approach.

Even more significantly, Soviet professions of an intent to limit expansionism in the Third World have subsequently been flagrantly ignored by Moscow. In the early 1970s, for example, many observers hailed "codes of conduct" agreed to by President Nixon and General Secretary Brezhnev, which were supposed to restrict military involvement in the Third World. But the period subsequent to that signing in the mid-to late 1970s witnessed one of the greatest bursts of Soviet expansionism since 1917—all of it in the Third World.

Further, while ideology is probably less important to current Soviet rulers than to earlier ones, it is still worth noting that communist doctrine specifically takes into account the possibility of, or even necessity for, an occasional temporary pause or *peredyshka* in Soviet efforts to expand the sphere of communist domination.

Another key question is how Moscow perceives what have been termed by Rand's Charles Wolf as "the costs of empire." A 1986 Rand study concluded that the U.S.S.R. averaged $37 billion a year (primarily hard currency costs) from 1980 to 1983 in supporting its overseas empire, which amounted to around 5.4 per cent of the Soviet GNP for those years. It is as yet unclear whether the Kremlin is concluding that these costs must be diminished and that the advantages of maintaining their current empire are not worth the costs involved. While some official rhetoric suggests this may be happening, Soviet actions thus far do not validate this thesis. It may also be true that Moscow is finding it increasingly difficult to choose between the advantages of encouraging radical forces and those of building bridges to moderate governments among the emerging middle-range powers of the world. However, as noted earlier, there have also been previous periods in which Moscow has conducted a two-tiered policy encapsulating normal relations with a government while at the same time either directly or indirectly working with radical factions seeking to undermine the very same government. It remains to be seen where the Soviets will end up on this important question.

The Western Policy Response

The United States and its allies should respond to Gorbachev's "new thinking" with a sophisticated multidimensional and multilevel approach. The outlines of such an approach should include:

- The encouragement of long-lasting structural changes in the Soviet domestic system leading to an open, pluralistic society. Such a society is morally preferable but it is also less likely to be inherently expansionist. Changes made thus far in the Soviet system could be reversed with ruthless totalitarian efficiency (although not without real cost to the Soviet body politic).
- Restraint on transferring militarily significant technologies to the Soviet bloc and on subsidized economic assistance. Significantly increased economic interaction, including the use of "untied" loans, should be conditioned upon long-lasting structural changes in key Soviet domestic and international policies. Paradoxically, a premature economic policy of liberalization by the West could hinder the process of Soviet change since it could make it easier for Kremlin leaders to avoid reaching difficult decisions to reallocate resources from its military and its overseas empire to economic development. Specifically, as U.S. Senator Bill Bradley has suggested:

    > The West . . . should treat its capital as a strategic asset and develop a plan and set of conditions for its flow eastward . . . the flow of Western capital should be limited and proportionate with the degree of systematic reform. . . . If we make reform a vigorous criterion for lending, we then encourage General Secretary Gorbachev to push ahead on his present course. Without Western capital and technology, the Soviets can increase domestic investment only by decreasing military spending. I question the wisdom—and the morality—of helping the Soviets avoid the choice between civilian investment and military buildups.[4]

- Maintaining U.S. support, where appropriate conditions exist, for anti-Soviet insurgencies against Soviet Union/Cuban-backed Third World regimes. This can be a geopolitically legitimate response to Soviet indirect aggression and also serves to raise the cost to Moscow of its overseas empire. Criteria for U.S. support include the nature, size, and potential effectiveness of the insurgent groups, as well as the nature of U.S. security interests. U.S. support can range from moral, diplomatic, and economic to the supplying of military aid. Wherever possible—as today in Nicaragua and Angola—the United States should support democratically-oriented forces. But in all cases, its friends will inevitably be more open to democratic change and respect for human rights than will a Soviet/Cuban supported communist regime.
- Openly working with democratic forces and factions within non-democratic regimes of the left and right to help them develop the infra-

structures for democracy. The United States should also, under appropriate circumstances, help pressure these regimes to become more democratic. Different types of pressure may be required for Leninist regimes than for traditional authoritarian regimes because of the structural differences between a Leninist power structure and that of traditional authoritarian regimes. Because of the relatively open nature of authoritarian regimes, and their orientation towards the Western world, their transformation into democratic systems by relatively peaceful means is a realistic possibility. Regimes based upon ideology and tightly controlled, as are most Marxist-Leninist regimes, as the events of June 1989 in the People's Republic of China regrettably demonstrated, are much less likely to be subject to such peaceful transitions.

- Keeping in mind that indigenous causes are at work in all situations where the East-West dimension exists. The United States should be careful to tailor its policies to the specific historical circumstances and local dynamics of the nation in question rather than imposing some abstract model on all such situations. Strong local forces such as nationalism and a Western cultural orientation may in some cases make Soviet success problematic.
- A readiness to meet any sign of genuine Soviet policy change in the Third World with a willingness to negotiate and find creative ways to reduce the Soviet overseas empire.

The U.S. long-term objective, and it may be very long-term, should be the establishment of a world order based upon the rule of law and peaceful competition between nations. There is no getting around the reality that this will require a Soviet Union in which communism no longer has its original operational content. As U.S. ambassador Max Kampleman has put it:

> No regime can be permitted to propagate its faith with the sword. A Soviet Union which desires to enter the 21st century as a respected and secure member of the international community must reject its old faith that the "irreconcilability" of our two systems means the "inevitability" of war and must repudiate violence as the instrument to achieve its vision of a new society.[5]

There are indeed signs of a rethinking of ideology in the U.S.S.R. Perhaps we are on the verge of changes of truly historical significance. But for U.S. policy to change significantly, there must be new Soviet behavior as well as "new thinking." The cautionary factors discussed earlier provided more than reasonable grounds for caution, but they do not call for rigidity. U.S. policy must be imaginative and flexible, and it must be ready to seize any opportunities that present themselves to encourage genuine and long-lasting change in the U.S.-Soviet relationship. While the principal determinants of Soviet developments are within the U.S.S.R., the United States and other nations can have an important influence at the margins. Thus, the United States and its friends should work for a future in which Third World nations can determine their own destiny and in which the U.S.-Soviet rivalry is played out through peaceful political, economic, and cultural competition.

Notes

1. Bruce Porter, *The U.S.S.R. in Third World Conflicts*, (Cambridge: Cambridge University Press, 1984).
2. As Professor Jiri Valenta has pointed out, regimes such as East Germany should properly be conceptualized as "junior partners," whereas a Cuba is more of a proxy.
3. Dennis L. Bark, ed., *The Red Orchestra: Instruments of Soviet Policy in Latin America and the Caribbean* (Stanford, CA: Hoover Institute Press, Stanford University, 1986).
4. U.S. Senator Bill Bradley, *The New York Times*, October 15, 1987.
5. Speech to Conference on International Peace sponsored by the U.S. Institute of Peace, at Airlie House, Airlie, Va., June 21, 1988.

Part Eight
Overview and Evaluation

16

Moscow's "New Thinking" and Third World Regional Conflicts: Some Conclusions

Jiri Valenta

The Geneva Accords on Afghanistan, signed in March 1988, and the subsequent Soviet military withdrawal from that country served as catalysts for the proliferation of other multilateral and bilateral negotiations among rival players in longstanding regional conflicts centering around Angola, Cambodia, and Nicaragua, but also Iran and Iraq. Subsequently, on December 22, 1988, accords were signed by the parties to the Angolan conflict, and there were the beginnings of preliminary regional dialogues among feuding parties in the Western Sahara and between the Koreas. As peace seemed to be breaking out all over in 1988-1989, many policymakers and analysts attributed the climate of compromise and incipient reconciliation in part to Mikhail Gorbachev's "new thinking" (*novoe myshlenie*) in foreign affairs, which encompasses a Soviet willingness to cooperate with the United States in seeking solutions to regional conflicts. Others argue, however, that Gorbachev's policy concepts and declarations need to be further tested in Afghanistan and beyond. They urge continuing caution, pending further Soviet deeds, and strict verification of any ensuing U.S. agreements with the U.S.S.R. and its allies regarding not only Afghanistan but also Angola, Cambodia, and Nicaragua.

Included in the "new thinking" is an acceptance of the U.S. notion that regional conflicts tend to jeopardize tranquil U.S./Soviet relations. Gorbachev, therefore, attaches great importance to their quick resolution, which he views as second only to U.S.-Soviet arms control negotiations. However, the long-term policy implications of the new approach toward the Third World are unclear. What is really new about Gorbachev's thinking regarding Leninist-oriented vanguard-party regimes and regional conflicts? How have Soviet

Third World policies been affected so far by the new concepts? Will they precipitate a substantive strategic or merely tactical shift in Soviet dealings with Leninist-oriented regimes? What should be America's and its allies' response and initiatives toward Gorbachev's innovative foreign policies?

The New Thinking: Conceptualization

Novoe myshlenie is at once the foreign policy corollary and a consequence of the domestic reform concept *perestroika* (economic and societal oriented political restructuring) and *perestroika's* by-product, *glasnost* (openness). Cornerstones of the new Soviet approach, the three concepts are easily misunderstood, in part because they are intertwined, but also because they are essentially attitudinal and so elude precise explanation. *Perestroika*, though used also in reference to world politics, applies basically to Soviet society, and in particular the economy. It describes the radical restructuring and replacement of the centralized Stalinist autocracy of the past with the much more decentralized Leninist vanguard-party structure. This is seen by Gorbachev and his supporters as an urgent necessity. In the matter of economic reform, the Soviet leadership have been guided by their study of the Hungarian and (until May-June 1989) the Chinese models of reform as well as Lenin's synthesis of the market and planned economy (New Economic Policy), which had been repudiated by Stalin after 1929. They claim that Leninism, original and undistorted, is the ideological source of *perestroika*.

Glasnost—a societal condition necessary for *perestroika*—is a policy concept denoting more open dialogue and the admissibility of past policy mistakes, made possible primarily through a relaxation of censorship. It is encouraged by the leadership more as a means for achieving *perestroika* than as an independent objective. Whatever the results of the ongoing Politburo debate over the limits of *glasnost* and *perestroika*, they are not intended to transform the U.S.S.R. into a Jeffersonian democracy but, as stressed often by Gorbachev and his supporters, to facilitate a renewal of Leninism.

The concept *novoe myshlenie* is used to conceptualize practical changes in the theory and practice of Soviet foreign policy, even though it is also used to describe changes in domestic affairs. (Conversely, foreign policy changes are at times referred to in terms of restructuring or *perestroika*.) The "new thinking" also involves a critical assessment of past Soviet foreign policy with the intention of arriving at new, creative approaches toward world affairs, particularly in the areas of nuclear arms control and regional conflicts. Like *perestroika*, it would not be possible without *glasnost*; and like *perestroika*, it envisages a return to original Leninist precepts. As explained by one Soviet official: "What is involved is realism in the evaluation of one's own interests, the elimination of dogma and stereotypes from them . . . in short . . . a return to Leninist policy."

The outcome of Gorbachev's domestic and foreign policy reforms is still very uncertain, all the more so because they represent a serious departure from the policies of the past, which are marked not only by the residues of Stalinism but also by the ideological sterility of the "old thinking" practiced under Leonid Brezhnev. To understand the deeper meanings and long-term potential of *novoe myshlenie* and *perestroika*, one must analyze their sources and the catalysts that crystallized them into being. While revolutionary in the immediate Soviet context, Gorbachev's reforms have precedents in the short-lived experiment of Alexander Dubcek during the Prague Spring of 1968, its survival in different form in Hungary in the 1970s, and its later resurrection by Deng Xiaoping in China in the late 1970s.

Notwithstanding the preceding experiments and models, "Gorbachevism" would have crystallized more slowly had it not been for various pressures from abroad (particularly through the so-called Reagan Doctrine), and, even more important, stagnating Soviet economic conditions. The systemic dysfunction of Soviet society in all its aspects, especially the economy, is recognized by Soviet writers as the most immediate cause of *perestroika*. Although some Soviet analysts were aware of the crisis earlier, its full extent was recognized by the Soviet leadership only in the wake of the accident at Chernobyl in 1986. The technological and organizational insufficiencies and disinformation (or lack of information) provided by the Soviets during this disaster caused worldwide outrage and multiple pressures, demonstrating overwhelmingly the need for pervasive systemic change. There had been a growing debate on the need for reforms within the Soviet academic community a few years before Gorbachev became general secretary, and the accident at Chernobyl helped to catapult it out into the open.

Another important catalyst for change, especially in the Soviet conceptualization of foreign affairs, was the realization that profound domestic reforms would require equally profound changes in foreign policy. *Perestroika* demands a marshalling of resources away from the enormous military build-up of the 1970s and 1980s and away from the support of the new Leninist allies acquired during the Brezhnev years, as well as a scaling down of existing commitments. It is estimated that as much as 25 percent of the Soviet budget is spent on Soviet defense and on maintaining the Soviet military and economic commitment to junior allies (Cuba and Vietnam) and Leninist-oriented regimes (Afghanistan, Nicaragua, Angola, Ethiopia, Cambodia, and South Yemen) in the Third World. Such overextension has made it difficult to channel resources to domestic reform projects. The financial burden of Soviet foreign policy has, of course, been exacerbated by the perceived need to respond to the U.S. military build-up and U.S. military support for anticommunist resistance groups struggling against the unpopular Leninist dictatorships brought into power with Soviet assistance.

As the Soviets see it, they cannot curtail their strategic build-up if the United States continues its own enormous program of military research and development. Thus, Gorbachev's flexible new arms control posture of 1986-1988 was partially motivated by his desire to preempt further advances of the Strategic Defense Initiative (SDI), or at least slow it down. Similarly, Gorbachev's announcement of a large reduction in the Soviet military budget in January 1989 may have been intended, in part, to elicit a like response from the United States.

Soviet commitments to new Leninist forces became prohibitive as of the late 1980s, when the Carter policy of supporting the freedom fighters in Afghanistan was extended, under Reagan, to include support for the anti-Leninist insurgencies in Angola, Nicaragua, and Cambodia. The new Soviet course has definitely been a response not only to this policy but also to the military aid to these same insurgencies, and political pressure on the U.S.S.R. by other countries: support by the People's Republic of China and the ASEAN nations for the resistance movements in Afghanistan and Cambodia, South Africa's support for the resistance movement in Angola, and support of the Afghan resistance by some Islamic and Western developing nations.

Like the Soviet military build-up, the Soviet activism of the 1970s, culminating in the Soviet invasion of Afghanistan and a long occupation, has considerably drained the scarce Soviet resources. Gorbachev admitted this in January 1989: "Why hide it: we are carrying large expenses . . . in connection with the situation in Afghanistan." At this time the Soviet budget deficit was at least $162 billion, or 11 percent of the Soviet GNP. It is not a coincidence that the "new thinking" should appear as this and other grim signs have convinced many Soviet officials that the "old thinking" of the Brezhnev era contributed significantly to Soviet economic and social stagnation.

Soviet analysts in the age of *glasnost*, therefore, have become increasingly critical of Brezhnev, especially because of his wasteful and unnecessary strategic and Third World policies. They now concede that Soviet "direct and indirect involvement in regional conflicts brings about enormous losses, exacerbating overall international tensions, justifying the arms race, and hampering mutually beneficial economic ties with the West."

Does the "new thinking" mean that Gorbachev, notwithstanding his Leninist rhetoric, is turning his back on Leninist theory and the long tradition of Russian and Soviet imperialism? His predecessors Brezhnev and Khrushchev, like Lenin, believed that peaceful coexistence is a specific form of class struggle that it is useful only as a prolonged tactic to postpone, but not prevent, the inevitable conflict between the capitalist and communist worlds. But Gorbachev and his supporters have put this theory in question, indirectly, by refuting the once accepted Von Clausewitzian dictum that war is a continuation of policy by different means. Now they emphasize nonviolence as the preferred norm in international community life.

They contend that the struggle between two opposing world systems is no longer a determining tendency of the present era, which should be characterized by common rather than individual security, military sufficiency instead of strict parity, and shared human values. These ideas are still being tested. Meanwhile, however, the withdrawal of Soviet forces from Afghanistan at the time of this writing and Soviet encouragement of the negotiation of other regional conflicts demonstrate an initial sincerity and a willingness to adjust what heretofore has been considered a very rigid, unalterable system of beliefs.

It is too early to celebrate a strategic change in Soviet international behavior, for the thinking of Gorbachev and his supporters, despite their declarations, does not yet encompass an unequivocal rejection of the Leninist belief in two competing world systems of which the imperialist system presumably provokes conflicts and therefore is the guilty adversary. The rejection of the notion of military struggle between them does not preempt other forms of struggle. Furthermore, the Soviets have never said, unambiguously, that they would stop supporting Leninist forces and allies throughout the world, who seem bent on struggle. So the potential for new conflicts still exists.

Second, given the Russian empire's historical traditions of conquest and expansionism, both later sanctioned by Leninist ideology, the proclaimed "new thinking" must be appraised in light of Soviet actions. The accords on Afghanistan and Angola are tentative beginnings. But in Afghanistan, it is still unclear whether the Soviets will ultimately accept a genuinely nonaligned regime, chosen by the Afghan people. And the accords on Angola, like the projected accords on Cambodia, will have to be tested through a gradual, two-year withdrawal of Cuban and Vietnamese forces from these countries. In Nicaragua and Ethiopia, meanwhile, the Soviet policy of supporting revolutionary regimes appears essentially unchanged by the "new thinking" as of mid 1989.

The element of pragmatism in Soviet thinking should not be underestimated. Gorbachev is a realist and he is scaling down the Soviet military commitment in selected Third World areas primarily because the military track, which had been consistently pursued, did not bring the desired results, even during its greatest intensification. Thus, the withdrawal from Afghanistan was preceded by the largest Soviet military offensive in almost a decade since the Soviet invasion, and yet it failed. Likewise, the 1988 accord on Angola was preceded by the largest Cuban military offensive since Fidel Castro, backed by the U.S.S.R., sent his troops there thirteen years ago. The 1988 bilateral negotiations between the Sandinista regime in Nicaragua and the resistance were also preceded by a large, well-planned military offensive, including a Sandinista intrusion into Honduran territory aimed at destroying the resistance's military and logistical supplies. Moreover, in Ethiopia and Syria the Soviet military commitment remains unchanged.

The Politburo debate on the new policies continues, and there seems to be no firm consensus. In spite of a strengthening of Gorbachev's position at the 19th All-Union Conference of the CPSU in June-July 1988, *perestroika*, *glasnost* and *novoe myshlenie* are still under attack. Senior Politburo member Egor Ligachev led the opposition prior to October 1988. He rejected radical *perestroika* somewhat indirectly, repudiated the excesses of *glasnost*, and tried to discredit the "new thinking" by rehabilitating the old concept of the "class character" of international relations. As Ligachev explained, "Any other presentation of the question [the other presentation being Gorbachev's and Shevardnadze's notion that class struggle no longer plays a leading role in international relations] just sows confusion among the Soviet people and among our friends abroad."

The Central Committee meeting of October 1988 was a temporary victory for Gorbachev in that Ligachev then lost his position as second secretary as well as his ideological portfolio, which was passed on to Gorbachev's ally, Vadim Medvedev. However, Ligachev retained a Politburo seat; and Gorbachev again hinted strongly at powerful dissent to his reforms the following January. Gorbachev's reforms are also resisted by some Politburo members responsible for security matters, the many rank-and-file party members who do not see the long-term benefits of the proposed radical changes, and additionally by Fidel Castro and other opponents of *perestroika* abroad such as the East German leadership.

Clearly the Kremlin struggle has not been decided. Some leaders fear that *glasnost* may be outpacing *perestroika* and could destabilize the Leninist system as open dissent grows in the absence of rapid improvement of the Soviet economy. Whether the reforms flourish will depend on Gorbachev's ability to build an ongoing consensus in the Politburo and ultimately score a clear-cut victory over his critics. His introduction of a new constitutional concept sanctioning a powerful presidency, presumably to be occupied by him, would allow him to consolidate power. Moreover, the March 1989 election of a new Congress of People's Deputies, its frank debate and policy resolutions, and the proceedings of the new Supreme Soviet in June-July 1989 were a major boost for the political restructuring of Soviet society. But this is not enough. Gorbachev must also deliver some tangible economic results of the reforms in the next two or three years. Given the uncertain conditions of Soviet internal politics, it is impossible to form firm, long-term conclusions about the longevity or potential of Gorbachev's reforms. Their success is not inevitable.

Soviet Junior Partners—Cuba and Vietnam—and Regional Conflicts

In spite of the many profound cultural, historical, and socioeconomic differences between Cuba and Vietnam, there are undeniable similarities in their political systems and their foreign behavior over the last twenty-five years. As junior partners of the Soviet Union, Cuba and Vietnam have played key roles in helping to usher in and consolidate a number of Leninist-oriented regimes— Nicaragua and (until October 1983) Grenada in the Caribbean Basin; Angola and Ethiopia in Africa; and Laos and Cambodia in Southeast Asia. This activity was especially evident in the late 1970s and throughout the 1980s when Cuba and Vietnam served as twin pillars of the Soviet-led interventionism on behalf of Leninist-oriented forces in the Third World, reinforcing Deng Xiaoping's notion of Vietnam as the "Cuba of the Orient" and the ensuing notion of Cuba as the Vietnam of the Caribbean. Clearly Gorbachev must cope with not only the legacy of the Brezhnev era but also the legacy of Brezhnev-supported Cuban and Vietnamese activism.

When comparing countries so varied, one must take into account the warnings of cultural and political relativists who caution against sweeping generalizations of comparative analysis that may obfuscate the uniqueness and specific conditions of individual countries. Cuba's predominantly Western political culture and deeply rooted caudillo tradition (shared to a degree by the Philippines) are vastly different from the Buddhist and quasi-Confucian tradition from which Vietnam's political culture descends.

Nevertheless, there are important parallels in the recent political developments in Cuba and Vietnam that derive from parallel geostrategic conditions and the similar ideological model both countries have adopted. In spite of their different paths to Leninism—gradually in Cuba after the victory of the anti-Batista revolution, and immediately in Vietnam when an experienced communist party seized power—both regimes embraced a political system constructed on the Leninist tenets of the vanguard (single and elite) party, democratic centralism (vertical command structure of party and state), and proletarian internationalism (a strategic alliance with the U.S.S.R. dictating multi-faceted support of its alliance partners). Herein lies one of the important distinctions between Leninist junior partners such as Vietnam and Cuba and Soviet client states such as India. Whereas Soviet and Indian foreign policy interests tend to coincide in some areas, India has not embraced the Leninist path of development. Nor has it become a full-fledged member of the worldwide Soviet alliance system.

During the Brezhnev era, Cuba and Vietnam evolved into two of the most militarized countries in the world, although ultimately dependent upon the Soviet Union's much greater military might and strategic cover in the event of potential confrontations with perceived hostile neighbors—the United States in the case of Cuba and the People's Republic of China in the case of Vietnam. However, neither Cuba nor Vietnam is an immediate neighbor of the Soviet Union. Because of this geographic reality and the fact that the revolutions in Cuba and Vietnam occurred without Soviet military assistance (unlike the revolutions in Eastern Europe and Mongolia), the Soviet influence, strong as it is, is more indirect. Cuba and Vietnam, unlike the Warsaw Treaty Organization countries, tend to act as voluntary rather than obligatory allies.

While voluntary allies, Cuba and Vietnam are not unconstrained, autonomous actors. The U.S.S.R., primarily because of its superior military and economic might, plays the dominant role in the alliance, especially concerning Cuban and Vietnamese foreign policy, over which Soviet wishes exert unusually strong influence. In the 1970s and 1980s, the projection of power by the Vietnamese and Cubans in pursuit of strategic goals shared with the Soviets, helped them cement strategic alliances with the U.S.S.R. At the same time, Cuba and Vietnam also influence Soviet foreign policy when it depends on large and lengthy deployments of their military forces. This has been the case in Angola since 1975, in Ethiopia since 1977, and in Cambodia since 1979.

The fact that Cuba and Vietnam have some autonomy and can influence Soviet foreign policy has made it easier for them to react independently to *perestroika, glasnost*, and *novoe myshlenie*. Thus far, Castro has rejected *perestroika* and *glasnost* on the grounds that Cuba, being at the doors of "imperialism," cannot commit the "strategic error" of "using capitalist methods." Castro sees *perestroika* and *glasnost* as a challenge to the ideological purity of the Cuban regime and to his own personal power as a socialist caudillo. He is especially annoyed by Soviet criticism of the serious difficulties confronting the Cuban economy and has publicly repudiated the suggestions of some colleagues and middle-level officials that "Gorbachevism" may provide a way out of Cuba's economic morass. He has vowed, instead, to continue his policy of "rectification" (based on orthodox communism), eschewing material incentives in favor of ideological rewards, maintaining iron discipline and eliminating potential challenges to his power, as demonstrated by the trial and execution of General Arnaldo Ochoa Sanchez in July 1989.

The new Vietnamese leadership of Nguyen Van Linh, meanwhile, has embraced *perestroika* unconditionally, possibly because of Linh's weaker position in the Vietnamese collective leadership (as compared to Castro's), and thus greater susceptibility to Soviet pressure, but also because of Hanoi's much graver economic conditions. Instead of being a source of revolutionary inspiration, Vietnam has become a source of migration by desperate boat people. The severe food shortages and possible starvation in Vietnam loom all the more starkly against the prosperous backdrop of Singapore and Thailand

and other ASEAN countries. The much needed "renovation," Hanoi's version of *perestroika*, has been praised by the Soviet leaders, and its by-product *glasnost* was used by the Vietnamese Politburo to criticize the "mandarinism" of the Vietnamese *nomenklatura*. Instead of generating public dialogue, as they have in Moscow, however, *perestroika* and *glasnost* appear to have become the new orthodoxy in Hanoi.

Cuba and Vietnam share a similar dislike of the Soviet "new thinking" in foreign affairs. Whereas Moscow finally relented on Afghanistan, there are no signs of self-criticism by Hanoi or Havana concerning their respective interventions in Cambodia and Angola. It was primarily Soviet subtle pressure that convinced them to negotiate these conflicts.

The fact that Cuba and Vietnam approach Gorbachev's reforms differently from Moscow suggests a transnational dialogue within the Soviet alliance system. Those who can be counted on to support Gorbachev's new course are the leaders of Hungary and Poland. Other communist countries, however—East Germany, Cuba, and perhaps now China (after June 1989)—disapprove or are confused by the Soviet policies, especially *glasnost* and the potentially detrimental effects it can have on stability in their countries through the lessening censorship in the media. Concern about the effects of media reporting were reflected in the remarks of Cuban leader Carlos Rafael Rodriguez, who complained to this writer in the fall of 1988 that Soviet newspapers were publishing "counterrevolutionary stories." The East German leadership, for similar reasons, forbade the distribution of the Soviet-published German language edition of *Sputnik*. Segments of the Czechoslovak leadership and members of the FSLN leadership of Nicaragua as well as the African National Congress (ANC) of South Africa are also among the ranks of those who disapprove of various aspects of the reforms.

Conflict in South Asia: Afghanistan

Among the regional conflicts involving the Soviet Union, the Afghan conflict is the only one in which the Soviets have taken unilateral steps toward a resolution. By doing so, they acknowledged two facts—one, that their invasion was an ideologically motivated error, a "mistaken prescription for the installation of socialism," and two, that superior military power cannot effectively consolidate a Leninist-oriented regime in the face of determined internal opposition (the mujahideen backed by strong outside support, in this case from the United States, China, and various Islamic countries).

The Soviet decision to withdraw regular military forces from Afghanistan was surely conditioned by the U.S. decision in 1986 to qualitatively upgrade military assistance to the Afghan mujahideen to include shoulder-held Stinger antiaircraft missiles. The resulting rise in the morale of the Afghan resistance and the increased military and economic costs of the war for the Soviets, especially the dramatic loss of aircraft and troop casualties, contributed to a decisive turn in the conflict. The Soviets coupled the military disengagement with a political plan for Afghan national reconciliation designed to broaden support for the pro-Soviet, Leninist-oriented regime in Kabul.

The U.S.-sponsored Geneva peace accords of April 1988—involving, in varying degrees, the Kabul government, Pakistan, the U.S.S.R., and the United States—set terms for the Soviet pullout and acted as a catalyst for subsequent negotiations processes in other regions. Even though the Soviet withdrawal was completed according to the timetable fixed by the accord, the durability of the agreement and, with it, the outcome of the conflict remain unclear, primarily because the accords excluded the Afghan resistance, a principal party to the conflict.

Military and economic costs were not the only factors contributing to the Soviet decision to leave Afghanistan. The isolationism brought on by the Soviet conduct in that war entailed such economic implications as Soviet ineligibility for Western multilateral and bilateral aid, and outside investment that Gorbachev desperately needs to carry out *perestroika*.

In the spirit of *glasnost*, Soviet writers are critically assessing the causes and development of the Soviet involvement in Afghanistan, and this has led to some national soul-searching, and to the search for a scapegoat as well. As Soviet analysts admit, the invasion was based on the mistaken ideological assumption that socioeconomic conditions in Afghanistan were ripe for revolution, i.e., that the Leninist party there had become a national force with broad popular support. The fierce resistance later disproved this assumption. As the Soviet Politburo came to believe that their plans for Afghanistan could not be imposed militarily, they shifted to political channels. The ensuing Soviet-sponsored national reconciliation program under Najibullah, handpicked by the Soviets to replace the compromised and thus unsuitable Babrak Karmal, sought to bring in a new coalition government including the Leninist-oriented party and noncommunist elements.

While promoting a policy of national reconciliation inside Afghanistan, the Soviets intensified their search for a diplomatic resolution of the conflict under U.N. sponsorship. Such efforts were enhanced by the signing of the Intermediate Nuclear Forces (INF) Treaty, which provided, among other things, for the removal of the SS-20 missiles located in the Soviet Far East. This helped create a conciliatory atmosphere conducive to negotiations.

Thus, on February 8, 1988, shortly after signing the INF agreement in Washington, Gorbachev announced that the Soviet Union would withdraw its troops from Afghanistan, with or without an accord. Such bold initiative surprised both Pakistan and the United States but also alarmed them, for without an agreement, the Soviets would have been free to withdraw exclusively on their own terms, without a timetable for withdrawal or stipulations ensuring Afghanistan's neutrality and nonalignment.

An agreement was definitely preferable. Necessarily drawn up in some haste, the accords had three substantial flaws: 1) They did not provide specifically for the withdrawal of Soviet advisers (KGB and military) or for the cessation of Soviet Air Force operations (originating in the Soviet Union) over Afghanistan; 2) they did not involve the mujahideen as negotiating partners; and 3) they did not provide for an end to military aid to the warring parties by their respective allies during the withdrawal. The Afghan resistance saw the accords as a betrayal and thus continued their struggle in their spite. Though a step forward, the accords evidenced a wide gap between the Afghan reality and the quasi-reality on which they were predicated. For this and other reasons, they cannot easily serve as a model for resolving other regional conflicts.

Yet some analysts see the recent Soviet policy on Afghanistan as a good example of Gorbachev's "new thinking." They believe the accords open the way for a dismissal of Kabul's Leninist regime, and that the Soviets will accept a new nonaligned government in Afghanistan.

Others see Gorbachev's approach as a scheme designed to provide a traditional breathing space (*peredyshka*), but still in keeping with the overall long-term Leninist strategy. According to the latter analysis, the Soviets are removing their troops from Afghanistan in order to alter world public opinion, which has been against them, and to weaken international support for the resistance. As this thinking goes, the lack of a central authority created by the Soviet exit will lead to a political vacuum and even political anarchy, a sort of "Lebanonization" of Afghanistan, with several groups of mujahideen warring among themselves along ideological, religious (Shiite/Sunni), and tribal lines. Eventually the war would be reduced, in the eyes of the world, to an internal conflict, devoid of direct Soviet participation. Having deflected world attention from their instigation of the conflict, the Soviets could then shift the blame for the continuing tragedy to the resistance, which, unable to create a stable government, might be depicted as a kind of brutal Khmer Rouge.

The real test of the "new thinking" and Gorbachev's sincerity will be whether the first scenario is allowed to develop, i.e., a nonaligned government is allowed to be established in Kabul. The Soviet general Kim Tsagolov, who served as a military adviser in Afghanistan between 1981 and 1984, was unsure about the survival of the Najibullah regime after completion of the Soviet withdrawal. This, however, does not necessarily mean there will be a quick takeover by antigovernment forces, a Vietnam type scenario. On the surface at least, the picture is different. The Soviet troops did not flee Kabul in 1988-1989 in the chaotic way that the American forces left Saigon in 1975. Nor has Gorbachev, faithful to the Soviet line, officially conceded defeat.

Meanwhile, unlike the invaders from North Vietnam, the Afghan resistance forces—which are genuine, indigenous guerrilla groups—remain seriously divided.

By the time of the final Soviet military withdrawal on February 15, 1989, the mujahideen were still unable to capture any major provincial capital. By contrast, the "guerrillas" of North Vietnam had become, by the end of the war, a regular conventional force under the centralized command of the Leninist party in Hanoi. It should be noted, however, that since signing the Geneva Accords, the Soviets have been increasingly reluctant to directly engage the resistance militarily. However, they have continued to support the Najibullah regime with extensive economic and military aid (including surface-to-surface SCUD tactical missiles and MIG 27 fighter-bombers), and before their withdrawal in February 1989, they continued the devastating saturation bombing of resistance positions with Backfire bombers stationed in Soviet territory. If the civil war continues much beyond the Soviet withdrawal, the bombardments could be resumed in defense of the Najibullah regime.

More evidence is needed before concluding that the Soviets are prepared to accept a resolution of the conflict that is acceptable to the majority of the Afghan people. As the deadline for the Soviet withdrawal approached, they did enter into direct talks with the resistance factions heretofore ignored, and with the exiled Afghan King Mohammed Zahir Shah, who is living in Italy. Both of these initiatives were Soviet attempts to partially salvage the Leninist regime in Kabul by incorporating some of its elements in a coalition government including the resistance and the royalists. Presumably the King could play the role of mediator in any eventual effort to build such a government, though this option appeared foreclosed at the time of writing.

During the course of 1989, a decisive role will be played also by neighboring Pakistan, where various political groups disagree about the kind of government they would like to see in Kabul, and there will be some input from India, which is apprehensive about the Kabul-Islamabad Moslem axis. That Pakistan is an important player is confirmed by the fact that Soviet Minister of Foreign Affairs Eduard Shevardnadze made a last-minute trip to Pakistan in January 1989 to solicit Islamabad's help in salvaging some future government role for the discredited Najibullah regime. Given the history of multiple and incessant Soviet pressures on Pakistan, Shevardnadze's supplicant mission betrayed an element of desperation. The death in August 1988 of Pakistani President Zia-ul Haq, a staunch supporter of the Afghan resistance, could still have unfavorable consequences for the resistance in their efforts to manage and solve the problems created by the long conflict. However, the unconditional withdrawal from Afghanistan of all Soviet forces, including advisory personnel, which was completed on February 15, 1989, and cessation of all military activities from the Soviet territory on behalf of Kabul's regime demonstrate a bona fide strategic dimension of the "new thinking" and its applicability in the peaceful resolution of other regional conflicts. Although the fate of the Najibullah regime is not yet decided as this book goes to press in summer 1989, it is unlikely there will be real stability in Kabul in the near future.

Other Regional Conflicts

The notion heard both in the United States and in the Soviet Union that the Geneva Accords on Afghanistan can serve as a model for settling the regional conflicts in Angola, Cambodia, and Nicaragua is somewhat nearsighted. There are similarities among these conflicts—especially the Leninist orientation of the vanguard party regimes in each country and their attempts to build strategic alliances with the U.S.S.R., Cuba, Vietnam, and other Soviet allies. There are, however, vastly different cultural, political, and socioeconomic conditions in the countries and in the surrounding regions that have differentiated the origins of the conflicts as well as the likely prescriptions for their resolutions. The Geneva Accords, while not exactly a model for conflict resolution, have served at least as an inspiration and a catalyst in bringing about the successful multilateral negotiations on Angola (including the MPLA/Labor Party regime, Cuba, South Africa, and the United States, but excluding the UNITA resistance) and the regional talks on Cambodia (including the Leninist PRK regime, the resistance, and their ASEAN neighbors). Some of the flawed aspects of the Geneva Accords, their exclusion of the resistance especially, influenced the Angolan negotiations, which were also barred to the resistance. Pressure by China, which supports the Khmer Rouge, prevented this from happening in Cambodia by July 1989.

The exemplariness of the Geneva Accords becomes especially elusive in view of the fact that the final resolution of the Afghan conflict still has to unfold. The accords are a hopeful beginning on the long road to peace; but if they fail because of their flawed nature—primarily the exclusion of a main party to the conflict—then they may become a model for how not to negotiate such conflicts.

Conflict in Africa: Angola, Namibia, Ethiopia

Angola. The Soviet/Cuban intervention in Angola in 1975— on behalf of the Leninist-oriented Movement for the Popular Liberation of Angola (MPLA) against its two rivals, the National Union for the Total Independence of Angola (UNITA) of Jonas Savimbi and the Front for the National Liberation of Angola (FNLA) of Holden Roberto—was the first large-scale Soviet-allied military intervention in the Third World. While the Soviet-backed Cubans were intervening from across the Atlantic on behalf of the MPLA, the South Africans were intervening, on a smaller scale, from the south (Namibia) on behalf of UNITA. (Although a logistical necessity for Savimbi, the South African assistance compromised him with other black African leaders and movements.) In the aftermath, 50,000 South African troops continued to occupy Namibia, where they confronted the MPLA's sister liberation organization, the Southwest African People's Organization (SWAPO), and provided military aid to UNITA in its continuing struggle against the MPLA, now calling itself the MPLA-Labor Party (a term suggesting its vanguard party orientation).

In spite of their many differences, the mujahideen in Afghanistan and Savimbi's UNITA in Angola became serious insurgency forces and evolved comparably in their struggles to overthrow Leninist-oriented regimes. However, unlike the mujahideen, who received bipartisan U.S. support as early as 1980, UNITA received such support only after 1985 when the Clark Amendment prohibiting American aid to UNITA was repealed. It was in part the persistent efforts of Assistant Secretary of State for African Affairs Chester Crocker to break this military stalemate that finally convinced Gorbachev to pressure Cuba and South Africa into serious negotiations.

A major difference between Afghanistan and Angola stems from the greater complexity of the policymaking process involving Angola. Whereas the Soviets and the puppet Najibullah regime negotiated as one unit vis-à-vis outside parties (Pakistan, and the United States), in Angola the Soviets had to reach an understanding with both the MPLA-Labor Party regime and Cuba before approaching the other side with one voice. For example, several months before the agreement was signed, the Cubans deployed an additional 15,000 elite troops to help conduct the largest campaign in the Angolan war, surely designed to influence the negotiations and to obliterate the UNITA forces if an agreement was not reached. It is difficult to know to what degree this campaign sprang from sheer Cuban initiative and what hand the Soviets had in the decision; and whether their support was a final concession to the Cuban adventurism. Whatever the facts, the Cuban ability to undermine implementation of the agreement on Angola should not be underestimated.

Some of the first signs of the Soviet "new thinking" on Angola and on Afghanistan surfaced in 1987 when Soviet officials expressed a more nuanced and more realistic position on the southern African region, to the displeasure of the MPLA and its sister organizations, Namibia's SWAPO and South Africa's African National Congress (ANC). Subsequently—concurrent with the changing Soviet position on Afghanistan—the U.S.S.R. made a much more definite shift, accepting the basic premises of linkage, i.e., the need to secure the withdrawal of both Cuban and South African forces from Angola and Namibia respectively, and the need to secure independence for Namibia according to the terms of U.N. Security Council Resolution 435. We know that the issue of Angola and Namibia was discussed at the Reagan/Gorbachev summit in Moscow in the spring of 1988, after which Chester Crocker held several meetings with Soviet officials to discuss a negotiated solution. It was in this period that the Soviets persuaded Cuba, by both arm-twisting and cajoling, to participate in multilateral negotiations with the MPLA-Labor Party regime and South Africa, with the United States chairing the negotiations and the U.S.S.R. acting as observer. Although the United States and the Soviet Union provided the major impetus, it is also true that Cuba, South Africa, and Angola were receptive to superpower mediation to end the continuous, very costly military stalemate. Finally, on December 22, 1988, the parties agreed on a timetable for the withdrawal of 50,000 Cuban troops, to begin in January 1989 and end in July 1990, when the final contingent would be withdrawn. The Soviet sigh of relief was almost audible as the Soviet Deputy Minister of Foreign Affairs responsible for handling regional conflicts, Anatolii Adamishin, praised the "spirit of realism" shown by the RSA (Republic of South Africa) government in the search for a resolution of the Angolan conflict.

The accords on Angola/Namibia are not flawless. Like their precedent, the Geneva Accords, they do not provide for negotiations with the indigenous insurgencies or subsequent power-sharing, although the Soviets did finally offer this solution to the Afghan resistance in January 1989. While the MPLA-Labor regime of Jose Eduardo dos Santos is prepared to reconcile with some of the rank-and-file members of UNITA, as it had made peace previously with elements of the now defunct FNLA, its earlier rival, until June 1989 it rejected a truce agreement and power-sharing with UNITA leaders, who it believes will eventually be defeated. The UNITA leadership, meanwhile, who represent a third of the population of Angola, have vowed to fight on until assured of a power-sharing role. Savimbi's arms supplies are estimated to enable him to maintain the present level of operations for at least another three years.

As with Afghanistan, the new approach on Angola, at least for the moment, is apparently aimed at stopping the flow of arms to Savimbi's forces, who are resisting the consolidation of power by the MPLA Leninist regime. The agreement does not provide for an end to South African support for UNITA. Nor does it specify that Angola should cease training ANC cadres at bases in Angola, which, if it should happen, would impose significant logistical difficulties on the ANC.

Ethiopia. While taking a flexible approach to Angola at the Moscow summit, Gorbachev refused to talk with President Reagan about Ethiopia, the most strategically located Soviet ally in Africa. The regime of Mengistu Haile Mariam, which is seriously challenged by resistance groups from the provinces of Eritrea and Tigre, ranks as the fourth largest recipient of Soviet military aid worldwide, behind junior allies Cuba, Vietnam, and client state Syria. The continuing Soviet military assistance to that brutal regime, like the transfers of advanced fighter aircraft to Syria and North Korea, suggests that the "new thinking" will be applied selectively and that the Soviet policy of supporting Leninist forces in the Third World has not been abandoned altogether. However, the series of military defeats of Mengistu's regime in late 1988-early 1989 have already brought some Soviet pressure on Addis Ababa to negotiate a settlement to the ongoing civil war.

Conflicts in Southeast Asia: Cambodia and the Philippines

Cambodia. The military stalemate in Cambodia, like the stalemates in Afghanistan and Angola, has convinced the Gorbachev leadership that the long military effort to consolidate the Leninist regime installed in Cambodia ten years ago is going nowhere. The effort has been blocked by the Cambodian resistance—which is supported by the People's Republic of China, Thailand, and other Southeast Asian nations, and more modestly by the United States.

The fact that Moscow must coordinate its activity in Cambodia with its junior partner Vietnam helps to explain in part the slower implementation of the principles of the "new thinking" there than, for example, in Afghanistan, where Moscow acts alone. (The pursuit of the diplomatic track in Angola was retarded for the same reason.) Thus, in spite of the psychological breakthrough of July 1988 at the multilateral Jakarta Informal Meeting (JIM-I) among the rival Cambodian factions, Vietnam, and members of ASEAN, and the Vietnamese announcement (April 1989) about the withdrawal of its military forces in September 1989, there is no conclusive evidence that Hanoi has decided to follow Moscow's example in Afghanistan, that is, withdraw its armed forces and resolve the conflict via political means.

The "new thinking" on Cambodia, Afghanistan, and Angola has been conditioned by the realities of brutal, seemingly unending, and finally stalemated civil wars. In Cambodia, the Soviet-backed Vietnamese blitz invasion of December 1978 quickly led to the installation of the pro-Vietnamese, pro-Soviet puppet regime of People's Republic of Kampuchea (PRK) under Heng Samrin (who had defected to Vietnam shortly before the invasion), but that regime has been kept afloat only through nine years of military occupation by 120,000 to 150,000 Vietnamese troops engaged in an antiguerrilla war against three resistance groups: the Khmer Rouge (numbering about 28,000-40,000), the followers of Prince Norodom Sihanouk (about 16,000), and the Khmer People's National Liberation Front of former Prime Minister Son Sann (9,000 men). The Sihanouk, Khmer Rouge and Son Sann groups make up the volatile Coalition Government of Democratic Kampuchea (CGDK). Like in

Afghanistan and Angola, the Soviets and their junior partners learned in Cambodia that an indigenous national resistance receiving substantial international aid can deny an occupier control of the countryside and gradually increase the cost of warfare to politically and economically unacceptable levels.

The costs have been high. Vietnamese war casualties—disclosed for the first time since 1979, after the Soviets announced their own casualties in Afghanistan—were approximately 50,000 dead and about an equal number of wounded in ten years. These figures greatly surpass the official Soviet count of casualties in Afghanistan for approximately the same time period: 13,310 killed and 35,478 wounded as of the spring of 1988, and about 15,000 killed by the final withdrawal date of February 15, 1989. The overall financial burden on the Soviet empire has been similarly high. Soviet military and economic aid to Vietnam is estimated at $4 to $5 million per day, and much of this amount is earmarked for Vietnam's campaign in Cambodia. With such costs, the Soviets and Vietnamese either had to revise their goals in Cambodia or score a decisive victory. They settled on the first alternative, as the latter would have required a large escalation of the war and the invasion of a sanctuary state supporting and harboring the resistance, in this case, Thailand. The Soviets had weighed the same choices before in Afghanistan, where a victory would have required the invasion of Pakistan, the main sanctuary of the mujahideen.

The Soviets made a definitive reassessment of their plans for Cambodia after Gorbachev came to power. Once considered irreversible, the Leninization of Cambodia was then gradually reassessed. The Soviets began to take a more subtle, diplomatic approach in search of a political settlement. Through these efforts, the U.S.S.R. has emerged as the key power broker in that regional conflict.

The Soviet efforts to broker the conflict in Cambodia (and the conflict in Angola) were of course conditioned by the foregoing previous negotiations on Afghanistan. Although the Geneva Accords could hardly serve as a model for resolving the very different Cambodian conflict, they were a useful precedent; for the real peace initiatives on Cambodia and Angola came only after the accords were signed in March 1988. Subsequently, in May, after the visit of Thailand's Premier Prem Tinsulanonda to Moscow, the Soviets made a special effort to induce Vietnam in the direction of multilateral negotiations. Whereas in 1984 Vietnam had flatly refused to join in ASEAN's proximity talks on Cambodia, they did agree to do so in spring 1988, when Moscow put pressure on them.

At the same time that the Vietnamese agreed to participate in the JIM-I talks, they were said to be ready to withdraw their troops from Cambodia, 50,000 by early 1989 and the remaining 70,000 by 1990—a timetable that is very similar to the Cuban timetable for withdrawal from Angola. They also recalled their high military command, presumably placing their remaining troops under the alternate command of the local PRK regime. Vietnam alleges that 50,000 of its troops were withdrawn by early 1989. Available evidence suggests, however, that they withdrew primarily from territories adjacent to Thailand and that Cambodian replacements temporarily took up these border positions. Because of the lack of international supervision, it is not clear whether the Vietnamese troops were redeployed elsewhere in the country. Thus Cambodia is still occupied by Vietnamese troops as of July 1989.

The Soviets apparently put pressure on Hanoi to withdraw its troops from Cambodia in 1989. The withdrawal is expected to help facilitate a much hoped for rapprochement with the People's Republic of China. However, there is no evidence that Moscow would like to entirely abandon the PRK regime. Nor would the Vietnamese ever cooperate with such a plan, and they have some say in the matter because of their jurisdiction over the Cam Ranh Bay naval facilities, which are very important to Soviet naval strategy in the Pacific.

Current Soviet policies in Cambodia are aimed at creating and supporting a national reconciliation coalition government headed by Prince Sihanouk. As envisioned by the Soviets, however, the PRK would wield the real power in such a coalition. This would explain the rationale behind the bilateral talks between Sihanouk and PRK Premier Hun Sen in Paris around the time of JIM-I; they were designed primarily to gain legitimacy for the Hun Sen regime and win over the Sihanouk faction while isolating the more bellicose Khmer Rouge, which the PRK government refuses to include in any coalition.

The JIM-I and JIM-II talks demonstrated that the Vietnamese until early 1989 were prepared to engage in cunning diplomacy—the well-known "talk/ fight, fight/talk" stratagem they employed during the Indochina war of 1960-1975—but that they were not seriously searching for a negotiated settlement of the conflict, under international monitoring and within a definite timetable. Vietnam, more than the U.S.S.R., is counting on the negotiations to divide the resistance forces and deprive them of vital external support, especially from China. Meanwhile the Vietnamese could perpetuate their control by incorporating units of Khmer-speaking Vietnamese within the ranks of the Cambodian armed forces. (As I suggested earlier, Cuba may be planning a similar strategy in Portuguese-speaking Angola.) However, the Khmer Rouge, like the resistance forces in Afghanistan and in Angola, have accumulated weapons stores sufficient to enable them to continue fighting for a long time, even if the Chinese and other outside assistance is terminated.

There are forces, nonetheless, that appear to push Vietnam toward an eventual strategic compromise on Cambodia: the Soviet "new thinking" in foreign affairs, which extends to the resolution of regional conflicts; the

Soviet desire for a rapprochement with China and the Chinese prerequisite that the Vietnamese leave Cambodia; the pressing need to scale down the Soviet economic and military overcommitment worldwide; and near-terminal economic conditions in Vietnam. The negotiations between senior Chinese and Vietnamese diplomats in January 1989, reportedly at the insistence of Moscow, and Gorbachev's summit with the Chinese leaders in Beijing in May 1989, furthermore, seem to indicate progress toward a political settlement. The JIM-II meeting in February 1989 and the Paris negotiations commencing in July of the same year constituted further small steps in the direction of political compromise. However the warring parties again disagreed on a key aspect of the accord—the make-up of an interim coalition government—and Vietnam again refused to agree to the international supervision of its troops withdrawals. Because of continuing Vietnamese obstinacy, in part motivated by the fear of a resulting rapprochement between the U.S.S.R. and China, the road toward a genuinely neutral Cambodia is going to be long and difficult.

The Philippines. The sincerity of the Soviet "new thinking" in international affairs may soon face another test in the Philippines, where the communist New People's Army rapidly gained strength prior to the February 1986 revolution, during the last years of the authoritarian regime of President Ferdinand Marcos. That conflict could escalate regionally, with prospects for both Soviet and U.S. involvement.

The fall of the Marcos dictatorship and the ascent to power of the democratic administration of President Corazon Aquino in February 1986 have resulted in a resurgent Philippine nationalism that is increasingly anti-American. This is manifested in growing opposition to the U.S. military facilities of Clark and Subic Bay. Under the banner of "new thinking," the Soviet Union has skillfully used the new political mood to help advance its strategic goal of reducing and eventually eliminating the American military presence from the Philippines. Until now, Soviet strategy has consisted of a major diplomatic offensive designed to improve Philippine/Soviet relations on the one hand, and on the other hand to influence to Soviet advantage the protracted and contentious U.S./Philippine review of the Military Bases Agreement (MBA) held in 1988. Moscow has encouraged popular sentiment against the U.S. bases and supported the enactment of antinuclear legislation by the Philippine Congress in 1988. Gorbachev even tried to link the closing of U.S. bases in the Philippines with the closing of Soviet bases in Vietnam. However, the bases in Vietnam are inferior and thus the U.S. losses would be greater. If the United States should be deprived of this last military foothold in the Southeast Asian region, Moscow could move a step closer to eventual military supremacy in the Asian-Pacific region.

Much attention has also been focused on the alleged Soviet direct and indirect support for the New People's Army (NPA) communist insurgency.

New evidence from captured documents suggests, for example, that the NPA maintains relations with a number of pro-Soviet Leninist regimes worldwide, including the Sandinistas. In spite of the evidence of increased contacts between the Soviets and the recently de-Maoised Communist Party of the Philippines (CPP), direct Soviet involvement so far appears to be limited to an occasional transfer of funds to the CPP-controlled trade unions, and a couple of weapons shipments perhaps through Libyan and Vietnamese intermediaries in the early 1980s under Brezhnev. The timing of a few of these shipments might have coincided with the weapons shipments to Leninist insurgents in other parts of the Third World such as El Salvador in Central America. Continuation of such interference (disputed by some) in the early 1990s seems unlikely, as Soviet state-to-state relations with the Philippines improve. It is through state channels that the Soviets can best influence their primary policy objective of removing the American military presence. Support now for the insurgency would jeopardize these efforts as well as provide a rationale for keeping the bases. Heeding the lessons of Cambodia, the Soviet Union is reluctant to engage in another protracted conflict in Southeast Asia, with all the inherent diplomatic and economic burdens.

A critical point could arrive if Manila decides at some point to terminate its military relationship with the United States, as this would seriously handicap the anti-insurgency campaign of the Philippine military. Should the insurgency then reach a "strategic stalemate," the U.S.S.R. and/or Vietnam might be tempted to provide military support for the NPA and thus tip the military balance in the insurgency's favor. Moscow's decision whether to do this would be determined on the basis of an assessment of its relationship with the CPP and possible American and regional responses to visible Soviet involvement.

Whether acting directly or through Vietnam, its junior ally in the region, Moscow's involvement could ultimately transform a civil war in the Philippines into another protracted Southeast Asian conflict, with the two superpowers providing varying degrees of support for the combatants. Such a conflict could increase the militarization of the Asian-Pacific region and seriously damage currently improving relations between the United States and the Soviet Union.

Regional Conflict in Central America: Nicaragua

The conflict in Nicaragua is the only one of the five conflicts examined in which the principal issue is not an invasion or large-scale intervention by the Soviets or Soviet allies. Unlike in Afghanistan, Cambodia, Angola, and Ethiopia, in Nicaragua there was no invasion or large-scale intervention designed to help a Leninist regime survive internal threats.

Some Conclusions 311

The regional conflicts discussed were all conditioned by explosive domestic and regional conditions, and this was especially true in the case of Nicaragua, where domestic conditions gave rise to an indigenous revolutionary force. It was this home-grown force and not a Soviet, Soviet/Cuban, or Soviet/Vietnamese intervention (the Afghan, Cambodian, and Angolan scenarios) that brought a Leninist-oriented regime to power in Nicaragua.

The Nicaraguan case is poorly understood precisely because it is rooted in two distinct kinds of civil war: the popular uprising of 1978-1979 against the hated Somoza regime, and the subsequent insurgency that developed in response to FSLN (Sandinista) rule in the 1980s. The Leninist nature of the Nicaraguan regime and its self-perceived strategic alliance with the U.S.S.R. and Cuba, conditions that are true as well of the other cases, are also poorly understood in the case of Nicaragua, and this has resulted in less than adequate support for the resistance from the United States.

For a clearer understanding of the FSLN orientation it is necessary to turn to the secret *FSLN Political-Military Platform* of 1977, * wherein FSLN goals are well-defined, albeit in language deceptive to the layman. Therein the FSLN elite is described as a Leninist vanguard and a strategic ally of the Soviet Union and Cuba. Avoiding, however, many of the mistakes of Leninist-oriented regimes such as Afghanistan, Cambodia, and Ethiopia—whose objectives were less camouflaged and more quickly executed—the Sandinistas followed a gradualist course, like some of the Eastern European Communists during the 1945-1948 period. From their Eastern European models, the Sandinistas learned the practicality of allowing superficial elements of political pluralism and a controllable amount of openness and of maintaining a mixed economy.

Because of the unique elements of the Nicaraguan situation, many observers tend to overlook or dismiss the important similarities it shares with the other regional conflicts. The similarities lie primarily in the Leninist orientation of the ruling vanguard parties, their organizational principle of democratic centralism, their pursuit of foreign policies designed to build strategic alliances with the U.S.S.R. and other Leninist states, and Soviet military aid to these regimes. While some Western analysts make light of these similarities and tend to see Nicaragua in a category by itself, which has justified the different U.S. policy vis-à-vis the Nicaraguan resistance, the Soviets openly recognize the common strains among these regimes, especially the importance of Soviet military support to their survival and progress.

---

*The original platform was introduced to U.S. scholars by Ambassador Alvaro Taboada, ISEES Ph.D. candidate and a contributor to this volume. For the complete text of the platform, see Valenta and Duran (eds.), *Conflict in Nicaragua: National Regional and International Dimensions*, pp. 287-318.

Although using different military tactics in Nicaragua than in Angola and Ethiopia—large arms transfers and sophisticated advisory assistance instead of direct military intervention—the U.S.S.R. and Cuba have sought the same objective there as elsewhere: to consolidate a Leninist regime. Prior to the Sandinista revolution, the primary Soviet objective in Central America, and all of Latin America, was to encourage nationalistic, i.e., anti-U.S., change by peaceful means (diplomacy, trade, and economic assistance). After the Sandinista victory of 1979, however, the Soviets switched to the Castro-Guevara recipe for forcing political change through violent revolution. With junior ally Cuba voluntarily playing the key role after 1979, the Soviets supplied massive economic aid and military assistance to encourage the consolidation of the Sandinista regime and the New Jewel Movement (NJM) regime in Grenada, and provided covert aid to other revolutionary guerrilla groups such as the FMLN in El Salvador. Soviet policies in the region shifted again dramatically before Gorbachev came to power, however, in part because of the encouragement and military support given to the democratic resistance in Nicaragua, the emergency program for El Salvador, and the U.S./OECS intervention in Grenada in October 1983.

One striking difference between the Nicaraguan insurgency and the insurgencies in Afghanistan, Angola, and Cambodia, is that the Nicaraguan resistance did not become a national force supported by a popular majority. Unlike the national liberation struggles of the seven factions of mujahideen in Afghanistan, the three broadly representative guerrilla factions in Cambodia, and UNITA's majority Ovimbundo ethnic group in Angola—all of which coalesced in response to a clear foreign aggression—the Nicaraguan struggle became a classic civil war in which most of the urban proletariat supported the Sandinistas and the majority of the peasants supported the resistance.

The viability of the Nicaraguan resistance as a fighting force has been further weakened by the on-again-off-again policies of the U.S. Congress and by the absence of vigorous support by Nicaragua's Central American neighbors, Costa Rica and Guatemala. The resistance has received consistent support only from Honduras. Such regional support, or lack of it, is critical. The Cambodian resistance was supported consistently by Thailand and also by other ASEAN nations; the Afghan mujahideen were supported by Pakistan and also by Iran; and UNITA was supported by South Africa and Zaire, and by the United States, which resumed aid to Savimbi in 1985. It is conceivable that if the United States and other regional actors had decided to fully support the Nicaraguan resistance, they would have done as well as the resistance groups in Afghanistan, Angola, and Cambodia.

When discussing the negotiations on Afghanistan and the precedent-setting Geneva Accords, it is easy to forget that the search for a diplomatic solution to the regional conflict in Central America began before Gorbachev came to power and before the "new thinking" was applied to Afghanistan and other regional hot spots. First, there were various bilateral negotiations between the United States and Nicaragua, prompted by the FSLN's search for assurances of U.S. nonintervention. This was the same kind of understanding that Fidel Castro had reached with the United States after the Cuban missile crisis in 1962, and he, as we know from a former Sandinista leader, heartily recommended it to the Sandinistas as the factor that had enabled him to stay in power. However, Washington's negative perceptions of FSLN internal and regional conduct got in the way of a *modus vivendi*. Meanwhile, between 1985 and 1987, there were also intermittent multilateral negotiations among members of the regional Contadora group (Mexico, Panama, Venezuela, Colombia). Their efforts, however, which were later supported by the Lima Group (Peru, Brazil, Argentina, Uruguay), led nowhere. Unlike the ASEAN countries, who backed up their diplomatic efforts with military support for the Cambodian resistance, the Contadora countries and most of the other regional actors did not back their search for peace with military/political support for the Nicaraguan resistance, and thus there was no real incentive for the Sandinistas to negotiate seriously.

Gorbachev's influence on the Nicaraguan conflict (and on the other conflicts) was apparent even before the accords on Afghanistan in spring 1988. First, Gorbachev pressured Nicaraguan President Daniel Ortega to respond positively to the peace plan of Costa Rican President Oscar Arias Sanchez and to the Esquipulas negotiations between Nicaragua and its Central American neighbors, both initiated in 1987. Later, in 1988, the Soviets were behind Ortega's decision to enter into negotiations with the Nicaraguan resistance, first through an intermediary and then directly. Whereas Soviet military aid to Nicaragua decreased only modestly in tonnage in 1988, the Soviets signalled the intention of decreasing their military support of the FSLN regime in early 1989.[1] Meanwhile, the United States cut all military aid to the resistance.

While pursuing this unexpected diplomatic track, the Sandinistas, like their comrades in Angola several months later, also embarked on a significant military initiative. In the spring of 1988, using the old Vietnamese "talking/fighting, fighting/talking" recipe, they pushed the resistance into Honduran territory. This offensive was followed by a few rounds of bilateral talks between the FSLN and the resistance, the last one in Managua. But after the U.S. Congress again cut off military aid to the resistance in the spring of 1988, this second round of talks also broke down. After that, amid serious political differences within the resistance leadership, most of the resistance forces retreated to Honduran territory. Meanwhile the FSLN played for time and waited out the rest of the Reagan administration. However, in the fall of 1988, when the Congress was said to be reconsidering aid to the resistance, the Sandinista regime suggested renewing the talks. Thus, the FSLN version of the "new thinking" is to fight whenever the resistance is lacking support and talk only as a tactic to prevent it from getting support, giving proof of lessons well learned from the Vietnamese. With skillful maneuvering, the Sandinistas successfully weakened and divided the resistance while influencing the U.S. Congress not to give them military support.

Beyond the Reagan Doctrine

The United States and its allies cannot afford to wait and see what will come from Gorbachev's rethinking of Soviet foreign affairs. As the "new thinking" has begun to be reflected in negotiations on arms control and regional conflicts, Western policymakers need to meet the Soviet initiatives with their own brand of innovative thinking. To begin, they must put the Gorbachev phenomenon in perspective, neither celebrating it nor dismissing it prematurely. The reforms were never meant to turn the Soviet Union into a Jeffersonian democracy, nor to deceive us into believing that they were. They were rather meant to improve the efficiency and decency of the existing one-party Leninist system and thereby ensure the viability of the U.S.S.R. as a superpower in world affairs. They have led to an ongoing relaxation of the coercive instruments of power and an apparent mellowing of the totalitarian structures, but still remain within the framework of a healthy Leninist autocracy. The long-term results of the reforms, however, are unclear, as Soviet domestic and foreign policies are in great flux due to the bold new propositions.

It is said that any fundamental democratization of Soviet society will be expressed externally, through a departure from the expansionist foreign policies that have characterized Russian and Soviet behavior for so much of history. However, even if the reforms take a decisive turn toward greater pluralism, as yet an unlikely scenario, the U.S.S.R. will continue in the next decade to be America's chief strategic and political rival. Pluralism does not guarantee fair play; nor does it constrain imperial ambitions, as the history of Great Britain demonstrates. Furthermore, pluralistic countries, including the English-speaking Western democracies, have been adversaries in the past. Britain and Canada clashed with the United States in 1812, and Britain and the United States engaged in gunboat diplomacy at the end of the last century.

The changes that have been introduced in the U.S.S.R. are not irreversible. They are resisted by the Soviet *nomenklatura* and are poorly understood by the great masses of Soviet people. Other equally serious attempts to restructure the Leninist system—which, like *perestroika*, were to be implemented with degrees of *glasnost*—were reversed by the chieftains of the *nomenklatura*: Stalin, for example, in the case of Lenin's New Economic Policies (NEP) of the 1920s, and Brezhnev in the case of Khrushchev's thaw of the

1950s and early 1960s. Though the current reforms are more comprehensive and better conceptualized than those preceding them, a number of their aspects are challenged by some communist leaders at home and abroad, as is their architect Gorbachev. Thus, while we should welcome the reforms, our own policies should not be contingent upon their success or upon Gorbachev's political survival.

What is needed is a U.S. foreign policy that is responsive above all to American national interests, which include discouraging the mushrooming of new pro-Soviet Leninist regimes while encouraging a gradual mellowing of those already in existence. U.S. policies must be cautious because of the uncertainty about the future of Gorbachev's domestic and foreign policy designs, yet flexible and bold, whenever necessary, because we can ill afford to miss available opportunities to build a constructive relationship with our principal adversary. In sum, we can hope, think, and even behave with optimism, as long as this does not prevent us from testing Soviet sincerity. How the Soviets decide to influence the course of various ongoing regional struggles and the efforts they make or do not make to bring about their resolutions will be the best gauge of Soviet intentions, whether they are in the interest of expansion or coexistence.

While welcoming *perestroika*, the United States should not pay for it. For now, available resources can best be used to maintain a strong defensive posture and to support anti-Leninist liberation struggles in regions where the Soviet Union has not yet decided to support meaningful compromises. While serving as an arsenal of democracy and an ally to the forces dedicated to curbing Soviet expansionism, however, the United States must also be a leader in the truly creative diplomacy needed to solve regional conflicts. Western initiatives have influenced the current negotiating trend, and they can continue to influence Soviet behavior if judiciously conceived and implemented.

Much more evidence is needed before we can conclude that traditional Soviet imperialism is no longer a threat to the Western and (bona fide) nonaligned nations, making the Reagan Doctrine obsolete. The most important test of Soviet sincerity will be the Soviet behavior in Afghanistan in the months and years ahead. The cessation of all military operations, including the bombardments of Afghan territory from bases inside the Soviet Union, and Soviet acceptance of a regime chosen by the Afghan resistance, irrespective of Moscow's preference, would signal good intentions. Such actions could also open the way to U.S./Soviet cooperation in the shared objective of ending the continuous chaos and anarchy on the Soviet Union's southern borders and preventing the spread of Islamic fundamentalism in Afghanistan. In the coming months, U.S. policymakers should seriously consider advising that the Western sanctions imposed at U.S. urging by the Coordinating Committee for Strategic Exports at the time of the Soviet invasion be waived for a period of a year or two; and then making the sanction waiver contingent upon continuing Soviet willingness to compromise on the issues of human rights and regional conflicts. Meanwhile, the West should continue to furnish military assistance to the mujahideen as long as the Leninist regime of Najibullah remains in power. Replacement of this regime by a regime acceptable to the Afghan people is the best insurance that the Soviets will not return.

In Afghanistan, U.S. policy should aim for the creation of a genuinely nonaligned government. In Angola, Cambodia, and Nicaragua, U.S. policy should first aim for the withdrawal of all communist allied forces and advisers, and then, power-sharing in coalition governments, including representatives of the resistance forces. The South African/Cuban Accords on Angola and Namibia of December 22, 1988, mediated by the United States and assisted by the Soviet Union, are a positive step toward the resolution of the Angolan conflict. The agreement excluded, however, Savimbi's UNITA, which has strong support among large segments of the Angolan population and has vowed to continue the struggle in spite of the accords. We must, therefore, continue to encourage further negotiations between the MPLA/Labor Party regime and UNITA. Should the MPLA-Labor Party regime refuse to continue the meaningful direct negotiations, that finally began in June 1989, we ought to continue to provide military aid to UNITA through friendly African nations, while also continuing the political and economic boycott of the existing regime. The Cuban/South African withdrawal from Angola/Namibia will take place throughout 1991, and it should be monitored through a strict verification regime so as to ensure that Cuban military personnel do not remain in the country under the guise of MPLA forces.

In Cambodia, we should continue to encourage national reconciliation through ongoing negotiations, while actively supporting the resistance forces of Prince Sihanouk and Premier Son Sann. The U.S. policy objective in Cambodia is not only to prevent the Khmer Rouge from coming to power, but also to end the Vietnamese occupation, remove the puppet regime in Phnom Penh, and gradually help bring into being a coalition government led by the universally respected Sihanouk and including all warring parties. Hanoi's propaganda that its intervention in Cambodia was motivated by human rights concerns is untrue. In the last decade human rights offenses have been committed by both sides in the conflict. Many leaders of the current Phnom Penh regime—including Prime Minister Hun Sen, who was an official of the Khmer Rouge—supported the infamous Pol Pot. As in Angola, the formal withdrawal of allied communist forces from Cambodia should not be the only objective in 1989-1991. We must also work with the Southeast Asian nations and the People's Republic of China toward a reliable system of monitoring the

Vietnamese withdrawal, the deployment of the international peacekeeping force in Cambodia, and general elections to take place after the Vietnamese withdrawal.

U.S. policymakers should be mindful of their encounters with the Vietnamese in the 1960s and 1970s and the likelihood that they will use a similar strategy: negotiating while fighting and continuing to infiltrate neighboring Cambodia. In searching for a lasting peace in Southeast Asia, we must avoid the mistakes that undermined other international agreements on the region: the 1954 Paris accord on Vietnam, the Laos settlement of 1962, and the Paris Peace Treaty of 1972. None of these agreements established verification measures sufficient to ascertain the withdrawal of all Vietnamese troops and advisers. And they were subsequently violated through Vietnamese infiltration and eventually open military intervention.

In Nicaragua, the long-term U.S. policy objective should also be power sharing, as remote as this objective might be in 1989. We must not forget that the Reagan Doctrine in support of anti-Leninist forces produced salutary results in three of four regional conflicts: Afghanistan, Angola, and Cambodia. In all three, Leninist-oriented regimes were forced to negotiate with the resistance forces they had formerly shunned. In Nicaragua, however, the negotiations with the resistance so far have not produced any serious initiative on the part of the Sandinista regime. The meager payoffs of the U.S. policies vis-à-vis Nicaragua in the 1980s were determined by several factors: a) different conditions from elsewhere (Afghanistan, Cambodia, Angola)—above all, the absence of large, communist-allied interventionist forces—and the related civil nature of the Nicaraguan war; b) the tendency of the U.S. executive branch to micromanage and mishandle—perhaps because of its very proximity—the only anti-Leninist insurgency in the Western Hemisphere; and, above all c) the absence of a bipartisan U.S. foreign policy, manifested in wavering congressional support for the resistance. With respect to Nicaragua, the old policy of passive containment will not produce perceptible changes in the Sandinista behavior. In February 1989, the Sandinistas negotiated an accord with their Central American neighbors that provides for the removal of the Contras from Honduras in return of the promised "democratization" of Nicaraguan society. However, the Sandinistas have a very poor record of fulfilling such promises. Thus, the U.S. bipartisan accord between the U.S. Congress and the Bush administration could become an important base for more coherent U.S. policies aimed at the resolution of the Nicaraguan conflict.

Nicaragua must become a much more important issue on the superpowers' regional conflicts agenda, and the agenda should include efforts to make the Soviets at least an informal party to the diplomacy, as they were in Angola, where their pressure on Cuba led to a negotiated solution. Finally, as Afghanistan, Angola, and Cambodia demonstrate, pressure by an armed resistance is crucial in preventing the consolidation of power by a Leninist regime. For other forms of pressure to be credible and effective in bringing about change in Nicaragua, U.S. policymakers should continue humanitarian aid for the resistance until the Sandinistas resume direct talks with the opposition and carry out the promised free election in early 1990.

In general, the problem remains, that while new areas of regional conflict may be gaining superpower attention, the old ones in Nicaragua and Cambodia in particular have remained unresolved as of Summer 1989. While the negotiated accords providing for the disengagement of the superpowers and/or their junior allies from Third World regional conflicts unquestionably serve to reduce the scope of these conflicts and lower the risk of a superpower confrontation, they do not directly address the domestic causes of the strife and usually do not directly involve (with the exception of Nicaragua in 1988 and Angola since the cease-fire of June 1989) the local combatants. As a result, as we can see in the cases of Afghanistan and Angola, regional conflicts are not resolved with ending military intervention by the Soviet or Soviet allied forces, but are rather suspended in uncertain cease-fires and/or transformed back into civil wars. While there has been steady progress in the disengagement of external powers, both the superpowers and their junior allies, actual peace through domestic political settlement of the conflicts has proved to be far more difficult to attain. The lasting peace can be achieved only through three-pronged negotiations involving not only the superpowers, but also the regional states and the civil war combatants.

The U.S. relationship with Moscow is destined to be highly competitive in the last decade of this century. Well-conceived policies can make a difference. In general, however, the struggle for *perestroika* and "new thinking" will be decided in Moscow. We must try to view these policies within their geopolitical context and determine whether the Soviet reforms will have any permanency before joining the rush of some of our NATO allies to subsidize *perestroika* or gain the economic advantages that would accrue from increased trade with the U.S.S.R. We *should* rush, however, to take advantage of the opportunities *perestroika* poses for finding resolutions to regional conflicts, in the anticipation that they could possibly be reversed or that the "new thinking" may have been conceived, in part, as a tactic for creating a breathing space, a *peredyshka*.

If the present era continues and Gorbachev demonstrates a continued commitment to resolving regional conflicts and opening up the Soviet system, positive economic incentives would be in line: not necessarily cheap credits, but assistance in training Soviet managers and helping them to develop marketing skills, and even trade concessions, e.g., granting of most-favored-nation status. This is not of great economic significance (because of the nature of Soviet exports), but of enormous psychological significance. We must recognize that the Soviet willingness to compromise is ultimately based on internal weaknesses and external setbacks. When the Soviet Union provides irrefutable evidence that it has ceased support for the growth of Leninist forces worldwide—what former Yugoslav communist leader Milovan Djilas called "international civil war"—we could declare a moratorium on the cold war and the Reagan Doctrine and work with the U.S.S.R. toward what George Kennan called our "common purpose." In the long run, Western policies must conciliate, not confront the U.S.S.R., for "appeasement from weakness and fear is alike futile and fatal," said Winston Churchill, while "appeasement from strength is magnanimous and noble and might be the surest and perhaps the only way to world peace."

Note

1. In October 1989, the Soviet Union appeared to be committed to a temporary reduction of arms deliveries to Nicaragua until the February 25, 1990 elections. However, the military aid from Cuba and East Germany to Nicaragua was said to continue unabated.

Appendix A

Geneva Accords on Afghanistan

The following is the text of the Geneva accords:
Palais des Nations, Geneva, April 14, 1988.
Bilateral agreement between the Republic of Afghanistan and the Islamic Republic of Pakistan on the principles of mutual relations, in particular on noninterference and nonintervention.

The Republic of Afghanistan and the Islamic Republic of Pakistan, hereinafter referred to as the high contracting parties,

Desiring to normalize relations and promote good neighborliness and cooperation as well as to strengthen international peace and security in the region,

Considering that full observance of the principle of noninterference and nonintervention in the internal and external affairs of states is of the greatest importance for the maintenance of international peace and security and for the fulfillment of the purposes and principles of the Charter of the United Nations,

Reaffirming the inalienable right of states freely to determine their own political, economic, cultural, and social systems in accordance with the will of their peoples, without outside intervention, interference, subversion, coercion, or threat in any form whatsoever,

Mindful of the provisions of the Charter of the United Nations as well as the resolutions adopted by the United Nations on the principle of noninterferences and nonintervention, in particular the declaration on principles of international law concerning friendly relations and cooperation among states in accordance with the Charter of the United Nations, as well as the declaration on the inadmissibility of intervention and interference in the internal affairs of states, of Dec 9, 1981,

Have agreed as follows:

Article I

Relations between the high contracting parties shall be conducted in strict compliance with the principle of noninterference and nonintervention by States in the affairs of other States.

Article II

For the purpose of implementing the principle of noninterference and nonintervention each high contracting party undertakes to comply with the following obligations:

(1) To respect the sovereignty, political independence, territorial integrity, national unity, security, and nonalignment of the other high contracting party, as well as the national identity and cultural heritage of its people.

(2) To respect the sovereign and inalienable right of the other high contracting party freely to determine its own political, economic, cultural, and social systems, to develop its international relations, and to exercise permanent sovereignty over its natural resources, in accordance with the will of its people, and without outside intervention, interference, subversion, coercion, or threat in any form whatsoever.

(3) To refrain from the threat or use of force in any form whatsoever so as not to violate the boundaries of each other, to disrupt the political, social, or economic order of the other high contracting party, to overthrow or change the political system of the other high contracting party or its governments, or to cause tension between the high contracting parties.

(4) To ensure that its territory is not used in any manner which would violate the sovereignty, political independence, territorial integrity, and national unity or disrupt the political, economic, and social stability of the other high contracting party.

(5) To refrain from armed intervention, subversion, military occupation, or any other form of intervention and interference, overt or covert, directed at the other high contracting party, or any act of military, political, or economic interference in the internal affairs of the other high contracting party, including acts of reprisal involving the use of force.

(6) To refrain from any action or attempt in whatever form or under whatever pretext to destabilize or to undermine the stability of the other high contracting party or any of its institutions.

(7) To refrain from the promotion, encouragement, or support, direct or indirect, or rebellious or secessionist activities against the other high contracting party, under any pretext whatsoever, or from any other action which seeks to disrupt the unity or to undermine or subvert the political order of the other high contracting party.

(8) To prevent within its territory the training, equipping, financing, and recruitment of mercenaries from whatever origin for the purpose of hostile activities against the other high contracting party, or the sending of such mercenaries into the territory of the other high contracting party and accordingly to deny facilities, including financing for the training, equipping and transit of such mercenaries.

(9) To refrain from making any agreements or arrangements with other states designed to intervene or interfere in the internal and external affairs of the other high contracting party.

(10) To abstain from any defamatory campaign, vilification, or hostile propaganda for the purpose of intervening or interfering in the internal affairs of the other high contracting party.

(11) To prevent any assistance to or use of or tolerance of terrorist groups, saboteurs, or subversive agents against the other high contracting party.

(12) To prevent within its territory the presence, harboring in camps and bases or otherwise, organizing, training, financing, equipping, and arming of individuals and political, ethnic, and any other groups for the purpose of creating subversion, disorder, or unrest in the territory of the other high contracting party and accordingly also to prevent the use of mass media and the transportation of arms, ammunition, and equipment by such individuals and groups.

(13) Not to resort to or to allow any other action that could be considered as interference or intervention.

Article III

The present agreement shall enter into force on May 15, 1988.

Article IV

Any steps that may be required in order to enable the high contracting parties to comply with the provisions of Article II of this agreement shall be completed by the date on which this agreement enters into force.

Article V

This agreement is drawn up in the English, Pashtu, and Urdu languages, all texts being equally authentic; in case of any divergence of interpretation, the English text shall prevail.

Done in five original copies at Geneva this fourteenth day of April 1988. (Signed by Afghanistan and Pakistan.)

Guarantees

Declaration on international guarantees.

The government of the Union of Soviet Socialist Republics and of the United States of America,

Expressing support that the Republic of Afghanistan and the Islamic Republic of Pakistan have concluded a negotiated political settlement designed to normalize relations and promote good neighborliness between the two countries as well as to strengthen international peace and security in the region,

Wishing in turn to contribute to the achievement of the objectives that the Republic of Afghanistan and the Islamic Republic of Pakistan have set themselves, and with a view to ensuring respect for their sovereignty, independence, territorial integrity, and nonalignment,

Undertake to invariably refrain from any form of interference and intervention in the internal affairs of the Republic of Afghanistan and the Islamic Republic of Pakistan and to respect the commitments contained in the bilateral agreement between the Republic of Afghanistan and the Islamic Republic of Pakistan on the principles of mutual relations, in particular on noninterference and nonintervention,

Urge all states to act likewise.

The present declaration shall enter into force on May 15, 1988. Done at Geneva, this fourteenth day of April, 1988, in five original copies, each in the English and Russian languages, both texts being equally authentic.

(Signed by the U.S.S.R. and the U.S.A.)

Bilateral Agreement between the Republic of Afghanistan and the Islamic Republic of Pakistan on the Voluntary Return of Refugees.

The Republic of Afghanistan and the Islamic Republic of Pakistan, hereinafter referred to as the high contracting parties,

Desiring to normalize relations and promote good neighborliness and cooperation as well as to strengthen international peace and security in the region,

Convinced that voluntary unimpeded repatriation constitutes the most appropriate solution for the problem of Afghan refugees present in the Islamic Republic of Pakistan and having ascertained that the arrangements for the return of the Afghan refugees are satisfactory to them,

Have agreed as follows:

Article I

All Afghan refugees temporarily present in the territory of the Islamic Republic of Pakistan shall be given the opportunity to return voluntarily to their homeland in accordance with the arrangements and conditions set out in the present agreement.

Article II

The Government of the Republic of Afghanistan shall take all necessary measures to ensure the following conditions for the voluntary return of Afghan refugees to their homeland:

(A) All refugees shall be allowed to return in freedom to their homeland.

(B) All returnees shall enjoy the free choice of domicile and freedom of movement within the Republic of Afghanistan.

(C) All returnees shall enjoy the right to participate on an equal basis in the civic affairs of the Republic of Afghanistan. They shall be ensured equal benefits from the solution of the land question on the basis of the land and water reform.

(D) All returnees shall enjoy the same rights and privileges, including freedom of religion, and have the same obligations and responsibilities as any other citizens of the Republic of Afghanistan without discrimination.

Article III

The Government of the Islamic Republic of Pakistan shall facilitate the voluntary, orderly, and peaceful repatriation of all Afghan refugees staying within its territory and undertake to provide, within its possibilities, all necessary assistance in the process of repatriation.

Article IV

For the purpose of organizing, coordinating, and supervising the operations which should affect the voluntary, orderly, and peaceful repatriation of Afghan refugees, there shall be set up mixed commissions in accordance with the established international practice. For the performance of their functions the members of the commissions and their staff shall be accorded the necessary facilities, and have access to the relevant areas within the territories of the high contracting parties.

Article V

With a view to the orderly movement of the returnees, the commissions shall determine frontier crossing points and establish necessary transit centers. They shall also establish all other modalities for the phased return of the refugees, including registration and communication to the country of return of the names of refugees who express the wish to return.

Article VI

At the request of the Government concerned, the United Nations High Commissioner for Refugees will cooperate and provide assistance in the process of voluntary repatriation of refugees in accordance with the present agreement. Special agreement may be concluded for this purpose between UNHCR and the high contracting parties.

Article VII

The present agreement shall enter into force on May 15, 1988. At that time the mixed commission provided in Article IV shall be established and the operations for the voluntary return of refugees under this agreement shall commence.

The arrangements set out in Articles IV and V above shall remain in effect for a period of 18 months. After that period the high contracting parties shall review the results of the repatriation and, if necessary, consider any future arrangements that may be called for.

Article VIII

This agreement is drawn up in the English, Pashtu, and Urdu languages, all texts being equally authentic. In case of any divergence of interpretation, the English text shall prevail.

Done in five original copies at Geneva this fourteenth day of April 1988. (Signed by Afghanistan and Pakistan).

Interrelationship

Agreement on the interrelationships for the settlement of the situation relating to Afghanistan.

1. The diplomatic process initiated by the Secretary-General of the United Nations, with the support of all governments concerned and aimed at achieving, through negotiations, a political settlement of the situation relating to Afghanistan, has been successfully brought to an end.

2. Having agreed to work towards a comprehensive settlement designed to resolve the various issues involved and to establish a framework for good neighborliness and cooperation, the Government of the Republic of Afghanistan and the Government of the Islamic Republic of Pakistan entered into negotiations through the intermediary of the Personal Representative of the Secretary-General at Geneva from 16 to 24 June 1982. Following consultations held by the personal representative in Islamabad, Kabul, and Tehran

from Jan. 21 to Feb. 7, 1983, the negotiations continued at Geneva from April 11 to 22 and from June 12 to 24, 1983. The Personal Representative again visited the area for high level discussions from 3 to 15 April 1984. It was then agreed to change the format of the negotiations and, in pursuance thereof, proximity talks through the intermediary of the Personal Representative were held at Geneva from 24 to 30 August 1984. Further rounds of proximity talks were held at Geneva from 20 to 25 June, from 27 to 30 August and from 16 to 19 December 1985. The Personal Representative paid an additional visit to the area from 8 to 18 March, 1986, for consultations. The final round of negotiations began as proximity talks at Geneva on 5 May, 1986, was suspended on 23 May, 1986, and was resumed from 31 July to 8 August, 1986. The Personal Representative visited the area from 20 November to 3 December, 1986, for further consultations, and the talks at Geneva were resumed again from 25 February to 9 March 1987, and from 7 to 11 September, 1987. The Personal Representative again visited the area from 18 January to 9 February at Geneva from 2 March to 8 April 1988. The format of the negotiations was changed on 14 April 1988, when the instruments comprising the settlement were finalized, and accordingly, direct talks were held at that stage. The Government of the Islamic Republic of Iran was kept informed of the progress of the negotiations throughout the diplomatic process.

3. The Government of the Republic of Afghanistan and the Government of the Islamic Republic of Pakistan took part in the negotiations with the expressed conviction that they were acting in accordance with their rights and obligations under the Charter of the United Nations and agreed that the political settlement should be based on the following principles of international law:

- The principle that States shall refrain in their international relations from the threat or use of force against the territorial integrity or political independence of any State, or in any other manner inconsistent with the purposes of the United Nations;
- The principle that states shall settle their international disputes by peaceful means in such a manner that international peace and security and justice are not endangered;
- The duty not to intervene in matters within the domestic jurisdiction of any state, in accordance with the charter of the United Nations;
- The duty of states to cooperate with one another in accordance with the Charter of the United Nations;
- The principle of equal rights and self-determination of peoples;
- The principle of sovereign equality of states;
- The principle that states shall fulfill in good faith the obligations assured by them in accordance with the charter of the United Nations.

Voluntary Manner

The two governments further affirmed the right of the Afghan refugees to return to their homeland in a voluntary and unimpeded manner.

5. The following instruments were concluded on this date as component parts of the political settlement:

A bilateral agreement between the Republic of Afghanistan and the Islamic Republic of Pakistan on the principles of mutual relations, in particular on noninterference and nonintervention;

A declaration of international guarantees by the Union of Soviet Socialist Republics and the United States of America;

A bilateral agreement between the Republic of Afghanistan and the Islamic Republic of Pakistan on the voluntary return of refugees;

The present agreement on the interrelationships for the settlement of the situation relating to Afghanistan.

5. The bilateral agreement on the principles of mutual relations, in particular on noninterference and nonintervention, the declaration on international guarantees; the bilateral agreement on the interrelationships for the settlement of the situation relating to Afghanistan will enter into force on 15 May 1988. In accordance with the time frame agreed upon between the Union of Soviet Socialist Republics and the Republic of Afghanistan, there will be a phased withdrawal of the foreign troops which will start on the date of entry into force mentioned above. One half of the troops will be withdrawn by 15 August 1988, and the withdrawal of all troops will be completed within nine months.

6. The interrelationships in paragraph 5 above have been agreed upon in order to achieve effectively the purpose of the political settlement, namely, that as of 15 May, 1988, there will be no interference and intervention in any form in the affairs of the parties, the international guarantees will be in operation, the voluntary return of the refugees to their homeland will start and be completed within the timeframe specified in the agreement on the voluntary return of the refugees; and the phased withdrawal of the foreign troops will start and be completed within the timeframe envisaged in paragraph 5. It is therefore essential that all the obligations deriving from the instruments concluded as component parts of the settlement be strictly fulfilled and that all the steps required to ensure full compliance with all the provisions of the instruments be completed in good faith.

7. To consider alleged violations and to work out prompt and mutually satisfactory solutions to questions that may arise in the implementation of the instruments comprising the settlement, representatives of the Republic of Afghanistan and the Islamic Republic of Pakistan shall meet whenever required.

A representative of the Secretary-General of the United Nations shall lend his good offices to the parties and in that context he will assist in the organization of the meetings and participate in them. He may submit to the parties for their consideration and approval suggestions and recommendations for prompt, faithful, and complete observance of the provisions of the instruments.

In order to enable him to fulfill his tasks, the representative shall be assisted by such personnel under his authority as required. On his initiative, or at the request of any of the parties, the personnel shall investigate any possible violations of any of the provisions of the instruments and prepare a report thereon. For that purpose, the representative and his personnel shall receive all the necessary cooperation from the parties, including all freedom of movement within their respective territories required for effective investigation. Any report submitted by the representative to the two governments shall be considered in a meeting of the parties no later than forty-eight hours after it has been submitted.

The modalities and logistical arrangements for the work of the representative and the personnel under his authority as agreed upon with the parties are set out in the memorandum of understanding which is annexed to and is part of this agreement.

8. The present instrument will be registered with the Secretary-General of the United Nations. It has been examined by the representatives of the parties to the bilateral agreements and of the states-guarantors, who have signified their consent with its provisions. The representatives of the parties, being duly authorized thereto by their respective governments, have affixed their signatures hereunder. The Secretary-General of the United Nations was present.

Done at Geneva, this fourteenth day of April, 1988, in five original copies each in the English, Pashtu, Russian, and Urdu languages, all being equally authentic. In case of any dispute regarding the interpretation the English text shall prevail.

(Signed by Afghanistan and Pakistan)

In witness thereof, the representatives of the states-guarantors affixed their signatures hereunder;

(Signed by the U.S.S.R. and U.S.A.)

Annex

Memorandum of Understanding

I. Basic requirements

(a) The parties will provide full support and cooperation to the representative of the Secretary-General and to all the personnel assigned to assist him.

(b) The representative of the Secretary-General and his personnel will be accorded every facility, as well as prompt and effective assistance, including freedom of movement and communications, accommodation, transportation, and other facilities that may be necessary for the performance of their tasks. Afghanistan and Pakistan undertake to grant to the representative and his staff all the relevant privileges and immunities provided for by the convention on the privileges and immunities of the United Nations.

(c) Afghanistan and Pakistan will be responsible for the safety of the representative of the Secretary-General and his personnel while operating in their respective countries.

(d) In performing their functions, the representative of the Secretary-General and his staff will act with complete impartiality. The representative of the Secretary-General and his personnel must not interfere in the internal affairs of Afghanistan and Pakistan and, in this context, cannot be used to secure advantages for any of the parties concerned.

II. Mandate

The mandate for the implementation of assistance arrangements envisaged in Paragraph 78 derives from the instruments comprising the settlement. All the staff assigned to the representative of the Secretary-General will accordingly be carefully briefed on the relevant provisions of the instruments and on the procedures that will be used to ascertain violations thereof.

Modus Operandi

III. Modus operandi and personnel organization

The Secretary-General will appoint a senior military officer as deputy to the representative, who will be stationed in the area, as head of two small headquarters units, one in Kabul and the other in Islamabad, each comprising five military officers, drawn from existing United Nations operations, and a small civilian auxiliary staff.

The deputy to the representative of the Secretary-General will act on behalf of the representative and be in contact with the parties through the liasion office each party will designate for this purpose.

The two headquarters units will be organized into two inspection teams to ascertain on the ground any violation of the instruments comprising the settlement. Whenever considered necessary by the representative of the Secretary-General or his deputy, up to 40 additional military officers (some 10 additional inspection teams) will be redeployed from existing operations within the shortest possible time (normally around 48 hours).

The nationalities of all the officers will be determined in consultation with the parties.

Whenever necessary, the representative of the Secretary-General, who will periodically visit the area for consultations with the parties and to review the work of his personnel, will also assign to the area members of his own office and other civilian personnel from the United Nations secretariat as may be needed. His deputy will alternate between the two headquarters units and will remain at all times in close communication with him.

IV. Procedure

(a) Inspections conducted at the request of the parties.

(i) A complaint regarding a violation of the instruments of the settlement lodged by any of the parties should be submitted in writing, in the English language, to the respective headquarters units and should indicate all relevant information and details.

(ii) Upon receipt of a complaint the deputy to the representative of the Secretary-General will immediately inform the other party of the complaint and undertake an investigation by making on-site inspections, gathering testimony, and using any other procedure which he may deem necessary for the investigation of the alleged violation. Such inspection will be conducted using headquarters staff as referred to above, unless the deputy representative of the Secretary-General considers that additional teams are needed. In that case, the parties will, under the principle of freedom of movement, allow immediate access of the additional personnel to their respective territories.

(iii) Reports on investigations will be prepared in English and submitted by the deputy representative of the Secretary General to the two governments, on a confidential basis. (A third copy of the report will be simultaneously transmitted, on a confidential basis, to United Nations headquarters in New York, exclusively for the information of the Secretary General and his representative.) In accordance with Paragraph 7 a report on an investigation should be considered in a meeting of the parties not later than 48 hours after it has been submitted. The deputy representative of the Secretary-General will, in the absence of the representative, lend his good offices to the parties and in that context he will assist in the organization of the meetings and participate in them. In the context of those meetings, the Deputy Representative of the Secretary-General may submit to the parties for their consideration and approval suggestions and recommendations for the prompt, faithful, and complete observance of the provisions of the instruments. (Such suggestions and recommendations will be, as a matter of course, consulted with, and cleared by, the representative of the Secretary-General.)

Inspection

(a) Inspections conducted on the initiative of the deputy representative of the Secretary-General.

In addition to the inspections requested by the parties, the deputy representative of the Secretary-General may carry out, on his own initiative and in consultation with the representative, inspections he deems appropriate for the purpose of the implementation of Paragraph 7. If it is considered that the conclusions reached in an inspection justify a report to the parties, the same procedure used in submitting reports in connection with inspections carried out at the request of the parties will be followed.

Level of participation in meetings.

The Deputy Secretary-General will participate at meetings of the parties convened for the purpose of considering reports on violations. Should the parties decide to meet for the purpose outlined in Paragraph 7 at a high political level, the representative of the Secretary-General will personally attend such meetings.

V. Duration

The deputy to the representative of the Secretary-General and the other personnel will be established in the area not later than 20 days before the entry into force of the instruments. The arrangements will cease to exist two months after the completion of all time frames envisaged for the implementation of the instruments.

VI. Financing

The cost of all facilities and services to be provided by the parties will be borne by the respective governments. The salaries and travel expenses of the personnel to and from the area, as well as to the costs of the local personnel assigned to the headquarters units, will be defrayed by the United Nations.

Published by the Embassy of Pakistan, Washington, D.C. 1980.

U.S. Statement

The United States has agreed to act as a guarantor of the political settlement of the situation relating to Afghanistan. We believe this settlement is a major step forward in restoring peace to Afghanistan, in ending the bloodshed in that unfortunate country, and in enabling millions of Afghan refugees to return to their homes.

In agreeing to act as a guarantor, the United States states the following:

(1) The troop withdrawal obligations set out in paragraphs 5 and 6 of the Instrument on Interrelationships are central to the entire settlement. Compliance with those obligations is essential to achievement of the settlement's purposes, namely, the ending of foreign intervention in Afghanistan and the restoration of the rights of the Afghan people through the exercise of self determination as called for by the United Nations Charter and the United Nations General Assembly resolutions on Afghanistan.

(2) The obligations undertaken by the guarantors are symmetrical. In this regard, the United States has advised the Soviet Union that, if the USSR undertakes, as consistent with its obligations as guarantor, to provide military assistance to parties in Afghanistan, the U.S. retains the right, as consistent with its own obligations as guarantor, likewise effectively to provide such assistance.

(3) By acting as guarantor of the settlement, the United States does not intend to imply in any respect recognition of the present regime in Kabul as the lawful Government of Afghanistan.

Rosanne Klass, "Afghanistan: The Accords," *Foreign Affairs* (Summer 1988), p. 945.

Appendix B

Agreements for Peace in Southwestern Africa

Document 1
Principles for a Peaceful
Settlement in Southwestern
Africa, July 20, 1988

Following is the text of the agreement initialed by delegations from Angola, Cuba, and South Africa in New York City on July 13, 1988. This statement was approved by their respective governments and released publicly by mutual agreement on July 20, 1988.

The Government of the People's Republic of Angola, the Republic of Cuba, and the Republic of South Africa have reached agreement on a set of essential principles to establish the basis for peace in the southwestern region of Africa. They recognize that each of these principles is indispensable to a comprehensive settlement.

A. Implementation of Resolution 435/78 of the Security Council of the United Nations. The parties shall agree upon and recommend to the Secretary-General of the United Nations a date for the commencement of implementation of UNSCR 435/78.

B. The Governments of the People's Republic of Angola and the Republic of South Africa shall, in conformity with the dispositions of Resolution 435/78 of the Security Council of the United Nations, cooperate with the Secretary-General with a view toward ensuring the independence of Namibia through free and fair elections, abstaining from any action that could prevent the execution of said Resolution.

C. Redeployment toward the North and the staged and total withdrawal of Cuban troops from the territory of the People's Republic of Angola on the basis of an agreement between the People's Republic of Angola and the People's Republic of Cuba and the decision of both states to solicit the on-site verification of that withdrawal by the Security Council of the United Nations.

D. Respect for the sovereignty, sovereign equality, and independence of states and for territorial integrity and inviolability of borders.

E. Non-interference in the internal affairs of states.
F. Abstention from the threat and utilization of force against the territorial integrity and independence of states.
G. The acceptance of the responsibility of states not to allow their territory to be used for acts of war, aggression, or violence against other states.
H. Reaffirmation of the right of the peoples of the southwestern region of Africa to self-determination, independence, and equality of rights.
I. Verification and monitoring of compliance with the obligations resulting from the agreements that may be established.
J. Commitment to comply in good faith with the obligations undertaken in the agreements that may be established and to resolve the differences via negotiations.
K. Recognition of the role of the Permanent Members of the Security Council of the United Nations as guarantors for the implementation of agreements that may be established.
L. The right of each state to peace, development, and social progress.
M. African and international cooperation for the settlement of the problems of the development of the southwestern region of Africa.
N. Recognition of the mediating role of the Government of the United States of America.

Document 2
Protocol of Brazzaville,
December 13, 1988

Delegations representing the Governments of the People's Republic of Angola, the Republic of Cuba, and the Republic of South Africa,

Meeting in Brazzaville with the mediation of the Government of the United States of America,

Expressing their deep appreciation to the President of the People's Republic of the Congo, Colonel Denis Sassou-Nguesso, for his indispensable contribution to the cause of peace in southwestern Africa and for the hospitality extended to the delegations by the Government of the People's Republic of the Congo,

Confirming their commitment to act in accordance with the Principles for a Peaceful Settlement in southwestern Africa, initialled in New York on 13 July 1988 and approved by their respective Governments on 20 July 1988, each of which is indispensable to a comprehensive settlement; with the understanding reached at Geneva on 5 August 1988 that is not superseded by this document; and with the agreement reached at Geneva on 15 November 1988 for the redeployment to the north and the staged and total withdrawal of Cuban troops from Angola,

Urging the international community to provide economic and financial support for the implementation of all aspects of this settlement,

Agree as follows:

1. The parties agree to recommend to the Secretary-General of the United Nations that 1 April 1989 be established as the date for implementation of UNSCR 435/78.

2. The parties agree to meet on 22 December 1988 in New York for signature of the tripartite agreement and for signature by Angola and Cuba of their bilateral agreement. By the date of signature, Angola and Cuba shall have reached agreement with the Secretary-General of the United Nations on verification arrangements to be approved by the Security Council.

3. The parties agree to exchange the prisoners of war upon signature of the tripartite agreement.

4. The parties agree to establish a Joint Commission in accordance with the annex attached to this protocol.

Annex on the Joint Commission

1. With the objective of facilitating the resolution of any dispute regarding the interpretation or implementation of the tripartite agreement, the parties hereby shall begin their work upon signature of the tripartite agreement.

2. The Joint Commission shall serve as a forum for discussion and resolution of issues regarding the interpretation and implementation of the tripartite agreement, and for such other purposes as the parties in the future may mutually agree.

3. The parties invite the United States of America and the Union of Soviet Socialist Republics to participate as observers in the work of the Commission. Furthermore, the parties agree that, upon the independence of Namibia, the Namibian Government should be included as a full member of the Joint Commission. To that end, the parties will extend a formal invitation to the Namibian Government to join the Joint Commission on the date of Namibian independence.

4. The Joint Commission shall be constituted within thirty days of the signing of the tripartite agreement. The Joint Commission shall establish its own regulations and rules of procedure for regular meetings and for special meetings which may be requested by any party.

5. The decision by a party to discuss or seek the resolution of an issue in the Joint Commission shall not prejudice the right of that party to raise the issue, as it deems appropriate, before the Security Council of the United Nations or to pursue such other means of dispute resolution as are available under international law.

6. The Joint Commission shall in no way function as a substitute for

UNTAG (including the monitoring role of UNTAG outside Namibia) or for the U.N. entity performing verification in Angola.

Document 3
Tripartite Agreement,
December 22, 1988
Agreement Among
The People's Republic of Angola,
The Republic of Cuba,
and
The Republic of South Africa

The governments of the People's Republic of Angola, the Republic of Cuba, and the Republic of South Africa, hereinafter designated as "the parties,"

Taking into account the "Principles for a Peaceful Settlement in Southwestern Africa," approved by the Parties on 20 July 1988, and the subsequent negotiations with respect to the implementation of these Principles, each of which is indispensable to a comprehensive settlement,

Considering the acceptance by the Parties of the implementation of the United Nations Security Council Resolution 435 (1978), adopted on 29 September 1978, hereinafter designated as "UNSCR 435/78,"

Considering the conclusion of the bilateral agreement between the People's Republic of Angola and the Republic of Cuba providing for the redeployment toward the North and the staged and total withdrawal of Cuban troops from the territory of the People's Republic of Angola,

Recognizing the role of the United Nations Security Council in implementing UNSCR 435/78 and in supporting the implementation of the present agreement,

Affirming the sovereignty, sovereign equality, and independence of all states of southwestern Africa,

Affirming the principle of noninterference in the internal affairs of states,

Affirming the principle of abstention from the threat or use of force against the territorial integrity or political independence of states,

Reaffirming the right of the peoples of the southwestern region of Africa to self-determination, independence, and equality of rights, and of the states of southwestern Africa to peace, development, and social progress,

Urging African and international cooperation for the settlement of the problems of the development of the southwestern region of Africa,

Expressing their appreciation for the mediating role of the Government of the United States of America,

Desiring to contribute to the establishment of peace and security in southwestern Africa,

Agree to the provisions set forth below.

(1) The Parties shall immediately request the Secretary-General of the United Nations to seek authority from the Security Council to commence implementation of UNSCR 435/78 on 1 April 1989.

(2) All military forces of the Republic of South Africa shall depart Namibia in accordance with UNSCR 435/78.

(3) Consistent with the provisions of UNSCR 435/78, the Republic of South Africa and the People's Republic of Angola shall cooperate with the Secretary-General to ensure the independence of Namibia through free and fair elections and shall abstain from any action that could prevent the execution of UNSCR 435/78. The Parties shall respect the territorial integrity and inviolability of borders of Namibia and shall ensure that their territories are not used by any state, organization, or person in connection with acts of war, aggression, or violence against the territorial integrity or inviolability of borders of Namibia or any other action which could prevent the execution of UNSCR 435/78.

(4) The People's Republic of Angola and the Republic of Cuba shall implement the bilateral agreement, signed on the date of signature of this agreement, providing for the redeployment toward the north and the staged and total withdrawal of Cuban troops from the territory of the People's Republic of Angola, and the arrangements made with the Security Council of the United Nations for the on-site verification of that withdrawal.

(5) Consistent with their obligations under the Charter of the United Nations, the Parties shall refrain from the threat or use of force, and shall ensure that their respective territories are not used by any state, organization, or person in connection with any acts of war, aggression, or violence, against the territorial integrity, inviolability of borders, or independence of any state of southwestern Africa.

(6) The Parties shall respect the principle of non-interference in the internal affairs of the states of southwestern Africa.

(7) The Parties shall comply in good faith with all obligations undertaken in this agreement and shall resolve through negotiation and in a spirit of cooperation any disputes with respect to the interpretation or implementation thereof.

(8) This agreement shall enter into force upon signature.

Signed at New York in triplicate in the Portuguese, Spanish and English languages, each language being equally authentic, this 22nd day of December 1988.

FOR THE PEOPLE'S REPUBLIC OF ANGOLA
Afonso Van Dunem
FOR THE PEOPLE'S REPUBLIC OF CUBA
Isidoro Octavio Malmierca

FOR THE PEOPLE'S REPUBLIC SOUTH AFRICA
Roelof F. Botha

**Document 4
Bilateral Agreement,
December 22, 1988**

Following is the unofficial U.S. translation of the original Portuguese and Spanish texts of the agreement with annex.

**Agreement Between The
Government of The People's
Republic of Angola And The
Republic of Cuba For The
Termination of The
Internationalist Mission of The
Cuban Military Contingent**

The Government of the People's Republic of Angola and the Government of the Republic of Cuba, designated hereof as the parties,
Considering,

That the implementation of Resolution 435/78 of the Security Council of the United Nations for the independence of Namibia shall commence on the 1st of April,

That the question of independence of Namibia and the safeguarding of the sovereignty, independence, and territorial integrity of the People's Republic of Angola are closely interrelated with each other and with peace and security in the region of southwestern Africa,

That on the date of the signature of this tripartite agreement shall also be signed by the Governments of the People's Republic of Angola, the Republic of Cuba, and the Republic of South Africa shall be signed, containing the essential elements for achievement of peace in the region of southwestern Africa,

That the acceptance of strict compliance with the foregoing will bring to an end the reasons which compelled the Government of the People's Republic of Angola to request, in the legitimate exercise of its rights under Article 51 of the United Nations Charter, the deployment to Angolan territory of a Cuban internationalist military contingent to guarantee, in cooperation with the FAPLA (the Angolan Government army), its territorial integrity and sovereignty in view of the invasion and occupation of part of its territory,

Noting,

The agreements signed by the Governments of the People's Republic of Angola and the Republic of Cuba on 4 February 1982 and 19 March 1984, the platform of the Government of the People's Republic of Angola approved in November 1984, and the Protocol of Brazzaville signed by the Governments of the People's Republic of Angola, the Republic of Cuba, and the Republic of South Africa on December 13, 1988.

Taking into account,

That conditions now exist which make possible the repatriation of the Cuban military contingent currently in Angolan territory and the successful accomplishment of their internationalist mission,

The parties agree as follows:

Article 1

To commence the redeployment by stages to the 15th and 13th parallels and the total withdrawal to Cuba of the 50,000 men who constitute the Cuban troop contingent stationed in the People's Republic of Angola, in accordance with the pace and time frame established in the attached calendar, which is an integral part of this agreement. The total withdrawal shall be completed by the 1st of July 1991.

Article 2

The Governments of the People's Republic of Angola and the Republic of Cuba reserve the right to modify or alter their obligations deriving from Article 1 of this Agreement in the event that flagrant violations of the Tripartite Agreement are verified.

Article 3

The parties, through the Secretary-General of the United Nations Organizations, hereby request that the Security Council verify the redeployment and phased and total withdrawal of the Cuban troops from the territory of the People's Republic of Angola, and to this end shall agree on a matching protocol.

Article 4

This agreement shall come into force upon the signature of the tripartite agreement among the People's Republic of Angola, the Republic of Cuba, and the Republic of South Africa.

Signed on the 22 December 1988, at the Headquarters of the United Nations Organization, in two copies, in the Portuguese and Spanish languages, each being equally authentic.

FOR THE PEOPLE'S REPUBLIC OF ANGOLA
Afonso Van Dunem
FOR THE PEOPLE'S REPUBLIC OF CUBA
Isidoro Octavio Malmierca

Annex on Troop Withdrawal Schedule

Calendar

In compliance with Article 1 of the agreement between the Government of the Republic of Cuba and the Government of the People's Republic of Angola for the termination of the mission of the Cuban internationalist military contingent stationed in Angolan territory, the parties establish the following calendar for the withdrawal:

Time Frames

Prior to the first of April, 1989 (date of the beginning of implementation of Resolution 435)	3,000 men
Total duration of the calendar Starting from 1st of April, 1989	27 months
Redeployment to the north:	
To the 15th Parallel	by 1 August, 1989
To the 13th Parallel	by 31 October, 1989
Total men to be withdrawn:	
By 1 November 1989	25,000 men (50%)
By 1 April 1990	33,000 (66%)
By 1 October 1990	38,000 (76%)
	12,000 men remain
By 1 July 1991	50,000 (100%)

Taking as its base a Cuban force of 50,000 men.

Published by the United States Department of State; Bureau of Public Affairs Office of Public Communication, Editorial Division (Washington, D.C.: December 1988). Editor: Sharon R. Haynes.

Biographical Sketches of the Editors and Contributors

Editors

JIRI VALENTA is director of the Institute for Soviet and East European Studies (ISEES) and professor of political science at the Graduate School of International Studies (GSIS), the University of Miami. He is the author, coauthor, and coeditor of eight books and/or monographs, including *Soviet Intervention in Czechoslovakia, 1968: Anatomy of a Decision; Eurocommunism Between East and West; Soviet Intervention in Afghanistan; Soviet Decisionmaking for National Security* (parts of which also appeared in Chinese); *Grenada and Soviet/Cuban Policy: Crisis and the U.S./OECS Intervention*; and *Conflict in Nicaragua: National, Regional, and International Dimensions*. Dr. Valenta has received fellowships from the Brookings Institution, the Rockefeller Foundation, the Council on Foreign Relations, the Woodrow Wilson International Center for Scholars, the National Endowment for the Humanitites, and the University at Uppsala, Sweden. He was a Fulbright fellow at the Colegio de Mexico in 1986 and he became a member of the Council on Foreign Relations in 1984. A frequent consultant to the U.S. government, Dr. Valenta has testified at hearings of the committees on foreign affairs of the U.S. House of Representatives and the U.S. Senate and at the hearings of the "Kissinger" Bipartisan Commission on Central America.

FRANK CIBULKA is a senior lecturer in political science at the National University of Singapore. His specialization is in Soviet and East European studies wherein his primary research interests are currently Soviet policy in Southeast Asia and Soviet-Philippine relations in particular. Dr. Cibulka has written a number of essays for books and journals on Soviet policy in the Asia-Pacific region.

Contributors

VERNON V. ASPATURIAN is the Evan Pugh Professor of Political Science and director of the Slavic and Soviet Language and Area Center, Pennsylvania State University, and a visiting distinguished professor at RAND Corporation and the UCLA Soviet and East European Studies Center in 1988-1989. He is the author and co-editor of many books on Soviet foreign policy and comparative communism including, among others, *The Soviet Union in the World Communist System, Process and Power in Soviet Foreign Policy, Eurocommunism Between East and West,* and *The Union Republics in Soviet Diplomacy.*

H. DE V. DU TOIT is a professor of national security at Rand Afrikaans University in Johannesburg, South Africa. He was an officer in the South African Defense Force from 1952 until 1977, when he retired, and most of this time he spent in military intelligence. In the last six years he was chief of staff intelligence with the rank of lt. general. The author of numerous essays, he is a member of the South African Academy of Sciences.

WILLIAM GRIFFITH is the Ford Professor of Political Science at the Massachusetts Institute of Technology and an adjunct professor of diplomatic history at the Fletcher School of Law and Diplomacy, Tufts University. The author of many books on communism, Dr. Griffith recently published a collective volume on Central and Eastern Europe. He has served as a consultant to the U.S. National Security Council and to the U.S. Ambassador to West Germany and is a member of the Council on Foreign Relations.

JERRY HOUGH is the James B. Duke Professor of Political Science at Duke University and a visiting senior fellow at the Brookings Institution. Dr. Hough has written several books, including *How the Soviet Union Is Governed, Generational Changes in the Soviet Union,* and *The Struggle for the Third World.*

SABAHUDDIN KUSHKAKI is the director of the Cultural Center of the Afghan Resistance in Islamabad and was a former minister of information of the Afghan government before 1973. Prior to the Communist takeover of the Afghan government in 1978, Mr. Kushkaki founded the first English newspaper in Afghanistan, *The Kabul Times,* and in 1968 established the first private daily newspaper in Kabul, *The Caravan.*

COLIN LEGUM was educated in South Africa and was active in journalism and politics there until 1949. He joined the *Observer* (London) in 1949 as Africa and Commonwealth correspondent and has served as editor of the *Africa Contemporary Record* since 1968 and as coeditor of the *Middle East Contemporary Survey* since 1977, while residing in the United Kingdom. Legum is the author of more than a score of books and has contributed chapters to many books written under the auspices of American and European universities.

C. WILLIAM MAYNES entered the Foreign Service in 1962, and in 1970 became a congressional fellow. In 1972 he began work for the Carnegie Endowment for International Peace as director of the International Organization Program. In 1973, he became the institution's secretary. Mr. Maynes became assistant secretary of state for international organizations affairs in January 1977 with responsibility for U.S. policy in the United Nations and its specialized agencies. Since April 1980, he has served as editor of *Foreign Policy*. He is a member of the Council on Foreign Relations.

DOUGLAS PIKE is a former U.S. Foreign Service officer and is currently director of the Indochina Archive and a professor at the University of California, Berkeley. He is the author of several authoritative studies of Vietnamese communism. His most recent publication is *Vietnam and the USSR: Anatomy of an Alliance*.

BHABANI SEN GUPTA is a research professor at the Centre for Policy Research, C.U.N.Y., New Delhi, India and Visiting Professor, Department of Political Science, Columbia University, New York City. He is a leading Soviet expert in India and the author of several books on communism and Soviet foreign policy.

ALI SHEIKH is a senior fellow and a Ph.D. candidate at the Institute for Soviet and East European Studies (ISEES), the Graduate School of International Studies, the University of Miami, Coral Gables, Florida. He is on leave from the Institute of Strategic Studies in Islamabad, Pakistan. While at ISEES, in 1986-1988, Sheikh was awarded two fellowships: one by the Earhart Foundation and another by the Social Science Research Council. He is the author of several articles for scholarly journals and newspapers dealing with Soviet policies toward Afghanistan, and Pakistan.

ALVARO TABOADA is a former FSLN Ambassador to Ecuador and currently a senior fellow and Ph.D. candidate at the Institute for Soviet and East European Studies, the Graduate School of International Studies, the University of Miami, where he is the recipient of an Earhart Foundation Fellowship. He is the author of several books and articles dealing with Latin American affairs and Soviet politics in Central America including a chapter in *Conflict in Nicaragua: A Multi-dimensional Perspective*. Previously, Ambassador Taboada was a visiting professor of general theory of the state at the Universidad Centroamericana, Managua, and a visiting professor in the doctoral program of history at the Pontificia Universidad Catolica del Ecuador, Quito. Actively involved in the struggle against the dictator Somoza, Ambassador Taboada was the chairman of the Christian Democratic party of Nicaragua prior to 1979.

KHIEN THEERAVIT is a professor of international relations, Faculty of Political Science, and director of the Institute of Asian Studies, Chulalongkorn University, Bangkok, Thailand. He has served as head of the Department of International Relations of the same university (1979), and as a member of the National Assembly and the Foreign Relations Committee (1974), and advisor to the prime minister of Thailand (1980). He has written numerous books and articles and six research reports, two of which received distinction awards from Thailand's National Research Council and from Chulalongkorn University.

BRUCE WEINROD is director of foreign policy and defense studies at The Heritage Foundation, Washington, D.C. His areas of focus include East-West relations and arms control. Prior to joining The Heritage Foundation, Mr. Weinrod served as legislative director to U.S. Senator John Heinz and also worked on the staff of the White House. Appointed by President Reagan, Weinrod was confirmed by the U.S. Senate as a member of the Board of the U.S. Institute of Peace in 1987. He is a public member of the U.S. delegation to the 1986-88 Vienna follow-up conference on the Helsinki Agreements and a member of the Council on Foreign Relations.

HOWARD WIARDA is a resident scholar and director of the Center for Hemispheric Studies at the American Enterprise Institute for Public Policy Research in Washington, D.C. He is also a professor of political science and adjunct professor of comparative labor relations at the University of Massachusetts in Amherst. His most recent books include, *In Search of Policy: The United States and Latin America*; *Rift and Revolution: The Central American Imbroglio*; and *Politics and Social Change in Latin America*. Dr. Wiarda is a member of the Council on Foreign Relations.

Index

Act of Contadora, 248
Adamishin, Anatolii, 165
Afanasiev, Victor, 177
Afghanistan, 6, 9, 36–38, 145, 282
   future options, 150–152, 150–153
   Geneva Accords on, 53–54
   Gorbachev's policy in, 132
   India-Pakistan conflict over, 54–58
   mujahideen leadership, 52, 69, 136, 140
   and Soviet "new political thinking," 129–138, 299–303
   Soviet withdrawal from, 34–35, 48, 72, 137–138
   U.S. policy toward, 315–316
Africa:
   Angola and Nambia, Soviet role in negotiations over, 164–165
   current Soviet policies on regional conflicts in, 167–169
   Horn of Africa Soviet policy, before Gorbachev, 161–164
   Southern African Societ policy, before Gorbachev, 159–161
   sub-Saharan, 106
African National Congress. *See* ANC
Agreements for Peace in Southwestern Africa, text of, 331–338
Amin, Idi, 38
ANC, 160, 165–166, 304–305
Andropov, Yurii, 174–175
Angola, 35, 38–39, 48, 52, 59, 72–73, 167–169, 266, 316
   and Reagan Doctrine, 269–270
   and Soviet "new thinking," 303–305
   Soviet policy toward, 164–165, 180–187
Aquino, Benigno, 216
Aquino, Corazon, 216, 218–220
Arbatov, Georgii, 50, 173
ASEAN (Association of Southeast Asian Nations), 91–92, 200–208, 220, 306, 312–313

Basic Requirements of Stable Coexistence (Arbatov & Cox), 50–51
Bender, Jerry, 186–187
Bogomolov, Pavel, 254
Bokassa, 38
Borge, Tomas, 241
Bovin, Aleksandr, 70
Brezhnev, Lenoid
   death of, 3–4
   foreign and military policy, 4–7, 11
   and internal development, 25
   principles governing Soviet-American relations, 47
   Third World ideology, 80–84
Brezhnev Doctrine, 105, 116, 176–178
Bukharin, Nikolai, 85
Bulichov, Ilia, 253
Bull, Hedley, 187

Cambodia, 39, 72–73, 270–271, 306–309, 316–317
Capitalism vs. socialism, 17–23
Carter, Jimmy, 69, 266, 268
Castro, Fidel, 48–49, 73, 79, 114, 117, 136, 161, 163–164, 174, 179–180, 242
Central America, 255–260
   decline of Inter-American system, 246–250
   "new thinking" and Soviet-Sandinista relations, 250–255
   Soviet-Nicaraguan relations, 240–246
   Soviet-Sandinista alliance, 237–240
Chace, James, 50
Chebrikov, Viktor, 16
China, 37, 49, 61, 82–83, 146
   future options for, 154–155
   and Kampuchea, 99–100
   and Moscow-Hanoi alliance, 97–98
   Soviet relations with, 209–210
Chissano, Eduardo, 165
Clark Amendment, 183, 184

Class struggle, 18–20
Clausewitz, Gen. Karl von, 17, 294–295
CMEA (Council for Mutual Economic Assistance), 94, 198
Co, Tran Quang, 228
Cold War, 103–108, 217
Commentary, 267
Communist Party of the Phillipines. *See* CPP
Communist Party Soviet Union. *See* CPSU
Constitution:
 of 1924, 10
 of 1936, 10
 of 1977, 9, 21
Contras, 37, 115, 271, 273
Costa Rica, 259
Council for Mutual Economic Assistance. *See* CMEA
Cox, Arthur, 50
CPP, 215–216, 224–232, 310
CPSU, 11
 19th Congress, 6, 9–10
 27th Congress, 19, 45, 129, 172, 176
 international policy goals, 172–179, 215
Crocker, Chester, 165, 305
Cuba, 38–39, 48, 79, 254
 depression in, 112
 distance from Soviets, 111
 divisiveness in, 112
 economy of, 110
 elan in, 110–111
 generational differences in, 111
 impact of *glasnost* and *perestroika*, 108–109, 112–114
 isolation of, 112
 leadership in, 110
 public attitudes in, 111
 role in Angola, 179–180
 social programs, 110
 and Soviet "new thinking," 297–299
 United States pull in, 111–112
Cuban Revolution, 239

Democratic Kampuchea. *See* DK
Demographic growth, 5
Demokratizatsiia, 66
Deng Xiaoping, 39, 73, 293, 297
Detente, 12–13, 60–61, 66, 69–70
DK, 206
Dobrynin, Anatolii, 14

Eastern Europe, 272

Economy (Soviet), 5
Eisenhower, Dwight, 267
El Salvador, 266
EPLF (Eritrean People's Liberation Front), 163
Ermacora, Felix, 133
Esquipulas Accord, 249
Ethiopia, 38, 167–169, 305–306

Far Eastern Economic Review, 210
FNLA, 161, 182–183, 303
Foreign policy (Soviet):
 Indochina in pre-Gorbachev era, 196–199
 Indochina under Gorbachev, 199–207
 and *perestroika*, 3
 restructuring of, 23–28
 and Soviet idology, 7–13
 and Third World, 273–275, 281–284
FRELIMO (Front for the Liberation of Mozambique), 161
Front for the National Liberation of Angola. *See* FNLA
FSLN, 311, 313
Fukuyama, Francis, 280–281, 283–284

Gandhi, Indira, 58
Gandhi, Rajiv, 58
Gavrilov, Vladimir, 253
Geneva Accords, 53–54, 135, 137–140, 148, 150, 202, 291, 303
 text of, 319–330
Gerasimov, Genadi, 127, 184
Glasnost, 46, 60–61, 66, 292–296
 and Afghanistan issue, 132–134
 impact on Cuba, 108–109, 112–114
 impact on Nicaraguan relations, 250–255
Glinkin, Anatolii, 253
Golan, Galia, 68
Goncharev, Victor, 166
Gonzales, Edward, 179
Gorbachev, Mikhail:
 Afghanistan policy, 132, 147–150
 Kampuchean peace initiatives, 199–207
 "new thinking" and foreign policy, 3–41
 "new thinking" on regional conflicts, 45–61
 Third World ideology, 84–87
 Third World policies, 65–75
 and Vietnam alliance, 95–96
Gorschkov, S.G., 162

Grenada, 6, 242, 243, 312
Gromyko, Andrei, 14, 47, 173, 200, 226
Guatemala, 248

Hammer, Armand, 133
Hanoi-Moscow axis, 94–97
Heinzing, Dieter, 196
Helsinki Accords, 12
Ho Chi Minh, 94
Hoffman, Erik, 171
Hough, Jerry, 68
Hungary, 267
Hun Sen, 205, 211, 308, 316

Iakovlev, Aleksandr, 7, 10, 105, 173
Ideology (Soviet)
    change in under Gorbachev, 13–15
    and Soviet foreign policy, 7–13
IMEMO, 70
Imperialism, 66
Imperialism: The Highest Stage of Capitalism (Lenin), 78
India, 54–58, 146
    future options for, 154
Indochina Report, 199
INF treaty, 9, 103, 119, 214, 300
Institute of Oriental Studies, 70, 81
Inter-American system, 246–250
Inter-American Treaty for Reciprocal Assistance. *See* TIAR
Intermediate Nuclear Forces. *See* INF treaty
Intifada, 72
Iran, 49, 69, 71, 145
    future options for, 154
Iran-Iraq War, 69
Iraq, 49, 71
Islamic Unity of Afghanistan Mujahideen. *See* IUAM
Israel, 72
IUAM, 151–152
Izvestiia, 46

Jakarta Informal Meeting. *See* JIM-I; JIM-II
Japan, 61
JIM-I, 306–308
JIM-II, 308–309

Kampleman, Max, 286
Kampuchea (Cambodia), 49, 52–53, 97–100
    Soviet policy in pre-Gorbachev era, 196–199

Kapitsa, Mikhail, 201, 218
Karmal, Babrak, 129
Kaunda, Kenneth, 184
Kennedy, Paul, 50, 104
Keynes, John Maynard, 67
Khmer, Rouge, 39, 49, 53, 73, 100, 197, 201, 203, 308
Khomeini, Ayatollah, 69, 71
Khrushchev, Nikita, 14–15
    and internal development, 25
    Third World policy, 79–80
Kirkpatrick, Jeane, 267
Kommunist, 105
Kosygin, Aleksei, 80
Kusumaatmadja, Mochtar, 203
Kuwait, 71

Latin America, 106
Lenin, Nikolai, 78–79, 82–87, 211
Leninism, 17–23, 106–107, 116, 149–150, 250–253
Liberation movements, 33–34
Ligachev, Egor, 7, 10, 14, 16, 17, 32, 47–48, 296
Linh, Nguyen Van, 204, 298
Linkage theory, 13, 47
Losyukov, Alexander, 222–224

Manglapus, Raul, 219, 221–223
Marcos, Ferdinand, 218
Marx, Karl, 82–86
Marxism, 17–23, 106–107
Medvedev, Vadim, 296
Malchor, Alejandro, 220
Mengitsu Haile Mariam, Lt. Col., 38, 69, 74, 162–163, 168–169, 305–306
Mercado, Orlando, 219
Mexico, 247
Middle East, 71–72
Military Bases Agreement (MBA), 221–224, 309
Military (Soviet), 26, 144–145
Ministry of Foreign Affairs, 11, 127, 199
MK. *See* ANC (African National Congress)
Movement of the People's Liberation of Angola. *See* MPLA
Mozambique, 38, 48, 59
MPLA, 39, 161, 164, 167, 180–188, 303–305, 316
Mujahideen, 52, 69, 136, 140

Najibullah, 37
Namibia, 38, 48–50
  Soviet policy on, 164–165, 180–187
NDF (National Democratic Front), 216, 229
New Economic Policy (NEP), 86
New Jewel Movement. *See* NJM
New People's Army. *See* NPA
Nicaragua, 35, 37, 53, 117, 228–229, 239–240, 255–260
  and Reagan Doctrine, 271
  Soviet military/economic aid, 243–246
  and Soviet "new thinking," 250–255, 310–314
  Soviet-Sandinista diplomacy, 240–243
  U.S. policy towards, 317–318
Nixon, Richard, 47, 48
NJM, 249, 312
Nomenklatura, 66, 314
Novoe myshlenie (new thinking), 66, 292–296
NPA, 215–216, 224–232, 309–310
NWFZ (nuclear weapon free zones), 128

OAS, 247
OAU, 174, 183, 189
OIC, 147
Ordonez, Sedfrey, 223
Organization of African Unity. *See* OAU
Organization of American States. *See* OAS
Organization of Islamic Conference. *See* OIC
Ortega, Daniel, 248, 258
Ortega, Humberto, 241
Ovchinnikov, Vsevolod, 177

Pakistan, 52–54, 145
  conflict with India over Afghanistan, 54–58
  future options for, 153
  Peshawar Seven, 55–56, 58, 140
  and Soviet Union, 129–138
Palestinians, 72
Partido Komunista ng Pilipinas. *See* PKP
PDPA, 129–141, 146, 151
Peaceful coexistence, 23–24, 47
People's Democratic Party of Afghanistan. *See* PDPA
People's Republic of China. *See* China
People's Republic of Kampuchea. *See* PRK
Peredyshka, 24
Perestroika, 3, 9, 46, 60–61, 66, 292–296, 314–315, 318

  impact on Cuba, 108–109, 112–114
  impact on Nicaraguan relations, 250–255
Perestroika (Gorbachev), 15–23, 178, 211
Peshawar Seven, 55–56, 58, 140
Phieu, Lt. Gen. Le. Kha, 209
Phillipines, 215–216, 309–310
PKP, 215, 218
Platt, Nicholas, 221
Poland, 6
Politics of Sea Power, The (Gorshckov), 162
Pol Pot, 53, 99, 197, 205, 270–271, 316
Ponomarev, Boris, 68
Porter, Bruce, 277
Portugal, 181–182
Pravda, 46, 70, 177, 210
Prem Tinsulanonda, 200–201, 204, 209, 307
Primakov, Evgenii, 29–32, 70, 105, 177, 178–179, 214–215
PRK, 204–206, 306–308
Problemy Ekonomiki, 105

Quang, Tran, 206

Raphel, Arnold, 55
Reagan, Ronald, 6, 11, 29, 40, 53, 84, 119, 167, 175
Reagan Doctrine, 52–54, 59, 175–176, 186
  and Afghanistan, 268–269
  and Angola, 269–270
  and Cambodia, 270–271
  evolution of, 265–268
  lessons of, 272–275
  and Nicaragua, 271
Redman, Charles, 186
Regional conflicts, 33–34
  Soviet resolution of, 35–41
Richardson, Elliot, 50
Risquet, Jorge, 180
Rogachev, Igor, 218–219, 222
Rosa Coutinho, Antonio, 182
Ruiz, Henry, 241
Ryzhkov, Nikolai, 16, 204

SACP, 159–160, 166
Salas, Rodolfo, 226
SALT treaties, 12
Sandinista Front, 37, 117, 238–260, 271
San Salvador, 259
Santos, Eduardo dos, 185
Saudi Arabia, 71

Savimbi, Jonas, 39, 185, 269-270
SDI, 294
Selassie, Haile, 161
Selected Works (Lenin), 211
Shahani, Leticia Ramos, 218
Shamir, Yitzhak, 72
Shcherbitskii, Vladimir, 16
Shevardnadze, Eduard, 7, 10, 23-24, 27, 31, 85, 127, 133, 200, 201
Shevchenko, Arkadii, 47
Shula-e-Javid, 155
Shultz, George, 133
Siad Barre, 74
Sihanouk, Norodom, 73, 100, 202, 204, 211, 273, 308
Simoniia, Nodari, 81-82
Singapore, 203
Sison, Jose Maria, 215, 226
Slovo, Jo, 166
Socialism vs. capitalism, 17-23
Sokolov, Oleg, 223, 226
Somalia, 74
Somali National Movement (SNM), 74
South Africa, 38, 48, 165-167, 180
South African Communist Party.
  See SACP
Southeast Asia:
  post Vietnam War developments, 91-94
  Soviet alliance with, 91-101
  Soviet-Phillipine relations, 216-232
  Soviet-Vietnam/Kampuchea relations, 195-211
South West African People's Organization.
  See SWAPO
Soviet Bloc, 5, 272
Soviet Union:
  Afghanistan, options for future relationship, 152-153
  African regional conflicts, current policy on, 167-169
  Angola/Namibia policy, 164-165, 180-187
  and Cuba, 108-119
  Marxist-Leninist ideology and Third World, 77-87
  and Pakistan, 129-138
  and Phillipines, 216-232
  South Africa policy, 165-167
  Third World policy and "new thinking," 68-69, 104-108, 171-180, 297-299, 299-303
  Third World regional conflicts, policies towards, 126-129, 143-155, 173-179
  and Vietnam alliance, 91-101
  Vietnam and Kampuchean conflict, 195-211
Stalin, Joseph, 14-15, 251
  and domestic development, 25
  Third World policy, 79
START, 214
Starushenko, Gleb, 165-166
Strategic Arms Reduction Talks.
  See START
Strategic Defense Initiative. *See* SDI
Suslov, Mikhail, 47
SWAPO, 160, 185, 254, 304

Thach, Nguyen Co, 196, 203, 209
Thailand, 2-3
Third World, 12
  changing Soviet relations with, 28-35, 104-108
  Gorbachev's policies on, 65-75, 171-173
  Marxist-Leninist ideology towards, 77-87
  and socialism, 22
  and Soviet foreign policy restructuring, 23-28, 273-275, 281-284
  Soviet resolution of regional conflicts in, 35-41, 173-179
Thurow, Roger, 184
TIAR, 247, 248
TPLF (Tigrean People's Liberation Front), 163
Treaty of Friendship and Cooperation (U.S.S.R. & Vietnam), 197-198, 217
Tri, Vo Nhan, 199
Trotsky, Leon, 85
Trung, Thai Quang, 199

UNITA (Union for the Total Independence of Angola), 52, 161, 164, 182-186, 254, 269, 272-273, 303-305, 312-313, 316
United Nations, 41, 172
  role in Gulf war, 49
United Nations Security Council, 46-47, 52
United States:
  detente policy, 69
  foreign policy and Soviet "new think-

ing," 277-287, 315-316
linkage theory, 13, 47
policies toward Third World countries, 188-189
and resolution of regional conflicts with Soviets, 39-40

Vietnam, 8, 48, 49, 93-94, 228
and Kampuchean conflict, 195-211
Soviet aid to, 208-209
Soviet alliance with, 91-101, 94-97
and Soviet "new thinking," 297-299
Vietnam War, 91-94

Volskii, Victor, 252-253
Vorontsov, Yurii, 136
Vorotnikov, Vitalii, 16

Wall Street Journal, 184
Watergate, 8
Western Europe, 61
Wolf, Charles, 284

Zahir Shah, 55, 133, 135
Zaikov, Lev, 16
Zia-ul Haq, Gen., 55-56, 58, 129-131, 140-141, 302